BECOMING DRACULA

THE EARLY YEARS OF BELA LUGOSI

VOLUME TWO

By Gary D. Rhodes and Bill Kaffenberger

Featuring photographs from the
collections of John Antosiewicz, Bill Chase,
George Chastain, Kristin Dewey, Roger Hurlburt,
Russell McGee, Dennis Phelps, and David Wentink

Copyright © 2021 by Gary D. Rhodes and William M. Kaffenberger, Jr.

All Rights Reserved.

This book may not be reproduced, in whole or in part, in any form (beyond that copying permitted by Section 107 and 108 of the U.S. Copyright Law and except by reviewers for the public press), without written permission from the publisher.

Designed by Steve Kirkham – Tree Frog Communication – www.treefrogcommunication.co.uk

Cover photo of Bela Lugosi and Hazel Whitmore in 1928, courtesy of the University of Washington Libraries, Special Collections, UW40898.

Back cover photo originally published in *Exhibitors Herald* on July 7, 1923.
Photo restoration by George Chastain. Original courtesy of Russell McGee.

Printed in the United States

Published by BearManor Media
1317 Edgewater Drive 110
Orlando, FL 32804
books@benohmart.com

Unless otherwise noted, all photographs come from the collections of
Gary D. Rhodes and Bill Kaffenberger.

Library of Congress Cataloguing-in-Publication Data
Rhodes, Gary D. and Bill Kaffenberger
Becoming Dracula: The Early Years of Bela Lugosi, Volume II / Gary D. Rhodes and Bill Kaffenberger

Includes bibliographical references and index
ISBN 978-1-62933-812-5 (hardcover)
ISBN 978-1-62933-811-8 (softcover)

1. Lugosi, Bela, 1882-1956. 2. Motion Picture Actors and Actresses–United States–Biography.
I. Rhodes, Gary D. II. Kaffenberger, Bill. III. Title.
PN2859.H86L835

Authors' Notes: Some images chosen for this book are of an imperfect quality, but they are reproduced herein due to their rarity and their importance to the narrative.

Dedicated to

Robert Cremer and Bela G. Lugosi

Acknowledgments

The authors would like to extend their gratitude to the various archives, libraries, museums and universities that kindly offered assistance during the research phase of this project: the Alexander Library of Rutgers University of New Brunswick, New Jersey, the American Heritage Center at the University of Wyoming, the Andover-Harvard Theological Library of Massachusetts, the Antigo Public Library of Antigo, Wisconsin, the Annenberg Rare Book and Manuscript Library at the University of Pennsylvania, the Ardmore Public Library of Oklahoma, the Bancroft Library at the University of California at Berkeley, the Billy Rose Theater Division of the New York Public Library, the Bundesarchiv in Berlin, the Chicago History Museum Research Center of Chicago, Illinois, the Chickasaw Regional Library System of Oklahoma, the Cleveland Public Library of Ohio, the D. C. Public Library of Washington D. C., the Department of Special Collections at the University of California at Santa Barbara, the Deutsche Kinemathek in Berlin, the Free Library of Philadelphia, the Harry Ransom Center at the University of Texas at Austin, the Hillman Library at the University of Pittsburgh, the Historical Society of Pennsylvania, the Howard Gottlieb Archival Research Center at Boston University in Massachusetts, the Hungarian Film Institute, the Hungarian Theater Museum and Institute of Budapest, Hungary, the Immigration and Naturalization Service, Interlibrary Loan at the University of Central Florida, the Kiplinger Research Library of Washington D. C., the Library of Congress of Washington, D. C., the Los Angeles Public Library, the Margaret Herrick Library of the Academy of Motion Picture Arts and Sciences, the Media History Digital Library, the Museum of History, Ethnography, and Fine Arts–Lugoj, Romania, the Museum of Performance and Design of San Francisco, California, the National Archives of the United States, the National Széchényi Library Theater History Collection of Budapest, Hungary, the New York State Historical Association, the Newark Public Library of New Jersey, the Pasadena Playhouse of California, the Pennsylvania Department of Education – Bureau of State Library, the Pest-Buda Restaurant of Budapest, Hungary, the Pickering Educational Resources Library at Boston University, the Research Service of the Budapest City Archives of Hungary, the San Diego Public Library of California, the Santa Barbara Public Library of California, the San Francisco Public Library, the Syracuse University Archives of New York, the University of Central Oklahoma, the University of Debrecen University and National Library, Arts and Sciences Library of Debrecen, Hungary, University of Pennsylvania Penn State Special Collections Library, and the University of Washington Libraries/Special Collections.

In addition, the authors would like to express their appreciation to the following individuals who have helped make this book possible: Carolyn Edgington Anderson, Tom Anker, Jerry Armellino, Dr. Bonhardt Attila, Leonardo D'Aurizio, Ellen Bailey, Wendy Barszcz, Marty Baumann, Scott Berman, Tom Brannan, Olaf Brill, Larissa Brookes, Duane Brower, John Brunas, Michael Brunas, Bob Burns, Joe Busam, Bart Bush, Petrina Calabalic, Paolo Caneppele, Jeff Carlson, Allison Carmola, Mario Chacon, Ross Clark, William Cornauer, Mária Cseh, Richard Daub, Kate Deeks, Frank J. Dello Stritto, Dorothy Demarest, Patricia Dew, Harald Dolezal, the late David Durston, the late Robert Ray Edgington, Ruth Edgington, Robert Edgington Jr., Michael Engel, Scott Essman, the late Philip R. Evans, the late William K.

Everson, Elena Filios, Fabian Fuerste, Lawrence Fultz, Jr., Shawna Gandy, Cheri Goldner, Julio Gonzalez, Emily Goodrich, the late Richard Gordon, the late Gordon R. Guy, Steve Haberman, G. D. Hamann, Warren G. Harris, Betsy L. Hendrix, Dóra Hicsik, Suzette Hinson, David J. Hogan, Suzanne Horton, Durham Hunt, Roger Hurlburt, the late Steve Jochsberger, Steve Kaplan, Amy Kastigar, Constance Kelly, Anthony Kerr, Nancy Kersey, Eugene Kirschenbaum, Robin Ladd, Rosemary Lands, Sierra Lepine, Frank Liquori, Bill Lord, Steve McFarland, Lauren Martino, Jeremy Megraw, David Merlini, the late Linda Miller, D'Arcy More, Dejan Mrkić, Peter Michaels, Jean-Claude Michel, Mark A. Miller, Deborah A. Mitchell, the late Lynn Naron, the late Randy Nesseler, Ted Newsom, Dr. James P. Niessen, Scott Nollen, John Norris, Jim Nye, Chris O'Brien, Marcus O'Brien, Margaret O'Brien, Dennis Payne, Victor Pierce, William Pirola, William V. Rauscher, Mike Ravnitzky, Robert Rees, Kate Reeve, Jeffrey Roberts, Barbara L. Rothschild, Dr. Andrea Rózsavölgyi, Becky Scarborough, Bruce Scivally, Joseph Shemtov, Samuel M. Sherman, Margaret Sides, Bettina Sinkó, Zoran Sinobad, Barb Smith, Don G. Smith, Lynette Suckow, Karin Suni, Vera Surányi, Graham Sutton, Dr. Andor Sziklay, László Tábori, Kirsten Tanaka, Dominika Tápai, the late Brian Taves, Maurice Terenzio, Mario Toland, Ádám Török, Nadine Turner, Elizabeth Van Tuyl, John Ulakovic, Judit Katalin Ulrich, Dr. Steven Béla Várdy, Jon Wang, Leo Wiltshire, the late Robert Wise, Laraine Worby, Valerie Yaros, Gregory Zatirka, and Péter Zsolt.

The authors would also like to offer their deepest thanks to a number of individuals who gave so much of their time and support that they proved crucial to this project's completion: the late Forrest J Ackerman, Gyöngyi Balogh, Matthew E. Banks, Buddy Barnett, Sidney Blackmer, Jr., the late Richard Bojarski, Tom Brannan, Olaf Brill, Kevin Brownlow, Mario Chacon, George Chastain, Ned Comstock, Michael Copner, Michael J. David, Jack Dowler, Edward "Eric" Eaton, John Ellis, Theodore Estes, Donald F. Glut, Michael Ferguson, Nelia Romero Florido, Phillip Fortune, Beau Foutz, Fritz Frising, Christopher R. Gauthier, Robert Guffey, Lee Harris, Cortlundt Hull, Elena Kaffenberger, Dr. Michael Lee, Russell McGee, Mark Martucci, Susan D. Mazza, Jerry McCoy, Lisa Mitchell, Tamara Nagy, David Nahmod, Constantine Nasr, Henry Nicolella, Donald Rhodes, Phyllis Rhodes, William Rosar, Noémi Saly, the late Richard Sheffield, Dr. Robert Singer, Anthony Slide, Carter Smith, Billy Stagner, David Stenn, Elemer Szasz, Adele Veness, and Glenn P. White.

Special recognition goes to the following: Dr. Mirjam Dénes for translating hundreds of Hungarian documents into English and providing many insightful comments and observations about Hungarian theater; Raymond E. Glew for assisting in our Budapest research; Dr. Ildikó Sirato, Edit Rajnai, and the staff of the National Széchényi Library Theater History Collection of Budapest, Hungary for their assistance in making available rare Hungarian theater playbills for our research; Mária Kórász and the Vasváry Collection at the Somogyi Library in Szeged, and Zsuzsa Köpösdi for her assistance in locating theatrical documents from the University of Debrecen University and National Library, Arts and Sciences Library of Debrecen, Hungary.

Likewise, we extend our deepest thanks to Bela G. Lugosi, Lynne Lugosi Sparks, and Lugosi Enterprises for their support and assistance; John Antosiewicz, Bill Chase, Kristin Dewey, Roger Hurlburt, Russell McGee, Dennis Phelps, and David Wentink for sharing photos from their collections; Tamás Gyurkovics, John Soister, and Tom Weaver for proofreading and providing insightful commentary on our rough drafts, as well as to Robert Cremer and Dr. Robert J. Kiss for proofreading and providing translations of several hundred German documents into English.

Likewise, we acknowledge the crucial contribution of Steve Kirkham, who devoted much time to creating the stunning layout for Volume Two of this project, and Ben Ohmart at BearManor Media, who has been so supportive of our research.

Gary D. Rhodes
Orlando, FL

Bill Kaffenberger
Los Angeles, CA

(Courtesy of John Antosiewicz)

Chapter 21

The Modern Hungarian Stage

"I want to see the future, to discover
what I must struggle for, what I must suffer."
– Madách, *Az ember tragédiája* (*The Tragedy of Man*)

In 1932, Lugosi described his reasons for leaving Europe in rather fanciful, even supernatural terms:

> I had been an actor in Hungary, and when I fled to New York, one of the first parts offered me was the role of Count Dracula in the play, *Dracula*, which was then about to be produced for the first time. And most strangely, this story dealt with the very subject, which has caused me to leave my native country – vampires of the night, and the strange legion of the undead....[1]

Lugosi's account notably avoided the political reasons that prompted his departure from Hungary. But it also truncated the years he spent in the United States before achieving fame in English-language theater.

A more accurate account might not only have dealt with politics and even perhaps his divorce from Ilona Szmik, but also of declining prospects for actors in his homeland. In 1921, one journalist wrote:

> Since Hungary lost two-thirds of its territory in the Great War, Hungarian artists have much less opportunity for a fine career at home. So, in the past couple of years, more and more Hungarians found out that America can provide such career opportunities which can never be found in the old continent.[2]

Lugosi had perceived such opportunities for some time, dating to his escape to Vienna or perhaps earlier. The fact that he spoke almost no English was a major barrier upon his arrival in America, but it simultaneously led him to find work with expatriates from his home country.

Despite the misgivings some retained about his political activities in Budapest, the Hungarian theatrical community in New York welcomed Lugosi. He immersed himself in local Hungarian restaurants and clubs and entertainment, embracing a culture exemplified by such artists as Duci de Kerékjártó, who regularly gave violin concerts in Manhattan in the early twenties.[3]

Most importantly, Lugosi joined a Hungarian-American theater company that, as one later article described, "played towns with large Hungarian populations. They would start in New York with a new play and after touring it, they would return for a new production and start all over again."[4] Journalist Zoltán Székely added:

> Béla Lugosi was a member of a company which, in the early 1920s, toured the towns and [small communities] where Hungarian people were living, and they performed the comedy entitled *Halló* [*Hello*, aka *Halló!*] by Imre Földes.
>
> ... I remember there were not more than twenty or twenty-five spectators in the audience. The actors had no money. Sometimes, after the performance, a well-to-do Hungarian invited the members of the company for dinner. Lugosi did not even have normal clothes, so he travelled to the next town for the next performance wearing the same costume he was wearing on stage, a hussar captain's uniform, with his little bundle hung over his bare sword. In the bundle [were] some make-up tools, and a piece of dry sausage might have been hiding [in there]. Those were all of his assets.[5]

The company that Lugosi joined was not the first of its type in New York. According to Hungarian theater historian Sándor Enyedi:

> Theatrical acting in Hungarian in America starts at the beginning of the 20th century. In the first Hungarian theatrical magazine in the U.S., entitled *Színházi Újság*, which was first published on 15 September 1921, a reader recalls the starting point like this: 'Sixteen years ago, a handful of enthusiastic actors gathered and held performances weekly or every other week. During daytime, they earned their living at the factory, and they held rehearsals in the evenings just from the fantastic love of their hearts [without pay]....' After the

Published in *Előre* on April 3, 1921.

end of World War I, in the shadow of the collapse of the Soviet Regime, new emigrant masses, including artists, left their homeland and tried their luck overseas.

The Fellegi sisters, Lola and Teri, arrived in the U.S. at that time, as well as the excellent baritone Lajos Rózsa, and Béla Lugosi, too. One theatrical performance came after the other: in many cities of the U.S., amateurs played together with professionals, and according to the theatrical paper mentioned above, the local Hungarians wanted to establish companies in three locations: in New York and its surroundings, in Chicago and in Cleveland. From their plans some temporary initiatives came to life, and Béla Lugosi, who had just arrived in New York, could hope that, after Vienna and Berlin, the places of his forced emigration, he could realize his artistic ideas in no other place but New York, in the U.S....[6]

And so, even if there was very little pay, even if the actors had to seek other employment to survive, their love of the theater drove them onward.

Various Hungarian-American cultural and artistic events competed for a relatively small number of audience members. In early January of 1921, for example, actor Károly Vidor (aka Charles Vidor) established a small Hungarian theater company in New York City. He had arrived in America approximately five months before Lugosi, having left Hungary where he was once trained in a government-run acting school. Like Lugosi, Vidor served in the military during World War I. And like Lugosi, Vidor came to America in hopes of pursuing an acting career. The *New York Times* explained the sad end of his dreams:

> Charles Vidor, a young actor and stage director of the Hungarian company recently presenting native plays at the Bramhall Theater... committed suicide by inhaling gas yesterday... Back of the death was a story of an adventure in art and ambition that failed, for it disclosed that Vidor, barely 22 years old, had tried to organize a national playhouse here... A company of amateurs, with himself as the only professional, failed to win its way; there came formidable competition in the arrival of a group of veterans of the Budapest stage – and down in the partly furnished studio the gas was turned on. Peace brought famine to Hungary and Vidor decided to try to satisfy his ambition in this city.
>
> Sixty or seventy prominent Hungarians provided the financial backing, but Vidor faced a difficult task... Starting with good houses, the receipts began to taper... but it was not until last Sunday, when the rival company made its debut, that the end of the young actor's great effort came into sight... Down in the People's House... the professionals presented their offering. It was a decided success – everybody in the Hungarian colony said so – and Vidor, watching the actors and actresses he had seen on the stage in Budapest, knew it... Vidor had appeared depressed and, in a flash of dramatic morbidness, he must have decided to surrender.[7]

The story is only partially correct. His depression also resulted from being romantically spurned by producer Ilona Fülöp.[8] Lugosi likely knew Vidor, even if only upon his arrival in

New York. By the time of Vidor's suicide, the professional competition included the Amerikai Magyar Színtársulat (American Hungarian Theater Company), as well as the company that Lugosi joined, the Modern Magyar Színpad (Modern Hungarian Stage).

Producer László Schwartz formed the Modern Magyar Színpad at the beginning of 1921 in order "to present dramatic works of the younger generation of Hungarian playwrights. It is also purposed to present American plays, in Hungarian versions, before sending them abroad."[9] Along with Lugosi, the company included such actors as Ilona Montagh (aka Ilona von Montagh), Kornélia Lőrincz (aka Cornelia Lőrinc), and István Papp (aka Stefan Papp), as well as graduates of the Dramatic Academy of Hungary.[10]

With the slogan "Hungarian Plays, in Hungarian, by Hungarians, for Hungarians," the troupe presented road show productions prior to opening at the People's House Theater with *Boldogság* (*Happiness*) on January 30, 1921. This apparently marked Lugosi's first performance with them.[11] A Hungarian-language newspaper in New York described the play as follows:

Published in *Előre* on February 19, 1921.

> After ten years of marriage, the sculptor Hiláry [Lugosi] discovers that he and his wife, Magda [Kornélia Lőrincz] do not understand each other. A relative of the wife, a certain painter called Olga [Ilona Montagh], comes to visit them, and the artist realizes that he and Olga understand each other very well. He falls in love with her. When the wife notices something, the husband asks her to send the guest away for the sake of both. Magda refuses, because she wants to test him. She says: they will see if he is strong enough to overcome his love toward the girl. He turns out to be not strong

Published in *Előre* on January 29, 1921.

enough. The girl leaves the house crying, the sculptor goes after her, but then he returns alone and rushes into the arms of his wife. The end of the play has been changed by the company, because in the original play the man will stay with the girl, and the wife will remain alone, since she thinks she has no right to stand in the way of other peoples' happiness.[12]

Despite the altered conclusion, response to the *Boldogság* production was far from positive:

> We went to the debut performance of the Modern Hungarian Stage feeling extremely curious because the directorship promised well-established artists from Hungary to the New York audience, which has been disappointed so many times in the past. There was no shortage of promises, and we knew that the directors were ambitious and energetic people, so we had the right to hope that the usual unpleasant incidents would be missing this time.
>
> And we ended up being disappointed. We have never seen such disorder in any Hungarian performance. Spectators were looking for their seats, and they couldn't find them. Several people held claim for the same seat, which, of course, led to unpleasant conversations.
>
> There was, however, one novelty: the doormen were quite successful in scolding the audience. A gentleman wearing a tailcoat – probably one of the directors – instead of using the orchestra's stage door, kept jumping on and off the stage, shoving the curtains aside. He definitely did a healthy workout. Instead of the promised start at 8pm the performance was commenced only at 9. Finally, it began, amidst the audience's continued impatient beating and applause.
>
> The theme of the play is weak. The plot is slow. The reason for the wife's resignation is not entirely clear. The inner struggle that builds up to self-sacrifice is entirely missing…
>
> Lugosi was too serious, as if he had been preparing for the big scene all along, and thus he missed out on many nice nuances. We could not believe his feigned nervousness. Nevertheless, he is a serious artist and we are looking forward to his future performances, knowing that we will receive a great deal….[13]

By contrast, a review of the company's performance of *Boldogság* in South Bethlehem, Pennsylvania described a very different experience:

> Yesterday was of great importance in the cultural life of Hungarians living in Bethlehem. … The audience, which has experienced so much disappointment in the past, filled the hall of the Hungarian House with feelings of skepticism. They had all the right to do so, since they have met so many regrettable events in the past.
>
> A few minutes after the curtain rose, all the skeptics in the audience wore a smile on their faces. This was a sign of a pleasant surprise. Even before the first act was over, the audience at Bethlehem realized that no Hungarian actors had ever conveyed so much beauty, goodness, and soul-lifting on the local stage as this troupe just did.

Béla Lugosi, Ilona Montagh, Kornélia Lőrincz, and István Papp played the lead roles. All of them are true artists who were not only born gifted, but who also possess the knowledge which belongs only to actors who have graduated from an acting academy and who regard acting as their vocation and as the sacred purpose of their life.

Beyond the enthusiastic applause and ovation, the audience has already found a way to get the Modern Magyar Színpad back in Bethlehem, as they assured the company right after the show that, in the event a second performance could take place, the theater would be so crowded that there would be no empty seats, not even for ghosts.[14]

After a rough start, the company had quickly improved, and soon achieved numerous successes, certainly more than previous Lugosi biographers have generally acknowledged.

Within a few weeks, Lugosi directed and starred in the Modern Magyar Színpad's production of *A kisasszony férje* (*A Young Lady's Husband*, aka *Almost Married*). It debuted at the Thirty-Ninth Street Theater on February 20, ostensibly as a benefit for the Hoover Fund for Suffering Hungarian Children.[15] The plot involved a young lady falling in love with a man who is against the institution of marriage, and so she must trick him into becoming her husband.[16] A critic for the *Amerikai Magyar Népszava* wrote:

> Those intelligent Hungarians who enjoyed the first performance of the Modern Magyar Színpad will be pleased to read the delightful news that the Hungarian theatrical company has finally reached success both in financial and artistic terms, which was enough to secure an upscale Broadway theater for its future performances.

Published in *Előre* on March 5, 1921.

Published in *Előre* on February 12, 1921.

> This move marks the beginning of a new era in the history of American Hungarian theater. The start of a row of such high-level performances like the best of Broadway companies; the beginning of the most celebrated Hungarian guest performances by the most celebrated Hungarian actors in the framework of the performances of the Modern Magyar Színpad, the perfect introduction of Hungarian art in America. This is the beginning of a new, agile and healthy American Hungarian art – but what is just as important is that this is the end to the outdated and noisy performances surrounded with many personal inconveniences which were unavoidable as long as Hungarian theatrical performances were lacking a professional, modern building and had to be played in rooms equipped with primitive stages.[17]
>
> ... [W]e have to admit that the soul and main driving force of the company is Béla Lugossi, a member of the Budapest Nemzeti Színház [National Theater]. Lugossi was one of the most popular and talented members of Hungary's number one theater, who, by bringing his talent to America, gave up his advanced position in [Budapest]. Numerous new opportunities had been rising in front of this outstanding artist, since Hungarian theater is flourishing all over the world. Lugossi gave up all these opportunities and left his old home.
>
> What Lugossi's art provides is so sophisticated, so heart-to-soul, that we cannot doubt that the Hungarians would feel this man to be flesh of their flesh, blood of their blood. ... By looking at him, we recognize ourselves. His Hungarian calls to us and gives us the most expensive, the most human gift: the soul. ... We hope that Lugosi will be surrounded by such great love as he experienced back home, and we wish that his successes will be many times bigger. We can only congratulate the directorship of the Modern Magyar Színpad for acquiring someone so powerful as Lugossi for the staff, and we believe that he will bring the theater to unprecedented and unexpected heights.[18]

While impressed with the sold-out production of *A kisasszony férje,* another critic was not so taken with Lugosi's performance:

> We had to realize with regret that this time Béla Lugosi, the director, overcame Béla Lugosi, the actor. He was too self-conscious and cold; we could not believe that he really loved his wife. The fun, the cheerfulness, the flattering humor did not suit his character. It seems that plays with serious social problems and dramas are more suitable for his talent, personality and temper.[19]

Nevertheless, *A kisasszony férje* was "applauded enthusiastically" at its next New York performance, staged at the Belmont Theater. As one journalist observed, "Any writer would be happy if this talented, little company performed his play."[20]

A critic for *Előre* discussed at length the performances in South Bethlehem and Philadelphia, Pennsylvania:

> After a successful performance in New York, the troupe left to conquer the public in the countryside with big hopes... with its previous performances, the company has

earned such a good reputation that its news spread rapidly not only around New York, but across the United States. Nothing proves this better than the board of directors [of the troupe] receiving countless invitations for longer country tours.

The performance at South Bethlehem exceeded all expectations. The actors experienced a real celebration in the small town, the Hungarian community [house] of which was packed with enthusiastic crowds. The quality of the performance was as high as the one in New York. The interplay of actors, the directing, and the excellent quality of the personification of the characters made the cheers and enthusiasm of the audience perfectly understandable.

The performance in Philadelphia was a success, too. The Mercantile Hall has never accommodated such a large and enthusiastic audience. The company enjoyed an endless ovation... At the end of the show, amidst the thunderstorm of applause, [the director] announced that he wanted to hold the next performance in a more prominent theater... The indifference of Hungarian people towards theater is thus broken. There is no doubt that the Modern Magyar Színpad plays an important part in reaching this [outcome].[21]

Published in *Előre* on March 19, 1921.

During the spring of 1921, with Lugosi as actor and often as director, the company toured in a number of other productions.

Critics did question the choice of *Fiú-e vagy leány?* (*A Boy or a Girl?*), believing it to be of a "light" or even low literary quality.[22] By contrast, they generally lauded the other plays, as this review of *Halló* indicates:

> To guarantee that the audience will get the high-quality performance that they expect, we have Béla Lugosi, the ex-heroic lover of the Nemzeti Színház, as the director of the play. Lugosi embraced this project with ambition and knowledge, both of which are essentials for the real

Published in *Előre* on February 24, 1921.

Published in *Amerikai Magyar Hírlap* on April 14, 1921.

artistic work. And the actors at his disposal are ready to achieve all that is possible in the given circumstances. We have all the reasons to say that the talent of Lugosi as director will again shine through the play, just as in his past directions.[23]

How about [Lugosi's] acting skills? He showed those on numerous occasions already, although we could never see the face of this par excellence artist exposed to such bright lights as we did on Sunday. He created a perfect illusion: it would never have crossed one's mind that under the Hussar Lieutenant [character] Béla Lugosi was hidden. The actor Lugosi can safely store his performance in the play *Halló* in New York as one of his best. And all the other actors can say the same about themselves, which is again thanks to Lugosi the director....[24]

When in New York, the troupe often held residence at the Belmont Theater, where they presented many plays from the touring circuit.[25] One local critic had high hopes, predicting that "the further activities of this organization may prove even more interesting, in view of the fact that Hungarian

Published in *Előre* on June 2, 1921.

playwrights of today are producing some of the most original modern drama, especially in the field of comedy."[26]

Those hopes were apparently realized, given subsequent reviews. Of *A kaméliás hölgy* (*Lady of the Camelias*, aka *Camille*), a critic told readers:

> A remarkable part of the success was to be [credited] to Béla Lugosi's acting and directing skills. In the role of Armand Duval, he proved to be an infinitely likeable character, and a strong, self-conscious, talented actor at the same time.[27]

However accurate it might be, Zoltán Székely's memory of a small audience and actors without pay seems to be only part of the story, one that featured many successes, even if they were critical more than financial.

And yet, for reasons that are not entirely clear, Lugosi ended his association with the Modern Magyar Színpad, probably after completing an April 1921 tour of *Halló* in Youngstown, Ohio, but perhaps later, as there is an indication he might have performed with the troupe in June.[28] After the summer of 1921, Lugosi's immediate future would continue to be in Hungarian-American theater productions, but not with László Schwartz's company.

Endnotes

1 "'Dracula' Heads Billings of South Main Theater." *Aberdeen American-News* (Aberdeen, SD) 7 Feb. 1932.

2 "Modern Magyar Színpad." *Előre* (New York) 18 Jan. 1921.

3 "Business Records." *New York Times* 15 July 1924.

4 "Lugosi in 1918 Fled Hungary." *Philadelphia Inquirer* 16 May 1943.

5 Halász, Péter. "Drakula." *Amerikai Magyar Világ* (New York) 20 Apr. 1969.

6 Enyedi, Sándor. *A Tragédia amerikai színpadi pályafutásához* (Budapest: Színháztudomanyie Szemle 12, 1983).

7 "Suicide of Actor Closes a Theater." *New York Times* 6 Feb. 1921.

8 "Öngyilkos lett az imádott leány mütermében." *Előre* 7 Feb. 1921.

9 Ibid.

10 Ibid.

11 "Hungarians Will Give Plays in Native Tongue." *New York Tribune* 19 Feb. 1921.

12 "Műveszet, Zene–*Boldogság*." *Előre* 1 Feb. 1921

13 Ibid.

14 "Műveszet –Zene–Színház, A Modern Magyar Színpad Sikere Bethlehemben." *Előre* 6 Feb. 1921.

15 "Laura Crews at the Garrick." *The Evening Telegram* (New York) 19 Feb. 1921.

16 "Művészet–Zene–Színház." *Előre* 23 Feb. 1921.

17 "Magyar Színtársulat a Broadwayn." *Amerikai Magyar Népszava* (New York) 2 Feb. 1921.

18 "Lugossi Béla Utja." *Amerikai Magyar Népszava* 15 Feb. 1921.

19 "Színház, Müveszet, Mozi – *A kisasszony férje.*" *Amerikai Magyar Népszava* 22 Feb. 1921.

20 "Színház, Müveszet, Mozi – A Modern Magyar Színpad vasárnapi előadása." *Amerikai Magyar Népszava* 8 Mar. 1921.

21 "A Modern Magyar Színpad South Bethlehem és Philadelphiai Előadásai." *Előre* 3 Mar. 1921.

22 "*Fiú-e vagy leány?*" *Amerikai Magyar Népszava* 15 Mar. 1921.

23 "A Modern Magyar Színház elődása." *Amerikai Magyar Népszava* 9 Apr. 1921.

24 "Színház, Müveszet, Mozi – *Halló!*" *Amerikai Magyar Népszava* 12 Apr. 1921.

25 "The Plays That Pass – Is the American Actor Without Honor in His Own Theater?" *The Daily Call* (New York) 13 Mar. 1921.

26 Ibid.

27 "Színház, Müveszet, Mozi – *A kaméliás hölgy.*" *Amerikai Magyar Népszava* 1 Mar. 1921.

28 See "Az Első Dráma." *Amerikai Magyar Hírlap* 9 June 1921. The Modern Magyar Színpad toured with the play *Szerelem vására*, appearing in Youngstown, Ohio on June 19, 1921, but without Lugosi.

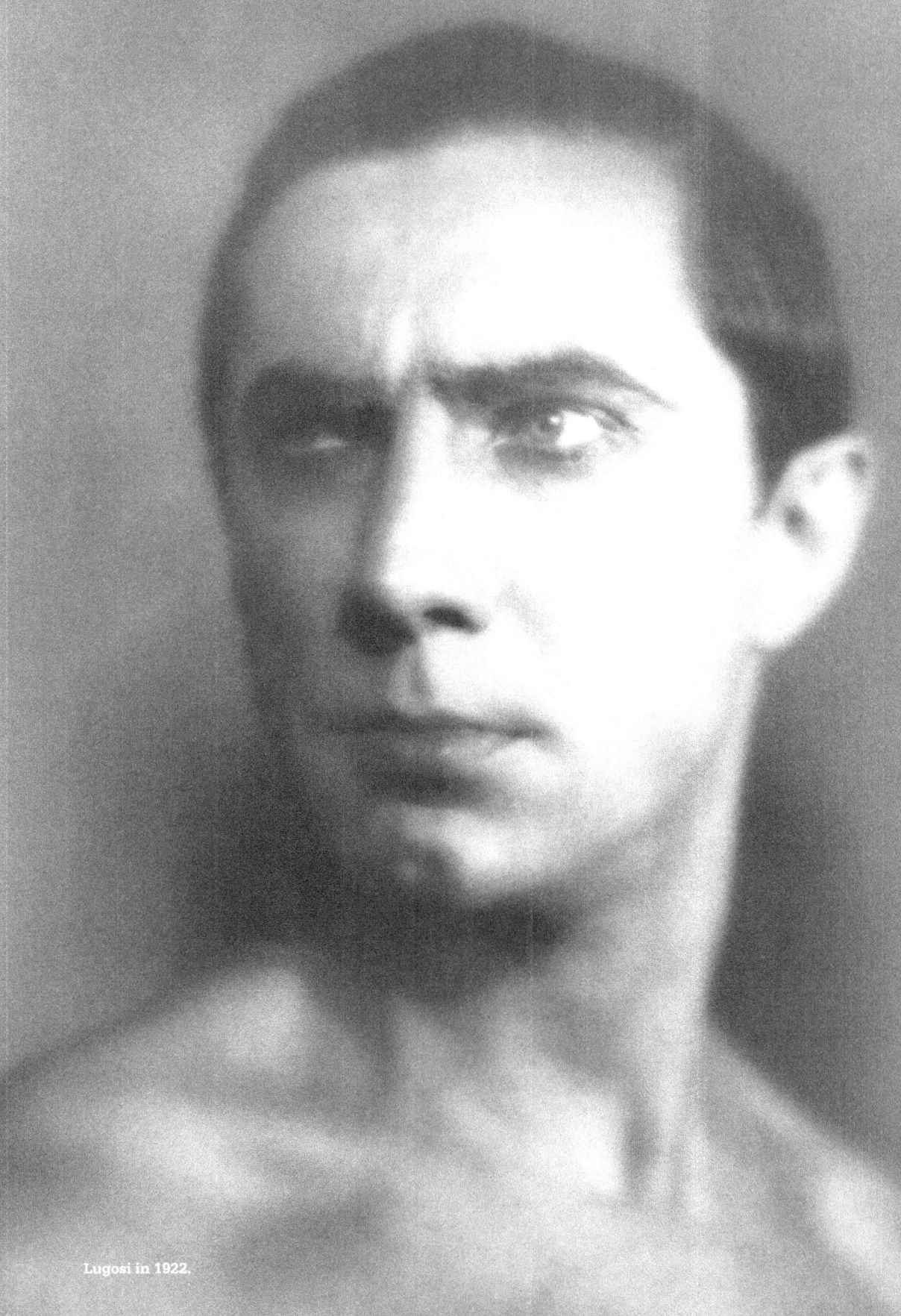

Lugosi in 1922.

Chapter 22

Unearthed

> "I shall then make known to you something
> of the history of this man, which has been
> ascertained for me. So then we can discuss
> how we shall act, and can take
> our measure accordingly."
> – Bram Stoker, *Dracula*

Once settled in America, Lugosi avoided bringing attention to his role in the Béla Kun government. But being a stranger in a strange land did not mean his past was buried. Some members of the Hungarian-American community in New York and elsewhere knew about his politics. Others confused him with the misdeeds of János "Béla" Lugosi-Buchter. Rumors spread, many of them hardly helpful to an actor looking to start a new life.

Lugosi did receive assistance from at least a few colleagues hoping to clear his name. In November 1921, the First Hungarian Literary Society of New York sent U.S. immigration officials a letter that declared:

> The Actors Trade Union [under the Kun regime] was founded in order to protect the rights of its members and *was not* involved in politics. The activities of the Trade Union were directed by officers elected by all the actors. Béla Lugosi was the paid secretary and was, as such, only an executor of decisions made by the leadership. We solemnly declare that Béla Lugosi did nothing except sacrifice his health, rising career, and family life to serve faithfully the interests of the actors for which recognition and gratitude should be due him. Under no circumstances did any of his actions shame or cause injury to the Hungarian people or nation.[1]

The statement is fascinating in part because it minimized Lugosi's actual position and power in the Kun government. More curious, though, is the fact the organization wrote anything. Lugosi had reported at Ellis Island on March 23, 1921.[2] The Literary Society wrote its letter supporting him approximately eight months later. The specific impetus is unknown, but presumably one or more persons had in the interim conveyed negative information about Lugosi to the American government, claiming his political past made him undesirable. It was the past made present. It was, as Stoker wrote in *Dracula*, the "odour of old earth newly turned."

Negative comments about Lugosi were not limited to a few Hungarians in America. In late March of 1921, only four days after Lugosi went to Ellis Island, one Budapest newspaper wrote:

> An American theatrical entrepreneur sends advertisements weekly to those newspapers published in Budapest. He floods the Hungarian population in America with the same news, in which, as his main attraction, he advertises 'the guest recital of Mr. Béla Lugosi, member of Hungary's Nemzeti Színház [National Theater], with attraction-seeking headlines. To be fair, Americans must also be informed of the fact that the Nemzeti Színház does not have a member called Béla Lugosi anymore.
>
> Once, he used to be a member of the cast, but in a totally unnoticeable way, and he appeared in roles with twenty-some words, then he was dismissed, and he had to flee from Hungary because of his communist practices. The Modern Magyar Színpad [Modern Hungarian Stage] in America has the right to advertise its illustrious guest accompanied by a rather unsuccessful portrait of comrade Lugosi; we have no objections to it, but neither the Nemzeti Színház nor Hungarian art in general have anything to do with him, who, in his own country could not become anything other than a guest of an internment camp.[3]

Such reportage – which underplayed Lugosi's role at the Nemzeti Színház – was clearly the result of anti-Kun and anti-communist sentiment in Miklós Horthy's Hungary. But it helped disinter Lugosi's political life from its grave, perhaps fueling anti-Lugosi forces in America, even if there were only a few of them.

It is evident that famed Hungarian singer and anti-socialist Ernő Király became Lugosi's most vocal critic in the early 1920s. In September 1921, Király came to America and toured cities with sizable Hungarian populations. A promoter in New York booked him on the same bill with Lugosi, who was to appear in a one-act play, most likely *Törvény* (*The Law*). In fact, Lugosi was booked to appear in a number of other cities with Király, including at least three in Ohio: Akron, Lorain, and Cleveland (where, according to the newspaper *Szabadság*, Lugosi was a "favorite of all [Hungarian-language] theatergoers.")[4]

Lugosi apparently had no problem with the arrangement, and neither did Király, at least at first. According to one Budapest newspaper:

> The concert of Ernő Király, held in New York on 4 September, had been greatly anticipated. Most tickets were sold weeks before, although the venue of the concert,

the Lexington Theater, can accommodate more than 3,000 spectators. In the evening of the concert a great number of Hungarian New Yorkers were stuck outside, so many people that they could have filled another big theater easily. Such interest seems natural.

Thanks to his phonograph disc recordings, Ernő Király is regarded as the most well-known Hungarian artist in America, even by those who have never seen him on stage. It would be hard to find a Hungarian home in America where the wonderful Hungarian [folk] songs by Ernő Király are not being listened to frequently. The audience eagerly applauded the artist, whose songs had an extraordinary effect on Hungarians who had to flee from their country.

Published in *Színházi Újság* on January 1, 1922.

At the time of his arrival, Ernő Király was informed of a rather inconvenient surprise: the organizers of the concert employed Béla Lugosi to play a role in a one-act drama which was incorporated in the concert without letting Király know about it. Since Ernő Király declared that he was not willing to appear with Lugosi, a new person was employed to play [Lugosi's role] in recent days. This made the communist fans of Lugosi start a protest against Király, but it turned out to be short lived.[5]

Another Budapest newspaper also reported on the incident, providing some additional information:

Why did a scandal happen during the concert of Ernő Király in New York? We have already written about an embarrassing incident that happened during the concert of Ernő Király in New York. The first report from New York has not provided detailed information, and thus we did not know what kind of group protested during the guest recital of the Budapest-based singer. In some American newspapers, which have just arrived, we can read what caused the protests.

Various actors with Hungarian roots living in America were expected to appear on stage during the concert of Ernő Király. One of them was Béla Lugosi, who left Hungary because of his behavior during the communist regime. Lugosi had a sad role in the

Published in Hungarian-American newspapers in 1921.

socialization process of theaters and in forcing actors to join the unions, and thus, Ernő Király – based on the reports of American magazines – was not willing to appear on the stage in Lugosi's presence.

However, one part of the audience demanded Lugosi's appearance, while another part protested against him, and when Lugosi finally appeared on stage, the turmoil erupted, and the audience disturbed the performance with loud interruptions. Finally, organizers had to turn to the police to control the situation, after which the concert went on without further disturbances.[6]

Király related further details to the Budapest newspaper *Világ*, which published his first-person account:

> When my ship arrived at the port of New York, my manager welcomed me. My first question was whether everything was all right. Yes – he said – we prepared the program and we will start the tour involving 12 Hungarian actors and actresses, with Béla Lugosi among them. I heard the news with great surprise, and I declared right away that I could not appear on the stage with Lugosi, and I am not willing to ... instead I'd prefer to return to Europe immediately. The manager assured me that he would deal with the problem, and I asked him to keep me from meeting Lugosi in person.
>
> I had already known that he is a quick-tempered, passionate person and so am I. I was also aware that he is physically stronger than I, so it would be rather inconvenient

to find myself in front of him. Fortunately, Lugosi did not come to find me; instead he called me, asking whether I was still sticking to my previous decision. When I said I was, he hung up without saying a word, and then he started plotting behind my back, which had particular effects on both of us, and had a rather ugly outcome for him.

He started attacking me in a newspaper called *Új Előre*, which is an extremist socialist one, published by Hungarians in America. He published one libelous article after the other, instigating the naïve and uninformed mass of Hungarian workers against me. That is why a fight, or better to say, a battle broke out in the audience during my first performance in New York.

The curtain rose, and I was already standing on the stage when Lugosi's comrades started a loud outcry accompanied with swearing. There were about two thousand people present in the audience, out of which about 100 people might have been the men of Lugosi. The majority of the audience received [this stunt] with indignation and they attacked those who were protesting. A disturbance erupted with fighting, a real war, where fists, clubs and boxers were equally employed.

Twenty-five people were beaten so badly that the ambulance had to carry them away. Twenty out of twenty-five injured, however, returned from the hospital to the audience after the injuries on their head and arms had been dressed. They had all the right to do so since America is a free country, and they had valid tickets, anyway. Thus, the storm broke out again, so the police were called, and fifty policemen came to the theater to march off those who were responsible for the disturbance.[7]

The veracity of Király's version of events is hard to determine. Obviously, he was someone who disliked Lugosi's politics vehemently.

Indeed, Király was a favorite of Miklós Horthy, the very man whose government was responsible for hunting down and murdering scores of political opponents during Hungary's "White Terror." Király allegedly admitted that he supported Horthy and "barks with the pack only because, if he did not, he would have been destroyed."[8] Whether or not that was true, it should be noted that Lugosi did not write any articles about the incident in *Előre*.

Moreover, the coverage in *Előre* did not libel Király, but instead reported the following:

> Hungarians in New York, especially workers, have been very excited for days, about the news which was spread about Király's concert...
>
> It is well-known that the Berger brothers, who are the managers of Király's tour in America, have been

Published in *Szabadság* on Sept 3, 1921.

announcing for weeks that Béla Lugosi and Ilona Montagh, two artists who are highly regarded by workers in America, would be featured in Király's concert program. It is also known that during the Hungarian Soviet Republic, Lugosi did beautiful cultural work. Like all cultural work, Lugosi's was an unforgivable crime in the eyes of Horthy's idiot officers and shrews...

Since the audience had already purchased the tickets for Király's concert, and it looked forward to the performance of Lugosi and Montagh just as much as to that of Király, if not more so, if Lugosi and Montagh had retreated for any reason from playing despite all the advertisements, it would have been an unpleasant surprise in itself. However, the widespread news about the reasons behind their cancellation did not cause surprise, but outrage in New York.

In the past few days, rumors were spread about Ernő Király's declaration upon his arrival in America, which was, by the way, based on the suggestions made by Márton Rátkai and Erzsi Tordai, and the content of which was that he was not willing to perform on stage with Lugosi because he would not bring risk to himself to be 'blamed' for working with an actor who 'compromised' himself during the Soviet Republic. What would they say 'back home' – he went on – if they found out he appeared on the stage with Lugosi?

The outrage of Hungarian workers in New York was just as boundless as Király's rhetoric was provoking....[9]

Published in *Előre* on August 20, 1921.

Apparently, Király's managers had announced for at least a few weeks that both Lugosi and Montagh would be on the concert bill. It is difficult to believe that Király knew nothing about it. It is also difficult to believe he could not foresee at least a small degree of controversy would result from refusing to appear with Lugosi, unless he hoped for that outcome in order to look anti-Lugosi (and thus anti-socialist and anti-communist) to Horthy and others in Hungary.

Shortly before the scheduled date of the concert, negotiations were held in the offices of *Előre* in an attempt to strike a compromise that would allow Lugosi to perform. According to that newspaper:

> **MEGVÁLTOTTA MÁR A JEGYÉT**
> # KIRÁLY ERNŐ ?
> egyetlen new yorki felléptéhez
> **Szeptember 4-én** este, pont **Lexington Theatre** Lexington Ave.
> 8 óra 30-kor és 51st Street
>
> VIDÉKI KÖRÚTJA:
>
> Hétfő, Szept. 5-én..South Bethlehem, Pa. .... Magyar Ház
> Kedd, Szept. 6-án Philadelphia, Pa. ....Labor Lyceum
> Szerda, Szept. 7-én..Trenton, N. J. .... Magyar Otthon
> Csütörtök, Szept. 8-án..Bridgeport, Conn........Rákóczi Hall
> Péntek, Szept. 9-én..New Brunswick, N. J. ....Szt. László Hall
>
> VÁLTSA MEG AZONNAL, HA JÓ HELYET AKAR KAPNI.

Above: Published in *Előre* on September 3, 1921.
Right: Published in *Előre* on September 4, 1921.

> # Fellép-e Lugosi és Montagh vasárnap a Király - koncerten?
>
> Az ELŐRE SZERKESZTŐSÉ-GÉBEN FOLYTATOTT TÁR-GYALÁSOK EREDMÉNYE
>
> A magyar munkásság résen áll minden fehér-kisérlet ellen
>
> Napok óta nagy izgatottságban tartja a new yorki magyarságot, különösen a munkásságot, a vasárnapi Király-koncerttel kapcsolatban elterjedt hir.
>
> Köztudomásu, hogy a Berger-testvérek, Király amerikai körutjának a rendezői, heteken át hirdették, hogy a Király-koncertek programján fognak szerepelni Lugosi Béla és Montagh Ilona, az amerikai munkás-

In yesterday's issue, we outlined the negotiations which had taken place in our editorial office on this matter. We wrote that Király's manager had promised that Lugosi would perform at the concert on Sunday night, and we wrote that Lugosi would perform according to the agreement. Király's manager, Mr. Berger, had promised that he and Ernő Király would visit our editorial office on Saturday and finally settle the case. Mr. Berger did not live up to this promise; instead he breached the agreement he had made to Lugosi and to us at the editorial office of *Előre*. ... If Hungarian-American workers' money is good enough for Ernő Király, why is he not happy for the company of artists on the stage who are truly praised by Hungarian-American workers?

... While writing these lines, a gentleman named Adorján Ötvös, who had allegedly been commissioned by Király to contact us, informed us by telephone that Király has had no intention of boycotting Lugosi, and that he is willing to declare

Gary D. Rhodes | Bill Kaffenberger

on the stage that he had no objections against him. However, based on the above facts and testimonials, we had to inform Mr. Ötvös politely and decisively that we can no longer believe what Mr. Király says, and, as far as we know the Hungarian workers in New York will not believe him either. He can make peace with Hungarian workers in New York for the gross insult in only one way: by appearing with Lugosi on the stage.[10]

If this account is to be believed, Király refused to work with Lugosi, then promised to work with him, and then changed his mind again.

In the end, Király apparently capitulated and Lugosi was allowed to perform, but not without Király's management interfering once again. According to *Előre*:

Published in *Előre* on September 5, 1921.

[A]s we approached the theater in the evening, we were shocked to see the driveway packed with cops, and even inside the theater one could see policemen everywhere. We tried to warn the police that their presence might agitate the workers even more, so if a disturbance erupts it will be their fault. We demanded that they leave, but the sensible advice found Mr. Berger & company [with] deaf ears again.

They just wanted to show off their strength. And indeed, they showed it.

When the curtain rolled up, a frenzy broke out, and it was such a strong one that it was something new even for the good old Lexington Theater....[11]

It is unclear whether or not Lugosi actually participated in the one-act play; he probably did, but the one existing review does not identify the actors who took part. However, Lugosi certainly did address the audience at the beginning of the program. *Előre* told readers:

> Lugosi was greeted with roaring applause when he appeared on the stage. He was truly celebrated by the workers of New York. He was the only one who had the chance to perform in real silence. Lugosi briefly summed up the details of the case, then said:
> 'Now it could be my turn to say that I'm not acting with Ernő Király. But I'm a worker on the stage, too, and I do what the audience orders me to do.'
> He then read a powerful poem about how deep Hungary has sunk in the mud, about workers being punished for the benefit of others, many of them dying for useless aims. The author would surely be pursued by Horthy's men, if he lived in Hungary, said Lugosi. We are sure that some 'white guards' took notes about the poem, so that they could denounce the author later. However, Lugosi, after having finished the recital, announced [sarcastically] that the poem was written by Mihály Vörösmarty, the author of the [patriotic Hungarian song] *Szózat*, who could not be arrested since he already died in 1855 in fear of the prospective 'white' punishment.
> Lugosi was celebrated by relentless applause from the audience, through whom workers were given a glorious gratification.[12]

And so Lugosi prevailed, at least according to a newspaper that was sympathetic towards him. All of the surviving evidence in this case is published in sources clearly biased towards one party or the other.

The Király controversy was likely a reason that the First Hungarian Literary Society drafted their letter in support of Lugosi in November of 1921. Then, wisely or not, in November of 1922, Lugosi recited poetry at New York's Lyceum Theater for a celebration of the anniversary of the Russian Revolution.[13] Afterwards, there is no evidence that he engaged in overtly political activity until World War II. If anything, Lugosi downplayed his political past during the rest of the 1920s and 1930s.[14]

Such a move might have been wise, as most audience members were less concerned with Lugosi's politics than they were his acting. In January 1922, *Új Előre* reported:

> Politics infiltrate the Hungarian community of actors, too. Béla Lugosi, who is unfamiliar with the workers' movement, is a thorn in the flesh of a couple of semi-talented, homesick emigrants. They do not want to play with him. Those who are reluctant to see Lugosi on stage complain about his political past, but not about his talent.[15]

Then, in November of 1927, a Hungarian-language newspaper published in Chicago underscored the need to keep Hungarian politics and theater separate:

> [W]e do not support the Hungarian theaters because the actors must eat, but because they amuse, educate, and keep alive Hungarian culture. As long as the theater is free of political partisanship, it is needless and perhaps destructive to air

the political views of the audience in connection with it. We must all admit that while the majority of Chicago Hungarians are against reactionary politics, there are some conservative, impartial Hungarians. It is wisest, therefore, to separate the Hungarian theater, the home of culture, from politics. We hope that the actors, too, will abstain from discussions....[16]

As Bram Stoker wrote in *Dracula*, "the dust had been much disturbed." It was time for it to accumulate once again, burying Lugosi's political past for as long as possible.

Endnotes

1 Quoted in Cremer, Robert. *Lugosi: The Man Behind the Cape* (Chicago: Henry Regnery, 1976). Emphasis in original.

2 *Inspector's Interrogation During Primary Alien Inspection*. Immigration Services. Ellis Island, New York. 23 Mar. 1921.

3 "Lugosi Ur." *Magyarország* (Budapest, Hungary) 27 Mar. 1921.

4 "Király Ernő." *Szabadság* (Budapest, Hungary) 3 Sept. 1921. The quotation about Lugosi being a "favorite" in Cleveland appears in "Király Ernő Szeptember 11-Én Clevelandban Lesz." *Szabadság* 23 Aug. 1921.

5 "Király Ernő Amerikában." *Pesti Hírlap* (Budapest, Hungary) 5 Oct. 1921.

6 "Miért volt botrány Király Ernő newyorki hangversenyén." *Pesti Napló* (Budapest, Hungary) 5 Oct. 1921.

7 "Király Ernő." *Világ* (Budapest, Hungary) 9 Nov. 1921.

8 "New York Munkásai Elégtételt Követeltek és Kaptak a Durva Sértésért a Király-Koncerten." *Előre* (New York) 7 Sept. 1921.

9 "Fellép-e Lugosi és Montagh vasárnap a Király – koncerten?" *Előre* 4 Sept. 1921.

10 "Király Ernő Vállalta a Horthy-Bunkó Szerepét a Munkásokkal Rokonszenvező Müvészek Ellen." *Előre* 5 Sept. 1921.

11 "New York Munkásai Elégtételt Követeltek és Kaptak a Durva Sértésért a Király-Koncerten."

12 Ibid.

13 "Orosz Forradalmi Emlékünnepet." *Új Előre* 5 Nov. 1922. [As of November 1, 1921, the publication *Előre* was retitled *Új Előre*.]

14 For more information on Lugosi's politics in America, see: Rhodes, Gary D. with Sheffield, Richard, *Dreams and Nightmares* (Narbeth, PA: Collectibles, 2007); Rhodes, Gary D. and Kaffenberger, Bill, *No Traveler Returns: The Lost Years of Bela Lugosi* (Albany, GA: BearManor Media, 2012); and Kaffenberger, Bill and Rhodes, Gary D., *Bela Lugosi In Person* (Albany, GA: BearManor Media, 2015).

15 Enyedi, Sándor. *A Tragédia amerikai színpadi pályafutásához* (Budapest: Színháztudományi Szemle 12, 1983), quoting *Új Előre* 4 Jan. 1922.

16 Untitled. *Magyar Tribune* (Chicago, IL) 4 Nov. 1927.

Chapter 23

The Tragedies of Man

> "I have responsibilities – great responsibilities that God imposes
> on me, that you [backward people] are not aware of, and
> unaware are the cross-trading Pharisees, too. I have
> great responsibilities that will promote a more
> beautiful, better, happier, and freer life."³⁴
> – Herman Heyersman, *Gettó* (*Ghetto*)

Having parted ways with the Modern Magyar Színpad (Modern Hungarian Stage) by mid-1921, Béla Lugosi became something more than an actor, more than a director. He started producing Hungarian-language plays as well. The date of this transition is somewhat difficult to determine, especially given that theater companies of the era generally took the summers off. At some point in August or September of 1921, though, Lugosi launched the next phase of his American career.

His first production was probably Ferenc Molnár's *Liliom*, a play that had been unsuccessful in Hungary when it debuted in 1909, but which captivated Broadway in the spring of 1921. The English-language version, translated by Benjamin Glazer, starred Joseph Schildkraut in the title role and Eva La Gallienne as Julie. The fact that a Molnár play was attracting large crowds to a New York theater might have heartened Lugosi that spring, giving him hope about his own future. As Benjamin Glazer wrote that year, "The Hungarian theater is only now being discovered in America. ... We scarcely know where to begin to choose, to admire, to praise."¹

Liliom's Broadway success certainly inspired Hungarian actor Márton Rátkai (aka Rátkay, aka Martin Ratkay) to mount a Yiddish-language version of the play at the Irving Place Theater in September of 1921.² It featured sets designed by Willy Pogány (aka Willi Pogány).³ Also in

```
! ! ! ALL STAR CAST ! ! !
         L I L I O M
   az amerikai magyar szinpadon!
  Molnár Ferenc világhirü darabjá-
nak szereposztása:
Liliom . . . . . . . . . . . . . . . Lugosi Béla
Juli . . . . . . . . . . . . . . . . Montagh Ilona
Mari . . . . . . . . . . . . . . . Váradi Juliska
Muskátné . . . . . . . . . . . . Thury Ilona
Ficsur . . . . . . . . . . . . . Horváth Lajos
Hordár . . . . . . . . . . . . . Erdélyi Emil
Hollenderné . . . . . . . . . . Kenesseyné
Hollender fia . . . . . Nyikos Zsigmond
Lujza, Juli lánya . . . . . . Winton Klári
Dr. Reich, öngyilkos . . . . . . .  —  —
Kádár öngyilkos . . . . . Darvas Károly
1. csendőr . . . . . . . . . . . . Tóth István
2. csendőr . . . . . . . . . . . . Nagy Lajos
Főkapitány az égben . . Hegedüs Lajos
Ajtónálló az égben . . . . . . . . . . Pataky
1. rendőr az égben . . . . . . . . . Hatvary
2. rendőr az égben . . . . . . . . .  —  —
Linz, pénztáros . . . . . . . Szalay Gyula
```

Published in *Színházi Újság* on September 15, 1921.

RÁTKAI MÁRTON

the cast was Egon Brecher, who would appear with Lugosi in *The Black Cat* (1934) and *Mark of the Vampire* (1935).[4]

Lugosi already knew Rátkai from their days in Hungary. The two men had appeared onstage together at the Király Színház (Royal Theater) in *A gésák* (*The Geisha*), which had a lengthy run in 1912.[5] Perhaps there was a rivalry between the two men; perhaps not. But one thing is certain: Rátkai was deeply involved in the union that Lugosi headed during the Béla Kun regime, even winning a seat on its executive committee.[6] Rátkai's name also appears on an official union letter signed by Lugosi.[7]

Liliom might have appealed to Rátkai for several reasons, not least being that he had been a supporting actor in the 1919 Hungarian film version directed by Mihály Kertész (Michael Curtiz). *Liliom* was never completed because Kertész left Hungary that year for Vienna.[8] Rátkai's work on the unfinished film probably led to false rumors in New York that he had starred in the Hungarian stage debut of *Liliom* in 1909.[9]

As late as 1920, Rátkai had appeared onstage in Budapest, and so – like Lugosi – he was a recent immigrant to America. According to one article, Rátkai had $200,000 to start a Hungarian theater troupe in New York City.[10] The investment dollars are not believable, both intrinsically (given the sheer value of that amount in 1921) and given that Rátkai did not remain in the United States for very long before returning to Budapest. Indeed, he seems to disappear from New York after 1922, after becoming "disappointed by America."[11]

Despite having participated in Lugosi's union, Rátkai did not have to leave Hungary in 1919. At a given point, he agreed with, or was at least not antagonistic to, the Miklós Horthy regime. And if the press accounts of Ernő Király's trip to America in 1921 are to be believed, Rátkai was not a fan of Lugosi's. It was probably Rátkai who advised

Király not to appear onstage with Lugosi. Rátkai was involved in arranging Király's American tour, and even met Király in person when he arrived at the docks in New York.[12]

And the timing of Rátkai's alleged $200,000 to begin his troupe might have been an effort, perhaps politically motivated, to go directly into competition with Lugosi. According to *Színházi Újság*:

> Márton Rátkai is a well known, talented artist. Budapest adores him, New York adores him, too. His only mistake is that he is a pioneer. He was pioneering with his debut in New York, when he tried to bring to success an unfamiliar and new genre, the special Budapest cabaret, which ... was not a mistake, but the time he chose was way too early.[13]

In the space of mere months, Rátkai organized three different, shortly-lived Hungarian-American companies, which seems to be an indication of their lack of success.[14]

Nevertheless, Rátkai did obtain the rights to stage *Liliom*. So did Lugosi, who staged *Liliom* in Hungarian rather than Yiddish in either August or September of 1921, making it the first time the play was performed in America in its original language. Here might have been another source of competition, even resentment, between Rátkai and Lugosi. For one performance, Lugosi had directed *Liliom*, and also starred in the title role. Ilona Montagh played Juli (aka Julie).

Published in *Előre* on August 24, 1921.

Alas, the Lugosi version is shrouded in a degree of mystery. More than one primary source from September 1921 mentions that it took place, having likely been produced by Ilona Fülöp, the woman for whom Károly Vidor (Charles Vidor) had committed suicide. One of the primary sources features a full cast list; another report was published in a Budapest newspaper.[15] But the sad fact is that many issues of Hungarian-American publications of the period no longer exist. The fate of *Színházi Újság* – a weekly publication that covered Hungarian theater and entertainment in New York – is particularly unfortunate. Very few issues from the early twenties survive.

Gary D. Rhodes | Bill Kaffenberger

Lugosi in *The Black Cat* (1934) with, from left to right, Boris Karloff, David Manners, and Egon Brecher. *(Courtesy of John Antosiewicz)*

As a result, the venue where Lugosi performed *Liliom* is unknown. It must not have been New York City, though, as the only known copy of the September 15, 1921 issue of *Színházi Újság* briefly mentions Lugosi's plans to stage a version in Manhattan with the same cast as in the earlier performance. Since there is no evidence of Lugosi helming a tour of *Liliom*, the version he did stage probably took place in a nearby city with Hungarian-American audiences, like Perth Amboy or Elizabeth, New Jersey.

The Lugosi production of *Liliom* in New York never happened, despite his popularity and the fact the English-language version was still playing Broadway in the autumn of 1921. What this means is unknown. Possible reasons include

RÁTKAI MÁRTON (A kegyelmes)
   Horthy rajza.

fallout from the Ernő Király incident and/or interference from Rátkai (who apparently had at least some money and would have been involved with the *Liliom* rights-holders) to Lugosi simply moving on to other projects. It is important to remember that, even though Molnár's name was paramount in Hungarian theater, the play *Liliom* had not yet become a traditional favorite among Hungarians or Hungarian-Americans. *Liliom* became much more important during and after 1921 than it had been before.

Notably, there are no known Lugosi productions from October through December 1921. But in 1922, he did perform with another theater troupe, the Amerikai Magyar Színtársulat (American Hungarian Theater Company). In mid-January 1922, he starred in *Királynőm, meghalok érted* (*My Queen, I Will Die For You*). Critical response to his performance was positive:

Published in *Amerikai Magyar Népszava* on January 11, 1922.

> Béla Lugosi played perfectly the role of the arrogant, violent army officer. In the scenes of the second act, when he keeps kicking the humble and despised Jewish teacher and mocks him with cruel, haughty words, but just a minute later, he embraces the same person with repressed feelings, like brothers do, he was wonderfully human in those moments, and his acting deserves [positive] appraisal.[16]

By the time of this performance, though, Lugosi had already returned to being his own producer.

For example, Lugosi produced, directed, and starred in Lajos Bíró's popular play *A sárga liliom* (*The Yellow Lily*) in New York City in early January of 1922. One journalist wrote about its importance:

> [An] interesting feature of the show will be the onstage appearance of Béla Lugosi, a former member of the Nemzeti Színház [National Theater]. Lugosi, who is well-known to Hungarians in New York and who was the central figure of numerous triumphant theater nights, will play one of his most satisfying roles this time ... his new show is gaining major interest.
>
> The Lugosi show is important not only as a theatrical event, but also as a social movement. The largest Hungarian societies and cultural circles in New York joined hands

Left: Published in *Amerikai Magyar Népszava* on December 25, 1921. Right: Published in *Színházi Újság* on January 1, 1922.

for this show. The audience in New York wants to enjoy Lugosi's art, and he found this direction to be the most appropriate to answer those expectations. ... This cultural event on New Year's Day opens a new chapter in the history of Hungarian theater in America.[17]

Two of the major Hungarian-language papers in New York were largely impressed with the result:

> Béla Lugosi played the role of the Archduke, and his acting brought to life the figure of the kind, young, eager man. He was elegant and light, and exceptional at the end of the first act, when he was playing the tired prince full of desires.[18] – *Amerikai Magyar Népszava*

> Lugosi played the role of the Grand Duke in an exquisite manner. He convinced us that he was the kind of thoughtless, brainless, parrot-talking, but snappy and pretty prince like the ones we all have heard of. Béla Lugosi provided a valuable performance

on Sunday evening, but we know he could have gotten more out of himself if he wanted to.[19] – *Új Előre*

Then, in late February, Lugosi produced, directed and acted in Herman Heyersman's *Gettó* (*Ghetto*). In the play, one character embodies conservatism and another liberalism.[20] Lugosi may well have seen parallels between their conflict and those that he had faced in Hungary. Critical response was again positive:

> Rafael (Lugosi) played on the highest octave of emotions in the audience's heart. His glowing, yet modestly veiled art made him so admired that no other Hungarian actor could compete with him in America.[21] – *Új Előre*

Published in *Amerikai Magyar Népszava* on February 23, 1922.

The massive room of the Central Opera House was filled by the audience at Béla Lugosi's Sunday performance. Heyersman's *Ghetto* was performed, a play that talks about the bitter and tragic struggle between two generations. ... Béla Lugosi played the role of the boy who was bitterly struggling against old, backward, rotten thoughts. His appearance within the sultry, moldy ambience of the play represented the power, the freedom, and development of the future, which will cross the narrow, limited, poor path of the old concepts. His voice, his sobbing, and his desire to get rid of the old [ways] were astonishingly realistic.[22] – *Amerikai Magyar Népszava*

Színházi Újság added that the play "deserve[d] praise," adding that Lugosi's performance was "beautiful."[23]

Of all of Lugosi's own Hungarian-language plays in America, the most important came in April 1922, when he produced, directed, and starred in a version of Imre Madách's 1861 classic *Az ember tragédiája* (*The Tragedy of Man*). Lugosi played Adam, Bella Pogány played Eve, Károly Davis played Lucifer, and Ilona Montagh played Hippia. Willy Pogány designed the sets, and a musical ensemble played music composed by the late Ferenc Erkel.[24]

By 1922, Lugosi knew *Az ember tragédiája* very well. He had performed in the play as early as February 13, 1903, during his tenure with the György Micsey Theater Troupe.[25] His first portrayal as Adam likely came on November 29, 1908, during his time in Debrecen, after which he played the role several times.[26]

Unlike *Liliom*, which was just becoming popular, *Az ember tragédiája* was likely the most beloved of all Hungarian plays. It remains unclear when Lugosi made the decision to stage it. However, once the news leaked out, it became a major topic of conversation, as Lugosi had "set out for an absolutely impossible mission."[27] After all, the Lugosi production was apparently the first time the play had ever been staged in America. *Amerikai Magyar Népszava* told readers:

Lugosi as Adam, the first man. As printed in *Színházi Újság* (New York) on March 15, 1922.

> Béla Lugosi, chief director of the performance, works day and night. Not to mention the scenario settings of the play [and] the training of the support staff consisting of 300 people takes up a huge amount of work. The performance of *Az ember tragédiája* requires such a huge staff that a whole team of assistants and stage managers will help Lugosi to ensure the fluency of the performance. Lugosi's directing and acting knowledge is already a guarantee of the perfection of the performance ... [T]he performance of *Az ember tragédiája* will be of the highest rank in every respect.[28]

The play premiered at New York City's Lexington Theater on April 8, 1922. A second performance was staged the next evening. Reaction in the Hungarian-American press was uniformly positive. A critic for *Amerikai Magyar Újság*, wrote:

> I do not think there was a single man who trusted in – sorry for the boastful expression – the artistic success of the New York performance of *Az ember tragédiája* ... Béla Lugosi is praiseworthy for this beautiful and honest attempt in New York. He might have been the only person who believed that they can provide something better than a poor country show, something more than a pale reflection of the colorful, dramatic piece, something more than a cliché of a poor oil print. ... If Lugosi would have done just that, if he would have provided no more than that, he would have still deserved

Published in *Amerikai Magyar Népszava* on March 11, 1922.

praise because he wanted to reach big things, and because he tried to approach the artistic with honesty and with eager desperation. ... This time, however, one has to talk seriously about this performance.

Lugosi, the director, was a surprise. He knew how to move the masses onstage, a couple of scenes were directed with a great intuition; the direction of the Egyptian scene and the French scenes was so fine that it surpassed the one we can see in the National Theater in Budapest ... [T]he overall impression suppresses these details, and we only mention the mistakes of the performance so that the director and actors can learn from it, and because such a serious and excellent production deserves serious criticism. ... This performance was a real cultural event and a great artistic sensation in the life of American Hungarians, and Lugosi has to be proud that this event is connected with his name. We have to admit: we did not expect so much from him, and the truth is that it was only his courage and enthusiasm that won the battle.

With such an acting quality, this actor would have a sensational success on the

 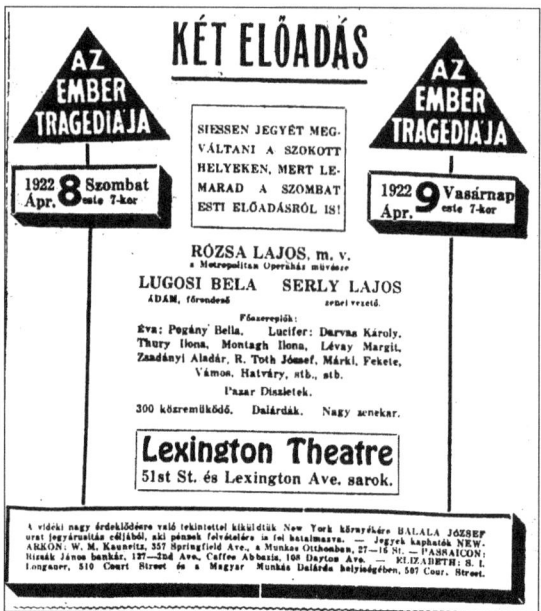

Left: Published in *Előre* on March 16, 1921. Right: Published in *Amerikai Magyar Népszava* on April 5, 1922.

best European stage, too. In big monologues, he was not preaching, but explaining, almost like a doctrine ... an incredible force breaks free of him and shakes the whole audience at the end of the scene: it was real acting from a great actor. ... Lugosi's Danton was sensational.[29]

Another article even suggested that Lugosi's Danton bested a depiction of the same character in a then-recent D.W. Griffith film.[30]

A critic at the *Amerikai Magyar Népszava* also praised Lugosi's latest production:

>...Béla Lugosi endured the trial by solving the incredibly difficult task, and he brought the impressive play to the Hungarians of New York in all its splendor, with majestic conviction and with perfect settings. We can hardly speak epithets which become so used and worn through theater reviews to properly describe performance, because this show is outstanding even within this year's unusually and sensationally lively and valuable season. We could not help but write columns of the greatness of each scene of the performance, the excellent work of all its actors [and] the outstanding qualities of Lugosi the director.
>
>... Besides Lugosi the director, Lugosi the actor did not remain in the shadow either. His voice, his mimics, and the feelings he conveyed perfectly matched the wide range of feelings which are characteristic of *Az ember tragédiája*. ... The surprising success and triumph of the performance means more than a good, a perfect performance. It means

that the Hungarian theater in America has come to a turning point under the leadership of Lugosi, because he successfully passed the great exam of theatrical direction....[31]

The Hungarian press was not alone in its applause, as the German-language *New Yorker Volkszeitung* praised the show, noting "The performance is enhanced by beautiful scenery and the musical accompaniment of a large orchestra which makes it worth seeing even for those who do not speak Hungarian."[32]

Lugosi was clearly happy about the support given to him and the production. In a personal letter to the newspaper *Új Előre*, he wrote:

> My colleagues! Now that I have succeeded in making a performance come to life that could be a cultural historical fact regarding Hungarians in America, I know that I would not have been able to make it happen without your enthusiastic, self-sacrificing, and successful endeavor, amongst all the insurmountable difficulties. Allow me to publicly express my deep gratitude and appreciation to you. And the fact that the income from the performances was greatly exceeded by the expenditures proves that we did not deny anything of what staging such a large-scale play demanded from the spiritually aspiring audience. The great artistic and moral success that I have gained through this performance is a source of my personal satisfaction.
>
> So, with the certainty that we will fight for our future successes together, and that in the future the public will not be fooled around by such wicked rumors such as that the [next] performance will be cancelled, or that it will be a cultural scandal, etc. I hope to remain your truest friend....[33]

The person or persons responsible for those "wicked rumors" is unknown. Perhaps it was Márton Rátkai. Perhaps they resulted from Lugosi's unrealized plans to stage *Liliom* in Manhattan.

Whatever the case, the frequency of Lugosi's roles in Hungarian-language theater productions dwindled. As the year 1922 progressed, he pursued new opportunities, including in the Hungarian community.

Endnotes

1 Glazer, Benjamin. "Discovering the Hungarian Theater." *Színházi Újság* (New York) 15 Sept. 1921.

2 Advertisement. *Előre* (New York) 24 Aug. 1921.

3 Jolo. "*Liliom*." *Variety* 23 Sept. 1921.

4 "*Liliom* Amerikai Színpadon." *Előre* 6 Sept. 1921.

5 "A Király-színházban." *Pesti Napló* (Budapest, Hungary) 7 Apr. 1912.

6   "Szakmozgalom." *Népszava* (Budapest) 13 Apr. 1919.

7   Typed and signed letter from Lugosi to the National Union of Actors. (HU MNL OL K 305-IV.-1919-10.-90700, Courtesy of the Hungarian National Archives).

8   Rode, Alan K. *Michael Curtiz: A Life in Pictures* (University Press of Kentucky: Lexington, KY, 2017).

9   Jolo, "*Liliom*."

10 "Legujabb." *Friss Újság* (Budapest, Hungary) 28 Sept. 1921.

11 Quoted in Fodor, Nándor. "Rátkay–Király–Küry." *Színházi Újság* (New York) 1 Jan. 1922.

12 "Fellép-e Lugosi és Montagh vasárnap a Király – koncerten?" *Előre* 4 Sept. 1921.

13 Fondor, "Rátkay–Király–Küry."

14 "Rátkai Ujabb Vállalkozása a 'Magyar Színház." *Színházi Újság* 1 Jan. 1922.

15 "All Star Cast!!!" *Színházi Újság* 15 Sept. 1921; "Színház és Zene." *Pesti Hirlap* (Budapest, Hungary) 19 Oct. 1921.

16 "Színház, Műveszet, Mozi." *Amerikai Magyar Népszava* (New York) 24 Jan. 1922.

17 "A Lugosi-Elöadás a Legújabb Szenzációja Magyar Amerikának." *Színházi Újság* 1 Jan. 1922.

18 "Színház, Zene." *Amerikai Magyar Népszava* 3 Jan. 1922.

19 "*Sárga liliom*." *Új Előre* 4 Jan. 1922.

20 "A Remélt Nagy Siker Jegyében Zajlott le a *Ghetto* előadása." *Új Előre* 28 Feb. 1922.

21 Ibid.

22 "*Gettó*." *Amerikai Magyar Népszava* 23 Feb. 1922.

23 *Színházi Újság* 1 Mar. 1922.

24 "Theater and Music." *New Yorker Volkszeitung* (New York) 9 Apr. 1922.

25 See Chapter 1 for more information.

26 See Chapter 4 for more information.

27 Enyedi, Sándor. *A Tragédia amerikai színpadi pályafutásához* (Budapest: Színháztudomanyie Szemle 12, 1983), quoting from *Amerikai Magyar Népszava* 10 Apr. 1922.

28 "*Az ember tragédiája*." *Amerikai Magyar Népszava* 18 Mar. 1922.

29 Enyedi, *A Tragédia amerikai színpadi pályafutásához*, quoting from *Amerikai Magyar Újság* (New York) 10 Apr. 1922.

30 Enyedi, *A Tragédia amerikai színpadi pályafutásához*, quoting from "*Az ember tragédiája*." *Amerikai Magyar Népszava* 10 Apr. 1922. The original article states, "Concerning Danton of the French Revolution, we can only wish that D. W. Griffith, the most famous filmmaker, could have seen Lugosi in this role. If he had seen him, he certainly would have asked Lugosi for the role of Danton, who is incomparably better, more rational, and convincing than the famous actor on the movie screen."

This comment apparently refers to Monte Blue, who portrayed Danton in D.W. Griffith's *Orphans of the Storm* (1921).

31 "*Az ember tragédiája.*" *Amerikai Magyar Népszava* 10 Apr. 1922.

32 "Theater and Music."

33 Lugosi, Béla. "*Az ember tragédiája* előadásának összes résztvevőihezl." *Új Előre* 13 Apr. 1922.

34 "Ma délután van a *Ghetto* előadása." *Új Előre* (New York) 26 Feb. 1922.

Lugosi as Dr. Mirakle, the exhibitor, in *Murders in the Rue Morgue* (1932). *(Courtesy of John Antosiewicz)*

Chapter 24

Film Exhibitor

> "I am not a sideshow charlatan, so if you expect
> to witness the usual carnival hocus-pocus,
> just go to the box-office and
> get your money back."
> – Dr. Mirakle, *Murders in the Rue Morgue* (1932)

In Robert Florey's *Murders in the Rue Morgue*, Dr. Mirakle (Lugosi) presents "Erik, the Ape-man" to Parisian carnival-goers. In Charles Barton's *Abbott and Costello Meet Frankenstein* (1948), McDougal's House of Horrors attempts to display the remains of Count Dracula (Lugosi), having obtained them from a European agent. After the passage of many years, when it came to Lugosi the horror film star, the exhibitor had become the exhibit.

Lugosi's efforts to carve out a career in America were not limited to acting, directing, and producing stage plays. In the autumn of 1922, he formed what one advertisement called "Lugossy Film," not a company to produce movies, but rather to screen them, to exhibit productions made in Hungary to Hungarian-American audiences. In order to do so, Lugosi turned to Mihály Hahn (aka Michael Hahn), who had brought some Hungarian film prints with him from Vienna to America.[1] Together with his wife Elisabeth, Hahn operated a film exchange in New York for many years that specialized in importing European productions.[2]

On November 5, 1922, "Lugossy Film" rented an auditorium at the Washington Irving High School in New York and presented an evening of Hungarian cabaret together with a movie entitled *Játék az esküvővel* (*The Wedding Game*). Live entertainment featured "Lugosi's first performance this season" in the one-act play *A gyászruhás nő* (*The Woman in Mourning Dress*).[3] According to the *Amerikai Magyar Népszava*:

Lugosi as Dracula, the exhibit, in *Abbott and Costello Meet Frankenstein* (1948). *(Courtesy of John Antosiewicz)*

The name of Béla Lugosi attracted a fair quantity of spectators to the Washington Irving High School. He appeared in a one-act play, which was greatly loved by the audience. His partner in the one-act play ... was [famed theater and film actress] Ferike Boros. He played skillfully in it. Then Irma Bráver sang a few songs, with a disciplined, orderly, beautiful voice. The rich baritone of Ferenc Zsolt created stormy applause and made him a favorite of the spectators. Then a Hungarian movie ... Ila Lóth is a nice and enjoyable vision on the screen, her naiveté and charm make her really similar to Mary Pickford. The audience laughed a lot at the intertitles, which turned out to be rather witty, and the participants applauded more than once during the screening.[4]

Ila Lóth – who had costarred onscreen with Lugosi in Hungary – never made a film titled *Játék az esküvővel*. It seems that Hahn and/or Lugosi retitled another Hungarian film with Lóth, perhaps to make it seem new or different, or – more likely, given the dearth of Hungarian silent films released in America – to avoid repercussions over screening a movie they didn't legally own or have the rights to exhibit.

Certainly the most fascinating and mysterious "Lugossy Film" event was the one that preceded *Játék az esküvövel*. On October 8, 1922, at the Washington Irving High School auditorium, Lugosi twice screened *Asszonyszivek Kalandora* (*The Adventurer of Women's Hearts*). Along with the screenings, Lugosi directed cabaret entertainment starring several Hungarian actors. But here Lugosi the film exhibitor also became Lugosi the film exhibit, as he was very definitely the star of *Asszonyszívek Kalandora*, a project hitherto unknown to historians. An advertisement referred to it as a seven-act film, but a published review clearly describes it as a two-act short subject.

According to the *Amerikai Magyar Népszava*, "the cabaret was satisfying enough" and "the actors ... received great applause." The same was less true of the film:

> [Fortunately it] does not represent the level of Hungarian cinematography anymore. We believe that the art of the Hungarian moving picture has already reached a much higher level than what it used to be like when this movie was made.[5]

By contrast, a critic for *Új Előre* enjoyed *Asszonyszívek Kalandora*. His review sheds a bit of light on its plot and origins:

> Mihály Hahn ... introduced a Hungarian film in his possession on Sunday afternoon and evening. ... The film featured Béla Lugosi. *Asszonyszívek kalandora*, a two-act drama, was shot in the early years of the war. There are a bit too many counts and barons, and hand-kissing servants in it, and its style is also not quite as simple as we like it today; nevertheless, it was interesting; the footage was beautiful, and the play of Lugosi and his three female colleagues had a strong impact on the audience. Lugosi appeared in front of the stage lights and thanked the [audience for the]

Published in *Amerikai Magyar Népszava* on November 3, 1922.

applause, which, as he said, was not for the film, not for him either, but for the hard work of the artists who made the movie come true.⁶

What is this undocumented Lugosi film?⁷ The tantalizing thought that Lugosi had produced his own short subject in America should be avoided, as there is absolutely no evidence that was the case. The comment about the film being made during World War I strongly implies it was produced in Hungary, as does an advertisement that promoted it as a "Hungarian recording."

Lugosi had starred in one short subject in Hungary, a comedy called *A régiséggyűjtő* (*The Antiquarian*, 1918). But its surviving plot synopses do not comport at all with *Asszonyszívek kalandora*. The two films belonged to different genres, with *A régiséggyűjtő* featuring three male leads and *Asszonyszívek kalandora* three female leads. And so the two are almost certainly not the same film.

Could *Asszonyszívek kalandora* instead be another Hungarian short film, one produced during the "early years of the war" that has languished in obscurity until now? That is possible. No film titled *Asszonyszívek kalandora* has ever been catalogued by silent film specialists in Hungary, nor has it surfaced in exhaustive searches of Hungarian industry trade publications or period newspapers. However, as film historian Gyöngyi Balogh has noted, some Hungarian shorts produced during the war may not have been screened, and thus no press or censorship records would have mentioned them.⁸

An important clue appears in an advertisement that promised *Asszonyszívek kalandora* would have both Hungarian and English intertitles.⁹ It seems likely that Hahn and/or Lugosi rechristened a pre-existing film as *Asszonyszívek kalandora* in America, even creating new intertitles that featured English. Why would anyone go to such trouble for a single Hungarian-American film screening?

Two images of film star Ila Lóth.

Published in *Amerikai Magyar Népszava* on October 31, 1922.

Lugosi in New York in the early 1920s.

In terms of the English language, Hahn probably hoped to rent the film print to American theaters. Along with the intertitles, the title card(s) for the film also probably featured English translations, thus allowing American exhibitors to screen the film, at least in the unlikely event anybody wanted to do so.

But the change of film title and intertitles likely stemmed from an additional reason, meaning that *Asszonyszívek kalandora* probably originated as one of Lugosi's Hungarian feature films, with someone like Hahn editing it down to a shorter length. The result would have simultaneously obscured its origins, much like the title *Játék az esküvővel* did for the

Published in *Amerikai Magyar Népszava* on October 7, 1922.

Published in *Előre* on October 8, 1922.

Ila Lóth feature, while also perhaps heightening the Lugosi content, making him even more the dominant star of whatever footage remained. The new title clearly placed emphasis on Lugosi the romantic lover. And new intertitles might have been necessary to better explain the edited and possibly altered storyline.

Surveying all of Lugosi's Hungarian feature films, it is possible that *Asszonyszívek kalandora* could have been an abbreviated version of either *Álarcosbál* (*The Masked Ball*, 1917) or *Leoni Leo* (*Leo Leoni*, 1917). Given the mention of three female leads, perhaps the most likely possibility would be *Küzdelem a létért* (*The Struggle for Life*, 1918). The fact that Lugosi was originally billed as Arisztid Olt in these two films might have been yet another reason for changing the title cards and/or intertitles.

As for the critic who reported that the film was produced during the "early years" of World War I, another question arises, as Lugosi signed up for military service in the summer of 1914. Theoretically, Lugosi could have appeared in a film prior to that time, or not long after returning to civilian life in 1916. But this comment might have been nothing more than Lugosi and/or Hahn's attempt to imply that a film produced in 1918 was a few years older than it was, thus explaining away what already seemed to be primitive production techniques by the standards of America in 1922. Perhaps. Here are the most logical explanations of this obscure entry in Lugosi's filmography. And certainly it should be treated as a unique film, even if it originates from pre-existing and repurposed footage. "Lugossy Film" had indeed exhibited a Lugosi film.

But these exhibitions came to an abrupt end. Whatever Lugosi's hopes had been, he only screened Hungarian films at two events. After that, Lugosi the exhibitor had to wait until Universal Pictures and *Murders in the Rue Morgue* in 1932, in which his character presented not cinema to audiences, but instead a "milestone in the development of life." As Dr. Mirakle, he would be responsible for murders and mad science. But he would also importantly advise Camille L'Espanaye (Sidney Fox), "Take a seat in front where you can see everything."

Endnotes

1 "In the Courts." *Film Daily* 30 Mar. 1923.

2 At a given point, perhaps much later, Hahn named his company the Danubia Distributing Corporation. See Alicoate, Jack, editor. "Exchanges." *The 1938 Film Daily Year Book* (New York: The Film Daily, 1938).

3 Advertisement. *Amerikai Magyar Népszava* (New York) 31 Oct. 1922.

4 "Lugosi Béla." *Amerikai Magyar Népszava* 7 Nov. 1922.

5 "Színház Művészet Mozi." *Amerikai Magyar Népszava* 10 Oct. 1922.

6 "Lugosi Filmen." *Új Előre* (New York City) 10 Oct. 1922.

7 One advertisement did refer to *Asszonyszívek kalandora* as being "seven acts" in length, but – given comments made by reviewers after seeing the film – that was apparently an error.

8 Balogh, Gyöngyi. Email to Gary D. Rhodes, 10 Mar. 2020.

9 Advertisement. *Amerikai Magyar Népszava* 7 Oct. 1922.

Published in the *Tampa Tribune* (Tampa, FL) on December 28, 1924.

Chapter 25

The Countess

When the magazine *Modern Screen* wrote about the "woman with yellow eyes" who allegedly plagued Lugosi just before World War I, they quoted him as follows:

In my [Hungarian theater company in New York] was a girl of my own race to whom I soon became attached. Strangely enough her name, too [like my first wife's] was Ilona. We became sweethearts and soon decided to get married. Once more I was in love and this time, I decided, no matter how many yellow eyes appeared in my audience, I would find happiness.[1]

But only two weeks after the marriage, so the story goes, Lugosi appeared onstage in Brooklyn. The woman with yellow eyes stared up at him from the front row. "So great was the shock of those glowing yellow orbs that his company thought Lugosi had been struck by an attack of heart trouble."[2]

The Ilona in this tale was Ilona Montagh, sometimes spelled "Ilona Montag." She was born in Hungary in December 1899. The place of birth is in question, as on different documents she listed Arad, Csanád, and Dombegyház.[3] Montagh was roughly the same age as Ilona Szmik, but looked quite different.[4] She stood 5 feet, 9 inches. And she had black hair and dark eyes.

Montagh knew she wanted to be an actress from an early age.[5] Early in her career, she received acclaim for portraying the lead female role in a Budapest production of *Lengyelvér* (*Polish Blood*).[6] And she appeared in at least two Hungarian films in 1916, *Házasság a Lipótvárosban* (*The Wedding in the Lipótváros*) and *A grófnő betörői* (*The Countess' Burglars*).

Then she moved to Berlin, playing the lead role in *Fehér báránykák* (*Little White Sheep*) at the Metropol Theater in June of 1917. An article in Hungary claimed:

After a difficult start, Ilona Montagh became one of Berlin's most celebrated actresses with astonishing speed. We are now being informed of her new successes. After Berlin she

was contracted to Dresden, and she pleased the audience with her very first appearance on stage, receiving the highest recognition from theatergoers and critics alike.[7]

On August 6, 1917, Montagh performed in the operetta *Königin der Luft* (*Queen of the Air*) at the Lessing Theatre in Berlin. A Hungarian theater publication reported, "Newspapers from Berlin praised in unison her sweet voice, lively movements, and adorable way of speaking."[8]

But according to Montagh, the production that gained her the most fame in Europe was *Schwarzwaldmädel* (*The Girl from the Black Forest*), which was staged in Budapest, Dresden, Hanover, Vienna and Berlin.[9] An article from 1924 recalled, "This show ran and ran, no rival ever getting within shooting distance of its record."[10]

Lugosi may well have met Montagh in Budapest. They might also have met in Berlin, where she not only worked on the stage, but also appeared in at least one German film, Emil Waldmann's *Juck und Schlau* (*Juck and Schlau*, 1920).[11] Even if they did not meet in Europe, they were likely aware of one another by reputation.

Montagh arrived in New York on January 6, 1921, not long after Lugosi reached the city.[12] She was 21 years old. A US immigration officer recorded that Gustave Amberg – who regularly staged German operas for American audiences – had paid Montagh's fare. Her initial residence was at the home of Amberg's friend Julius Kessler, a Hungarian who made a fortune in the whiskey business.[13] Once Prohibition began, Kessler devoted his time to philanthropic activities.[14]

Amberg presumably knew about Montagh's success in Berlin and wanted to present her to American audiences, as well as in Canada, it would seem, as there is a report that she appeared onstage in Ottawa in early February 1921.[15] But Amberg's plans came to an abrupt end when he died on May 23, 1921.[16] As for Montagh, perhaps she continued to stay at Kessler's home, but her stated reason for being in the US had crumbled. "Bad luck began to decorate her with all sorts of jinx-insignia," a journalist later wrote.[17]

Published in the October 31-November 6, 1920 issue of ***Színházi Élet***.

MONTAG ILONA   MONTAGH ILONA

Left: Published in the May 2-8, 1920 issue of *Színházi Élet*. Right: Published in the December 2-8, 1923 issue of *Színházi Élet*.

Montagh's acquaintance (or, as the case may have been, re-acquaintance) with Lugosi came fairly quickly. The two performed together in *Kisasszony férje* (*A Young Lady's Husband*) at the Thirty-Ninth Street Theater on February 20, 1921.[18] One article promoted her as being a "well-known prima donna."[19] And a critic reported her "spicy charm and fresh cheekiness were delightful."[20] She subsequently appeared with Lugosi in other productions, as chronicled in Chapters 21 through 23.

In America, Montagh falsely claimed to have been born into "one of the most aristocratic families in Buda-Pesth."[21] She began calling herself a "Countess" and generally rendered her name with a nobiliary particle: Ilona von Montag (or sometimes Ilona Von Montagh or Ilona de Montagh). She apparently reinvented her origins every bit as much as Lugosi had, if not more so. (It is worth noting that newspaper coverage of a 1922 party referred to him as "Bela von Lugosi."[22])

Lugosi's romance with Montagh probably began when the two appeared together in *Kisasszony férje*.[23] One journalist claimed, "Theirs was a spontaneous, fiery match, in which love of their mutual art and for each other vied."[24] The two married on September 7, 1921.[25] "A prospect of bliss which seemed too good to be true," another newspaper article reported, adding, "It was."[26] Years later, Lugosi recalled that the marriage lasted fourteen days.[27] Montagh maintained that it was "two months of boredom."[28] It could have been even longer before the two separated.[29]

Lugosi apparently hoped Montagh would become the mother of his child. "I wanted a wife to preside over a quiet home," he bemoaned.[30] She countered that Lugosi was "a perfect sweetheart but a poor husband, and he failed in every way to measure up to the high standards

Left: Published in the *Vancouver Sun* on January 30, 1921.
Above: Published in *Előre* on February 17, 1921.

he set for himself" when wooing her.[31] Topping the list of failures was his extreme jealousy.[32]

As of November 1921, Montagh began appearing in productions without Lugosi, presumably due to the breakup. That month, she sang in the operetta *Bruder Straubinger* (*Brother Straubinger*) at the Manhattan Opera House; then, in January 1922, she starred in the operetta *Rund um die Liebe* (*All About Love*) in Brooklyn.[33] Soon thereafter, she appeared in the Central Park Opera House's *Falusi Menyecskék*

Ilona Montagh in America. Photo distributed to newspapers on November 12, 1924.

(*Village Brides*), which starred famed primadonna Klára Küry.³⁴

The two might have reconciled for a time in 1922. They did perform together in Madách's *Az ember tragédiája* (*The Tragedy of Man*) in April of that year, with Lugosi as Adam and Montagh as Hippia.³⁵ In it, Madách wrote, "joy is but a fragile flower, foredoomed to fade." Only one month later, the Hungarian-American press announced that Montagh would hold a farewell recital at the Rand School in New York, as she was leaving America to resume her career in Paris.³⁶

Though tickets were sold, the recital didn't take place. Montagh said she was bedridden with appendicitis and announced that ticket vendors were responsible for the refunding of money to would-be audiences. "I leave it to the public to judge this customer treatment," she said, promising to refund money to anyone who had bought tickets directly from her.³⁷ She added that a contract awaited her

Above Top: Published in *Új Előre* on March 23, 1924.
Above Bottom: Published in the *New York Sun* on April 29, 1924.

in Paris, but she doesn't seem to have left the United States, at least not that year. And the number of her known performances in America dwindled dramatically.³⁸

If Montagh is to be believed, she was the one who left Lugosi, not the other way around. She claimed that Lugosi started a bizarre campaign to win back her affections. At first he kidnapped her beloved dog Fleurette, returning the pet so that he could speak with her. Then his actions grew stranger:

> No sooner had Ilona recovered from Fleurette's vanishing that she began to act as an unwilling shock-absorber for other strange attentions. Weird voices informed her over the phone at unearthly hours that she had better hurry and mend her absent husband's heart as soon as possible, or else!
>
> Ilona was more perturbed when the New York press began to develop a strange interest in her private life. Not once, but a half a dozen times, reporters pled for interviews, and she politely admitted them. But they threw off all pretense of being news-gatherers, and

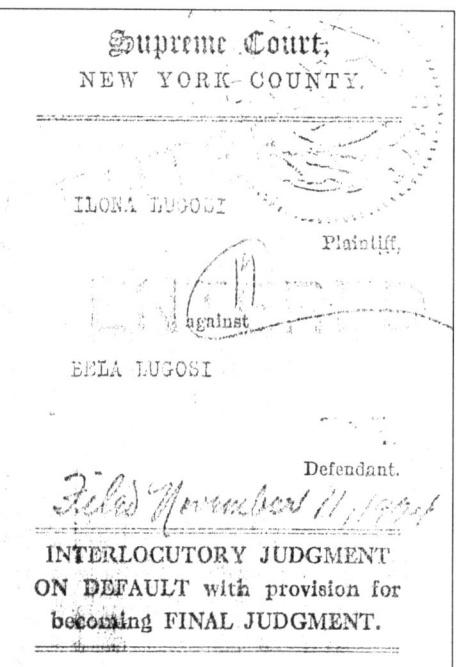

candidly told her that they were emissaries from her desolate mate.

Shortly after this, Ilona embarked for the theatre—alone. At the corner a strange man sprang out at her, uttering incoherent words and making peculiar gesticulations. The gist of his mumbled discourse was that Madame should, must, would take back Béla Lugosi.[39]

Scared out of her senses, Ilona was about to yell for the police when, to her astonishment, the stranger accomplished the equivalent of a quick nocturnal shave by feverishly snatching off his facial decorations.[40]

Underneath the "bogus set of whiskers" was Lugosi, a disguised advocate for himself. Montagh stormed off, apparently unimpressed.

But the "end was not yet." A week later, while Montagh rode in a bus, she felt her ankles go cold. Reaching down, she discovered her legs had been shackled together by a cord. Apparently Lugosi had been in the seat behind her and crouched onto the bus floor to reach her ankles. He then sat beside her and tied her wrists together. "Would she come back to him? Would she have mercy?" Montagh somehow managed to escape, fleeing from the bus and disappearing into the night.[41] At least that was the story she told.

Montagh brought her divorce suit before Judge William P. Burr on October 24, 1924. She blamed the action not on Lugosi stalking her or his jealousy, but rather "a raid on Lugosi's apartment, where she found an unknown woman."[42] The raid occurred on Montagh's birthday in May of 1924, perhaps resulting from her having hired a private detective.[43] Realizing that reconciliation was impossible, the actress stated "with tears in her beautiful, dark eyes" that she wanted no money from Lugosi, only her freedom.[44]

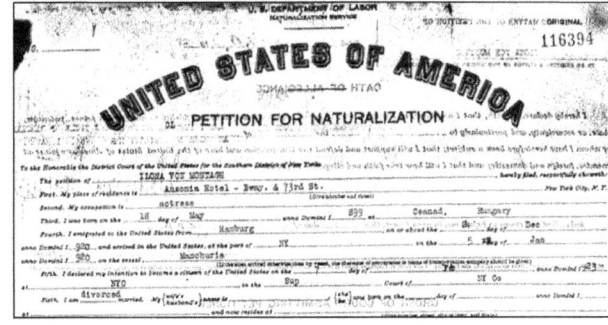

The judge believed the charge of adultery against Lugosi and stipulated that he could not remarry anyone during Montagh's lifetime without the permission of the court. The divorce became final on February 13, 1925.[45] "She Quits the 'Valentino of the Stage,'" one news item headlined.[46]

The news quickly reached Hungary, where a journalist wrote the following account:

> Those who can still remember the gloomy Bolshevik era, might not have forgotten about Béla Lugosi either. ... His wife, Ilona de Montagh, started divorce proceedings. [Montagh] is now living in Paris, and she is not asking for any kind of maintenance. Lugosi did not have any objections, so the divorce has been pronounced. The *New York Review* reports that two Hungarian actors, namely Géza Huszár and Aladár Gerő, had been the testimonials of Lugosi being caught on some unlawful entertainment with a blonde lady in his apartment.[47]

Here is a contradiction, though. Montagh claimed that she discovered Lugosi with a brunette.

Montagh's tale seems problematic in other respects. It is possible that she could have gone to Lugosi's apartment in 1924, even if the two separated by her choice in 1921, and even if she had spurned his attempts at reconciliation, but that seems unlikely. It also seems unlikely that she would have waited months to file for divorce if she was indeed so outraged to discover Lugosi with another woman in May of 1924. Whatever the truth of her stories, including of Lugosi's infidelity, the blonde/brunette may have been nothing more than a concoction that both parties agreed upon in order to obtain a divorce.

Montagh perhaps did move to Paris at some point, as a newspaper account claimed. But if so, she returned to America by 1927, at which time she applied for naturalization, which she was granted in January 1928.[48] There is a record of her going abroad after that time, with one ship manifest reporting her return to New York in April 1932. She was still in New York City in 1935, when the press reported the following:

> Laughing defiantly at her plight, Mrs. Ilona von Montagh Lugosi, former actress and divorced wife of Béla[49] (Dracula) Lugosi, Hungarian film star, was a prisoner in the East

67th Street Station last night charged with shoplifting.

She and a companion, Mrs. Irene Humphrey, 30, a widow, who shares a penthouse apartment with Mrs. Lugosi at 40 E. 58th St., were accused of stealing four gowns valued at $64.85 from B. Altman & Co.'s store at 34th St. and Fifth Avenue.

According to John F. Larkin, head of the Altman detective force, both women came to the dress department and asked to see some gowns. Once inside a fitting room, he declared, the pair slipped the dresses in paper bags under their arms and strolled out. Women detectives, who had been watching, arrested them.

At the station house they laughingly explained, police said, they had done it 'on a bet.' Neither was able to produce the required $500 bail at a late hour last night.[50]

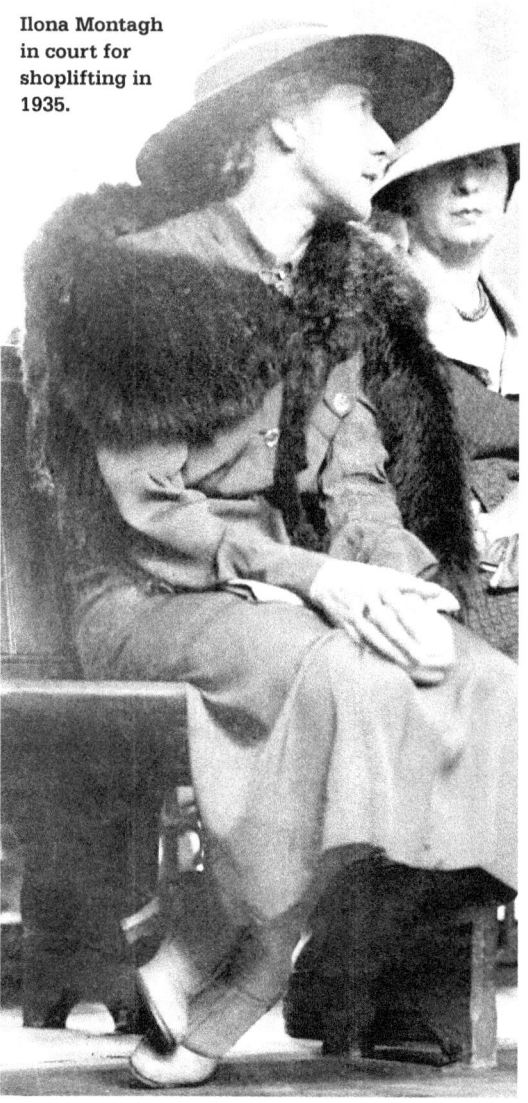

Ilona Montagh in court for shoplifting in 1935.

Montagh soon changed her story from the "bet" excuse, claiming the theft was "just a publicity stunt for a book I'm writing."[51]

When the case reached the court on August 7, 1935, she was still referring to herself as Countess Ilona von Montagh. She appeared wearing silver fox cape and (allegedly) a diamond bracelet.[52] She changed her story again and admitted to the shoplifting charges. As a first time offender, she apparently received a suspended sentence.[53]

Nothing more was heard of Montagh in the United States. There was a rumor she spent time in a mental institute. There were also rumors that she had returned to Hungary; even Lugosi believed this to be true. The name "Ilona Montagh" does turn up in Hungarian voter registration documents from 1945, a "housewife" married to one Gézáné Csanak.[54] Perhaps this is her, or perhaps not.

Mysteries abound. Probably there was no Woman with Yellow Eyes, though it isn't impossible that Montagh was the inspiration for her story, if she and Lugosi did meet in Hungary, Germany, and America.

But if so, that wasn't how Lugosi described her. *Modern Screen* quoted him as saying, "I determined to fight through and continue to love my second Ilona." But the Woman with Yellow Eyes decreed, "Let this woman you have married go."[55] Maybe the fictitious tale helped Lugosi to claim he left Montagh, rather than admitting she had left him.

Nevertheless, Lugosi told a different journalist a more concise account of his affection for the Countess: "I shall never love again."[56]

Endnotes

1   Chrisman, J. Eugene. "Masters of Horror – Karloff and Lugosi." *Modern Screen* Apr. 1932.

2   Ibid.

3   In terms of Dombegyháza, it is necessary to explain that the ship manifest actually reads "Dombezzliara," which was presumably a misspelling/misunderstanding made by whomever recorded Montagh's data.

4   When Montagh applied for US citizenship in 1923, she gave her birthplace as Csanád.

5   "Wild Wooing Tactics of a Temperamental Adonis." *Tampa Sunday Tribune* (Tampa, FL) 28 Dec. 1924.

6   "Monthag [sic] Ilona." *Színházi Élet* (Budapest, Hungary) 12-19 Aug. 1917.

7   "Montágh Ilona." *Színházi Élet* 6-12 Apr. 1919.

8   "Monthag [sic] Ilona."

9   "Wild Wooing Tactics of a Temperamental Adonis."

10 Ibid.

11 Her film *Juck und Schlau* (1920) also starred Anna Müeller-Lincke and Hans Laskus. See the announcement in *Lichtbild-Bühne* 28 July 1920.

12 "Montagh Ilona megérkezett Amerikába." *Világ* (Budapest, Hungary) 16 Jan. 1921.

13 Ship Manifest for the *Manchuria*.

14 "Julius Kessler, 85; Long a Distiller." *New York Times* 11 Dec. 1940: 27. [An example of Kessler's philanthropic work close to the time that Montagh came to the US would be his involvement in a million-dollar drive to help suffering children in Hungary. See "Plan Found to Save Starving Children." *New York Times* 30 Sept. 1919: 16.]

15 "Aradi színésznő Newyorkban." *Körösvidék* (Békéscsaba, Hungary) 19 Feb. 1921.

16 "$7,500 Willed by Word of Mouth." *New York Times* 1 June 1921.

17 "Wild Wooing Tactics."

18 On February 19, 1921, the *New York Tribune* referred to the play as *A Young Lady's Husband*. That same day, the *New York Evening Telegram* called the play *Almost Married*. Robert Cremer translates the title of this play as *Husband of the Miss*. See Cremer, Robert. *Lugosi: The Man Behind the Cape* (Chicago: Henry Regnery, 1976). *Little Miss Bluebeard* is the English title for Avery Hopwood's American adaptation of Gábor Drégely's *Kisasszony férje* (*A Young Lady's Husband*).

19 "Hungarians Will Give Plays in Native Tongue." *New York Tribune* 19 Feb. 1921.

20 "Színház, Műveszet, Mozi – *A kisasszony férje.*" *Amerikai Magyar Népszava* (New York) 22 Feb. 1921.

21 Ibid.

22 "An Informal Dance." *Brooklyn Daily Eagle* 1 May 1922.

23 Holmes, Ralph. "Great Stage Lover Is Poor Husband." *Detroit Evening Times* (Detroit, MI) 15 Nov. 1924.

24 "Wild Wooing Tactics."

25 "Wife of Heights Actor Asks Divorce – Bela Lugosi Unfaithful, She Charges." *New York American* (Washington Heights) 26 Oct. 1924.

26 "Wild Wooing Tactics."

27 Hopper, Hedda. "Bogey Men-About-Town." *Washington Post* 14 Jan. 1940.

28 Mefford, Arthur. "Lugosi Wins Heart of Clara Bow, Says Second Wife, Seeking Divorce." *The Daily Mirror* (New York) 5 Nov. 1929.

29 Cremer, *Lugosi: The Man Behind the Cape*.

30 "Haunted Honeymoon of the 'Vampire Man's' Society Bride." *Hamilton Evening Journal* (Hamilton, OH) 12 Oct. 1929.

31 "Wild Wooing Tactics."

32 Cremer, *Lugosi: The Man Behind the Cape*.

33 "Theater und Musik." *New Yorker Volkszeitung* (New York) 25 Nov. 1921; "Theater und Musik." *New Yorker Volkszeitung* 23 Jan. 1922.

34 Advertisement. *Amerikai Magyar Népszava* (New York) 11 Jan. 1922.

35 See *Színházi Újság* (New York) 15 Mar. 1922.

36 "Montagh Ilona Párísha megy." *Új Előre* (New York) 19 May 1922.

37 "Miért Maradt El Montagh Ilona Előadása." *Új Előre* 15 June 1922.

38 She apparently did perform at the Stuyvesant High School Auditorium in *Nani* on March 30, 1924. See: Advertisement. *Amerikai Magyar Népszava* 20 Mar. 1924.

39 For the sake of internal consistency, we have added a diacritic mark to the name Béla. It did not appear in the original article.

40 "Wild Wooing Tactics."

41 Ibid.

42 "Wife of Heights Actor Asks Divorce."

43 Ibid. Mention of the detective appears in Cremer, *Lugosi: The Man Behind the Cape*.

44 Ibid.

45 *Ilona Lugosi, Plaintiff, against Bela Lugosi, Defendant. Interlocutory Judgment on Default with Provision for Becoming Final Judgment.* Supreme Court, New York County. County Clerk Index No. 28365/1924. [In this paperwork, the "Final Judgment" is dated 13 Feb. 1925.]

46 "She Quits the 'Valentino of the Stage.'" *International News* Photo Caption 12 Nov. 1924.

47 "Lugosi Béla Newyorkban." *Pesti Hírlap* (Budapest, Hungary) 12 Jan. 1925.

48 Montagh's petition for naturalization is dated June 16, 1927.

49 For the sake of internal consistency, we have added a diacritic mark to the name Béla. It did not appear in the original article.

50 "Dracula's Ex and Pal Held for Shoplift." *New York Daily News* 21 June 1935.

51 "Bela Lugosi's Ex Laughs at Theft Charge." *New York Daily News* 22 June 1935.

52 "One Time Countess Held Under Bond on Shoplifting Charge." *Chicago Tribune* 22 June 1935.

53 "Countess Admits Shoplifting Charge." *Pittsburgh Press* 7 Aug. 1935.

54 Registers of Voters, Budapest City Archives, Budapest, Hungary, available in HU BFL-XV.20.6-IV.1404-8230-0720.

55 Chrisman, "Masters of Horror – Karloff and Lugosi."

56 "Haunted Honeymoon of the 'Vampire Man's' Society Bride."

Lugosi in *The Red Poppy* (1922).
(Courtesy of David Wentink)

Chapter 26

Broken Ribs

"Bela Lugosi is a newcomer of quite splendid mien,
romantically handsome and young."[84]
– *New York Times*

"[S]he had been squeezed too roughly in a
realistic love scene by Bela Lugosi, the
male vamp of the production."[85]
– *Zit's Theatrical Newspaper*

The vivacious Claire once thrived in the underworld, but she left behind her life of crime and married a Russian Prince. Secretly visiting The Red Poppy, a cabaret dive in the Paris slums, Claire encounters an "Apache" thief, a Spaniard named Fernando. The two dance and fall in love. Fernando visits Claire's home with the intent to rob it, as he imagines she is merely a servant working there. After learning the truth, Fernando is shot dead by the Prince's secretary, and Claire recommits to her unexciting married life.

The story is André Picard and Francis Carco's *Mon Homme* (*My Man*), as produced in Paris in 1921 with a cast of 46. Their three-act play became a "continental sensation over night, and rights for its production in other European cities were briskly bid for."[1] Henry Baron, who had produced *The Rubicon* with Estelle Winwood in the spring of 1922, secured a contract for the American production. He adapted *Mon Homme* into English, renamed it *The Red Poppy*, and immediately cast Winwood as Claire.[2]

Soon thereafter, Bela Lugosi won the role of Fernando. In 1925, Lugosi explained, "Possessing a good reputation in Hungary, I naturally thought that the going would be easy

Estelle Winwood in the 1920s, as photographed by Nicholas Ház, who also took the portraits of Lugosi for *The Red Poppy*.

in New York. But it was not. I may say it is not."[3] Publicity man/producer Nelson Lingard discovered Lugosi, and suggested that Henry Baron cast him in *The Red Poppy*.[4] Where did Lingard see him? Lugosi recalled that his success in the 1922 version of *Az ember tragédiája* (*The Tragedy of Man*) directly paved the way to *The Red Poppy*.[5]

"This will be Mr. Lugosi's first attempt to portray a role in the English language," one newspaper announced.[6] A later story claimed that Baron granted Lugosi's wish of four months to learn his lines with the help of an English coach.⁷ Initially, the two men had to talk in German to understand each other.⁸

Lugosi's stories about learning English varied somewhat, though in some measure they might all be correct. In one case, he spoke of an English-speaking woman with whom he fell in love:

> [S]he started to teach me English, and in six months I could speak it well enough to get a role in an American play. I had to play the role of a foreigner, as I still had quite an accent, but I got by very well.⁹

In another interview, Lugosi said that he took an apartment in Washington Heights to concentrate on learning the language.¹⁰ On yet another occasion, he remembered buying a dictionary and reading newspapers.¹¹

Once hired for *The Red Poppy*, Lugosi worked for three weeks with a language coach named Arthur Lubin. To a large degree, Lugosi learned his dialogue phonetically, and would later claim that he was the only member of the cast who knew his lines perfectly at rehearsals.¹² In one interview, Lugosi described his process:

> Would you like to know what I have found is the best way for my work toward perfecting a characterization since I have been in this country? I first get a part in my own Hungarian, thinking it out as though I were going to act it in my native tongue ... you see? I study it and seek to perfect it as

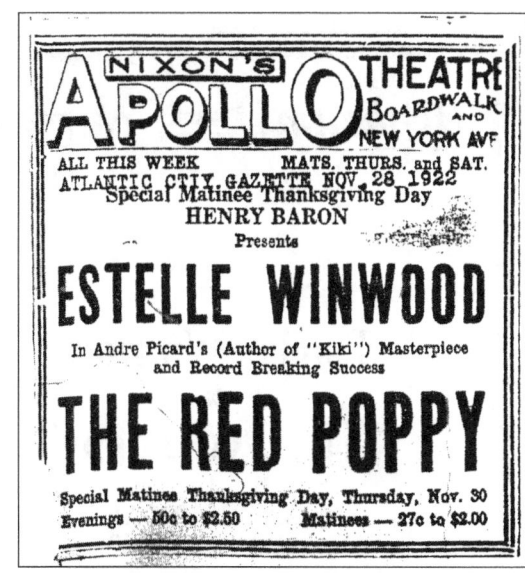

Above Top: Published in the *Atlantic City Gazette* (Atlantic City, NJ) on November 28, 1922. Above Bottom: From Estelle Winwood's personal scrapbook. *(Courtesy of the Billy Rose Theater Division of the New York Public Library)*

Gary D. Rhodes | Bill Kaffenberger

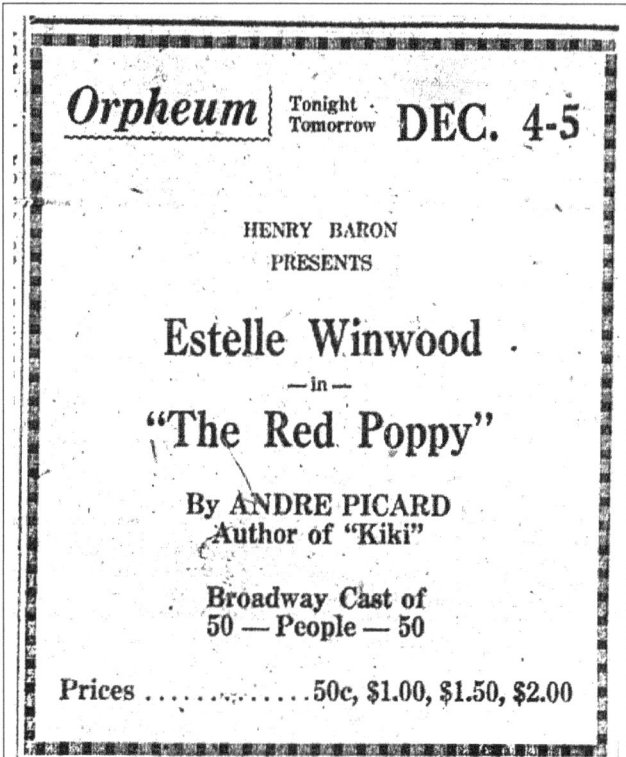

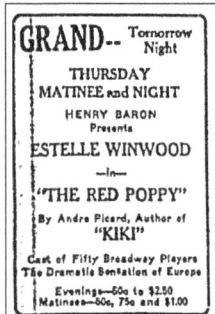

Above Left: Published in *The Evening News* (Harrisburg, Pennsylvania) on December 4, 1922. Above Right: Published in *The Evening News* (Harrisburg, Pennsylvania) on December 4, 1922.
Left: Published in the *Wilkes-Barre Times-Leader* (Wilkes-Barre, Pennsylvania) on December 5, 1922.
Right: Published in the *Wilmington Daily Commercial* (Wilmington, DE) on December 4, 1922.

though I were going to act it in Budapest for Hungarian audiences. Then, when I begin to feel quite at home in it, I begin to concentrate on the English diction, so that I may speak the part as it should be spoken for the American audiences.[13]

Lubin – who went on to become a notable Hollywood director and worked with Lugosi on the film *Black Friday* (1940) – might well have suggested this approach. Lugosi also recalled that working on *The Red Poppy* led him to "put [his] mind on learning the language."[14]

On November 27, 1922, the play debuted at the Apollo Theater in Atlantic City, New Jersey, the first of a series of tryout cities. Two of the three reviews were positive:

Publicity portrait of Lugosi for *The Red Poppy*.
(Courtesy of John Antosiewicz)

Publicity portrait of Lugosi for *The Red Poppy*.
(Courtesy of John Antosiewicz)

The piece has many merits as drama and even as spectacle. It offers opportunities and with a capable cast should have a future. ... The cast was headed by Estelle Winwood, who did some very dramatic moments without filling the part as it could be filled, but who succumbed in artistic importance to the striking performance of Bela Lugosi, a newcomer over here.[15] – *Variety*

Colorful, exotic, thrilling in intensity of scene and situation, the play lends itself to [Winwood's] swaying grace of movement, her lilting clearness of voice, whose inarticulate expression of pain at the very end leaves us with an unforgettable memory.

From Estelle Winwood's personal scrapbook. *(Courtesy of the Billy Rose Theater Division of the New York Public Library)*

... It is [in Act Two] that we meet Fernando, played by Bela Lugosi with wonderful intensity and sincere expression. ... [He] gives a performance which fairly flames with the fire of passion forged at the anvil of strength. Taken all in all, *The Red Poppy* is a most artistic production and one decidedly worth seeing.[16] – *Atlantic City Gazette-Review*

There are two dominant figures in the cast – Estelle Winwood and Bela Lugosi, the latter a Hungarian actor who ... achieves an artistic triumph. ... Until Fernando enters, the scene is tolerable. As a sample of staging it is not at all striking. Lugosi infuses a new spirit in the act. ... *The Red Poppy* does not suggest a plant that will thrive luxuriously on our soil. Its morale, its French allusions, its general tone are against it. But Bela Lugosi is there 99 percent.[17] – *Atlantic City Press*

After closing on December 2, the company moved to the Orpheum Theater in Harrisburg, Pennsylvania, for December 4 and 5. One local article wrongly claimed that Lugosi had previously appeared in the play in Paris.[18] Local critics praised the cast while remaining unimpressed with the play:

Too primitive for the American public, full of contradictions and impossible in theme to them.... Bela Lugosi carries off all of the honors of the play and aids Miss Winwood and Betsy Ross Clarke to portray their parts with a realism, which could not help bring out involuntary drawn breaths of sheer amazement. The play is a little slow in starting its growth, but by the second act it bursts into full bloom, withering away again in the third act. There is a lack of something forceful in the rounding out process....[19] – *New York Clipper*

The Red Poppy ... is an aimless exotic, somewhat futile melodrama whose principal interest lies in the fact Estelle Winwood plays the lead... Without dramatic tension or even moments of exciting action the play begins and ends with nothing accomplished and with its interest depending entirely on its bizarre situation. There are flashes of good acting and humor.[20] – *The Patriot*

Playbill for *The Red Poppy* at the Greenwich Village Theater.

The Red Poppy lacks lightness. It's just a little too dark, by which we mean that it's just a little too heavy.[21] – *The Evening News*

Bela Lugosi, in time a probable better Valentino of the screen together with Estelle Winwood and Betsy Ross Clarke, portrayed their parts with ... realism.[22] – *Harrisburg Telegraph*

The Red Poppy next played at the Grand Theater in Wilkes-Barre, Pennsylvania, on December 6 and 7. Once again, critics and audiences seemed to have preferred the actors to the play:

The Red Poppy may have been one of the successes of the Paris stage, but the English version given at the Grand last night would never prove it... Estelle Winwood as the star had several emotional scenes with Bela Lugosi that were depended upon to create sensational effect, but they did not fulfill the intended hope, as the audience was never carried away with the surroundings enough to enter late the spirit of the occasion.[23] – *Wilkes-Barre Record*

The Red Poppy, heralded as a study in emotions, failed to thrill a fair-sized audience at the Grand last night... It is devoid of anything that has the earmarks of a success... The cast, for the most part, was above average....[24] – *Wilkes-Barre Times-Leader*

The company then shifted to The Playhouse in Wilmington, Delaware, on December 8 and 9, for the final tryout performances. Reviews were generally positive:

> The staging has been magnificently done by B. Iden Pyne and the artistic wardrobe is worthy of a better play. ... The story ... is without reason, as it begins and ends nowhere.[25]
> – Billboard

> To say the play hasn't merit and is not clever in some parts would be to do it an injustice. ... Bela Lugosi, as Fernando, gives an admirable portrayal of the part of the fiery lover, who bows his hitherto unconquerable will to the compelling power of [Winwood's character].[26] – The Evening Journal

> Wilmington playgoers received with much enthusiasm last night, in advance of its New York opening, a romantic melodrama that seems destined to repeat there the success which it had in Paris, where it had scored a long run... Bela Lugosi, as Fernando, the fiery lover, acted with vigor and intelligence. A slight accent mars the effectiveness of his delivery.[27] – The Evening News-Journal

While in Wilmington, Lugosi spoke to a reporter about having attended a football game in New York. He added that Hungary's national sport was "wolf baiting," in which teams of men tried to approach and then escape hungry wolves. The reporter quoted Lugosi at great length, which suggests his skills at English might have been improving.[28]

The Red Poppy finally opened in New York on December 20, 1922, not on Broadway as originally announced, but at the Greenwich Village Theater, the result of a "last-minute booking."[29] The press drew attention to Winwood and Lugosi, as well as to the "spiked cuff" that George A. Lawrence wore onstage; it was a "leather band fastened around the wrist" that held a "number of steel spikes sharpened to needle point[s]."[30]

New York critics were mixed in their views, but negative notices outnumbered the positive:

> On the whole, *The Red Poppy* is an excellent play ... It should be with us for a long time to come.[31] – The Morning Telegraph

> It is often interesting, in several places rather exciting, and in a great many places merely dull and claptrap melodrama.[32] – New York Sun

> *The Red Poppy* will not cause your pulse to beat, but it has a few moments of theatrical effectiveness.[33] – New York American

> [*The Red Poppy*] is a flashy sort of melodrama that would seem hopelessly and mechanically artificial and altogether trivial if it were not played interestingly....[34] – New York Daily News

Above: Lugosi and Winwood in *The Red Poppy*. *(Courtesy of the Billy Rose Theater Division of the New York Public Library)*

Right: *The Red Poppy*. *(Courtesy of the Billy Rose Theater Division of the New York Public Library)*

Andre Picard ... and Francis Carco have here written a joyous French melodrama of the underworld, of approved theatrical pattern, with all the endearing absurdities hallowed by tradition.[35] – *New York Call*

The production reminds the audience of many of the old-time melodramas in which a man or woman was killed every few minutes.[36] – *Brooklyn Standard Union*

Whatever the original French play, *Mon Homme*, may have been, the production by Henry Baron in English ... reveals a very crumpled blossom. How curiously outmoded the play is....[37] – *New York Evening Telegram*

A gaudy and sensational Parisian melodrama, done into a rough-hewn show for New York audiences, was produced with some little difficulty at the Greenwich Village Theater last evening–but produced, nevertheless.[38] – *New York Herald*

The Red Poppy aims to be exciting, but, in its present production at least, hardly succeeds.[39] – *Brooklyn Daily Eagle*

The Red Poppy is a show for those who are not too particular, of whom it is said that they are numerous.[40] – *New York Tribune*

The new play at the Greenwich Village Theater doesn't seem to me to have any discoverable virtue–of even the most arrantly popular sort. ... French trash, no worse than ours, perhaps, but much less convincing.[41] – *New York Globe*

It proved far worse than could have been expected.[42] – *The Evening World*

Devoid of drama of any sort, pitifully played by all concerned and cluttered up with fake 'atmosphere,' the play is an unspeakable atrocity.[43] – *Billboard*

The Morning Telegraph claimed on December 23 that the play was "drawing large audiences from all parts of the city."[44] That was important, as seating capacity at the theater was "limited."[45] Even if the show had sell-out crowds, it could still only generate a profit of $500 a week.[46] The margin for error was narrow.

Lugosi – whose character did not appear onstage until Act Two – received largely favorable reviews:

In this particular part Lugosi seems to be the living ideal of the author, and the role seems to have been tailored to him, but one thing can be said, and that is in Lugosi the American stage has gained one of the greatest actors that Europe ever sent to this country.[47] – *The Morning Telegraph*

Lugosi and Winwood in *The Red Poppy*.
(Courtesy of the Billy Rose Theater Division of the New York Public Library)

[Estelle Winwood] is effectively aided by a tall Hungarian named Bela Lugosi, a good-looking boy who suggests the Lou Tellegen of a half dozen years ago. Young Lugosi plays intensely as an Apache....[48] – *New York Daily News*

A new comer to our stage, Mr. Bela Lugosi, of the National Theater, Budapest, plays the important role of 'Spanish Fernando' to our great satisfaction, making that Apache a happy blend of Liliom, 'Bilge' Smith, and the lover by Robert Warwick in *To Love*.[49] – *New York Evening Journal*

[T]he Spaniard, splendidly played by Bela Lugosi, late of the National Theater, Budapest, [along with Estelle Winwood] sweep through those fine passions that are fed by brutal blows and stranglehold kisses, putting to shame the life of the merely tubbed and tailored. ... Equally convincing is his passion of kicks and clenches. In the final scene he is not without a touch of the truly noble spirit. Here is an actor of fine achievement and possibly greater promise.[50] – *New York Times*

Bela Lugosi is a distinct acquisition to the play, for he has personality as well as histrionic training.[51] – *New York Call*

A tall, sallow, lugubrious and earnest person, with luscious eyes and an accent, [Lugosi] strove last night to please.[52] – *New York Tribune*

It was a 'type' part into which [Lugosi] fitted admirably, and he was generously applauded.[53] – *The Evening Mail*

Bela Logosi [sic], an actor from Budapest who makes his American debut in the role of the lover, is picturesque, has a good voice and considerable power.[54] – *Brooklyn Daily Eagle*

From Estelle Winwood's personal scrapbook. *(Courtesy of the Billy Rose Theater Division of the New York Public Library)*

[Lugosi] cuts a good figure and plays an ideal criminal very impressively. He also has enough passion. But how little satisfaction such plays provide. Their passions in the Parisian cellar cabaret should really impress nobody. One would welcome seeing the Hungarian performer Bela Lugosi in a different role, which would offer him a greater opportunity for interpretation.[55] – *New Yorker Volkszeitung*

This Budapest actor looked the part well enough and was duly arrogant. But even he could not bring romance to a play that was all rot, and what's more, tiresome rot.[56] – *The Evening World*

[Estelle Winwood] is wooed by a towering new actor from Budapest, whose heavy Teutonic speech makes it just a little hard for the audience to believe that he really is the mysterious Spaniard, Fernando. He is, indeed, the most mysterious Spaniard we have encountered in the theater.[57] – *New York Herald*

Of course a play like *The Red Poppy* offers him a chance to show his mettle as an actor, but his accent, though it sounded Spanish enough to our untrained ears, enabled us to catch only every other word he was saying. However, we heard what he said when he crushed the blond Winwood in amorous ecstasy – we heard it through his pantomime, which spoke louder than words.[58] – *New York Sun*

There is a big cast, and dominating them all is a new actor from Budapest, Mr. Bela Lugosi, who has an excellent stage presence and has every qualification for [a leading player] save a command of the English language.[59] – *New York Evening Telegram*

Bela Lugosi displayed vigor, dramatic power and intelligence. I should say that he will be an acquisition to our stage. His English is still a trifle indistinct, but not more indistinct than that of many native actors.[60] – *New York American*

I think [Lugosi] is a member of Hebrew Actors Union, Number One. His English is badly broken, but he spoke as intelligibly as Windsor P. Daggett's best in comparison to the mumbling, word-swallowing and general inarticulateness of the other members of the company, including especially Miss Winwood.[61] – *Billboard*

Bela Lugosi, a newcomer to the American stage, struggled with an obvious linguistic handicap and only occasionally overcame it.[62] – *New York Post*

[Lugosi's] figure is admirable, but his voice seemed rather empty last night.[63] – *New York Globe*

Good judges have praised him. The present deponent reserves judgment, except to say that in *The Red Poppy*, Mr. Lugosi is unimpressive.[64] – *Town Topics*

> **"RED POPPY" CUTS MATINEE**
> **No Extra Performance on Christmas Day.**
>
> Contrary to the custom of recent years of giving a Christmas matinee, Henry Baron has decided to let the members of "The Red Poppy" Company, the present attraction at the Greenwich Village Theatre, enjoy the holiday at home with their families and friends.
> The regular Thursday and Saturday matinees, however, will be given.
> "The Red Poppy," which is by André Picard, the author of "Kiki," has caught the popular taste, and despite its presentation so far downtown this sensational French melodrama is drawing large audiences from all parts of the city.

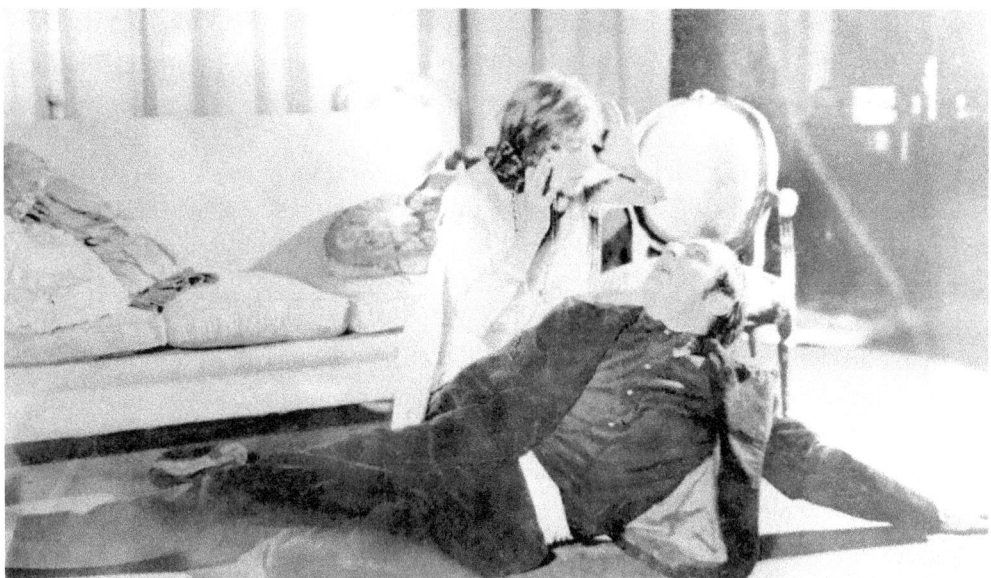

Above Top: Published in *The Morning Telegraph* (New York) on December 23, 1922.
Above: Lugosi and Winwood in *The Red Poppy*. *(Courtesy of the Billy Rose Theater Division of the New York Public Library)*

Years later, Lugosi spoke of the play fondly, recalling his favorable reviews, particularly Alan Dale's for the *New York American*. He once said that the cast of the play even gathered around him to congratulate him for receiving that review.[65]

Problems for *The Red Poppy* arose by December 23, 1922, when *The Morning Telegraph* reported the surprising news that no matinee would be given on Christmas Day. Henry Baron claimed this was to allow the cast to "enjoy the holiday at home with their families and friends."[66] Actors received salary checks on December 23, but were told not to cash them for two days. Those who ignored that request learned that funds weren't available.[67] *Variety* explained the source of the troubles:

> With the house taking first money of the slender receipts, the management was placed in the hole for funds to defray running expenses in addition to salaries. ... The lack of funds became evident last week when the advertisements for the attraction in the dailies were dropped.[68]

Here was presumably the real reason for the cancelled Christmas matinee.

Actors' Equity got involved, with one of its employees visiting the Greenwich Village Theater every day after the problems emerged. His efforts to help "pilot the company out of the chaotic financial position" encouraged the actors to stay together, with the intent to move to the Nora Bayes Theater on Broadway.[69] On December 29, *Variety* wrote, "house small and narrow profit possible only if capacity drawn. Doubtful if it can stick unless getting Broadway house."[70]

The show closed at the Greenwich on December 30, the stated plan being to take a short break before moving to the Nora Bayes. *Variety* reported, "Stopped suddenly Saturday. Stayed week and three days, drew very little money."[71] Then, on January 5, 1923, the break became permanent. By that time, some actors had dropped out of the play, and the company was disbanded.[72] *The Red Poppy* had been staged in New York only fourteen times.

During the "break," the press published stories about Estelle Winwood's injury. One article claimed that she sought help from a chiropractor after her back was injured during a "rough Apache dance." She "fell heavily across a chair [and] in addition to the fall was kicked in the back."[73] *Zit's Theatrical Newspaper* told a different version of events. Winwood was unable to act onstage because:

> [s]he had been squeezed too roughly in a realistic love scene with Bela Lugosi, the male vamp in the production. According to report, Bela had crushed her ribs and the region adjacent to her vertebral column with exceedingly realistic violence the evening before with the result she was unable to walk with anything resembling dignity. It took the united efforts of three chiropractors several hours of intermittent adjustments to put the star's ribs back in place again.[74]

In this version, Winwood returned to work, only to suffer again in a subsequent performance when Lugosi's "grizzly-bear ferocity" dangerously pushed a rib "against her vital organs."[75]

Retellings heightened the drama. In 1924, a journalist wrote, "Such a realist was the temperamental Adonis that one night he verged on roughness and pop! went two of Miss Winwood's ribs." Winwood explained, "It was the sort of thing that might happen to anyone."[76] The article even featured an X-ray photograph of the fractured bones. Another story maintained Lugosi actually broke her ribs.[77] Yet another claimed the injury caused her to "retire from the cast."[78]

In the 1970s, Winwood dismissed those stories. She told Robert Cremer, "The dance in the café was rough, all right. Bela threw me all over the place and twirled me on tabletops, but nothing happened to me. I didn't even break a fingernail."[79]

In its review of *The Red Poppy*, the *New York Sun* wrote, "these are no ordinary embraces which Miss Winwood must receive nightly in the name of art."[80] And yet Winwood was not injured. Here was a publicity story, of course, nothing more than a fiction. But the timing of its invention is important to understand. Winwood and Lugosi apparently remained committed to the play until the company disbanded. Tales of her injury provided a fanciful excuse for the closure at the Greenwich and the break before the planned move to Broadway.

Sets and props were held prisoner at the Greenwich due to Baron's failure to pay the rent he owed.[81] And Actors' Equity shut down his next show, *My Aunt From Ypsilanti*, when he failed to satisfy them by posting a bond to protect cast members; Equity specifically cited his prior failure on *The Red Poppy*.[82]

Despite all of these problems, though, Lugosi did achieve success in the play. It launched his English-language career and garnered him favorable notices and even some fans. *Billboard* quoted one female audience member who gushed, "He's so masculine."[83]

He was something of a Romeo once again, a romantic lead, a "male vamp" who had bitten the Big Apple.

Endnotes

1. *The Red Poppy* at Orpheum Tonight." *The Evening News* (Harrisburg, PA) 4 Dec. 1922.

2. "Estelle Winwood in *Bon [sic] Homme*." *The Morning Telegraph* (New York) 16 Nov. 1922.

3. Untitled clipping. *The Morning Telegraph* 25 Feb. 1925.

4. "The Final Curtain." *Billboard* 12 June 1937.

5. Fried, Alexander. "Those Chilling Horror Roles! Bela Lugosi Loves 'Em." *San Francisco Examiner* 15 Aug. 1943.

6. "*The Red Poppy* at Orpheum Tonight."

7. Shaffer, Rosalind. "Talkie Language Difficulties Met." *San Francisco Chronicle* 28 July 1929.

8. Coons, Robbin. "News from Hollywood." *Asbury Park Evening Press* (Asbury Park, NJ) 29 Oct. 1930.

9. "Political Upheaval in Hungary Sent Bela Lugosi to Hollywood." *Niagara Falls Gazette* (Niagara Falls, NY) 11 Dec. 1930.

10 "Mastery of English Put Lugosi on Way to Stardom." *Los Angeles Record* 14 July 1928.

11 Fried, "Those Chilling Horror Roles!"

12 The claim about rehearsals appears in the article "Lugosi's First Portrayal in America a Triumph," as published in the pressbook for the 1936 film *Postal Inspector*. A copy of the pressbook is archived at the New York Public Library for the Performing Arts, Dorothy and Lewis B. Cullman Center.

13 "Bela Lugosi Plays Count." *Los Angeles Record* 23 June 1928.

14 Tildesley, Alice L. "I Can't – But They Did, and How!" *Seattle Times* 18 Oct. 1931.

15 Scheuer. "*The Red Poppy*." *Variety* 8 Dec. 1922.

16 "*The Red Poppy* Proves Thrilling." *Atlantic City Gazette-Review* (Atlantic City, NJ) 28 Nov. 1922.

17 "*The Red Poppy* at the Apollo of Decidedly French Favor." *Atlantic City Press* (Atlantic City, NJ) 28 Nov. 1922.

18 "*The Red Poppy* at the Orpheum Tomorrow Night." *The Courier* (Harrisburg, PA) 3 Dec. 1922.

19 "*Red Poppy* Thrills." *New York Clipper* 13 Dec 1922.

20 "*Red Poppy* Aimless; Some Good Acting." *The Patriot* (Harrisburg, PA) 5 Dec. 1922.

21 "*The Red Poppy* Slow in Growth." *The Evening Times* (Harrisburg, PA) 5 Dec. 1922.

22 Robertson, Max. "*Red Poppy* Is Well Received." *Harrisburg Telegraph* 5 Dec. 1922.

23 "*The Red Poppy* at the Grand." *Wilkes-Barre Record* 7 Dec. 1922.

24 "*The Red Poppy*." *Wilkes-Barre Times-Leader* 7 Dec. 1922.

25 "*The Red Poppy* Blooms." *Billboard* 16 Dec. 1922.

26 "Princess Lured By Apache Love." *The Evening Journal* (Wilmington, DE) 9 Dec. 1922.

27 "Estelle Winwood in *The Red Poppy*." *The Evening News-Journal* (Wilmington, DE) 9 Dec. 1922.

28 "Wolf Baiting Great Hungarian Sport." *The Evening News-Journal* 9 Dec. 1922.

29 "*The Red Poppy* in the Village." *The Morning Telegraph* 21 Dec. 1922.

30 "Introduces 'Spiked Cuff.'" *Billboard* 6 Jan. 1923.

31 Marsh, Leo A. "*The Red Poppy* an Excellent Play." *The Morning Telegraph* 21 Dec. 1922.

32 "*The Red Poppy* Opens." *New York Sun* 21 Dec. 1922.

33 Dale, Alan. "*The Red Poppy* Has Episodes of Interest." *New York American* 21 Dec. 1922.

34 Mantle, Burns. "*Red Poppy* Flowers Under Miss Winwood." *New York Daily News* 21 Dec. 1922.

35 Castellun, Maida. "The Stage." *New York Call* 22 Dec. 1922.

36 "*The Red Poppy* Recalls Old Melodrama Days." *Brooklyn Standard Union* 21 Dec. 1922.

37 "*The Red Poppy* a Bit Crumpled." *New York Evening Telegram* 21 Dec. 1922.

38 Woollcott, Alexander. "The Reviewing Stand." *New York Herald* 21 Dec. 1922.

39 Pollock, Arthur. "*The Red Poppy*." *Brooklyn Daily Eagle* 22 Dec. 1922.

40 Hammond, Percy. "The Theaters." *New York Tribune* 21 Dec. 1922.

41 Macgowan, Kenneth. "The New Play." *New York Globe* 21 Dec. 1922.

42 Darnton, Charles. "The New Plays." *The Evening World* (New York) 21 Dec. 1922.

43 James, Patterson. "Greenwich Village Theater, New York." *Billboard* 6 Jan. 1923.

44 "*Red Poppy* Cuts Matinee." *The Morning Telegraph* 23 Dec. 1922.

45 "*The Red Poppy* Blooms No More." *The Morning Telegraph* 6 Jan. 1923.

46 "*Red Poppy* Stops." *Variety* 5 Jan. 1923.

47 Marsh, "*The Red Poppy* an Excellent Play."

48 Mantle, Burns. "*Red Poppy* Flowers Under Miss Winwood – Actress Saves Play by Her Adaptability." *New York Daily News* 21 Dec. 1922.

49 West, Julia. "Estelle Winwood as Star of *The Red Poppy* Is Fascinating." *New York Evening Journal* 21 Dec. 1922.

50 Corbin, "The Play."

51 Castellun, "The Stage."

52 Hammond, "The Theaters."

53 Craig, James. "*The Red Poppy*." *The Evening Mail* (New York) 21 Dec. 1922.

54 Pollock, "*The Red Poppy*."

55 "Theater, Film, and Art." *New Yorker Volkszeitung* 24 Dec. 1922.

56 Darnton, "The New Plays."

57 Woollcott, "The Reviewing Stand."

58 "*The Red Poppy* Opens."

59 "*The Red Poppy* a Bit Crumpled"

60 Dale, "*The Red Poppy* Has Episodes of Interest."

61 James, "Greenwich Village Theater, New York."

62 "The Play." *New York Post* 21 Dec. 1922.

63 Macgowan, "The New Play."

64 *Town Topics* 28 Dec. 1922.

65 Shirley, Lillian. "Afraid of Himself." *Modern Screen* Mar. 1931.

66 "*Red Poppy* Cuts Matinee."

67 "Where Poppies Blow." *Billboard* 3 Feb. 1923; "*The Red Poppy* Blooms No More."

68 "*Red Poppy* Stops." *Variety* 5 Jan. 1923.

69 "*Red Poppy* Not to Open." *Billboard* 23 Jan. 1923

70 "Broadway Hits." *Variety* 29 Dec. 1922.

71 "Shows In N.Y. And Comment." *Variety* 5 Jan. 1923.

72 "*The Red Poppy* Blooms No More."

73 "Estelle Winwood Recovers and *Red Poppy* Will Reopen." Article dated 6 Jan. 1923 and included in Winwood's personal scrapbook, which is archived at the New York Public Library for the Performing Arts, Dorothy and Lewis B. Cullman Center.

74 "*Red Poppy* Star Needs Doctoring After Embraces."

75 Ibid.

76 "Wild Wooing Tactics of a Temperamental Adonis." *Tampa Sunday Tribune* (Tampa, FL) 28 Dec. 1924.

77 Cremer, Robert. *Lugosi: The Man Behind the Cape* (Chicago: Henry Regnery, 1976).

78 Mefford, Arthur. "Lugosi Wins Heart of Clara Bow, Says Second Wife, Seeking Divorce." *The Daily Mirror* (New York) 5 Nov. 1929.

79 Cremer, *Lugosi: The Man Behind the Cape*.

80 "*The Red Poppy* Opens."

81 "*Red Poppy* Stays Off." *Variety* 12 Jan. 1923.

82 "Equity Stops Baron Show." *New York Clipper* 11 Apr. 1923.

83 James, "Greenwich Village Theater, New York."

84 Corbin, John. "The Play." *New York Times* 21 Dec. 1922.

85 "*Red Poppy* Star Needs Doctoring After Embraces." *Zit's Theatrical Newspaper* 5 Jan. 1923.

Published in the *Moving Picture World* on August 4, 1923.

Chapter 27

The Vulture

"I consider [*The Silent Command*] an effective,
intensely interesting and inspiring picture
that should stir the patriotism
of every true American."[49]
– General John J. Pershing

"It is a story of the Panama Canal,
of plotters, vampires and 'secret orders.'"[50]
– *Exhibitors Herald*

Captain Decatur (Edmund Lowe) was a great naval officer, entrusted with important national secrets about the Panama Canal. He was also an ethical and beloved family man, married with two children. But Decatur falls prey to Benedict Hisston (Lugosi), a sinister figure in international intrigue, a "vulture who feeds on war." Working for mysterious "foreign powers" in an effort to destroy the Canal, Hisston hires the alluring Peg Williams (Martha Mansfield) to "vamp" Decatur. The "tongue of scandal" ruins Decatur's reputation. Peg carefully weaves a "silken net" around him, making it seem as if he is reckless and insubordinate. Dishonorably discharged, Decatur loses everything, including his wife.

Here is the plot of *The Silent Command* (1923), Lugosi's first American film. However, this was not the first time that the wider American public had seen Lugosi's image on the screen. L & H Enterprises of New York City released *Daughter of the Night* (1921, aka *A Daughter of the Night*), an edited version of the German Lugosi film *Der Tanz auf dem Vulkan* (1920). Announced as "completed" in October of 1921,[1] the film received a favorable

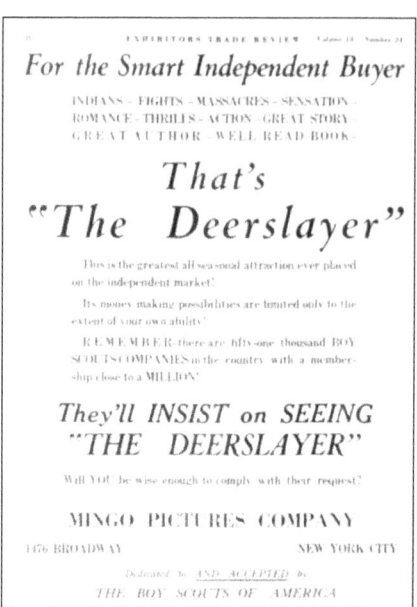

Left: From the pressbook for *The Silent Command* (1923). Above: Published in *Exhibitors Trade Review* on May 12, 1923.

review that same month in *Exhibitors Trade Review*.[2] It went into wide release in America as of early 1922.[3]

In like manner, Mingo Pictures released an abbreviated version of Lugosi's German film *Lederstrumpf* (*Leatherstocking*, 1920), with some trade publications believing that Mingo had actually produced the movie.[4] Under the title *The Deerslayer*, it was screened on November 15, 1922,[5] and then offered for wider American distribution at least by January 20, 1923.[6] Mingo promoted the film as being "dedicated to and accepted by The Boy Scouts of America." Grosset & Dunlap even published a "photoplay" edition of the film that featured images of Lugosi as Chingachgook.[7] Both of these Lugosi German films were still in general release when *The Silent Command* went into production.

William Fox produced *The Silent Command* in early 1923. The famed movie mogul and raconteur had been born in Tolcsva, Hungary in 1879 under the name Wilhelm Fuchs. His family immigrated to America when he was less than a year old. Fox grew up in New York City's Hungarian community, which might be how he learned about Lugosi.[8] Later, he might have even seen Lugosi in *Az ember tragédiája* (*The Tragedy of Man*) or *The Red Poppy*. At any rate, Lugosi signed a contract to play Benedict Hisston, a vulture, yes, but a particularly dapper vulture who smokes cigars, wears evening clothes, and ingratiates himself with key figures in American politics. To the press, he joked about the fact he was appearing in a navy propaganda film when his home country had no navy.[9]

One-time actor and stage director J. Gordon Edwards directed *The Silent Command*. Fox considered him to be "ideal." The two had worked together for years, Edwards having

directed such Theda Bara movies as *Camille* (1917), *Cleopatra* (1917), and *Salomé* (1918).[10] He also directed the infamous Fox film *The Queen of Sheba* in 1921.

Edwards, Lugosi, Edmund Lowe, Henry Armetta, and others departed New York for Panama on February 21, 1923 to shoot exteriors for *The Silent Command*.[11] It was there that Edwards directed the fight scenes aboard ship between Lugosi and Lowe. The two actors would later work together in *Women of All Nations* (1931), *Chandu the Magician* (1932), *Gift of Gab* (1934), and *The Best Man Wins* (1935). Scenes at Hisston's headquarters (or at least the exteriors of it) were apparently shot during the trip as well. And the crew filmed at the Panama Canal with the permission and assistance of the US Navy.

On March 15, 1923, the company boarded the *S. S. Metapan* to return to America. Edwards then shot interiors in New York City at Fox's eastern studios.[12] Martha Mansfield acted with Lugosi during what became some of the final days of her life. A former Ziegfeld Follies actress who appeared with John Barrymore in *Dr. Jekyll and Mr. Hyde* (1920), Mansfield died from burn injuries on November 30, 1923. Her costume caught fire on the set of her last movie, *The Warrens of Virginia* (1924).

Above: Original artwork of the film's "conspirator" as compared to Lugosi, the actor who played him. From the pressbook for *The Silent Command*.

By the end of June 1923, *The Silent Command* had moved into post-production.[13] It was completed by approximately July 22.[14] The film features a number of fascinating images, such as footage of the Atlantic fleet. It even includes something of a subtle commercial for Fox newsreels, as the characters project one of them at a gathering, complete with its opening titles.

Onscreen credits misspelled Lugosi's first name as "Belo." Publicity materials referred to him as "Bela," but generally gave him sixth billing. Nevertheless, his role is secondary only to Lowe's. Their prolonged fight scene is fast-paced and exciting, and Hisston's death by

Lugosi in *The Silent Command*.

drowning remains compelling. More fascinating is an extreme close-up of Lugosi's eyes, one that prefigures the same in such films as *Dracula* (1931), *White Zombie* (1932), and *Bride of the Monster* (1955).

Prior to its official release, Fox screened *The Silent Command* for a number of Washington D.C. officials. Among them was Theodore Roosevelt, Jr., the Assistant Secretary of the Navy, who sent Fox the following note on July 31, 1923:

> I saw your film, *The Silent Command*, today, and I wish to congratulate you on the excellent lesson it teaches. This country is a republic and therefore we will have the exact measure of national defense that the average citizen considers necessary... In your film you show clearly the great importance to our country of the navy and the Panama Canal. What you have done is of real educational value and I hope the film may be widely shown throughout the country.[15]

Military interest in *The Silent Command* continued. As a tribute to the American Navy, the film was screened in many cities as a part of Navy Day celebrations on October 27, which also happened to be the anniversary of Theodore Roosevelt's birth.[16]

The film's pressbook promised "Love, Intrigue, and the High Seas," adding that audiences would experience:

A scene from *The Silent Command*. (Courtesy of John Antosiewicz)

The thrills of nature in its maddest mood. Terrific, awe-inspiring storms at sea where mighty ships are tossed about like corks on the angry waves comprise only *a part* of the terrific tornado of action that permeates *every foot* of this sensational drama.[17]

In addition to the usual array of posters and lobby cards, the pressbook also touted a 15,000-word novelization of the film that could run in local newspapers, chapter by chapter, to help build advance excitement.

Chicago's Monroe Theater screened *The Silent Command* on August 31, 1923, but the film had its official premiere at New York City's Central Theater on September 2, 1923.[18] Special 24-sheet posters were printed, more than 300 for New York City and about half that many in Chicago.[19] Of the eleven major daily newspapers in Manhattan, only the *Times* and the *Post* seemed particularly hesitant about the film.[20] Most critics praised its stirring patriotism and action scenes. Presumably the large delegation of Navy officials that attended the New York premiere felt the same way.[21]

Reviews in trade publications were largely favorable, as the following excerpts indicate:

> The picture has been well made, and the action moves along swiftly up to the stirring climax. There are many scenes aboard battle ships and much waving of the American

flag. Edmund Lowe made a splendid Captain Decatur and he was given excellent support by Bela Lugosi, as the villain....²² – *Exhibitors Herald*

It has dash and action, thrills and suspense, combined with an absorbing story which has a novel and unexpected twist, and there is a continual increase in the tempo up to a whirlwind climax.²³ – *Moving Picture World*

[T]he picture is good entertainment by reason of its thrills, suspense and love interest... The storm at sea and the fight between Hisston and Decatur are very realistic.²⁴ – *Exhibitors Trade Review*

A glorification of the American Navy is on view... [R]ecommended to anyone suffering from an indifferent patriotism. Told in a melodramatic manner, it commands attention by virtue of its crescendo of events once the slow introductory scenes have passed....²⁵ – *Motion Picture News*

Published in *Exhibitors Trade Review* on November 3, 1923.

Bela Lugosi a new screen villain and a convincing one. ... *The Silent Command* is fine entertainment from the box office standpoint. It has all the elements of audience appeal necessary to make it a satisfying number.²⁶ – *Film Daily*

As a thrill provider where they want that sort of entertainment, the picture is there. Otherwise it's just a meller.²⁷ – *Variety*

Less kind was *Billboard*, which told readers, "This is the sort of picture which causes the spectator to fear that the orchestra is going to play *The Star-Spangled Banner* every few minutes."²⁸

Ballyhoo for *The Silent Command* was important for exhibitors across the nation, just as it was for all Hollywood features of the era. The pressbook touted ideas like borrowing Navy equipment to display in the theater lobby, inviting local Navy recruiting officers to screenings, and awarding free tickets to the best local essays on patriotism. It also suggested:

At comparatively small expense, a low, underslung automobile could be hired and a carpenter employed to build a compo-board body constructed like a ship. Driven through the city, this would attract wide attention and the public would learn quickly from banners that *The Silent Command* was playing at your theater.[29]

As usual, some theater managers put pressbook ideas into practice, while others invented their own publicity gimmicks.

For example, when *The Silent Command* premiered in Philadelphia on December 9, 1923, the theater featured a program produced with the involvement of naval officers stationed at League Island.[30] Navy recruiters in Chicago posted announcements that read, "Join the U.S. Navy and see the World. Before You Start Your Trip, See *The Silent Command*."[31] And the Fox Terminal Theater in Newark, New Jersey, decorated the entrance and lobby with flags and bunting resembling the American flag.[32]

Theater manager reports published in the trade press varied greatly from the enthusiastic to the unimpressed, from the successful to the disastrous:

> The best advertisers for this picture were the fans who saw it the first night. We shouted the merits of the picture from the housetops, but that shout was a whimper compared to the mouth-to-mouth advertising it received after its first screening. It's just the sort of a picture that we need every so often to stimulate our patriotism.[33]

> A wonderful picture that will please all audiences. ... If this is a sample of the other Fox specials, bring them on.[34]

> A dandy picture that you can go the limit on and you will sure please them.[35]

> A 'whip' of a picture. You owe your people a run of this.[36]

> Splendid in every respect. Business above average. Suitable any day.[37]

> Exploited heavily and opened to big business for four-day run. ... Receipts for engagement, however, fell short of expectations.[38]

> I believe this to be the best special on Fox program this season. However, I lost money on it.[39]

Published in *Moving Picture World* on September 22, 1923.

From the pressbook for *The Silent Command*.

It won't stand dissection by any critical audience, and you want to go light on your promises, for it won't make good on too strong exploitation. First day, fine; second day, sad. The local critics claimed it 'didn't ring true' and the fight on the ship got more laughs than any other part of the film, and it was not intended to be a comedy scrap.[40]

After reading reports in the *Herald* from other places where this picture had been shown, I really thought I had something worthwhile, but to my surprise I found it to be just a common ordinary picture and a poor one at that.[41]

Super special, should have been named soup special and that Lemon Soup. A very ordinary program picture. They can sell this or call it special if they want to but they are merely killing the exhibitors' confidence in future releases....[42]

The Silent Command is rather naïve melodrama. Its characters are superficially drawn, and its story scarcely will arouse much suspense in the minds of sophisticated movie patrons who have become accustomed to the more artistic films of the past few years.[43]

These views are hardly encompassing of the entire country and its millions of filmgoers. However, a pattern seems to emerge in the reportage. *The Silent Command* performed better in small towns and rural America than it did in large cities.

Perhaps the most unusual screening took place in Bellaire, Ohio, where the theater manager reported:

Some of the storm at sea scenes were taken from a Fox news view of a storm in Chili and we had the weekly the same night as the feature with both the identical scenes of the small vessel at the mercy of a storm.[44]

Studios during the Classical Hollywood Era regularly relied on stock footage of places and events that were too difficult or costly to shoot for their new movies. But it would have been extremely rare for an audience to see the stock footage in its original context at the very same screening as seeing its new, repurposed form. Here fiction and nonfiction met in the same images, the result probably limiting the impact of both.

As for Lugosi, critics and exhibitors commented surprisingly little about him. The most extensive comments about his performance appeared in New York's Hungarian-American newspaper, *Amerikai Magyar Népszava:*

For us, the only interesting thing in the film was Bela Lugosi's acting. The artist plays one of the leading roles, the most intriguing one. Lugosi did powerful and valuable acting in this role, which resembled much more theatrical acting than acting in a movie. It was subdued, interesting and original. He looks gorgeous in the movie, which will most certainly bring him great success. He was the best and most outstanding among

the actors. His acting is the strong point of the movie, which makes it worth watching.[45]

... The movie is a propaganda film of the maritime agency. A skillful recruiter with a happy ending: 'Come join us buddy, be a sailor.' We do not like such dramatized circulars, especially if it is filled with the most absurd nonsense. Logic and psychology are unknown notions in this film.[46]

Above Top: Published in *Exhibitors Herald* on September 29, 1923. Above: Published in *Exhibitors Herald* on November 10, 1923.

To appreciate Lugosi but remain skeptical of patriotic propaganda: here is a clear example of existing within a culture and yet simultaneously remaining outside of it. Most immigrants well understand that position, just as Lugosi would have. But his journey to becoming an American star – rather than a Hungarian or Hungarian-American star – was underway.

Concurrent with the release of *The Silent Command*, Lugosi gave an extensive English-language interview to his local newspaper, the *Bronx Home News*, from his apartment at 30 Fairview Avenue in the Washington Heights neighborhood. In the early 1920s, Washington Heights became a magnet for artists of all sorts. Asked why he chose that particular neighborhood, Lugosi explained:

> You must first know that I live two lives – a professional one and a private one. In my profession, I try to be other people, but in my private life, I am myself. Then I want to do what I want to, associate with whomever I want. Were I to live downtown, my studio would constantly be full of people that come there, not to see me, but to get something from me. This way, I know that anyone who takes the trip way up here has come for the sake of my company, and not for what help I can offer him.
>
> Of course, this does not mean that I am not ready to help people at all times. Besides, the spot where I live is one of the most beautiful in the city. It has a fascination all its own. One block to the south is the city, with its pulsating, never-ceasing life, and one block to the north is beautiful Nature. I like the people that live here.[47]

Lugosi also commented on the efforts of some Washington Heights residents to establish a local theater troupe:

> Wouldn't it be possible… for the civic organizations of the community to subsidize the theater to an extent that it need not become a purely commercial venture? I should like to see a place where the true art of the theater could be presented on the Heights.[48]

Subsidized theater was not particularly distant from the type of nationalized theater Lugosi had endorsed in Hungary. But Lugosi was definitely focused on the future of his career, an English-language acting career.

Perhaps he sought a happy ending in his new country. After all, Captain Decatur had one. *The Silent Command*'s twist is that Decatur's superiors gave him exactly what the title suggests, a "silent command." He was never actually dismissed from the Navy, just as he never cheated on his wife. It was all a ruse, so that he could get close enough to the spies to foil their dastardly plans. At the end of the film, the heroic Decatur returns to officer status and the loving arms of his wife and family. He had thus moved "from the pit of degradation to the pinnacle of honor!"

Endnotes

1 "A Frank Statement of Fact." *Exhibitors Trade Review* 15 Oct. 1921.

2 Ibid. While an allusion was made to Lugosi's character, his name was not mentioned in the review or the cast list. In fact, only Lee Parry (billed as Eleanor Parry) was shown in the cast list at the top of the review.

3 A two-page advertisement appeared in the 19 Nov. 1921 edition of *Exhibitors Trade Review*. The 15 Apr. 1922 edition of *Motion Picture News* reported "an increase in demand for [the] historical drama as evidenced by [the] success in placing [it] with some of the best exchanges throughout the country."

4 "Mingo Makes "*The Deerslayer*." *Exhibitors Trade Review* 4 Nov. 1922.

5 Ibid.

6 "Mingo, New Firm, Completes Picture." *Moving Picture World* 30 Jan. 1923.

7 Advertisement. *Exhibitors Trade Review* 12 May 1923.

8 Krefft, Vanda. *The Man Who Made the Movies* (New York: Harper Collins, 2017).

9 Smith, Don G. "The Road to Dracula: The Bela Lugosi Scrapbook." *Scarlet Street* No. 12 (Fall 1993).

10 "Fox Objective Is Ideal Directors." *Exhibitors Herald* 14 Aug. 1920.

11 "Edwards Going to Panama." *Film Daily* 20 Feb. 1923.

12 "U.S. Navy Drama Underway at Fox Studios." *Motion Picture News* 2 June 1923.

13 "Cuts and Flashes." *Film Daily* 26 June 1923.

14 "Eastern Notes." *Film Daily* 22 July 1923.

15 "N.Y. Premiere for *Silent Command*." *Motion Picture News* 18 Aug. 1923.

16 "Fox Early Releases Meet with Success." *Moving Picture World* 17 Nov. 1923.

17 *The Silent Command* pressbook.

18 Before being screened in Chicago and New York City, *The Silent Command* acted as the premiere film when Oakland's Fox Theater first opened its doors on August 25, 1923. Among the luminaries present was Tom Mix, who rode his horse Tony "through the lobby and down the center aisle." See "Fox Opening Oakland Theatre Acquires Continental Chain." *Moving Picture World* 8 Sept. 1923.

19 "Special 24 Sheets for Fox Film." *Moving Picture World* 8 Sept. 1923.

20 "*The Silent Command* – Fox Central." *Film Daily* 7 Sept. 1923.

21 "Fox Makes 1923 Debut on Broadway with Opening of Big Productions." *Moving Picture World* 15 Sept. 1923.

22 "*The Silent Command*." *Exhibitors Herald* 15 Sept. 1923.

23 "*The Silent Command*." *Moving Picture World* 15 Sept. 1923.

24 D. R. "*The Silent Command*." *Exhibitors Trade Review* 15 Sept. 1923.

25 Reid, Laurence. "*The Silent Command*." *Motion Picture News* 15 Sept. 1923.

26 "*The Silent Command*." *Film Daily* 9 Sept. 1923.

27 "*The Silent Command*." *Variety* 6 Sept. 1923.

28 "*The Silent Command*." *Billboard* 22 Sept. 1923.

29 *The Silent Command* pressbook.

30 "Two Impressive Ceremonies Mark Philadelphia Opening." *Moving Picture World* 15 Dec. 1923.

31 "Recruiting Tie-up Boosts *The Silent Command*." *Motion Picture News* 15 Sept. 1923.

32 "Saying It With Flags Over In Newark." *Moving Picture World* 10 Nov. 1923.

33 "What the Picture Did for Me." *Exhibitors Herald* 6 Oct. 1923.

34 "What the Picture Did for Me." *Exhibitors Herald* 13 Oct. 1923.

35 "What the Picture Did for Me." *Exhibitors Herald* 24 Nov. 1923.

36 "What the Picture Did for Me." *Exhibitors Herald* 29 Dec. 1923.

37 "Straight from the Shoulder Reports." *Moving Picture World* 19 Jan. 1924.

38 "What the Picture Did for Me." *Exhibitors Herald* 3 Nov. 1923.

39 "What the Picture Did for Me." *Exhibitors Herald* 26 Jan. 1924.

40 "Straight from the Shoulder Reports." *Moving Picture World* 22 Dec. 1923.

41 *"The Silent Command." Exhibitors Herald* 18 Oct. 1924.

42 "What the Picture Did for Me." *Exhibitors Herald* 27 Dec. 1924.

43 *"The Silent Command* – Fox Strand, Cincinnati." *Film Daily* 30 Dec. 1923.

44 What the Picture Did for Me." *Exhibitors Herald* 23 Feb. 1924.

45 *"The Silent Command." Amerikai Magyar Népszava* (New York) 4 Sept. 1923.

46 Ibid.

47 "Bela Lugosi, Young Hungarian Actor, Joins Washington Heights' Growing Artists' Colony." *Home News* (The Bronx, New York) 2 Sept. 1923.

48 Ibid.

49 Quoted in *The Silent Command* pressbook, which is archived at the New York Public Library for the Performing Arts, Dorothy and Lewis B. Cullman Center.

50 "Digest of Pictures of the Week." *Exhibitors Herald* 15 Sept. 1923.

> FESTVORSTELLUNG
>
> Zur Feier des 25-Jährigen Stiftungsfestes
>
> des
>
> # DEUTSCHEN VEREINS
>
> der
>
> Columbia Universität
>
> ## DIE SORINA
>
> von Georg Kaiser
>
> Regie: Bela Lugosi
>
> BRINCKERHOFF THEATER
> Broadway and 119th St.
> NEW YORK CITY
>
> Dezember 19, 20, 21
> 1923

Playbill for *Die Sorina*.

Chapter 28

Leaving the Nest

"[Don Juan] believes neither in Heaven,
nor the saints, nor God, nor the Werewolf."
– Molière

As 1923 came to a close, Bela Lugosi forged ahead with plans to become an English-speaking actor, to the extent that he apparently enrolled in a course on English at Columbia University in New York.[1] He came to know the university well, thanks to being involved in the Deutscher Verein (German Society), particularly its German-language production of Georg Kaiser's play *Die Sorina* (*The Sorina*).[2] Kaiser was the most famous dramatist of German Expressionism; his 1912 play *Von morgens bis mitternachts* (*From Morn to Midnight*) was adapted into an Expressionist film of the same name in 1920, while Lugosi was living in Berlin.

For *Die Sorina*, Lugosi started as one of a staff of "competent coaches and advisors,"[3] then became the sole coach of the play,[4] and eventually its director.[5] Students from Barnard College and the Columbia University School of Journalism formed the cast. A surviving playbill listed performances for December 19-21, 1923.[6]

Nevertheless, Lugosi continued his efforts to leave ethnic theater behind him, so much so that by February of 1925, the publication *A Hét* wrote, "Unfortunately, Lugosi rarely appears before the Hungarian audience that each of his performances is a real event. ... The audience is familiar with Lugosi's great qualities, and it is certain that if he were to play more often, he could preserve those theatre-goers of the Hungarian theatre who would otherwise leave."[7]

The transition Lugosi was making was not particularly easy. In 1924, producer Irving Davis offered him a contract to serve as director of the play *The Right to Dream*. Presumably Davis thought Lugosi was qualified due to having directed Hungarian and German plays in

A Fata Morgana egyik tipikus jelenete. A darabot hétfőn diszelőadáson mutatják be a Lyceum Theatre-ben

Published in *Amerikai Magyar Népszava* on April 12, 1924.

America. But Davis quickly fired Lugosi, accusing him of being unable to function in that capacity. Lugosi in turn sued Davis for breach of contract and requested a jury trial. In May 1924, just before the play opened on Broadway, the jury decided in favor of Davis, believing allegations that Lugosi had fabricated his connections and misrepresented his talent.[8] Why Davis really fired Lugosi is hard to determine; perhaps Lugosi's limited English-language skills were to blame.

By the time of the verdict, Lugosi had returned once again to ethnic theater. In April of 1924, he directed a production of *Fata Morgana* at New York's Lyceum, and acted as emcee for the same.[9] His participation was hardly surprising. Lugosi's plans to break into English-language theater had not kept him from remaining a part of the Hungarian-American artistic community. Its members included Lajos Bíró, author of *A sárga liliom* (*The Yellow Lily*) and one-time member of Count Károlyi's government. Bíró was in attendance at *Fata Morgana*.

Opening night was apparently quite festive, turning into a "celebration by Hungarians in New York."[10] A report further noted:

> A group of women and men, all dressed in traditional Hungarian garments, turned the theater's lobby into a colorful vision... The show was sold out, and one could only

HUNGARIAN NIGHT AT "FATA MORGANA"

The Hungarian societies of this city are taking charge of Monday night's performance of "Fata Morgana," by the Hungarian dramatist, Ernst Vajda, and making a gala night of its opening at the Lyceum theatre. The celebration will be as nearly like such an occasion in a Budapest theatre as possible. Official hosts will be Willy Pogany, the artist; Emil Kiss, the banker, and Lajos Biro, the dramatist. Master of ceremonies is the well-known Hungarian actor, Bela Lugosi.

SZINHAZ ES ZENE

LUGOSI Béla, akit a Theatre Guild a "Fata Morgana" egyik fontos szereplésére szerződtette és aki a Lyceum Theatreben április 14-én már föl is lép a nagy gála estén. Lugosit mindnyájan ismerjük az az ő belekapcsolása mindenrészre nyereség művészi szempontból.

A FÉSZEK, amely pár hétre beszüntette működését, e hó végén nyitja meg uj helyiségeit. Lugosi Béla, akit a Fészek vezetősége a klub átszervezésére kért meg, hetek óta szakadatlanul dolgozik, hogy a Fészeknek megfelelő uj otthona teremtsen. Az uj helyiségében az átalakitási munkálatok már javában folynak és a Fészek tagjaira a hónap végén kellemes meglepetés vár. A klub vezetőségének uj tervezetében minden garancia megvan arra, hogy a Fészek klub ezután zavartalanul és fokozottabb mértékben folytathatja munkáját és biztosra vesszük, hogy a már biztos alapokra helyezett irók és

Left: Published in the *New York Daily News* on April 10, 1924. Center: Published in *Új Előre* on April 13, 1924. Right: Published in *Amerikai Magyar Népszava* on May 11, 1924.

hear Hungarian speech in the crowded theater. The atmosphere was so genuinely Hungarian, that when I heard actors on the stage not speaking in Hungarian, I was almost surprised.[11]

... After the second act ... a spectacular group of people appeared on stage. Hungarian women and men in traditional attire marched in. The group was led by Bela Lugosi, Master of Ceremonies, who greeted the actors on behalf of The Fészek, interpreted the gratitude of Hungarians towards them, and provided them with three gorgeous tulip wreaths with golden ribbons.[12]

Most notably, Lugosi was an important member of New York's Fészek Club, also known as "The Nest," which had co-sponsored *Fata Morgana* with the Theater Guild. The organization provided a forum for actors, artists, and musicians, who often met at the Hungaria Restaurant. Some of its actors appeared in *Fata Morgana*.[13] Due in part to that performance, the Fészek asked Lugosi to become its leader, which he did in April 1924:

Bela Lugosi, who was asked... to reorganize the club, has been working tirelessly for weeks to create a suitable, new home for [The Fészek]. The remodeling work of the new place is well underway, and the members will be pleasantly surprised at the end of the month, when they will finally see the result. In the new management plan, the continuation of its even higher activity is firmly guaranteed, and we are confident that the club of already well-established writers and artists will not only be the center of Hungarian society in America, but it will promote Hungarian art widely among Americans, too.[14]

P. M. A.—A. E. A. Minimum Contract.

STANDARD FORM

ACTORS' EQUITY ASSOCIATION
115 WEST 47TH STREET
NEW YORK CITY

Agreement made this ......9th...... day of ......May......, 1924

between ....(hereinafter called "Manager")

and ......BELA LUGOSSI...................(hereinafter called "Actor")

Agreement of Employment
1. The Actor and the Manager agree that this contract is entered into independently of any other contract between any Equity member and any producer and of any other contract or contracts, affiliation or understanding of any character whatever other than the agreement dated September 6, 1919, between Producing Managers' Association and Actors' Equity Association.

The Manager engages the Actor to render services in * ......"THE WERWOLFE"......

upon the terms herein set forth, and the Actor hereby accepts such engagement on the following terms:
* (Here state the name of the part and of the play in which the Actor is to appear; also if he is to be required to understudy.)

Opening Date
2. The date of the first public performance shall be the ......on or about the 19th......day of ......May...... 1924, or not later than fourteen days thereafter. Employment hereunder shall begin on the date of the beginning of rehearsals and shall continue until terminated by such notice as is herein provided.

Compensation
3. The Manager agrees, as compensation for services hereunder, to pay the Actor the sum of ......THREE HUNDRED...... Dollars ($..300.00..) every week from the date of the first public performance of the play.

(Courtesy of the Billy Rose Theater Division of the New York Public Library)

In addition to firing the Board of Directors (save for Willy Pogány), Lugosi quickly rented a four-story building for the club at 54 West 55th Street.[15] The Fészek thus had a large headquarters, complete with a basement. As of May, the city's phonebook gave the club as Lugosi's address, so he was likely living there as well.

May of 1924 also marked Lugosi's next opportunity to appear in an important English-language production: Rudolf Lothar's three-act comedy *The Werewolf*, adapted from the German by Gladys Unger.[16] J. J. Shubert believed the play – first staged in Berlin in 1921 as *Der Werwolf* – had real potential for Broadway; he acquired the rights while he was abroad.[17] Two years earlier, the *New York Times* came to the opposite conclusion, thinking an American production would face backlash due to the plot's "six seductions and no end of merry quips about rape and the like."[18]

Lothar – an Austrian born in Hungary – did not write about a supernatural werewolf, but rather one who was all too human, something of a male counterpart to the "vampires" that actresses like Theda Bara played onscreen. The plot unfolds in a castle in Spain, where the Duchess of Capablanca becomes convinced that the spirit of the late Don Juan is responsible for recent sexual attacks on pretty young women. Her psychic investigates and determines instead that the astral projection of a famous professor is responsible. The Duchess attempts a rendezvous with the professor, but soon learns the real culprit is neither spirit nor astral projection: it is Vincente, her butler. He is not discharged.

Lugosi was cast as Vincente, perhaps due to the positive reviews he received in *The Red Poppy*. He signed his Actors' Equity standard minimum contract with the Shubert organization on

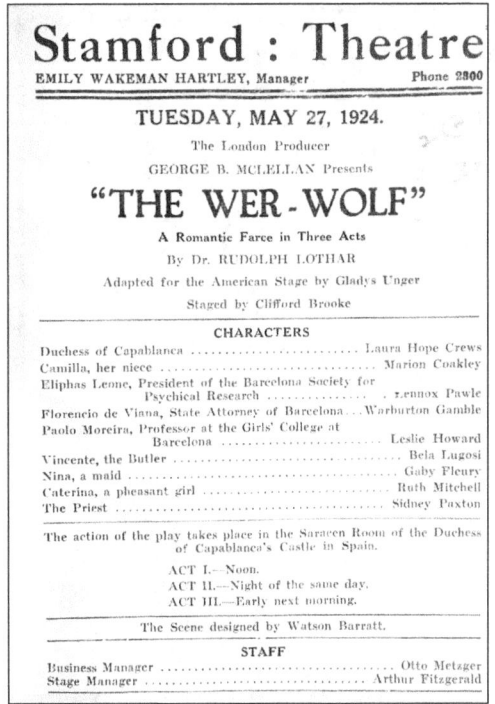

Left: *(Courtesy of the Billy Rose Theater Division of the New York Public Library)*. Right: Published in the *Stamford Advocate* (Stamford, CT) on May 26, 1924.

May 9, 1924. He agreed to a salary of $300 weekly, with $30 of that amount per week being paid directly to his agent.[19] The contract's other terms were hardly favorable. Though the production management had to pay his transportation from and back to Manhattan while playing other cities, Lugosi had to rehearse for up to four weeks without pay.[20]

That said, the first public performance occurred less than three weeks after Lugosi signed his contract. The cast also included Laura Hope Crews as the Duchess and Leslie Howard as the professor. Clifford Brooke staged the play, which was produced by George McClellan.[21] The first tryout performance was staged in Stamford, Connecticut, on May 27, 1924, where programs spelled the title as *The Wer-Wolf*, but newspaper ads spelled it *The Werewolf*.[22] The *Stamford Advocate* mentioned Lugosi in the cast, but did not otherwise comment on him.[23] A critic for *Variety* said the play "made a rather unusually favorable impression," adding that it was "aided considerably by the excellent playing of the cast."[24]

The play then opened in Buffalo, New York, at Shubert's Teck Theatre, where it ran from May 29 to 31, 1924. Lugosi received ninth billing in local advertisements.[25] While pleased with particular scenes, the *Buffalo Express* critic was not amused by the overall effect of the play:

> *The Werewolf*, a farcical comedy... proved an utterly stupid and unnecessarily questionable play on which were wasted the talents of a remarkable company.... vulgarized when there was no need to be vulgar, suggestive when it might just as well

Left: Published in the *Buffalo Courier* (Buffalo, New York) on May 28, 1924. Right: Published in the *Buffalo Times* (Buffalo, New York) on May 31, 1924.

have been simply funny. An example of a really good play gone wrong. The audience laughed a lot, was bored much of the time, disgusted occasionally, and, as the performance progressed, was lost in wonder why such a production and such a cast had been bestowed upon such material.

The possibilities of *The Werewolf* are endless. It would be easy with such a plot to turn out one of the lightest and most entertaining farces instead of the vapid and spineless play disclosed last night.... Bela Lugosi plays Vincente, the butler, with excellent effect.... The play is said to be headed for New York. It should stop outside for some weeks to allow of complete revision....[26]

The *Buffalo Evening News* added that, while the play was "far from perfect" and needed "considerable pruning," Lugosi played his part "commendably."[27]

After Buffalo, *The Werewolf* opened on June 1, 1924, at the Adelphi Theater in Chicago. That the Adelphi had once been a burlesque house seemed fitting given the play's subject matter.[28] The *Chicago Tribune* responded:

Published in the *Chicago Tribune* on May 25, 1924.

... A gay tale for the smoking-room is this, with the fable out of the Decameron, and its overlay of ribald satire on the psychic cults, the night listeners and the astral bodies. Besides, *The Werewolf* is what is called good theater....[29]

On June 2, the *Chicago American* told readers the play was "smoothly acted by an expert cast."[30] Two days later, the *Chicago Evening Post*

Lugosi in *The Werewolf*. *(Courtesy of the Billy Rose Theater Division of the New York Public Library)*

Gary D. Rhodes | Bill Kaffenberger

judged Lugosi to be "exceedingly good"; that same day, the *Chicago Daily News* said he was "efficient."[31]

But things had already changed dramatically, in more than one sense of the word. On June 2, 1924, the *Chicago Tribune* reported:

> Louis Bennison, who was to have acted the butler, was ill; Mr. Lugosi, who had been rehearsing it, was seen in it; and he will be relieved later in the week by Vincent Serrano. Mr. Lugosi, evidently a good actor, was a bit heavy; and his dialect was not a beneficence in a cast which varied uncommonly in its attitude toward English diction.[32]

Leslie Howard in *The Werewolf*. *(Courtesy of the Billy Rose Theater Division of the New York Public Library)*

Then, on June 6, 1924, the *Chicago Tribune* added, "Vincent Serrano... took over last night the role of the ... butler ... in succession to Bela Lugosi, whom we should like to see again."[33] Moreover, a clipping in Leslie Howard's personal scrapbook entitled "This Week in Chicago" and dated "June 15 to 21, 1924" clearly lists Serrano's name in the cast, not Lugosi's.[34]

To be sure, Lugosi's name continued to appear in at least a few subsequent publications. On June 27, 1924, for example, the *Daily Northwestern* listed Lugosi in the role of Vincente.[35] Cartoon drawings of the play's actors published in the *Chicago Daily News* on June 21, 1924, includes Lugosi's name, but under artwork clearly depicting Serrano. These were apparently errors resulting from publicity materials printed while Lugosi was still in the company. Indeed, the October 1924 issue of *Motion Picture Classic* went so far as to claim that Lugosi was in the Broadway cast, which was certainly not the case.[36] When *The Werewolf* premiered at Manhattan's 49th Street Theater on August 25, 1924, Serrano was very definitely playing what began as Lugosi's role.[37]

It seems probable that Lugosi didn't play Vincente after June 4, 1924, though curiously a surviving program bearing the handwritten date of June 8, 1924, still credits Lugosi as playing the role. It would be easy to presume that the printer had not yet provided new playbills, but the curiosity here is that Lugosi's name seems to be on

Published in the *Chicago Daily News* on June 21, 1924.

a small slip of paper pasted on *top* of the original page, as if he was replacing someone else.[38] The handwritten date is hardly reliable, but the program could indicate that Lugosi did appear in the play on one or more occasions after June 4. Perhaps Lugosi – who had received largely favorable reviews – became Serrano's understudy. Nevertheless, there is absolutely no proof or indication that he did.

By contrast, the preponderance of evidence suggests he left *The Werewolf* after June 4, 1924, and thus severed his connections with the Shubert organization. Why did he leave? Perhaps he was fired due to his limited English-language skills, though it should be repeated, he had received largely positive reviews and had played the part in Stamford, Buffalo, and (briefly) Chicago, so it's hard to believe these problems would not have manifested earlier. Possibly he had some argument or difficulty with the producer or director, though there is no evidence of the same. Or perhaps something else happened. *Variety* claimed:

> The Adelphi attraction drew a premiere gross of around $1,400, but it promises little here. Wednesday's matinee was called off and money refunded because it didn't look as if there was over $30 worth of patronage present for this performance.[39]

The dreadful first week might have caused the Shubert organization to take action. Ticket prices were certainly cut by the second week.[40] Replacing a cast member might have been one way the producers took proactive steps to save the play.

If Lugosi chose to leave on his own, or if the Shubert organization fired him without just cause, either party would have broken the contract, though that hardly means it didn't happen. In fact, the surviving copy of Lugosi's contract is curious in that no production manager of record co-signed it, spaces for the same having been left blank. Here is possibly an oversight that has no meaning, or perhaps it is an error that helped allow either party to sever ties with the other.

Why would Lugosi have wanted to leave? Perhaps he wanted to return to New York, where his wife Ilona Montagh was by that time planning to divorce him. Perhaps, though the two had been separated since 1922 or even 1921; whether Lugosi was still attempting to reconcile with her as late as June 1924 is unknown. Or perhaps he was eager to return to New York due to financial problems with the Fészek Club. On July 14, 1924, the club filed a lien against Lugosi in the amount of $142.70, which might have been for rent he owed for whatever room(s) he used as a residence at 54 West 55th Street.[41] And if he ended his relationship with the Shubert organization on amicable grounds, they may have even paid for his return trip to Manhattan as per the contract.

It does seem that Lugosi was probably back in New York City by early October of 1924, perhaps to deal with legal problems from the Fészek Club, or perhaps to deal with his impending divorce. On or around October 4, the court served Lugosi with a summons and verified complaint regarding Montagh's petition for divorce.[42] Unfortunately the paperwork does not record where Lugosi was at the time, but given that they located him, it would seem likely that he was in New York. At that time, his former cast members were still performing in *The Werewolf* on Broadway, where it had its final performance on November 29.[43]

Publicity still for *He Who Gets Slapped* (1924). Lon Chaney is in the middle; Lugosi was misidentified as the clown on the left. *(Courtesy of Forrest J Ackerman)*

By contrast, Lugosi may well have not wanted or needed to return to the city in June. In fact, facing divorce over a failed marriage and owing money to his friends might have been exactly what Lugosi would have wanted to avoid. And neither problem would necessarily have been logical reasons to leave *The Werewolf* by choice, if for no other reason than to keep his salary of $300 per week, with the possibility the same would continue if the play opened on Broadway and/or elsewhere. (For example, there was discussion in the press of an extended tryout on the West Coast in the summer of 1924. That production never happened.[44])

At any rate, the reason for Lugosi's departure from *The Werewolf* remains in question, as do his whereabouts from approximately June 5 to October 1924.[45] As a result, those months might constitute one of the greatest mysteries of his American career.

Flash forward to the 1950s. Lugosi befriends a teenager named Richard Sheffield, one of his biggest fans. They meet often between 1953 and 1956, during which time Sheffield carefully examined Lugosi's personal scrapbooks and files, which brimmed with still photographs. Decades later, Sheffield told film historian Gary D. Rhodes that he was surprised no Lugosi filmographies listed *He Who Gets Slapped* (1924), as he distinctly recalled seeing in Lugosi's collection an 8x10 photograph that depicted the film's star, Lon Chaney, together with Lugosi, both in clown makeup.

Two publicity stills from *He Who Gets Slapped* (1924). Richard Sheffield believed the man in the front row, second from left, might be Lugosi. *(Courtesy of Forrest J Ackerman)*

Rhodes responded that historians had no knowledge that Lugosi had ever worked with Chaney in any film. Sheffield remained resolute that he had seen the photograph, that it was definitely from *He Who Gets Slapped*, and that the clown resembling Lugosi must have been him, as Lugosi did not collect photographs from films in which he didn't appear. Sheffield added that he never thought to ask Lugosi about the photograph.

Legendary filmmaker Victor Sjöström (aka Victor Seastrom) directed *He Who Gets Slapped* for MGM. Along with *The Hunchback of Notre Dame* (1923) and *The Phantom of the Opera* (1925), the film became one of Chaney's great successes, both financially and artistically. But *did* Lugosi act in it, even as a bit player or an extra? If so, it marked an important onscreen moment, one in which the Man of a 1000 Faces appeared alongside the cinema's future Dracula.

He Who Gets Slapped was produced in California between June 17 and July 28, 1924. Lugosi would have had the ability and presumably the money (given his recent paychecks from *The Werewolf*) to purchase a train ticket and arrive in Los Angeles. There can be no doubt that he knew how to purchase a train ticket; after all, he was able to go from New Orleans to Manhattan with no trouble upon his initial arrival in America. The journey from Chicago to LA would have taken him only a few days.

With major troubles in New York and perhaps being fired from *The Werewolf*, Lugosi could have seen Los Angeles as a very attractive destination because of the opportunity to act in Hollywood films, meaning silent films where his accent and limited English would not have been a problem, as it possibly was with *The Werewolf*. When he expressed his desire to immigrate to America to his first wife in 1919, he might have already been thinking of Hollywood films as much or more than he was of the New York stage.

Would Lugosi have traveled to Los Angeles to work as an extra in clown makeup? No, absolutely not. But he might have decided to try his luck in Hollywood temporarily before having to return to New York in the autumn of 1924 due to the divorce proceedings. After all, he had already appeared in a key role in *The Silent Command* (1923).[46] In fact, he may have been planning to be in Hollywood for several weeks as part of the cast of *The Werewolf*, given rumors of the West Coast tryouts. He might well have known people already in Hollywood, including fellow Hungarian immigrants, contacting them before or after leaving the cast of *The Werewolf*.

Perhaps he was even offered a substantial role in a movie being filmed in Hollywood, one that could have led him to leave *The Werewolf* by his own choice, or – in another possible scenario – to provide a much-needed salary after being fired. Consider the following quotation from February 1925, in which Lugosi describes that situation:

> I received an offer of a contract to appear on the screen. I was playing in a stage production at the time and, acting on advice, I named a figure that doubled my stage salary when I gave my answer.
>
> The producer went mad. He claimed that I was unknown. That I wasn't worth that much. After he had publicized me, yes, perhaps. But not then. But I was told to double

my stage salary when talking to picture people. I didn't know that years of stage training and study counted for little.[47]

Was this a reference to the summer of 1924? That is difficult to say. But if this incident or one of a similar type meant he traveled to Los Angeles, the outcome could have been that no role or contract materialized. As a result, Lugosi became an extra in *He Who Gets Slapped* and possibly other films in order to make enough money to return to New York for the divorce proceedings and pay back some or all of his debts.

Possibly. It must be noted that all known surviving documents and evidence would certainly allow for the possibility that Lugosi was in Los Angeles for a few months, and that he could have been there by the time *He Who Gets Slapped* went into production. There is no compelling evidence that this could not have happened.

By contrast, there is no compelling evidence that Lugosi did journey to Los Angeles at the time or that he appears as a clown in *He Who Gets Slapped*. In 1928, one journalist even claimed that Lugosi had never been to the West Coast prior to that very year.[48] But of course if Lugosi's trip in 1924 was brief and essentially a failure, he might not have wished to mention it.

At any rate, in the 1990s, Rhodes suggested to Sheffield that he might have been mistakenly recalling a photograph from another film, specifically *The Mask* (aka *Punchinello*, produced in 1926, but not released until 1929) in which Lugosi did appear as a clown, including in stills with another actor in clown makeup. In retrospect, it is also possible that Sheffield saw a still from *Women Everywhere* (1930), a film with which Lugosi was involved and that did feature a clown (albeit one not played by Lugosi).

But even after examining images from *The Mask*, Sheffield remained certain that the still he saw depicted Lugosi and Chaney as clowns and that it was from *He Who Gets Slapped*. Viewing the film on home video, Sheffield was convinced he saw Lugosi. He also investigated still photographs from the movie and believed he saw Lugosi without clown makeup as an extra in two of them, and with clown makeup in another. But in the case of the latter, while the clown does look similar to Lugosi, it is in fact Ford Sterling. Might Lugosi have owned this photograph, even though he wasn't in it? Perhaps. Or perhaps Sheffield had seen some other image from the film, one that did show Lugosi.

Two points must be stated. Based on the known archival record, it is certainly *possible* Lugosi was an extra in *He Who Gets Slapped* and perhaps other Hollywood films shot in the summer of 1924. By contrast, there is absolutely *no* convincing evidence he was.

Maybe Lugosi appeared in a Lon Chaney film. Maybe not. Maybe it was a ghost; maybe it was astral projection. Or maybe the butler did it.

Endnotes

1 Shirley, Lillian. "Afraid of Himself." *Modern Screen* Mar. 1931. Columbia University does not have any record of Lugosi's registration, but that does not at all mean he was not a student in a course, which could have operated as an extension course or even informal tutorials.

2 The press repeatedly referred to the German Club by the name "Deutscher Verein." The cover of the playbill for *Die Sorina* refers to it as "Deutschen Vereins."

3 "Many Aspirants Report for Verein Play Cast." *Columbia Spectator* (New York) 18 Oct. 1923.

4 "Verein Play Progressing." *Columbia Spectator* 26 Oct. 1923.

5 "Verein Finally Names Cast of *Die Sorina*." *Columbia Spectator* 14 Nov. 1923.

6 "German Club to Present Play." *Barnard Bulletin* (New York) 23 Nov. 1923.

7 Enyedi, Sándor. *A Tragédia amerikai színpadi pályfutásához* (Budapest: Színháztudomanyie Szemle 12, 1983).

8 *Lugosi vs. Hubert Henry Davis*. Municipal Court of the City of New York, Borough of Manhattan, Third District. New York City, New York. 21 May 1924.

9 On April 15, 1924, the *New York Sun*'s article "*Fata Morgana* Has Gala Performance at Lyceum" reported: "Lugosi, in the company of the Hungarian Writers and Artists Club and friend Willy Pogány, banker Emil Kiss and dramatist Lajos Bíró, waxed eloquent to a packed house: 'When the Hungarian soldier leaves his native country, he carries with him a little packet of the homeland soil. Thus, you can appreciate the delight of so home-loving a people as we Hungarians are at having here before us, with all its romance, all its charm – the Puzsta. *Fata Morgana* – the Mirage – this vision of the Great Hungarian Plain – a miracle – this time not of nature but of consummate art! As all stars shine more brightly on the Puzsta and vie with each other in brilliancy, so do the members of this cast: these tokens of appreciation which the Hungarian Writers and Artists Club, called The Nest, offers to its most prominent members, express our gratitude to all ... whose genius and vision have made our dreams come true.'"

10 "Színház-Zene-Művészét-Mozi." *Amerikai Magyar Népszava* (New York) 16 Apr. 1924.

11 Ibid.

12 Ibid.

13 For more information on the Fészek Club, see Cremer, Robert. *Lugosi: The Man Behind the Cape* (Chicago: Henry Regnery, 1976).

14 "A Fészek." *Amerikai Magyar Népszava* 11 May 1924.

15 "West 55 Street Rental." *New York Sun* 29 Apr. 1924.

16 The American press of 1924 often spelled his name as "Rudolph Lothar."

17 "Shubert's *Werwolf* [sic]." *Variety* 14 May 1924.

18 Woolcott, Alexander. "Second Thoughts on Berlin Nights." *New York Times* 23 July 1922.

19 P.M.A. – A.E.A. Minimum Contract Standard Form, Actors' Equity Association, "*The Werewolfe*" [*sic*], signed 9 May 1924. This contract is archived at the New York Public Library for the Performing Arts, Dorothy and Lewis B. Cullman Center.

20 Ibid.

21 "3-Day Tryout." *Variety* 21 May 1924.

22 The Stamford program is archived at the New York Public Library for the Performing Arts, Dorothy and Lewis B. Cullman Center.

23 "Stamford Theater." *Stamford Advocate* (Stamford, CT) 26 May 1924.

24 "*The Wer-wolf* [*sic*]." *Variety* 4 June 1924.

25 Advertisement. *Buffalo Express* (Buffalo, NY) 18 May 1924.

26 "*The Werewolf* is a Satire on Astral Romance." *Buffalo Express* 30 May 1924.

27 "*The Werewolf* Opens 3-Day Try-Out Here." *Buffalo Evening News* (Buffalo, NY) 31 May 1924.

28 When it was a burlesque house, the venue was known as the Columbia. See Warren, George C. "Behind the Back Row." *San Francisco Chronicle* 7 June 1924.

29 Donaghey, Frederick. "Here's a Bold Gay Piece of German Make – And It's Nothing for the Facile Blusher." *Chicago Tribune* 2 June 1924.

30 Cormack, Bartlett. "*The Werewolf* Is New Comedy at the Adelphi." *Chicago American* 2 June 1924.

31 Collins, Charles. "O How European the Clark Street Drama Is Getting!" *Chicago Evening Post* 4 June 1924; Crolius, Margaret Mann. "Audacious Romance Is *The Werewolf*." *Chicago Daily News* 4 June 1924.

32 Ibid.

33 "Another New Play in Chicago's List: News of the Stage." *Chicago Tribune* 6 June 1924.

34 Leslie Howard's scrapbook is archived at the New York Public Library for the Performing Arts, Dorothy and Lewis B. Cullman Center.

35 Levy, Raymond L. "Second Balcony." *Daily Northwestern* (Evanston, IL) 27 June 1924.

36 *Motion Picture Classic* October 1924.

37 *The Werewolf* ran on Broadway for 112 performances before closing on or about December 1, 1924.

38 This program exists in the collection of the Chicago Historical Society.

39 "Chicago's Loop Down to Cases, with $12,000 Highest for Dramas." *Variety* 11 June 1924.

40 "Twin Theaters $24,000-$20,000 with Duncan Sisters and *Nanette*." *Variety* 18 June 1924.

41 "Business Records." *New York Times* 15 July 1924.

42 *Ilona Lugosi, Plaintiff, against Bela Lugosi, Defendant. Interlocutory Judgment on Default with Provision for Becoming Final Judgment.* Supreme Court, New York County. County Clerk Index No. 28365/1924. For more information on the divorce, see Chapter 25.

43 An advertisement in the 29 Nov. 1924 edition of the *New York Daily News* indicated that the production was in its final week, with November 29, the last day of the week, likely marking the last performance. Subsequent issues listed advertisements for the next production, *Badges*, which opened on 3 Dec. 1924.

44 On June 14, 1924, the *Bakersfield Californian* claimed that the comedy "... will open here shortly after a tryout in neighboring cities...."

45 The winter edition of the 1924 New York City phonebook lists Lugosi's address as the Fészek Club, but that might have little meaning. It could have been simply a carryover of the same address that appeared in the May 1924 phonebook. Or it could have been published upon his return to New York during or after October 1924.

46 He had also appeared in *The Rejected Woman* (1924), which is discussed in Chapter 29.

47 Untitled clipping. *The Morning Telegraph* (New York) 25 Feb. 1925.

48 Waite, Edgar. "Dracula Practices Mysteries Off Stage." *San Francisco Examiner* 26 Aug. 1928.

Lugosi in *The Midnight Girl* (1925). *(Courtesy of John Antosiewicz)*

Chapter 29

The Gateway to Dreams

*"It is wonderful what tricks our dreams play us,
and how conveniently we can imagine."*
– Bram Stoker, *Dracula*

On June 22, 1924, the *Chicago Tribune* published a fascinating report about provincial British theater:

It is said that women fainted and men begged the actors to let up when a dramatization of Bram Stoker's *Dracula* was recently acted in an English town. ... The novel had a bit of vogue when new.[1]

First published in America in 1899, Stoker's novel *Dracula* (1897) had remained in print during the years that followed. News of this Hamilton Deane stage production indicated that the vampire story had entered a new phase. This new phase also included Amy Lowell's lengthy poem *A Dracula of the Hills* (1923)[2], and the use of the name "Dracula" to label German serial killer Fritz Haarmann, whose real-life crimes were reported in the American press in 1924.[3] Dracula was now bigger than a novel; the character was slowly becoming part of popular culture.

Even earlier, American film studios of the type where Lugosi wanted to work had considered adapting Stoker's *Dracula* for the screen. Universal thought about doing so as early as 1915[4], but in 1923, studio founder Carl Laemmle, Sr., believed it was "a little too gruesome to screen well."[5] He apparently changed his mind, because in 1925 the press claimed that Universal would produce a film version starring Arthur Edmund Carew, who had appeared in such movies as *Trilby* (1923) and *The Phantom of the Opera* (1925).[6] These efforts were all in addition to Tod Browning hoping to direct a film adaptation in 1920.[7]

How much or little Lugosi knew about Dracula in the mid-1920s is difficult to say. Probably it was very little, perhaps no more than he knew in Hungary. What is clear is that Lugosi remained resolute in his mission to leave ethnic theater and become a presence in English-language productions, particularly in films made by major American studios. It was not an easy dream to fulfill. In a 1925 interview, Lugosi said:

> There is one thing that stands out in reference to the making of picture productions here ... That is, here personality counts more than ability. I say this with no intent to criticize or to decry. But naturally such a proceeding struck me as peculiar when in Hungary and Germany, skill and ability count for everything on the screen and the stage.[8]

During the course of 1924 and 1925, Lugosi did act in three released feature films. All of them were shot on the East Coast, and fortunately all of them survive.

The Rejected Woman (1924)

By early December of 1923, Distinctive Pictures had signed Lugosi to play an important supporting role in John Lynch's story *Blood and Gold*.[9] The industry press referred to Lugosi as the "Hungarian Barrymore," a "distinguished European actor" who had "appeared in many foreign films and in Fox's *The Silent Command* [1923]."[10] The stars of *Blood and Gold* were Conrad Nagel, who would later appear with Lugosi in *The Thirteenth Chair* (1929), and Alma Rubens, who is now largely remembered for her real-life drug addiction and tragic death.[11] She replaced Jetta Goudal, who was originally announced as the film's lead.[12] Bit players included "a dozen New York society men and women whose fortunes run into the millions."[13] For the

Left: Published in *Exhibitors Herald* on May 31, 1924. Right: Published in *Amerikai Magyar Népszava* on May 4, 1924.

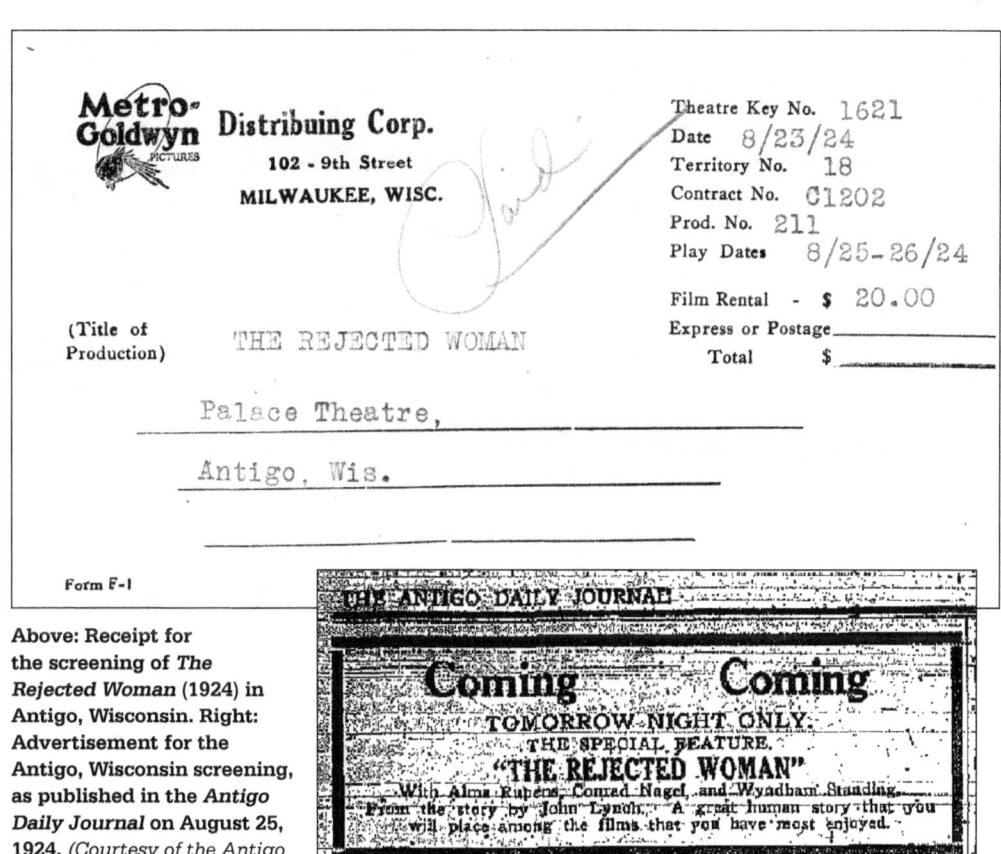

Above: Receipt for the screening of *The Rejected Woman* (1924) in Antigo, Wisconsin. Right: Advertisement for the Antigo, Wisconsin screening, as published in the *Antigo Daily Journal* on August 25, 1924. *(Courtesy of the Antigo Public Library)*

director, Distinctive hired Albert Parker, who had previously helmed *The Haunted House* (1917) and *Sherlock Holmes* (1922).

Production work began at the end of 1923, allegedly taking five months to complete.[14] Along with Distinctive's own studios in the Bronx, locations included New York's Ambassador Hotel and Sherry's restaurant, as well as the *S.S. Paris*, a French ocean liner.[15] The cast and crew also filmed at Trembling Mountain near Quebec, Canada, leaving for that location on December 27.[16] One newspaper article reported that Lugosi and another member of the company had a minor accident during the snowbound shoot, falling through an air hole in the ice.[17]

At a given point in early March of 1924, Distinctive changed the film's title to *The Rejected Woman*.[18] Its plot finds Diane Du Prez (Alma Rubens) meeting wealthy American John Leslie (Conrad Nagel) "somewhere in Canada." They fall in love, much to the chagrin of Diane's local suitor Jean Gagnon (Lugosi). Learning of his father's death, John must return to New York. Diane's father (George MacQuarrie) becomes angry with her for scandalously spending time alone with John. He sends her to be with her aunt in New York. One of the film's intertitles declares that Manhattan is "The Gateway to Dreams." But John's newfound position at his father's company makes a reunion with Diane impossible. Dunbar (Wyndham Standing) quickly falls in love with Diane and schemes to keep her away from John, but she rejects him.

Despite false accusations and lies, "hasty judgment and false pride," Diane eventually reunites with John, leaving Gagnon literally out in the cold.

Distinctive approved the final cut of The Rejected Woman by mid-April of 1924,[19] just in time to screen it at the Hotel Astor in New York on April 17. An unimpressed critic from *Exhibitors Herald* viewed it that night, telling readers that its "story can only be considered logical by a great stretch of the imagination."[20] Goldwyn Cosmopolitan agreed to distribute the film, premiering it at New York's Capitol in May.[21] The city's critics varied in their response, variously calling it "absurd" (*Evening World*), "hokum" (*Herald-Tribune*), and "absorbing" (*Telegram*).[22] Their response was more consistent when it came to praising the actors and the wintry scenes filmed in Canada. Nevertheless, the Capitol reported that *The Rejected Woman* "wasn't strong enough to hold up in [a] Broadway pre-release house."[23]

The industry trade press offered somewhat more complimentary views, if only because their critics realized the film might have greater appeal in smaller cities and towns:

> [It is] a strongly dramatic story that holds the attention from the first flash to the final fadeout. It should appeal to every type of audience and prove an excellent box-office attraction. ... With its intriguing title, its virile story, excellent acting and production values, we believe that you will find *The Rejected Woman* a thoroughly worthwhile attraction that will satisfy the great majority of your patrons.[24] – *Moving Picture World*

> This is not a bad picture, but it will not create any unusual talk among those who will see it. It is fairly interesting from start to finish, it contains a good amount of human interest, and some thrills. But the production is as lavish as are many of the super-specials. ... Good in the main for high-class patronage.[25] – *Harrison's Reports*

> ... ought to make money for the exhibitor wherever it is shown. It is extremely up-to-date in the true sense of that phrase as applied to showmanship angles, making the most of radio and aeroplane, offering elaborate settings, society atmosphere contrasted sharply with the frozen, snow-covered wastes of northern Canada, melodramatic incidents and romantic love interest. This is the sort of thing which is bound to please nine out of ten movie patrons.[26] – *Exhibitors Trade Review*

Advertisement for the Hungarian release of *The Rejected Woman*, published in *Nyírvidék* on August 9, 1925.

The best box office angle is in the title. That might mean something ... As a hokum production in the cheaper grade of house it will serve well enough, but as a pre-release in a main stem it runs for Sweeney.[27] – *Variety*

The industry press may well have been correct. A critic in St. Louis decried everything in *The Rejected Woman* for being as "standard with the movies as Ivory is to soap."[28] By contrast, an exhibitor in the small town of Southington, Connecticut, said, "our audience had nothing but praise. Personally thought this [was] one of the finest pictures of the year."[29] And a theater manager in Illinois called it "dandy," featuring "about everything ... a movie fan wants."[30]

Despite its melodramatic and sometimes illogical plot, *The Rejected Woman* does have merit. Rubens gives a very restrained performance. The location filming is impressive, and the story's pacing is effective. And Lugosi is particularly memorable as the French Canadian, a spurned lover deemed not exciting enough for a woman yearning to see the world. When he sees Diane and John together through the window of a cabin, his subtle expression exemplifies believable aches of lost love.

Daughters Who Pay (1925)

After a short stint with *The Werewolf* in 1924, and the end of his marriage to Ilona Montagh, Lugosi found work in another movie filmed in New York. Banner Productions scheduled *Daughters Who Pay* at least as early as September 1924, initially attaching Burton L. King as

A scene from *Daughters Who Pay* (1925).

Above Sonia, the sensational cabaret dancer, entertains the elite while the secret service men wait outside to arrest her as a spy.

To the left a close-up of Marguerite de la Motte, who plays a dual role in Banner's "Daughters Who Pay," a thrilling romance.

To the left John Bowers, the millionaire hero, rushes off to rescue his sweetheart from the Bolsheviks who have her in their power. Right, Sonia vamps her sweetheart's father in order to secure immunity for her brother.

"Daughters Who Pay"

A Banner Production featuring two beautiful women and the villainies of Russian anarchists

Published in *Exhibitors Trade Review* on February 14, 1925.

director.³¹ The company intended the project to be the fourth of its "Big Four" feature releases, planning from the start to distribute it on a states-rights basis (a system whereby a copyright holder sold the film to theaters locally or territorially) as early as January 1925.

Samuel J. Briskin and George H. Davis, the two directing heads at Banner, briefly changed the title of *Daughters Who Pay* to *The Lady of the Night* in November 1924, apparently because another company was producing a film with a title similar to *Daughters Who Pay*.³² But Banner reverted to *Daughters Who Pay* the following month when they learned that MGM was producing a film called *Lady of the Night*, which went on to be released in 1925.³³

By November of 1924, George Terwilliger became the final choice to direct *Daughters Who Pay*. His screen credits date to at least 1910 and continued into the sound era; he would later direct the voodoo film *Ouanga* (1936, aka *The Love Wanga*).

Daughters Who Pay went into production on December 22, 1924, at the Whitman Bennett Studios in Yonkers, New York.³⁴ Production seems to have been held up briefly because stars John Bowers and Marguerite De La Motte arrived from the West Coast later than expected.³⁵ De La Motte had previously played opposite Douglas Fairbanks in *The Mark of Zorro* (1920) and Lon Chaney in *Shadows* (1922); Bowers was probably best known for starring in *Lorna Doone* (1922) with Madge Bellamy. Also in the cast was veteran actor J. Barney Sherry, who had appeared in such movies as *The Forest Vampires* (1914), *The Devil* (1915), and *Go and Get It* (1920).

Lugosi in *Daughters Who Pay*.

A scene from *Daughters Who Pay*.

At the end of February 1925, *Moving Picture World* reported that shooting on *Daughters Who Pay* – as well as another Banner movie called *Speed* (1925) – was finished. Both films were then in post-production.[36] Of *Daughters Who Pay*, *Variety* told readers, "it is constructed not to leave anything out that might strike the fancy of the state right buyer."[37] Whether or not that was accurate, Banner released *Daughters Who Pay* to the states-rights market in the spring of 1925, at least one month later than they had originally hoped.

William B. Laub wrote the story and adapted it for the screen; he also edited it.[38] In its plot, Sonia Borisoff (De La Motte) is the "sensation of Broadway," a Russian dancer at the Club Royale. She is also part of a Russian spy ring led by Serge Romonsky (Lugosi), who intends to use Soviet propaganda and his "sinister power" to undermine America's faith in its own government.[39] Romonsky loves Sonia, but she prefers the American Dick Foster (Bowers), son of the wealthy Foster, Sr. (Sherry). Dick's father disapproves of the romance, and even tries to buy Sonia off.

The film's secondary story features a meek woman named Margaret Smith (De La Motte), whose brother has embezzled money from Foster, Sr. Sonia offers to break off her affair with Dick if Foster, Sr. forgives Smith's brother. The Department of Justice later bursts into Sonia's home and arrests the Russian spy ring. Romonsky escapes and, realizing Sonia is a double agent, lures her to a rural home in order to have her murdered. Dick arrives just in time to

 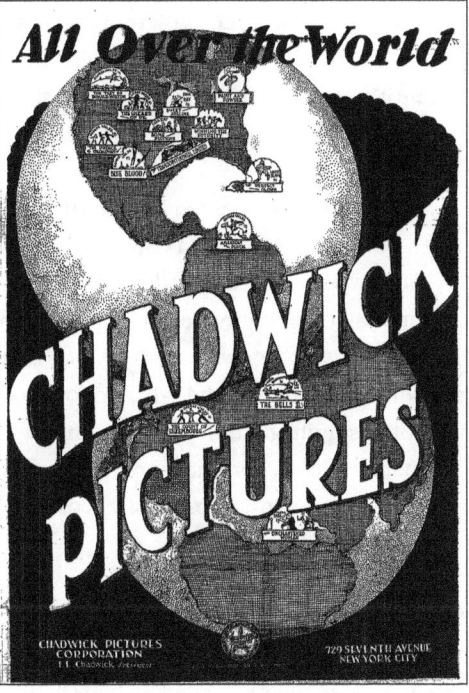

Left: Trade publication advertisement. Right: Published in *Moving Picture World* on February 27, 1926.

save Sonia, shoot Romonsky, and learn the truth: Sonia and Margaret are the same woman, something Foster, Sr. has already come to understand.

A critic for the *Exhibitors Herald* believed that *Daughters Who Pay* featured "fast action in the last scenes."[40] Overall, though, the industry reviews were less than enthusiastic:

> The story is thrilling, the acting adequate, and the suspense well sustained, so plausibility may be dispensed with. ... should prove satisfactory entertainment for audiences not too highly sophisticated, which are more interested in fast-moving action and colorful characters than in plausibility.[41] – *Moving Picture World*

> A romantic melodrama, with a complicated plot the threads of which are so tangled it is by no means an easy job to 'get the straight' of the yarn, but strong on thrills and going fast all the time. ... The title sounds as if it should have a box-office pull, but it has little to do with the course of events... The interior settings are attractive and the photography as a whole is excellent.[42] – *Exhibitor's Trade Review*

> *Daughters Who Pay* gets more complicated as it goes along and it is seldom very convincing entertainment. The development is episodic and not at all smooth.[43] – *Film Daily*

> If you want to put this picture over you must ask people to come just to see how foolish, how illogical, how uninteresting some pictures can be. You should tell them that this one is a prize lemon, and that if they should come they would have a rare opportunity to poke fun at it.[44] – *Harrison's Reports*

Reviewers largely ignored Lugosi, though he was likely one of the actors *Variety* had in mind when noting, "There were a couple of Russian heavies that didn't amount to much."[45]

Those who believed *Daughters Who Pay* to be improperly titled are correct; it is not, for example, an exploitation tale of flappers gone wrong. And despite the threadbare explanation of why Margaret knows how to dance and speak Russian, the storyline remains contrived melodrama. That said, the sets and location shoots in the snow are more than adequate. De La Motte is quite good in the film, and her scenes with Lugosi are appropriately tense, as he alternately tries to dominate and woo her. When he draws cards to see which of his minions will kill Sonia, Lugosi's Romonsky is particularly memorable.

The Midnight Girl (1925)

Lugosi had barely completed work on *Daughters Who Pay* when he agreed to appear in *The Midnight Girl*, originally announced as *The Street Singer*. Chadwick Pictures, an independent production company headed by I. E. Chadwick, used its Long Island studios to shoot the film, as well as some locations in Manhattan.[46] *The Midnight Girl* became the sixth of a total of nine "de luxe special productions" on the Chadwick season for 1924-25.[47]

Garrett Fort – who later worked on the scripts for *Dracula* (1931), *Frankenstein* (1932) and *Dracula's Daughter* (1936) – wrote the original story for *The Midnight Girl*. In it, theater impresario Nicholas Harmon (Lugosi) foregoes his "wanton" romance with fading opera diva Nina (Dolores Cassinelli) and pursues the talented young singer Anna (Lila Lee). An intertitle explains, "Harmon always figured that the woman he *hadn't* kissed was always worth two of those he already had." But his stepson Don (Gareth Hughes) loves Anna as well, and intervenes when Nicholas tries to take advantage of her. During a dramatic struggle, Anna fires a gun at Nicholas, but the bullet hits Nina. Only then does Nicholas realize he loves Nina. She survives, and all four characters enjoy a happy ending.

Wilfred Noy, who was Leslie Howard's uncle, directed *The Midnight Girl*, which was shot by two cinematographers, one of them G.W. "Billy" Bitzer, who had for many years famously collaborated with D. W. Griffith. Production began during the last week of January of 1925.[48] The shoot finished around the end of February.[49] Chadwick then released the movie on a states-rights basis.[50]

The Midnight Girl reveals a more limited budget than Lugosi's other surviving American silent films, and not just because it lacks the spectacle of major location shoots. For example, an intertitle claims we see "New York's Great Opera House," language presumably meant to conjure images of the Metropolitan, but the stage and seating depicted are so small that it looks more akin to a neighborhood movie theater. That's in addition to a particularly melodramatic story.

Cast and crew of *The Midnight Girl* (1925). *(Courtesy of John Antosiewicz)*

Nevertheless, *The Midnight Girl* is enjoyable, in part due to Lugosi's sheer amount of screen time. And the film features some striking images, including Lila Lee wearing costume wings and hanging from a clock in a nightclub, her performance causing her to become known as the "Midnight Girl." Lugosi appears with a Svengali-esque goatee that accentuates his lustful advances. When Lugosi and Lee sit together, a striking edit crosses the 180-degree line to show his spider-like fingers moving across her back. Particularly effective are extreme closeups of his face as he attempts to molest her, the imagery recalling German Expressionism and being prescient of a similar scene with Lugosi and Louise Currie in *Voodoo Man* (1944).

The industry trade press considered *The Midnight Girl* to be average or above, depending on the critic, but Lugosi received greater praise than he had for any of his previous American films:

> Well suited for [a] certain type patronage. Has angles and atmosphere that will appeal although story itself is of a conventional nature. ... The manager who assures the singer a career if only, etc., is a most familiar character. He appears again in *The Midnight Girl*, and gives Lila Lee, as the girl singer, plenty to worry about when she finds he has her cornered in his apartment.[51] – *Film Daily*

> This production directed by Wilfred Noy who also collaborated on the scenario should provide pleasing entertainment for the average theater patron... The story introduces several sure-fire melodramatic situations... Bela Lugosi gives an exceptionally satisfactory performance in the heavy role of the hero's philandering father.[52] – *Moving Picture World*

Chadwick's production of *The Midnight Girl* proves to have an often-screened plot and generally good cast. The theme, old hokum that it is, is the kind that lends box-office value to a picture. Except in theaters entertaining very sophisticated audiences, the opus will make some money. ... Bela Lugosi is excellent as the philandering producer of operas.[53] – *Billboard*

Clever acting and elaborate dance scenes. The lascivious Nicholas is the dominating influence throughout, and Bela Lugosi makes a deep though somewhat unpleasant impression in this strong part... much of the action passes in the luxurious abode of Nicholas....[54] – *The Bioscope*

As for movie fan magazines, *Photoplay* called *The Midnight Girl* "reasonably entertaining."[55] Exhibitor reports as published in the industry press varied:

As usual, another bum one. Why waste Lila Lee on junk like this? Chadwick seems to think all you have to do is take some well-known star with a bunch of hams and then you have a box office knockout. If you want us independent exhibitors to boost independent product, give us something to boost. ... The cabaret scenes were done very good – that's all.[56]

Above Top: Published in *Moving Picture World* on April 11, 1925. Above: Published in *Film Daily* on June 15, 1919.

Published in *Moving Picture World* on January 3, 1920.

> This was a good one day picture. A great improvement over most of the pictures I have had from this exchange....[57]

> Pretty fair program picture but the first reel contains the filthiest title and scene I ever saw in a picture. Cut it out before showing. Tone, doubtful. Sunday, no. Special, no. Fair appeal.[58]

Mention of the "filthiest" intertitle probably refers to one about Nina that reads, "She spared no artifice to hold him." Onscreen visuals at that point show Nina scantily clad, observing Harmon observing her.

Worse news than any critical response was the fact that *The Midnight Girl* faced two lawsuits. In September 1925, the Adolf Philipp Film Corporation sued Chadwick for plagiarism and sought $100,000 in damages. Philipp had written an operetta of the same title and staged it in 1913-14, though *Variety* noted that he had himself adapted it "from the French [original] of Paul Hervé and Jean Briquet."[59] The press generally referred to Philipp's *The Midnight Girl* as a "musical comedy" and "musical farce." Philipp then adapted his play into a two-reel short film in 1919.[60] He alleged that Chadwick stole more than his title; the company also stole his plot. In actual fact, the two stories are largely different from one another.[61] But that isn't what caused Philipp's lawsuit to fail. His copyright was faulty, and so he lost.[62]

Then, in 1926, famed opera singer Nina Morgana brought suit against Chadwick because Dolores Cassinelli's character in *The Midnight Girl* was named Nina Morgana.[63] Morgana – famed for being a protégée of Caruso and an important soprano at the Metropolitan Opera – asked for $25,000 in damages, alleging she had been "held up to public contempt" because the character Nina posed "with sparsely clad and even semi-nude men and women" in the film. She was also insulted because, in a publicity tagline, the character declares that she "sold her soul to become a prima donna." As a result, Chadwick instructed its film laboratory to "remove the name Nina Morgana from all film [prints] and substitute another name."[64] The character was renamed Mimi Divito, although two of the intertitles on surviving prints still say "Nina."[65]

Lugosi was not involved in either lawsuit. Rather, he had played three roles in American films in the space of a year, one unsuccessful French lover and two heavies, a Russian spy and an American philanderer. The three films have deficits, to be sure, but out of them emerges the most striking image of all of Lugosi's American silents. In *Daughters Who Pay*, Lugosi's Romonsky embraces De La Motte's Sonia, who dances with a rose in her teeth. He kisses her passionately, only to draw back and realize a stream of blood is running down from his lip.

The image looks as if it could have come from a vampire movie. As an intertitle in *The Midnight Girl* suggests, "The Hands of Time are ever writing a diverse destiny for us, the Children of the Hours."

Published in the *York Dispatch* (York, Pennsylvania) on May 27, 1925.

But certainly the blood on Lugosi's lip is prophetic of nothing. It just appears compelling in retrospect. *Daughters Who Pay* was not a vampire movie. After all, as Jonathan Harker says in Stoker's novel, "This startled me, but as the effect was only momentary, I took it that my eyes deceived me straining through the darkness."

Lugosi in *Daughters Who Pay* (1925). (Courtesy of the George Eastman Museum)

Endnotes

1 "This-and-That." *Chicago Tribune* 22 June 1924.

2 "The Book Column." *The Capital Times* (Madison, WI) 13 June 1923.

3 "*Dracula* in Reality." *Atlanta Constitution* 21 July 1924.

4 Koszarski, Richard. Email to Gary D. Rhodes, 26 Apr. 2012. Koszarski made notes regarding the 1915 consideration of a *Dracula* film while examining Universal's legal files in the mid-1970s.

5 Quoted in "Inside Stuff – Pictures." *Variety* 25 Apr. 1951.

6 "Behind the Screen in Movies." *Indiana Evening Gazette* (Indiana, PA) 18 Feb. 1925. Another article did not mention Universal, but instead claimed, "A well-known producer has evinced a desire to star Mr. Carew if he can find a suitable vehicle. Bram Stoker's *Dracula* and several books which offer colorful characterizations are under consideration for the versatile Carew." See "Carew Seeks Story." *Los Angeles Times* 29 Mar. 1925.

7 "Little Theatre Film?" *Oakland Tribune* 19 Dec. 1920.

8 Untitled clipping. *The Morning Telegraph* (New York) 25 Feb. 1925.

9 "Lugosi in Distinctive's Latest." *Film Daily* 2 Dec. 1923.

10 "Bela Lugosi Engaged for *Blood and Gold*." *Motion Picture News* 8 Dec. 1923.

11 For more information on Alma Rubens, see Rhodes, Gary D. and Alexander Webb, editors. *Alma Rubens, Silent Snowbird* (Jefferson, NC: McFarland, 2006).

12 "Alma Rubens Lead in *Blood and Gold*." *Motion Picture News* 1 Dec. 1923.

13 "Wealthy Society People Appear with Screen Stars in *Rejected Woman*." *Helena Daily Independent* (Helena, MT) 6 Jan. 1925.

14 "Titled *Rejected Woman* – Distinctive Production Will Be Released in April." *Moving Picture World* 15 Mar. 1924.

15 Ibid.

16 "Screen Stars Are Back From North." *Davenport Democrat and Leader* (Davenport, IA) 17 Feb. 1924.

17 Ibid.

18 "Cuts and Flashes." *Film Daily* 7 Mar. 1924.

19 "Final Cutting." *Exhibitors Herald* 19 Apr. 1924.

20 "All Brands of Hokum Used in This Picture." *Exhibitors Herald* 10 May 1924.

21 "Astor Showing for Distinctive." *Film Daily* 14 Apr. 1924.

22 "Newspaper Opinions." *Film Daily* 8 May 1924.

23 "*Dorothy Vernon* and *Girl Shy* Kept Main Stem Interested." *Variety* 14 May 1924.

24 "The Rejected Woman." *Moving Picture World* 3 May 1924.

25 "The Rejected Woman." *Harrison's Reports* 24 May 1924.

26 "*Rejected Woman* Should Make Good." *Exhibitors Trade Review* 10 May 1924.

27 "The Rejected Woman." *Variety* 7 May 1924.

28 Quoted in "Newspaper Opinions." *Film Daily* 9 June 1924.

29 "Rejected Woman." *Moving Picture World* 2 Aug. 1924.

30 "Rejected Woman, The." *Exhibitors Herald* 15 Nov. 1924.

31 "To Direct Banner Films." *Moving Picture World* 6 Sept. 1924.

32 "Start Last of Series Soon," *Film Daily* 20 Nov. 1924; "*Lady of the Night* Fourth of Banner Big 4 Series." *Motion Picture World* 13 Dec. 1924.

33 "Start New Banner Prod. Soon." *Film Daily* 14 Dec. 1924; "*Daughters Who Pay* Fourth in Banner 'Big Four' Series." *Moving Picture World* 27 Dec. 1924.

34 "Stars Dash to East Studios to Start *Daughters Who Pay*." *Moving Picture World* 3 Jan. 1925.

35 "*Daughters Who Pay* Fourth In Banner 'Big Four' Series." *Moving Picture World* 27 Dec. 1924.

36 "*Speed* and *Daughters Who Pay* Released in March." *Moving Picture World* 28 Feb. 1925.

37 "Daughters Who Pay." *Variety* 13 May 1925.

38 "Laub Busy on Editing." *Film Daily* 27 Feb. 1925. It is possible that Leota Morgan had written the original story on which *Daughters Who Pay* was based, with Laub adapting the same for the film's screenplay. Trade reports are contradictory on this point.

39 Some contemporary press accounts referred to Lugosi's character by the name "Oumansky," but onscreen intertitles make clear that his name was "Romonsky."

40 "New Pictures." *Exhibitors Herald* 13 June 1925.

41 "*Daughters Who Pay.*" *Moving Picture World* 30 May 1925.

42 "*Daughters Who Pay.*" *Exhibitors Trade Review* 20 May 1925.

43 "*Daughters Who Pay.*" *Film Daily* 10 May 1925.

44 "*Daughters Who Pay.*" *Harrison's Reports* 4 Apr. 1925.

45 "*Daughters Who Pay.*" *Variety* 13 May 1925.

46 "Chadwick Now Preparing to Complete Schedule." *Exhibitors Herald* 28 Feb. 1925.

47 "Nine De Luxe Chadwick Specials." *Moving Picture World* 10 May 1924; "New Chadwick Picture." *Moving Picture World* 24 Jan. 1925.

48 "Chadwick Rushing Studio Work." *Exhibitors Trade Review* 31 Jan. 1925.

49 "Chadwick Now Preparing to Complete Schedule." *Exhibitors Herald* 28 Feb. 1925.

50 "State Righters Eager for Chadwick Program." *Moving Picture World* 18 July 1925.

51 "*The Midnight Girl.*" *Film Daily* 12 July 1925.

52 "*The Midnight Girl.*" *Moving Picture World* 28 Mar. 1925.

53 "*The Midnight Girl.*" *Billboard* 28 Mar. 1925.

54 "Criticisms of the Films." *Bioscope* (London, England) 22 Oct. 1925.

55 "*Midnight Girl.*" *Photoplay* May 1925.

56 "What the Picture Did for Me." *Exhibitors Herald* 20 June 1925.

57 "What the Picture Did For Me." *Exhibitors Herald* 5 Sept. 1925.

58 "Independents – *Midnight Girl* – R. J. Reif, Star Theater, Decorah, Iowa." *Moving Picture World* 22 Aug. 1925.

59 "With the Press Agents." *Variety* 1 Aug. 1913.

60 Philipp had tried to develop a film deal for some of his plays, *The Midnight Girl* among them, as early as 1916. See "World Signs Adolf Philipp." *Variety* 1 July 1916.

61 "$100,000 for Plagiarism." *Variety* 16 Sept. 1925.

62 "Nina Morgana Wants $25,000 for Use of Name." *Variety* 3 Mar. 1926.

63 An intertitle in surviving prints actually refers to the character as "Nina Morgan," not "Nina Morgana."

64 "Character's Name Brings $25,000 Damage Action." *Variety* 10 Feb. 1926.

65 One of the two intertitles that says "Nina" uses a different font style from the rest of the film, which suggests that it dates from a different era than the other.

Lugosi in *Arabesque* (1925).
(Courtesy of David Wentink)

Chapter 30

Bizarre and Beautiful

> "A vampire scene, in which an Arabian 'wild woman' seduces the sheik, is the rawest and most inexcusable thing here in years."
> – *Variety*

Bela Lugosi starred in *The Red Poppy* in 1922. As one journalist reported, "he waited three years before again appearing in an English speaking part."[1] It came in the Broadway play *Arabesque*, written by Cloyd Head and Eunice Tietjens, with music by Ruth White Warfield. Wunderkind Norman Bel Geddes not only acted as its scenic designer, as he had already so successfully for a number of plays, but also as its director.[2] He also formed a corporation with Richard Herndon to co-produce this spectacular and sumptuous "comedy-drama."

Herndon originally encouraged Geddes to drop the project, believing it to be "underwritten." Head and Tietjens drafted two new scenes, which was enough to allay the concerns.[3] Of the rehearsals, which were underway at the Manhattan Opera House in September 1925, Eunice Tietjens recalled, "It seemed to us that half of the extra people in New York were disposed about the stage."[4] And then there were the stars. Lugosi, whom *Variety* called the "Hungarian Barrymore," portrayed the Sheik of Hammam.[5] Playing opposite him was Hortense Alden as Laila; she had appeared on Broadway in Ferenc Molnár's *Liliom* in 1921.

In *Arabesque*, the sensuous Laila seduces the Sheik of Hammam, who for the sake of cultural politics is betrothed to M'na (Sara Sothern). More trouble surfaces when Ahmed Ben Tahar (Curtis Cooksey) wants M'na to become his own wife. In the rivalry that follows, Ahmed wins the beautiful M'na's affections. All of this unfolds against the backdrop of forty speaking roles and around sixty extras. The press observed:

Lugosi working on *Arabesque*. Seated at the table beside him are (in order, from right to left) Eunice Tietjens, Cloyd Head, Norman Bel Geddes, Sara Sothern, and Curtis Cooksey.
(Courtesy of John Antosiewicz)

The locale of the play is in a small village in Tunisia, which lies on the edge of the Sahara Desert. The people of Tunisia comprise Arabs, Jews, Bedouins, ... Moroccans, and Senegambians [sic], and representatives of these nationalities are prominently cast in this remarkable play. These people are simple, kindly folk, living a life, which has changed little since the time of Abraham. ... Across the desert the camel caravans come in the old way. Into the village come the Bedouins, those sons of the earth who are like magnificent hawks, with their lithe beautiful women.[6]

Head and Tietjens had allegedly spent the previous winter in the actual village on which the one in the play was based.[7]

With Geddes as director, the key character in *Arabesque* became the setting. Changes unfolded rapidly without need of closing the curtain. As the *New York Herald-Tribune* described, "These changes are made by darkening the stage ... and as a window is substituted for a doorway and an exterior dissolves into an interior the characters continue speaking."[8] Vibrant, colorful lighting bathed the alternating scenes, creating a simultaneously exotic and erotic atmosphere.

Head and Tietjens were afraid that Geddes had "submerged" the dramatic line of the story, drowning it in "scenery and mechanics." Tietjens remembered that Lugosi and Sara Sothern "tried to help," lobbying for improvements to their characters. According to Tietjens, "Bela Lugosi had authority and power."[9] Rewriting thus "went on and on," which made the actors "half crazy with the constant rearrangement of their lines."[10] Rehearsals lasted for five weeks, one more than planned, with Geddes aided by four assistant directors.[11]

Arabesque then opened for tryout performances in Buffalo, New York, on October 5, 1925. Critics were guarded in their praise:

Published in the *Buffalo Courier* on October 4, 1925.

> *Arabesque* is pre-eminently a series of exquisitely beautiful pictures made by the master hand of Norman Bel Geddes – dark figures silhouetted on the roof tops against an amethyst sky, lanterns in the dark, rose, flame, turquoise blue, jade green and violet robes against gray walls. The play is a perfect feast of color; a marvelously beautiful spectacle. Unfortunately, the Teck stage, large as it is in itself, and enlarged as it was last night, extending away out over the orchestra pit, was still too small for the show. ... The show stands as a real achievement in scenic art, in spite of minor trouble last night. ... Bela Lugosi, one of Hungary's leading actors, did a fine, dignified piece of work, and was, incidentally, a sheik to satisfy the heart of any flapper – tall and stern and handsome. His splendid voice and excellent diction were not the least attractive part of his performance.[12] – *Buffalo Courier*

> To endeavor to describe *Arabesque* is well nigh as hopeless a task as to paint a word picture of a sunset, for there is a wealth of color and a detail of stage craftsmanship of new standard. ... There is an abundance of color at every moment in the production and its sheer magnificence is compelling. ... And yet there is something lacking. That something Monday caused the audience to refuse to accept the production seriously. There were giggles at just the wrong time and laughter when it was evident the moment was a dramatic one. Many openly expressed the view the production is intended to be accepted as burlesque, and yet such a conclusion is unthinkable. ... The cast is one of rare excellence ... Sara Sothern ... Curtis Cooksey ... Bela Lugosi ... are only a few of those who play with distinctions their difficult roles.[13] – *Buffalo Evening News*

> A rare bird indeed, and so overladen with its own rich plumage it is difficult to distinguish quite whether it is fowl, fish or fancy. ... Remove the vivid oriental brilliancy of the setting and *Arabesque* becomes a bit of bottle glass. ... The action transpires

before a shifting background of brilliant kaleidoscopic settings. ... The effect is uncanny and highly effective though bewildering because unique. ... Bela Lugosi played the sheik with restraint.[14] – *Variety*

After closing in Buffalo on October 10, 1925, the company moved to the Wieting Theater in Syracuse for October 12 to 14. Reviews varied:

> It is a play of giant and lovable people with a love story of ... power.[15] – *Syracuse Journal*

> One should not get the preconceived notion in this respect that the play is in any sense a picture play, filled with bogus properties and made theatrical by stage tricks. It is far removed from that; indeed, throughout one is impressed by the absolute sincerity of the players and the producers, and the entire absence of hokum and the bringing in of something sensational to stir applause. ... Curtis Cooksey and Bela Lugosi have the principal men parts. They invest the play with a primitive vigor characteristic of the desert, but the work of each is marked by repression which merits praise.[16] – *Syracuse Evening Herald*

> Its artistry is undeniable. As to its ultimate success or failure on Broadway, that depends on two things. If there are a sufficient number of metropolitanites ... that crave the esthetic, the beautiful and the unusual, then *Arabesque* ... is destined to succeed. If on the other hand, the Great White Way's clientele cannot understand *Arabesque* – is unable to grasp its poetry, its romance, its daring stagecraft, then ... it is destined to find an early death. ... So profuse has been the use of spectacle ... that the story is not always clear.[17] – *Syracuse Daily Telegram*

Above Top: Published in the *New York Herald-Tribune* on October 22, 1925. Above: Published in the *New York Times* on October 25, 1925.

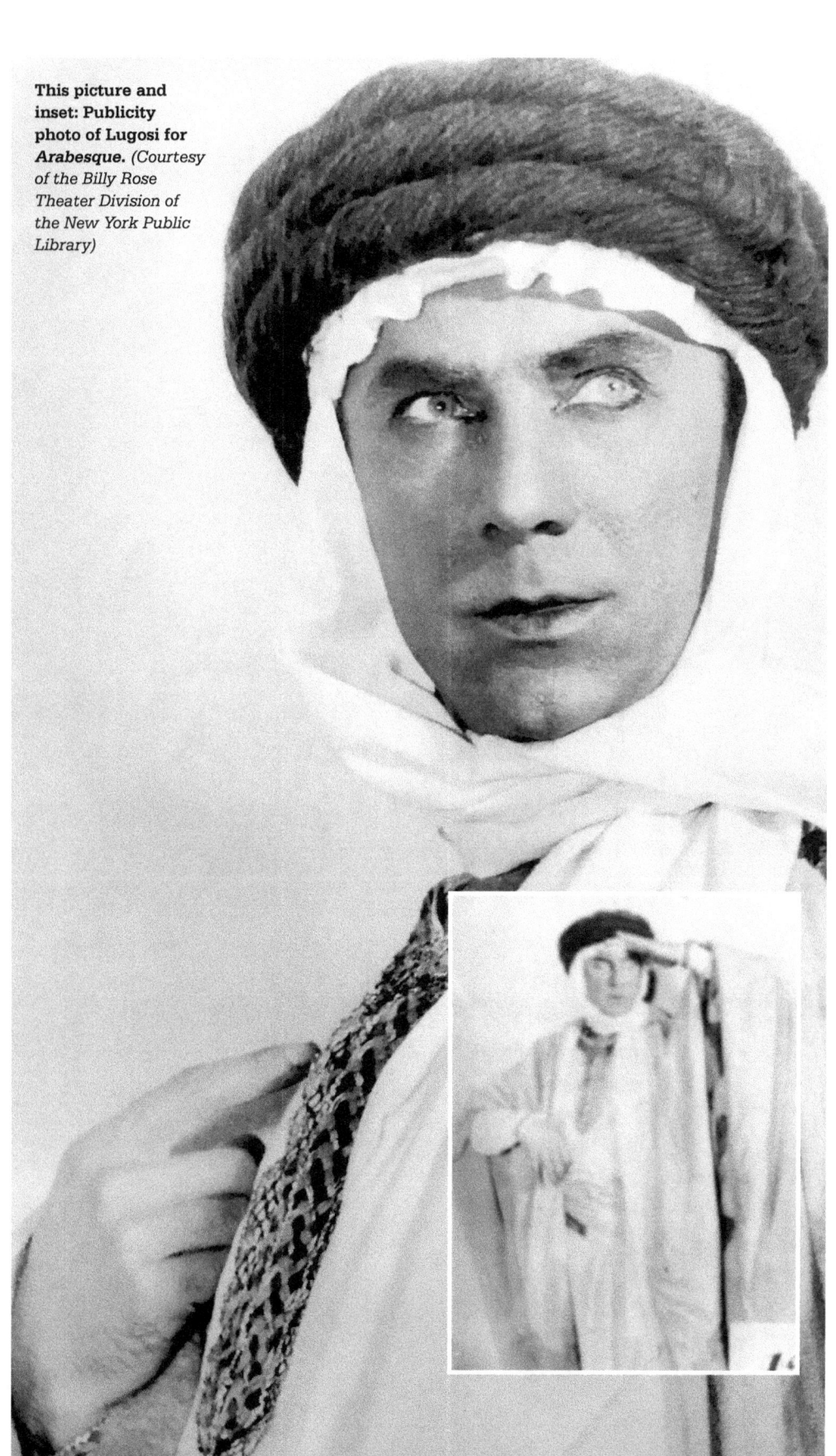

This picture and inset: Publicity photo of Lugosi for *Arabesque*. *(Courtesy of the Billy Rose Theater Division of the New York Public Library)*

Publicity photo of Lugosi for *Arabesque*. *(Courtesy of John Antosiewicz)*

```
+++++++++++++++++++++++++++++++++++++++++++++++++++
              PROGRAM CONTINUED
UNDER THE HAYSTACK, AHMED BEN TAHAR,
                                       CURTIS COOKSEY
He, who carries the Haystack off, Abdullah........Sarat Lahiri
SHEIK OF HAMMAM, A MINOR OFFICIAL,....BELA LUGOSI
Short Orderly, who carries umbrella...............M. Garboat
THE PEARL IN A BED OF OYSTERS, M'NA....SARA SOTHERN
THE MOTHER OF THE PEARL, MA-BOUBA.....OLIVE WEST
Coppersmith ................................Raphael Kadous
The Herdsman who gets his hair cut............Hamad Bisher
Woodpeddler ................................Ismut Hassen
THE SHEIK'S MOTHER WHO WOULD LIVE IN TUNIS,
                                          JULIA RALPH
THE SHEIK'S SISTER.......................NAOE KONDO
The Sheik's Aunt.......................Yetta Malamude
                              {.....Beine Lehassen
                              |..Mustapha Hantoot
Five Dancing Boys at the wedding.......{....Maetar Lehadder
                              |Mohammed Houssain
                              {....Hamad B. Omar
                              {....B. A. Fripp
Three Arab Guests.........................{Lackaye Grant
                              |Claude Dougal
THE PROFESSIONAL MATCHMAKER, HALIMA..HELEN JUDSON
An Innocent Bedouin, near the door..............John Brewster
The Public Letter Writer.........................Prince Singh
A Negro Servant Woman......................Elsie Winslow
Grain Vendor.................................James Gaylor
The Subcaid...............................William Skavlan
THE CAID OF NADOUR, A SUPERIOR OFFICIAL,
                                    ETIENNE GIRARDOT
                              {Florence Brinton
Four Bridesmaids........................{Elsbeth Herbert
                              |.....Helen Kim
                              {.....Rona Fray
The Muezzin................................Yuji Itow
         _____
         PROGRAM CONTINUED ON NEXT PAGE
+++++++++++++++++++++++++++++++++++++++++++++++++++
```

```
                    ARABESQUE
  "And the story goes that the bride did not veil, but spoke to him
with her naked face."—Baba Youssef.
                      SCENE 1
  The Moorish cafe in Hammam-el-Kedime, where Ahmed ben Tahar,
late sergeant in the French Army, sees the face of the pearl, M'na, and
finds a talisman, and where the Sheik meets a Bedouine desert-cat, Lalla.
                      SCENE 2
  The house of Mabouba, where the Sheik's Mother, sent by her son,
pays a visit of inspection to consider M'na—whom the Sheik had seen
on the roof-tops by Mabouba's design, and with whom he has fallen
in love; and what happened at the interview.
                      SCENE 3
  A navel of the desert, where the wandering Bedouins reveal that
they are not only thieves but murderers and where they discover that
they have lost a talisman taken from the dead man. Here the Sheik,
thinking they are only petty thieves, finds again the Bedouine and
makes an unwritten bargain.
                      SCENE 4
  The house of Mabouba, set for the wedding of her dead son to
collect the money which according to custom was due him at his wedding.
Here Ahmed learns that the Bedouins have murdered the Caid's nephew;
and his wits sharpened by jealousy, baits the Sheik, whose traffic with
the Bedouins he suspects.—Also, Mabouba's own funeral, held to convince
the Sheik's mother that Mabouba will be an unobtrusive mother-in-law,
and how the scheme worked in spite of an unwelcome interruption.

              Intermission Ten Minutes.
```

Above: From the playbill for *Arabesque*.

Tietjens recalled that, by the time the Syracuse tryouts ended, the show's "mechanics had been perfected, the beauty heightened, and all that remained of the play totally lost."[18] *Arabesque* became scenery over story, style over substance.

The play debuted on Broadway, not at the Century Theater, as originally planned, but instead at the National.[19] Opening night was on Lugosi's birthday, October 20, 1925; he was 43 years old.[20] While acknowledging *Arabesque*'s scenic beauty, critical response was largely (though not uniformly) negative:

> To anyone with an eye for the picturesque it will be a delightful study in glowing and busy life, reproduced enthusiastically and convincingly by Mr. Geddes. ... *Arabesque* is evidence of a great amount of labor brought to agreeable and successful accomplishment.[21] – *Wall Street Journal*

> As far as the eye can reach, *Arabesque*, that vivid and gala splurge of spectacle which has begun to play at the National Theater, is one of the most amazing and exciting achievements American stagecraft has ever made.[22] – *New York Sun*

> ...*Arabesque*, with its conscientious production and its laborious attention to detail, cannot be overlooked.[23] – *New York American*

> ... an unusually sumptuous, prodigal and lavish costume spectacle, *Arabesque* flashed forth in a bewildering array of color, novelty, daring and much that is truly art. ... The costuming is dazzlingly and amazingly vari-colored and magnificent; so are the props, which were beautifully designed. ... The book, however, never keeps pace with either

Above Left: Published in the *New York Herald-Tribune* on October 25, 1925. Above Right: Published in the *Brooklyn Eagle* on October 18, 1925.

the direction or the mounting. It is a stupid torrent (no, that is too swift – a vapid river) of words. No ideas, no sense of progression, no tension – just words, and none of them of any consequence... Had it been produced on an ordinary scale, it would have been yawned at and walked out on – it was anyway, to some extent.[24] – *Variety*

It's an entertainment that will necessarily make an appeal as a spectacle more than for its dramatic value. In drama it falls short.[25] –*New York Herald-Tribune*

As spectacle it is lavish and beautiful, leaving nothing to be desired; but other elements of good stage entertainment appear to have received insufficient attention.[26] – *The Stage*

With none to gainsay him, Mr. Geddes has provided an evening of interesting experiment, offering great pictorial beauty, a scene or two plainly designed to be daring, and extremely little in the way of drama. ... Certainly it was an emasculated text that was offered last night - a text trimmed to a point that made the story at times incomprehensible.[27] – *New York Times*

There are those who will claim *Arabesque* an artistic triumph. There are those who will wonder what it is all about. There are those who will be bored to tears. This reviewer stands with the last named.[28] – *The Daily Mirror*

Scene from *Arabesque*.

Scene from *Arabesque*.

Above: Scenes from *Arabesque*.

It is rather a three-ring circus in a rainbow tent ... told in dialogue of rather tony description, dialogue that is shot through, however, with lines often sharp and beautiful and, occasionally, witty. The plot of the affair starts off bravely enough to swim through the sea of loveliness, but almost before the first episode passes it is sunk without a trace.[29] – *New York Evening Post*

Arabesque is a colorful spectacle, but it seems to me that this is not enough to give the public. There should be something like an engrossing plot, some true drama, character study, acting, anything to give the play life. ... The stage of *Arabesque* is set for a remarkable play which is never acted.[30] – *Columbia Spectator*

Mr. Geddes has undoubtedly achieved interesting effects with his one setting, which he converts into ten different locales with the aid of lighting and decorative fabrics. ... All that is lacking, perhaps, is a play.[31] – *New Yorker*

Norman Bel Geddes has seized upon a scanty and almost excruciatingly unimportant little comedy as an excuse for him to come thumping into the theater with another multitudinous, eye-filling pageant.[32] – *New York World*

On opening night, the audience gave Geddes an ovation, but only 617 of 1,154 seats were filled.[33] Subsequent performances were even more poorly attended. Only 542 seats were sold on October 22, only 215 on October 23, only 293 for October 24's matinee, and only 357 for October 24's evening performance.[34]

Negative reviews and slow ticket sales were not all that Geddes and Herndon had to worry about. Backlash came over the play's more scandalous scenes. The *Post* observed, "There is a dance by a corps of undressed males which gave first nighters a gasp."[35] And the *World* described the "spectacle of nude young men covered with the very best butter who writhed interminably in a talented manner."[36]

Lugosi in *Arabesque*.

But it was the seduction scene with Lugosi and Alden – played without music and in a state of partial undress – that drew most of the shocked comments:

> It seemed hardly necessary in portraying the manners of the Tunisian Arabs to go quite so conscientiously and explicitly into detail concerning the seduction of a sheik. Buffalo audiences are not easily shocked, but the passage last night first shocked the house into a tense silence and then sent it into a fit of nervous giggles. Expressions of disgust were numerous.[37] – *Buffalo Courier*

> [T]here is a seduction scene toward the end of the first act which startles with its frankness and for which Norman Bel Geddes has called down upon himself an avalanche of attack.[38] – *New York Sun*

[P]robably something should be said about the brief crisis of orgiastic passion to which the audience is treated toward the end of Act One when a Bedouin girl so visibly and explicitly seduces a Sheik that the scene loses all the menace of suggestion and becomes faintly comical.[39] – *New York World*

Suffice it to say that the desert scene, at least, contains a thermometer-breaking interlude of amour, replete with snaky undulations of the female form divine and much caressing of thighs that will be talked about and gasped at for quite a spell.[40] – *New York Daily News*

[T]here is a bit which transcends and out-extremes anything this greying stage-reporter has ever witnessed elsewhere. It is not describable in these columns. It is a vamping bit in which a Bedouin girl, dressed down to the utmost finesse of nakedness (she would be far less conspicuous were she utterly naked) straddles a sheik, who lies full-length on a

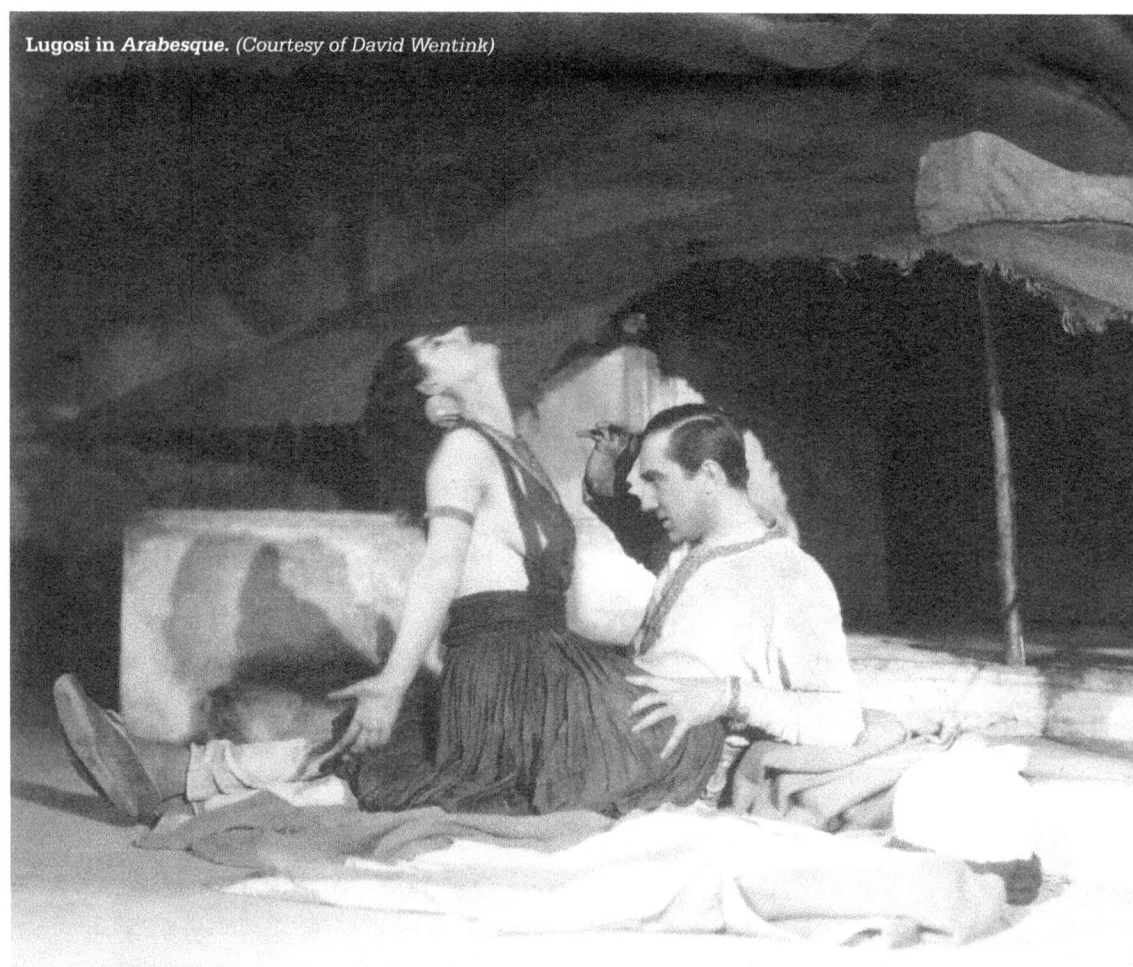

Lugosi in *Arabesque*. *(Courtesy of David Wentink)*

cloak on the floor of a savage tent at midnight, alone with her. Only the blackout saves what might have gone further, and not much further if it never blacked out. To further stamp the incident, the girl, in a prayer in the next act, begs of Allah such things as make the ears tingle, sending home the fact that the blackout was not a finale.[41] – *Variety*

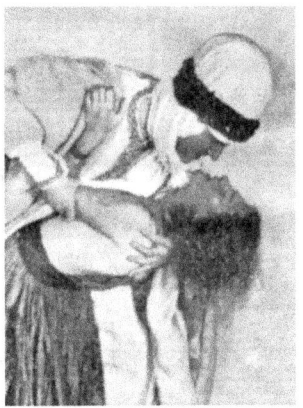

Publicity photo of Lugosi for *Arabesque*.

The outcry was strong enough that Geddes addressed the issue formally, just five days before the show closed:

> It is utterly ridiculous to attach the seduction of the Sheik by the Bedouin girl in the third scene ... on the ground of vulgarity. The scene is a definite link in the story, and I have purposely left out all cheap sensationalism. ... it is a truthful portrayal of a wild girl of the desert who has been born as sensuous as an animal and whose last thought would be concealment of the fact. ... I have seen girls of this type do things much worse than this Bedouin does in *Arabesque*, and I am not hypocritical enough to deny it.
>
> ... Personally I am fully satisfied with the results of the scene. Hortense Alden and Bela Lugosi play it so satisfactorily that the audience sits in tense silence every night for at least five minutes and then breaks into a queer little nervous sound which is not laughter but something akin to it, which indicates the complete grip the actors hold over the imagination of the onlooker.[42]

Not everyone was offended, of course. The *New York Sun* described the scene as "lovely."[43] And the *Daily News* even joked that Alden and Lugosi had to put "all their trust in the electrician who blots out the moon on cue."[44]

During the show's run, a journalist from the *New York Herald-Tribune* took Lugosi to lunch at a Hungarian restaurant. Lugosi allegedly hadn't eaten or slept for two days, but he was eager to share his acting philosophy:

> I do not care that my private face should be handsome, as long as I can buy several dollars worth of grease paint and make a good face for the stage. That is what is important, is it not?[45]

The journalist added that, despite the fact that Lugosi spoke English onstage "without the trace of an accent," he still seemed to have some "difficulty with the American language."[46]

Lugosi could take heart in receiving largely favorable notices, at least when critics bothered to mention the actors:

Then there is the Sheik of Hamman, acted superbly by Bela Lugosi....⁴⁷ – *New York Telegram*

If Lugosi keeps on with such a nice job, we'll soon see him among the best actors of the English language theater in America.⁴⁸ – *Új Előre*

Olive West, Victor Hammond, Bela Lugosi, Sara Sothern, and Curtis Cooksey acquit themselves splendidly in [the] leading roles.⁴⁹ – *The Daily Mirror*

There are several prominent players in the terrific cast.⁵⁰ – *New York Herald-Tribune*

The performance is quite sufficient, with the principal roles in the hands of Sara Sothern, Hortense Alden, Curtis Cooksey, and Bela Lugosi.⁵¹ – *New York Times*

Published in *Új Előre* on October 29, 1925.

Bela Lugosi makes an impressive Sheik. Lugosi looks capable of some fine things if he could better adapt his accent to Anglo-Saxon pronunciation.⁵² – *Billboard*

The sheik ... is overplayed and underdone by Bela Lugosi, but he gets the idea across.⁵³ – *Variety*

The acting of most of the one hundred odd roles is mediocre or worse.⁵⁴ – *The Stage*

Though no critic negatively singled Lugosi out, the *World* believed all of the performances were "uncommonly bad."⁵⁵

Arabesque closed on November 7, 1925, after only 23 performances in New York. Its first week gross of just under $10,000 was "not impressive."⁵⁶ Only $8,000 during the second week damned the play to the category of "no chance." Going dark meant a "considerable loss," as *Arabesque* had cost $69,000, more than double the original plans.⁵⁷ It also marked the end of the Geddes-Herndon corporation, apparently at the request of Herndon, who complained that Geddes had "too much temperament."⁵⁸

Despite the play's early closure, Lugosi had gained measurably by the experience. He had not only made his Broadway debut, but he did so in a production that allowed him to build on his work as Fernando in *The Red Poppy*. He was a dark, foreign lover, a Hungarian Barrymore vamping and being vamped in a play that was special, despite its shortcomings. It was scenery to be seen.

As the *New York Post* observed, *Arabesque* was a "thing purely of the eye, which manages to achieve the warmth of life, a spectacle bizarre and beautiful."[59]

Endnotes

1   "Mastery of English Put Lugosi on Way to Stardom." *Los Angeles Record* 14 July 1928.

2   At times Norman Bel Geddes was credited as "Norman-Bel Geddes" and, more commonly, as "Norman Bel-Geddes." For the sake of internal consistency, this book opts for "Norman Bel Geddes."

3   Tietjens, Eunice. *The World at My Shoulder* (New York: MacMillan, 1938).

4   Ibid.

5   "*Arabesque* Rehearsing; 40 Speaking Roles in Play." *Variety* 23 Sept. 1925.

6   "*Arabesque*." *Lockport Union-Sun & Journal* (Lockport, NY) 5 Oct. 1925.

7   "*Arabesque*, At Wieting Comedy, Takes 100 People." *Syracuse Journal* (Syracuse, NY) 10 Oct. 1925.

8   "*Arabesque* Presented As Expensive Spectacle." *New York Herald-Tribune* 21 Oct. 1925.

9   Tietjens, *The World at My Shoulder*.

10 Ibid.

11 "*Arabesque* to Employ Many Tunisians." *New York Herald-Tribune* [Clipping contained in the file on *Arabesque* at the Free Library of Philadelphia.]

12 "Offerings of the Week at Buffalo's Playhouses." *Buffalo Courier* (Buffalo, NY) 6 Oct. 1925.

13 "At the Playhouses." *Buffalo Evening News* (Buffalo, NY) 6 Oct. 1925.

14 "*Arabesque*." *Variety* 14 Oct. 1925.

15 "*Arabesque* Most Unique Play Yet." *Syracuse Journal* 12 Oct. 1925.

16 "Crossroads of Civilization On Weiting Stage." *Syracuse Evening Herald* (Syracuse, NY) 13 Oct. 1925.

17 Bahn, Chester B. "*Arabesque*, Pageant of Life, Is Poetry and Daring Stagecraft." *Syracuse Evening Telegram* (Syracuse, NY) [Clipping contained in the file on *Arabesque* at the Free Library of Philadelphia.]

18 Tietjens, *The World at My Shoulder*.

19 "*Arabesque* Rehearsing; 40 Speaking Roles in Play."

20 During the play's run on Broadway, ticket prices for matinees were – "for the first time on record" – the same as for evening performances. See "$5 Matinees." *Variety* 28 Oct. 1925.

21 "From Africa's Burning Sands." *Wall Street Journal* 22 Oct. 1925.

22 "All the Perfumes of Arabia." *New York Sun* 21 Oct. 1925.

23 Dale, Alan. "Tunisian Comedy with Queer Dances and Strange Types." *New York American* 24 Oct. 1925.

24 "*Arabesque*." *Variety* 28 Oct. 1925.

25 "*Arabesque* Presented As Expensive Spectacle."

26 "The American Stage." *The Stage* (London) 12 Nov. 1925.

27 "*Arabesque* Reveals Pictorial Beauty." *New York Times* 21 Oct. 1925.

28 "Red Heat Romance." *The Daily Mirror* (New York) 22 Oct. 1925.

29 "*Arabesque* at the National Theater." *New York Post* 21 Oct. 1925.

30 "The Suburbs Of Columbia." *Columbia Spectator* (New York) 4 Nov. 1925.

31 "Critique." *New Yorker* 7 Nov. 1925.

32 Woollcott, Alexander. "The Stage." *New York World* 21 Oct. 1925.

33 National Theater, New York City, Box Office Statements, October 20-24, 1925. [Available in the Theater Collection, Free Library of Philadelphia, Pennsylvania.]

34 Ibid.

35 "*Arabesque* at the National Theater."

36 Woollcott, "The Stage."

37 "Offerings Of The Week At Buffalo's Playhouses." *Buffalo Courier* 6 Oct. 1925.

38 "Norman Bel-Geddes Replies." *New York Sun* 2 Nov. 1925.

39 Woollcott, "The Stage."

40 Mantle, Burns. "*The Enemy* a Thunderous Echo; *Arabesque* Picturesque Drama." *New York Daily News* 22 Oct. 1925.

41 "Plays On Broadway." *Variety* 28 Oct. 1925.

42 Ibid.

43 "All the Perfumes of Arabia."

44 Mantle, Burns. "Wail of the Angels Is Heard Here About." *New York Daily News* 31 Oct. 1925.

45 "A Sheik, a Lovely Lady and a Grand Duchess on Parade." *New York Herald-Tribune* 25 Oct. 1925.

46 Ibid.

47 "*Arabesque* Is Sumptuous; Also Rich, Rare and Racial."

48 Simon, Kein. "*Arabesque* keleti történet 10 képben." *Új Előre* (New York) 31 Oct. 1925.

49 "Red Heat Romance."

50 "*Arabesque* Presented As Expensive Spectacle."

51 "*Arabesque* Reveals Pictorial Beauty."

52 "The New Plays on Broadway." *Billboard* 31 Oct. 1925.

53 "*Arabesque*." *Variety* 28 Oct. 1925.

54 "The American Stage."

55 Woolcott, "The Stage."

56 National Theater, New York City, Box Office Statements, October 20-24, 1925. [Available in the Theater Collection, Free Library of Philadelphia, Pennsylvania]; "Sextet of Shows Leave." *Variety* 4 Nov. 1925.

57 "Sextet of Shows Leave."

58 "Herndon-Geddes Split." *Variety* 25 Nov. 1925.

59 "*Arabesque* at the National Theater."

Lugosi in a photograph that might be from *Open House* **(1925).** *(Courtesy of David Wentink)*

Chapter 31

Closed House

Steel magnate Lloyd Bellamy (Ramsey Wallace) induces his wife Eugenie (Helen MacKellar) to help his business; she must "charm the men from whom he is seeking orders."[1] After she reluctantly agrees, her "feminine wiles" rapidly convince Basil Underwood (Albert Andruss) to award her husband a "coveted contract."[2] And then there is Sergius Chernoff (Bela Lugosi), a Russian who not only places a large order for steel, but also falls in love with Eugenie. By that time, though, she has already turned her attentions to yet another businessman.

So goes the plot of *Open House* (1925), which marked Lugosi's second appearance on Broadway. His key scene unfolded as follows:

> Chernoff, believing Bellamy has sold him $400,000 of defective rails, plans to avenge himself by compromising Eugenie. He tricks her into coming to his apartment. In a scene that throbs with emotion, the husband breaks in with detectives. Eugenie, angered, declares she has been unfaithful.[3]

But in actuality, she has not been. In Act Three, Eugenie announces her abiding love for her husband, who has learned never to involve her in his business. And Chernoff realizes the rails he purchased were not defective. The "curtain falls on a note of general happiness."[4]

Samuel Ruskin Golding, well known in New York as an attorney, wrote and produced *Open House*.[5] Together with co-producer Louis I. Isquith, he hoped to premiere the show on Broadway on November 2, 1925. For reasons that aren't entirely clear, that date had to be postponed by nearly six weeks.[6]

Golding held the first tryout performance at Reade's Broadway Theater in Long Branch, New Jersey, on the night of October 22, 1925.[7] Lugosi was not yet in the cast; at that time, H. Paul Doucet played Chernoff.[8] The show then moved to the Savoy in Asbury Park, New Jersey for October 23,

Above Left: Published in *The Daily Record* (Long Branch, NJ) on October 22, 1925. Above Center: Published in *The Daily Home News* on October 23, 1925. Above Right: Published in the *Detroit Times* on November 8, 1925.

with the local newspaper calling the play "excellent" and giving Doucet a "commendation."[9]

The company then staged *Open House* in New Brunswick on October 26, 1925, with the *Daily Home News* praising Doucet's "spirited grace."[10] From there, *Open House* played Trenton on October 27 and 28 before moving to Cincinnati for the first week of November.[11] From November 8 to 16, the company played Detroit.[12] A local review called Doucet "excellent" and the play "incredible."[13] As for Lugosi, he was starring in *Arabesque* until it closed on November 7.[14]

And so the question is really why Golding replaced Doucet with Lugosi. Perhaps it was due to the rehearsals that Golding held in October 1925.[15] With the exception of Helen MacKellar, the cast reported their unpaid salaries to Actors' Equity in November. Golding countered that he had not "originally" used all of the allotted time, and so he was entitled to what amounted to a second set of rehearsals.[16] Had Doucet grown weary of lack of payment? Perhaps. For reasons unknown, the role of Chernoff became Lugosi's by December. Announcing his appearance, one newspaper recalled his work in *The Werewolf* in 1924.[17]

Open House had a final tryout at the Windsor Theater in the Bronx on December 7, 1925.[18] It was the first tryout hosted by John Cort's new "neighborhood" theater.[19] It was also the first time Lugosi appeared in the show. "Indications only mediocre," *Variety* reported.[20]

When *Open House* finally made its Broadway debut at Daly's 63rd Street Theater on December 14, 1925, reviews were largely unfavorable:

Right: Published in the *New York Daily News* on December 13, 1925.

There are elements of merit in *Open House*. It is an interesting play. Mr. Golding has avoided the fault of most new playwrights, 'talkiness,' and the development of his situations is fairly well effected.[21] – *New York Telegram*

As Chernoff, Bela Lugosi does an excellent piece of work…. The staging is mediocre, with cordials that bubble when poured and a tendency toward lengthy telephone soliloquies.[22] – *New York Sun*

It is a naïve and awkward melodrama with which Helen MacKellar [struggled] last night…. The plot is developed with little ingenuity and much artificiality. … In her support Guy Hitner and Bela Lugosi manage to make two clichéd roles - the one the family doctor and friend, the other the Russian admirer - recognizable and even bearable.[23] – *New York Times*

And that any play in which the accused wife, without valid excuse or reason, jeopardizes her own and her children's happiness by openly declaring herself a wanton merely for the sake of [drama] cannot possibly impress an audience as being anything but shoddy fiction… Ramsey Wallace is a plausible husband… and Bela Lugosi a manly sort of intriguer.[24] – *New York Daily News*

Knowing the author of *Open House* [is] a practicing attorney, it may be unfair to take advantage of him to say that his drama is plastered heavily

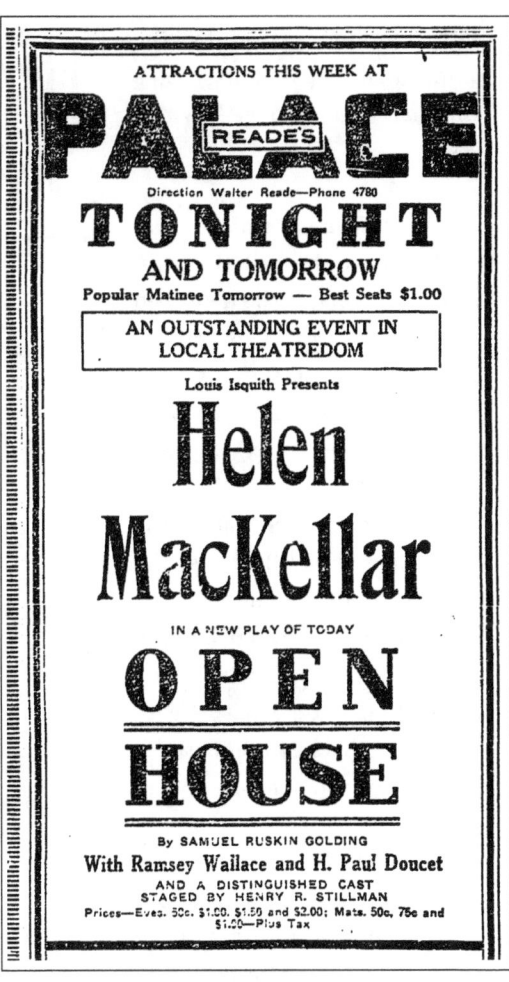

Top: Published in the *Trenton Evening Times* (Trenton, NJ) on October 27, 1925.
Above: Published in the *New York Daily News* on December 13, 1925.

with emotion naïve as the unimaginative psychology of a criminal court room.²⁵ – *New York Post*

Open House, which was produced for the first time last night ... can hardly be described as a success. ... Guy Hitner and Bela Lugosi support Miss MacKellar fairly well.²⁶ – *Brooklyn Standard Union*

Miss Helen MacKellar as the wife, Ramsey Wallace as the husband, and Bela Lugosi as the rival play their parts, I believe, in precisely the manner in which Mr. Golding would have them. More than that he cannot ask.²⁷ – *New York Evening Journal*

Top: Published in the *New York Times* on December 12, 1925. Above: Published in *Új Előre* on January 28, 1926.

Helen MacKellar is the star of the piece and is awarded this department's weekly prize of 'it is a pity to see an actress of her quality in a play of such cheapness.'²⁸ – *New Yorker*

Bela Lugosi, as the Russian villain, lacks the spirit required in the character he represents. His foreign dialect proves a handicap, especially in the excited scenes, and his laboring over words in order to pronounce them clearly cannot help becoming monotonous after a while.²⁹ – *Billboard*

[T]he casual auditor will probably find slim novelty in the proceedings.³⁰ – *New York World*

It was hardly an auspicious event. The play is mechanical and consistently tedious.³¹ – *New York Herald-Tribune*

I give *Open House* until Saturday night.³² – *The Morning Telegraph*

One trade publication claimed that some of New York's critics didn't even bother to see the show, which probably accounts for the lack of reviews in some newspapers.³³

Many would-be audience members didn't see *Open House* either. *Variety* speculated that the first week's gross was "probably under $5,000."[34] After the second week, the same publication predicated that conditions for a "run" did not seem "favorable."[35] After three weeks, *Open House* moved from Daly's to the Criterion Theater, by which time its weekly gross was apparently under $3,000.[36]

Rather than solve problems, the change of venue created even more. Golding had originally agreed to move the show to the Comedy Theater, but decided against it because its lobby needed construction work. Settlement talks fell apart and the matter headed to court.[37] The judge didn't require *Open House* to close at the Criterion, because Golding had never actually signed a contract with the Comedy.[38]

Then, in mid-January 1926, *Variety* reported that no one in the cast had received salary checks for the prior week, save for Ramsey Wallace, who nevertheless quit the show, being replaced by George MacQuarrie.[39] Golding gave the company an impassioned speech about his "strained" resources, promising to pay everyone within a few days. The others agreed to forge ahead without filing claims with Actors' Equity.[40]

On January 27, *Variety* reported that the show's gross for the prior week had allegedly climbed to $6,000, but that still wasn't enough "to stick."[41] By early February, the Criterion announced that *Open House* was in its eighth and final week at the venue.[42] Despite Golding's best efforts, the show had been a "loss."[43] It closed after 73 performances in New York City, but going dark didn't end the troubles.

Actors' Equity sued Golding in 1927 because he still hadn't paid salaries owed to several cast members. A total of $912.63 was due, to be split among seven

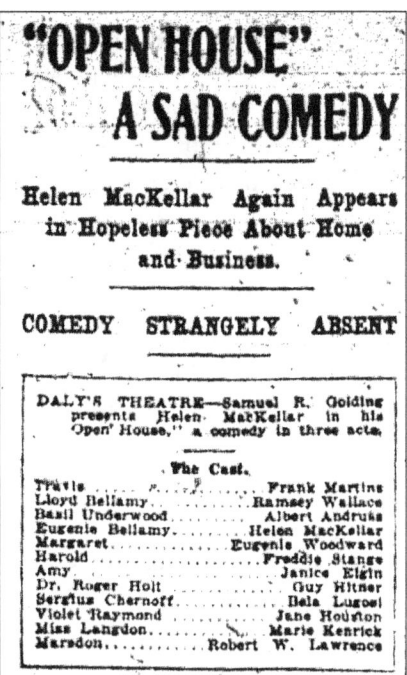

Top: Published in *The Morning Telegraph* (New York) on December 15, 1925. Above: Published in the *New York Evening Journal* on December 15, 1925.

actors, one of them Lugosi.[44] This news came after Famous Players negotiated for the screen rights to *Open House* without proceeding to produce a film version.[45]

For Lugosi, the show must have been disappointing, at least in some respects. Its money troubles were reminiscent of those that caused *The Red Poppy* (1922) to close. Nevertheless, Lugosi had still made gains in the English-speaking theater world. He was no longer an actor with one Broadway credit to his name. He was now a recognizable Broadway star. As the *New York Telegram* told readers:

> Mr. Lugosi ... was his suave and finished self, reminding one of the easy dignity with which he carried through his role of the Sheik in that fascinating and extravagant failure, *Arabesque*, only so recently.[46]

Endnotes

1 Garrick. "The New Plays." *New York Evening Journal* 15 Dec. 1925.

2 Mantle, Burns. "Outsiders Breaking In." *Chicago Tribune* 27 Dec. 1925.

3 Ibid.

4 Ibid.

5 Ibid.

6 "*Open House* Opens Nov. 2." *Billboard* 17 Oct. 1925; "Activities of Coming Shows." *Billboard* 24 Oct. 1925.

7 "*Open House* Opens at Broadway Tomorrow." *Long Branch Daily Record* (Long Branch, NJ) 21 Oct. 1925.

8 "In *Open House*." *Billboard* 31 Oct. 1925; "*Open House* Opens." *Variety* 4 Nov. 1925.

9 "The Play." *Asbury Park Evening Press* (Asbury Park, NJ) 24 Oct. 1925.

10 "*Open House* Play Not So Good as Cast." *The Daily Home News* (New Brunswick, NJ) 27 Oct. 1925.

11 "*Open House* Has Shore Premiere." *Asbury Park Evening Press* 23 Oct. 1925; Advertisement. *Trenton Evening Times* (Trenton, NJ) 27 Oct. 1925.

12 Advertisement. *Detroit Times* (Detroit, MI) 8 Nov. 1925.

13 "*Open House* Incredible." *Detroit Times* 8 Nov. 1925.

14 For more information on *Arabesque*, see Chapter 30.

15 "Helen MacKellar's Latest." *Variety* 21 Oct. 1925.

16 "*Open House* Comes In." *Variety* 18 Nov. 1925.

17 "News-Notes of the Stage." *Chicago Tribune* 13 Dec. 1925.

18 "Bronx Theater Tryout House." *New York Daily News* 4 Dec. 1925.

19 "Cort's First Tryout." *Variety* 2 Dec. 1925.

20 "Shows and Comment." *Variety* 16 Dec. 1925; "Cort Isn't Worried." *Variety* 16 Dec. 1925.

21 "Helen MacKellar Starred in *Open House*." *New York Telegram* 15 Dec. 1925.

22 "A Comedy Drama." *New York Sun* 15 Dec. 1925.

23 "*Open House* a Naïve Play." *New York Times* 15 Dec. 1925.

24 Mantle, Burns. "*Open House* and Ambitious Backers." *New York Daily News* 19 Dec. 1925.

25 "*Open House* at Daly's 63d Street Theater." *New York Post* 16 Dec. 1925.

26 "Manhattan Theaters – *Open House* at Daly's Sixty-third Street." *Brooklyn Standard Union* 15 Dec. 1925.

27 Garrick, "The New Plays."

28 "Critique." *New Yorker* 2 Jan. 1926.

29 Gillette, Don Carle. "The New Plays on Broadway." *Billboard* 26 Dec. 1925.

30 "The Business Woman." *New York World* 15 Dec. 1925.

31 "*Open House* Mechanical and Consistently Tedious." *New York Herald-Tribune* 15 Dec. 1925.

32 Forbes, John. "*Open House* a Sad Comedy." *The Morning Telegraph* (New York) 15 Dec. 1925.

33 "*Open House*." *Variety* 10 Feb. 1926.

34 "Shows in N.Y. and Comment." *Variety* 23 Dec. 1925.

35 "Shows in N.Y. and Comment." *Variety* 30 Dec. 1925.

36 "Shows in N.Y. and Comment." *Variety* 13 Jan. 1926.

37 "*Open House* in Court, Goldings Booking Jam." *Variety* 13 Jan. 1926.

38 "No *Open House* Order." *Variety* 10 Feb. 1926.

39 "Changes in Casts." *Billboard* 30 Jan. 1926.

40 "*Open House*, No Salary, but Show Continues." *Variety* 20 Jan. 1926.

41 "Shows in N.Y. and Comment." *Variety* 27 Jan. 1926.

42 "Shows in N.Y. and Comment." *Variety* 3 Feb. 1926.

43 "Shows in N.Y. and Comment." *Variety* 10 Feb. 1926.

44 "Equity Sues Sam Golding." *Billboard* 9 Apr. 1927.

45 Mantle, Burns. "Theater Notes." *New York Daily News* 4 Jan. 1926. On December 16, 1925, *Variety* wrote that *Open House* was not suitable for film adaptation because it couldn't possibly "inspire a director" or be "fashioned interestingly" for the screen.

46 "Helen MacKellar Starred in *Open House*."

Portrait of Lugosi published 1927 in the Hungarian-American newspaper *Az Ember*.

Chapter 32

Returning to the Nest

> "We hear the blind and aimless galloping
> Of an errant rider from days gone by:
> The shackled souls of sunken forests moan,
> As ancient marshes waken with a sigh."
> – Endre Ady, *Az eltévedt lovas* (*The Lost Rider*)

American films and plays had allowed Lugosi to leave the confines of the Hungarian-American theater community. To a large degree, he had become – or was certainly trying to become – "Bela Lugosi," rather than "Béla Lugosi." And he was working with English-speakers who knew little or nothing of his role in Béla Kun's government, or of him being confused with János "Béla" Lugosi-Buchter, or of his controversy with Ernő Király.

However, some of them might have heard about a man named János Lugossy (not to be confused with Lugosi-Buchter), also known as John Lugosy, who made headlines across America in the late summer of 1924. This Lugosy – a "dark, somber man of 37, always in debt" – murdered a person who had loaned him money, dismembered the corpse, and crowded its remains into a metal vat that he hid in his basement.[1] A married man, Lugosy was having several affairs and probably killed at least one other man as well.[2] A "general alarm" was issued for him in New York, but the press reported that Lugosy might well have escaped to Hungary, his home country, or perhaps to Germany, or South America.[3] He was never captured.[4] Not unlike the conclusion of *Bowery at Midnight* (1942), in which police discover Professor Brenner's (Lugosi) basement/graveyard, New York police began digging up Lugosy's basement, believing they might discover another corpse. Though there is certainly no evidence that anyone confused the murderer with the actor, the news once

DIG FOR CLEWS.—Following discovery of love letters from several women in cellar of missing John Lugosy, where mutilated body of Aaron A. Graff, 72, was found in box, police yesterday dug up floor for other evidence. Story on page *

Published in the *New York Daily News* on August 26, 1924.

again brought negative attention to the Lugosi/Lugossy/Lugosy name in the Hungarian-American community.[5]

And it was to that community that Lugosi returned, somewhat unexpectedly and temporarily, in the mid-twenties. He had made a concerted effort to leave ethnic theater behind him in an effort to reach the broader American public. It was a desire to break with the past, professionally even if certainly not personally, but his was a difficult journey for many reasons, including financial.

In early 1925, a brief article in *Új Előre* announced the formation of a new theatrical troupe featuring Lugosi, Lola Grill and Ilona Thury.[6] Jenő Vass was the director, and Jenő Siposs the producer. József R. Tóth – who had appeared (possibly with Lugosi) in the Star film *Radmirov Katalin* (1917) – was the company's manager.[7] The first production was *Forradalmi nász* (*The Revolutionary Wedding*), a play that Lugosi knew well from his days in Debrecen in 1909 and 1910.

One newspaper claimed that Lugosi would "benefit from the one-week-long break given to him by Famous Players Studios [to join the troupe] ... he will perform on Hungarian stage

The basement graveyard in *Bowery at Midnight* (1942). *(Courtesy of John Antosiewicz)*

again...."⁸ Lugosi did not work for the Famous Players-Lasky Corporation in 1925; the reference here must have been to Chadwick Pictures and the film *The Midnight Girl* (1925), which could have been filmed in part at the Famous Players studio in New York. Lugosi worked on *The Midnight Girl* just before the *Forradalmi nász* tour.⁹

Forradalmi nász tells a story set during the French Revolution. A Marquis is condemned to death immediately after marrying his wife. As a courtesy, the couple is allowed to spend one night together. The desperate wife asks a soldier named Marc-Arrán to change places with her husband. The soldier is in love with her, so he agrees. The husband flees, and the soldier spends the night with the wife, but he is a gentleman and does not try to woo her. The wife is amazed by how much he loves her, and she willingly invites him to her bed. They spend the night together, and the soldier dies the next day happily.¹⁰

Advance publicity for the tour played up Lugosi's long absence from the Hungarian-language stage:

> A festive performance will be held on Thursday night at the New Street Workmen Circle. The guest performance of Hungary's greatest, most talented dramatic actor, Béla Lugosi, will turn the evening into a celebration on 5 February... Béla Lugosi will be most warmly welcomed by the Hungarians of New Brunswick, and he will certainly deserve such admiration. His art will sparkle in the lead role of the fabulously beautiful

Above Left: Published in *Amerikai Magyar Népszava* on February 5, 1925. Above Top Right: Published in *Amerikai Magyar Népszava* on February 10, 1925. Above Right: Published in *Amerikai Magyar Népszava* on January 30, 1925.

drama... Lugosi's name is already well known in America as a movie star, and he is highly appreciated not only by us Hungarians, but by Americans, too.[11]

The performance... will be the sensation of the Hungarian theater season. Theatergoers of New York City and its surrounding area await this Sunday night's performance ... with unparalleled interest. There are many reasons for such excitement. The play itself is a masterpiece. It is as if the author of the play wrote the part [of Marc-Arrán] for Béla Lugosi.[12]

Forradalmi nász opened on January 30, 1925 in Northampton, Connecticut, and then moved on to Bridgeport, Passaic, Lyons Farms, Philadelphia, Trenton, New Brunswick, Newark, and Perth Amboy. Most reviews were positive:

The Sunday performance [in Passaic] had an unprecedented interest from all directions. The center of attention is Béla Lugosi. Lugosi earned such success on the English-speaking stage and in the realm of cinema, which has been unprecedented by Hungarian actors. His majestic figure, his superb voice, his acting skills and his talent

Top Left: Published in *Amerikai Magyar Népszava* on January 24, 1925. Top Right: Portrait of Lugosi from the mid-to-late 1920s. Above Left: Published in *Új Előre* on February 4, 1925. Above Right: Published in the *Freeport Daily News* (Freeport, New York) on April 14, 1926.

make his place among the best ... he plays the role [of Marc-Arrán] with great empathy and with even greater success. Possibly we have never seen Lugosi in a more suitable role. In cities [where *Forradalmi nász* is staged] all the scenes he plays in are honored with great applause by the audience, and after the last act is over, he is being called on stage ten or even fifteen times.[13]

The tour culminated at New York's Cort Theater on February 8. Two different critics acclaimed Lugosi's performance:

Top: Published in *Amerikai Magyar Népszava* on September 25, 1926. Above: Published in *Amerikai Magyar Népszava* on October 2, 1926.

Unfortunately, Lugosi rarely appears before the Hungarian audience, but that makes each of his performances a real event. It is perhaps one of the great problems of Hungarian theater in America that we can scarcely see our most talented and most significant actors, the stars are missing, the most popular artists do not have a word; they are leaving, which might be beneficial for them, but it is harmful to the audience and to the theater culture. The audience is familiar with Lugosi's great qualities, and it is certain that if he were to play more often, he could attract those theatergoers of the Hungarian theater who would otherwise not attend.[14] – *A Hét*

The leading role was played by Béla Lugosi in an excellent way, with great dramatic power, and faithfully to the role's character. Of course, Lugosi was outstanding; he dominated the stage even in the scenes when he was not speaking at all, and when he spoke, his voice was strong and warm at the same time. The audience celebrated Lugosi with enthusiasm, and they would certainly appreciate it if Lugosi escaped from American movies more often and came to play on the Hungarian stage....[15] – *Amerikai Magyar Népszava*

One of the reviewers reported, "the troupe will set off on [another] tour soon," but that was not to be.[16] There were no more plays, and no more performances. A third reviewer might have reported a possible reason. Although he praised Lugosi's "high quality [and] mature acting," the critic condemned the rest of the company giving a "low-level performance."[17]

For Lugosi, the *Forradalmi nász* tour probably provided much-needed funds. And the final performance did not mark the end of his brief return to the Fészek (Nest). In May of 1925, for example, he performed at *Ady-est*, a poetry reading held in honor of Hungarian poet Endre Ady, who had died in 1919.[18] Presumably Lugosi read at least one poem during the celebration.[19] Then, in December of 1925, Lugosi co-directed *Az Arábiai éjszaka cabaret* (*The Arabian Night Cabaret*). The event, presented for one-night only at New York's Yorkville Casino, featured guest artists wearing Arabian-style costumes, presumably influenced by Lugosi's performance in the Broadway play *Arabesque* (1925).[20]

Lugosi made no more formal Hungarian-American public performances or appearances until April 14, 1926, when he gave a radio interview on WGBS in New York City.[21] On the same short program were Hungarian portrait artist Arthur Halmi and Hungarian soprano Evelyn Novak.[22] More than anything else, the show is notable for being Lugosi's first documented work on the radio.

Appearing at a celebration for Hungarian singer/actress Ilona Thury in October 1926 became a signal of an era that was coming to a close.[23] Eight months later, on June 18, 1927, Lugosi was an honored guest at the "Hungarian Bohemians Sensational Summer Costume Ball," held at New York's Ritz-Carlton Hotel. The attendees included Vilma Bánky, Lajos Bíró, Mihály Kertész (Michael Curtiz), Sándor (Alexander) Korda and Mihály Várkonyi (Victor Varconi).[24] What costume Lugosi wore that night is unknown, but on other nights he took to wearing another guise, that of an actor in English-language plays.

Lugosi would never again act in a Hungarian-language play in New York or anywhere else on the East Coast. To return to the Fészek was not possible. He had to leave, in the lonely pursuit of an English-speaking career. As Endre Ady wrote in his poem *Az eltévedt lovas*:

> The errant rider from long ago
> Follows the path along the recent swale;
> There is no light, there are no burning lamps,
> There are no villages along the trail.

Endnotes

1. "What Has Happened to Justice?" *New York Daily News* 20 Feb. 1927; "Missing Man Slain, Body Dismembered and Sealed in Vat." *New York Times* 23 Aug. 1924. Some press accounts referred to the metal vat as a "box" or "trunk."

2. "Seek Graff Murder Clue in Baltimore." *New York Times* 25 Aug. 1924; "Find Love Letters in Graff Murder." *New York Times* 26 Aug. 1924; "Another Woman Enters Graff Case." *New York Times* 28 Aug. 1924; "New Vat Discussed in Graff Mystery." *New York Times* 29 Aug. 1924.

3. "Vat Murder Bares Another Mystery." *New York Times* 24 Aug. 1924.

4. "What Has Happened to Justice?"

5. "Tömeggyilkossággal gyanusitja a rendőrség Graff gyilkosát." *Amerikai Magyar Népszava* (New York) 26 Aug. 1924; "Lugossy Veszekedő Ember Volt – Mondja Megkerült Üzlettársa." *Amerikai Magyar Népszava* 28 Aug. 1924; "Lugossy János hir szerint New Yorkban tartózkodik." *Amerikai Magyar Népszava* 28 Aug. 1924.

6. "Új színtársulat." *Új Előre* (New York) 18 Jan. 1925.

7. "Színház–Művészét–Mozi." *Amerikai Magyar Népszava* 31 Jan. 1925.

8. "*Forradalmi nász*." *Magyar Hirnök* (New Brunswick, NJ) 29 Jan. 1925

9. The article "Chadwick 'Heavy' Returns to Stage" (*Exhibitors Trade Review* 21 Feb. 1925) discusses Lugosi's work in *The Midnight Girl* and in *Forradalmi nász*, which it refers to as *Hymen in Revolt*.

10. Hegedűs, Gyula. "*Forradalmi nász*." *Nyugat* (Budapest, Hungary) 1909 / 1. Sz.

11. "*Forradalmi nász*." *Magyar Hirnök* 29 Jan. 1925.

12. "Színház–Művészét–Mozi." *Amerikai Magyar Népszava* 7 Feb. 1925.

13. "Színház–Zene–Művészét–Mozi." *Amerikai Magyar Népszava* 5 Feb. 1925.

14. Quoted in Enyedi, Sándor. *A Tragédia amerikai színpadi pályafutásához* (Budapest: Színháztudományi Szemle 12, 1983).

15. "Színház–Művészét–Mozi–*Forradalmi nász*." *Amerikai Magyar Népszava* 10 Feb. 1925.

16. Ibid.

17. "*Forradalmi Nász*." *Új Előre* 11 Feb. 1925

18 *A Hét* 16 May 1925.

19 Enyedi, Sándor. *A Tragédia amerikai színpadi pályafutásához* (Budapest: Színháztudomanyie Szemle 12, 1983).

20 "Az Arábiai éjszaka December Hó 12-Én." *Új Előre* 6 Dec. 1925

21 "On the Air." *Nassau Daily Review* (Long Island, NY) 14 Apr. 1926.

22 "Tomorrow on The Air." *Trenton Evening Times* (Trenton, NJ) 13 Apr. 1926.

23 Advertisement. *Amerikai Magyar Népszava* 25 Sept. 1926; Advertisement. *Amerikai Magyar Népszava* 26 Sept. 1926; Advertisement. *Amerikai Magyar Népszava* 2 Oct. 1926.

24 "A nyári szezon szenzációja lesz a június 18-iki bohémbál." *Amerikai Magyar Népszava* 9 June 1927.

Publicity portrait of Lugosi for *The Devil in the Cheese*.

BECOMING DRACULA

Chapter 33

Parmesan

> "There has always been a feeling that one must be wary of cheese, particularly at night, in the interest of sleep. It is not a matter of conviction with us but of vague caution."
> – *The Devil in the Cheese* playbill

Tom Cushing's play *The Devil in the Cheese* has a wonderfully evocative title, with its story somewhat reminiscent of Edwin S. Porter's film *Dream of a Rarebit Fiend* (1906). In the play, Father Petros (Lugosi) convinces Quigley (Robert McWade), an archeologist, to undertake a dig near an old Greek monastery. Quigley brings his daughter Goldina (Linda Watkins) to keep her away from a suitor named Jimmie Chard (Fredric March).

After discovering and eating an ancient, "mummified" piece of Parmesan cheese, Quigley has a crazy dream in which he literally goes inside his daughter's head. An Egyptian deity gives him a personally guided tour of Goldina's thoughts, her imagination. "Damned spookiest thing I've ever done," Quigley says. Along with witnessing fanciful scenes of gorillas and cannibalism on a shipwrecked island, Quigley comes to understand how much Jimmie means to his daughter.

When Quigley's nightmare ends, another begins. Father Petros is actually leader of a gang of bandits, threatening everyone's lives unless they pay him a ransom. As one character has already observed, "this is just the spot for a murder!"

After arriving by airplane, Jimmie rescues the group, thus becoming a hero. The fanciful comedy-drama reaches a happy ending, as opposed to the bittersweet finale of Cushing's earlier play *Laugh, Clown, Laugh* (1923), which was adapted into a Lon Chaney film of the same name in 1928.[1]

The Devil in the Cheese debuted for one week at the Pasadena Playhouse in California in November 1925, at which time Bram Nossen played Father Petros.[2] After that, Cushing expended much time and effort to open the show on Broadway.

As of April 1926, longtime theatrical producer Charles Hopkins announced plans to open a theater bearing his name, one that would eventually become home to a permanent company.[3] The small, 300-seat venue had earlier been known as The Punch and Judy. The inaugural play was to be *The Devil in the Cheese*, slated to open on September 6 of that same year. Its title immediately went up in lights on the theater exterior, advertising it four months in advance.[4]

But September 6 came and there was no opening. What caused the delay is unknown. As of October, the Hopkins briefly provided a home to a different play, *Tragic 18*.[5]

Changes in the cast and behind-the-scenes personnel probably caused the holdup.[6] After all, it wasn't until the autumn, possibly as late as November, that famed scenic designer Norman Bel Geddes, creator of *Arabesque* (1925), became attached to the show.[7]

When Lugosi – who was living at 48 West 49th Street at the time – joined *The Devil in the Cheese* is unknown. He and some of his costars like Dwight Frye (who played Quigley's friend) could have been cast as early as the summer. Rehearsals for *The Devil in the Cheese* began in September, but were suspended until early November.[8] After a cumulative total of four weeks, Hopkins paid actors full salaries to rehearse until opening night.[9]

Delays continued, with the excuse in late November being that Charles Hopkins would not open the show until he was:

Top: Playbill for the Pasadena run of the play. *(Courtesy of the Billy Rose Theater Division of the New York Public Library).* **Above: Scene from *The Devil in the Cheese*.** *(Courtesy of the Billy Rose Theater Division of the New York Public Library)*

fully satisfied that the piece is ready for presentation. Until this point is reached, and everything to the slightest detail is in accordance with the producer's wishes, no opening date will be considered."[10]

At roughly the same time, the Helene Pons Studios were painting costumes based upon Geddes' colorful designs.[11]

When *The Devil in the Cheese* finally opened on December 29, 1926, critical reaction was largely unenthusiastic:

> After weeks of titillating expectancy, Mr. Hopkins finally introduced the Cushing opus, naively labeled as a comedy, although more aptly denoted as a 'melodramatic fantasy.'[12] – *Variety*

> [T]he play could be described as a successful psychoanalytical farce. – *The Morning Telegraph*[13]

> Mr. Cushing's exercise in craniology is often diverting in an extravaganza way, a sweet endeavor to emphasize the golden dreams. It is what may be called a 'clever' play, being more 'novel' than is the custom of the drama. – *New York Herald-Tribune*[14]

> *The Devil in the Cheese*, which has been ripening for so many months in Charles Hopkins's Theater, proved last night to be a good-natured piece of foolery, and managed to be genial and fairly amusing in spite of its young cumbersomeness.[15] – *New York Sun*

Top: Scene from *The Devil in the Cheese*. *(Courtesy of the Billy Rose Theater Division of the New York Public Library).* **Above: Artwork of Dwight Frye, published in the *New York Times* on February 27, 1927.**

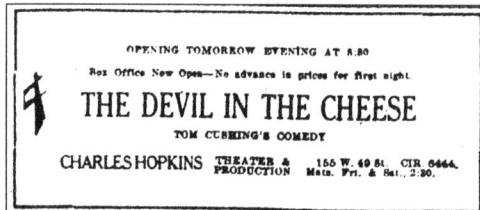

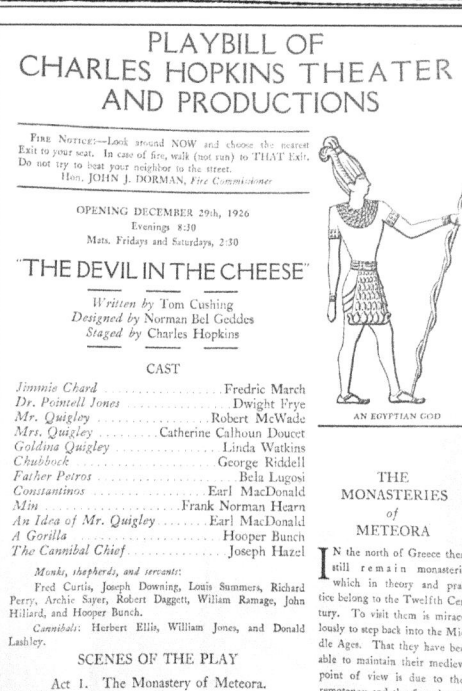

Top: Published in the *New York Evening Journal* on December 28, 1926. Above: *(Courtesy of the Billy Rose Theater Division of the New York Public Library)*

[I]t is a distracting, diverting nightmare which somehow holds you and makes you laugh and sends you away at the finish more and more convinced that wonders, even in the theater, seem never to cease.[16] – *New York Evening Journal*

I stepped into the Charles Hopkins' Theater the other evening for a rather belated view of *The Devil in the Cheese*, and found it to be a harmless, amusing little comedy with an atmosphere of the amateurish about it. One is introduced to the inside of a young girl's head.[17] – *The Rye Chronicle*

Of the new productions, *The Devil in the Cheese* by Tom Cushing, is most amusing and imaginative ... it is sheer fantasy and whimsy. Two of its acts are written a bit too heavily....[18] – *The Western Weekly*

[I]t is an innocuous little comedy, slightly offensive because of a vein of inept whimsicality.[19] – *New Yorker*

It is the sort of comedy that should go well with the boys and girls home for the holidays, but it is not likely to do much [for] their chaperones.[20] – *New York Daily News*

Realism and phantasy have gone into the brewing of the play, producing a mixture well-meaning if amateurish. The second act takes place inside a girl's head and hasn't much to offer. Her thoughts are simple and pretty. She thinks of cooking cannibals, shipwrecks, babies and her boy friend while her father looks on at her thoughts. [The play] shows a pleasant immaturity, is amiably literal, uninspired altogether.[21] – *Brooklyn Eagle*

Humdrum prefaces and postludes to these middle scenes take too much of the action and deaden what seems, otherwise, a charming fantasy.[22] – *New York Evening Post*

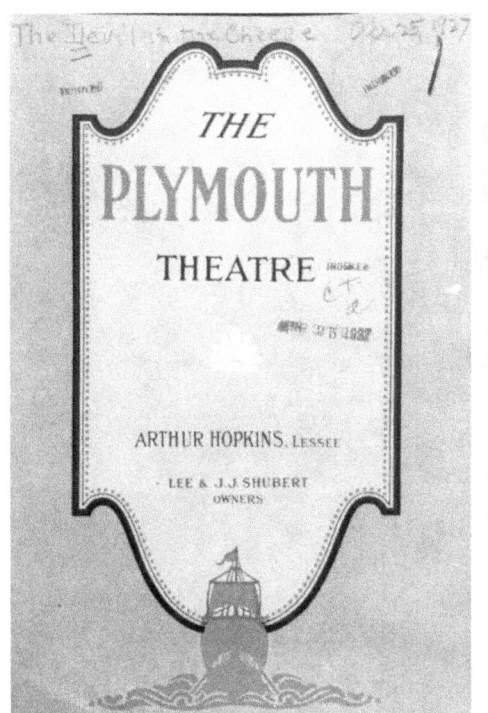
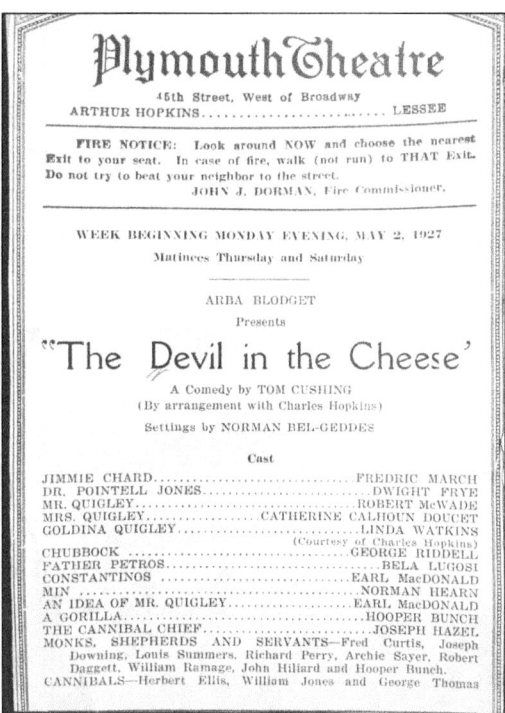

Above: *(Courtesy of the Billy Rose Theater Division of the New York Public Library)*

Unfortunately, the result does not justify the rumored necessary preparation, many changes to find the right cast and the drawn-out schooling for desired effect. ... *The Devil in the Cheese* is by no means a total loss unless it be financially so, for it is mildly amusing.[23] – *Billboard*

It is, I suspect, a somewhat fresher and more spirited comedy than it seemed in its badly paced first performance. But then I also suspect that in retrospect it boils down to considerably less of a play than Mr. Cushing thought he was writing.[24] – *New York World*

I am constrained to assert that judged as a premeditated satire *The Devil in the Cheese* misses every chance of being successful, and by no inconsiderable margins. ... As entertainment, *The Devil in the Cheese* is probably superior to anything now running on Broadway, with the exception of *The Pirates*; which is damning with faint praise but telling the truth. But all these added together do not make a satire or even a witty comedy.[25] – *Columbia Spectator*

In spite of an alluring title and one beautiful setting by Norman Bel Geddes, this fantasy ... seems inept and awkward. [Geddes'] designs and one or two good bits of acting remove *The Devil in the Cheese* from pure amateurishness.[26] – *New York Times*

Gary D. Rhodes | Bill Kaffenberger

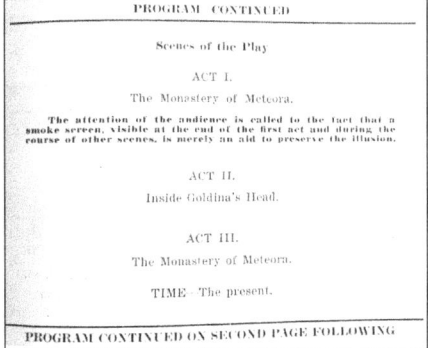

Above Top: From the playbill during the play's run at the Plymouth. Above: Scene from *The Devil in the Cheese*. Right: Scene from *The Devil in the Cheese*. *(Courtesy of the Billy Rose Theater Division of the New York Public Library)*

I have decided the less said about cheese the better.[27] – *New York American*

Perhaps the greatest praise came not from a newspaper critic, but from William Lyon Phelps, a professor of English Literature at Yale University. He recommended *The Devil in the Cheese* as "brilliant, witty, diverting – two hours of unalloyed delight."[28]

Similarly, when asked if there were any comedy plays worth seeing, the Reverend Doctor S. Parkes Cadman wrote an endorsement in the *Brooklyn Eagle*: "Yes, there is one that is simply bubbling over with true humor, and what is more, it is clean. It is *The Devil in the Cheese*. It is a beautiful situation, very cleverly worked out. I am happy to commend it, because one of the great needs of our unrelaxing [sic] life is to know when to laugh."[29]

For Lugosi, Father Petros offered a dual role, the monk being a disguise for a bandit actually named Kardos. He appears onstage at length in Acts One and Three, with some of his dialogue being particularly funny, and some of it being menacing. When asked if the rooms leak, Petros responds, "Why not? Old Monastery. 1210." He has moments of anger, as when he declares, "I would cut the throats of every one of the [Persians] – from ear to ear." And once he reveals his true self, he declares, "Here I am the big man! I do what I want! These hills never speak afterwards!"

As had been the case with *Arabesque* and *Open House*, Lugosi received better notices than the play:

Scenes from *The Devil in the Cheese*. *(Courtesy of the Billy Rose Theater Division of the New York Public Library).*

Now Lugosi is once again in front of the American public, and his performance is his greatest artistic portrayal.[30] – *Az Ember*

Bela Lugosi impersonates a Greek brigand, masked under the habit of a monk, better than I have ever seen a character of the mind portrayed. – *New York Herald-Tribune*[31]

Bela Lugosi is imposing….[32] – *Billboard*

As the bandit, Mr. Lugosi acts with an authority and cadence worthy of better things.[33] – *New York Times*

[The play] might have been more happily borne if, with the exception of the deft Dwight Frye and the swaggering Bela Lugosi, the play had been more appropriately cast….[34] – *New York Telegraph*

Bela Lugosi is neatly impressive as the chief robber.[35] – *New York Daily News*

Bela Lugosi was that *rara avis*, a convincing bandit chief.[36] – *The Morning Telegraph*

Miss Lugosi suggests a miniature Phyllis Povah, and that means to you whatever it means to you.[37] – *New York World*

One of the principal characters is acted by one Bela Lugosi, a handsome Hungarian actor. He looks quite picturesque in the black garb of a Greek monk, and later in the colorful attire of a bandit chief. But if I can believe my eyesight, Lugosi does not look like a woman in the play at all, despite the fact that he wears a skirt as the bandit. ... His name is 'Father Petros' and he has a long black beard that even Shaw may envy. Consider then, my surprise when the next day I saw in the review of the *New York World* that 'Miss Lugosi looks like a miniature Phyllis Povah.'[38] – *Brooklyn Daily Eagle*

In an apparent accident, the *New York World* compared Lugosi to this actress, Phyllis Povah.

How famed critic Alexander Woollcott, of the *New York World*, managed to refer to Lugosi as "Miss" is something of a mystery, especially after having previously reviewed Lugosi in *Arabesque*.

As for *The Devil in the Cheese*'s box-office potential, *Variety* published the following on January 5, 1927:

> Commercially, this one is hard to figure. On form, it shouldn't last, but when one considers that Hopkins pools his house and attraction, it makes it easier. It even makes possible the rather heavy overhead in the intimate Hopkins playhouse. For that reason it is very likely Hopkins will prolong *The Devil in the Cheese* for a run.[39]

The prediction proved correct. On January 19, *Variety* reported *The Devil in the Cheese* was generating only a "little" business.[40] But then it unexpectedly sold out for much, if not all, of February.[41] And so the company began giving three matinees weekly instead of two.[42]

Variety attributed the newfound success to "extra advertising." *Billboard* particularly noted the use of radio promotions.[43] According to the *Evening Post*, there was also an additional reason: "management accredits this record to the recent publicity attached to the drive against 'objectionable' plays, inferring that it indicates a desire on the part of the people to see good and clean comedy."[44]

By the beginning of March, rumor had it that *The Devil in the Cheese* was doing so well that it might move to a larger theater.[45] According to the *New York Sun*, "one of the members of the cast, Dwight Frye, has had his faith in his profession restored. [The play] is giving him the longest run of his career."[46] All seemed to be going very well.

Scene from *The Devil in the Cheese*. *(Courtesy of John Antosiewicz)*

On April 25, the move finally happened, from the Hopkins to the Plymouth Theater.[47] The first week's gross was a "moderate" $8,000.[48] On May 6, the cast (presumably with Lugosi) performed excerpts of the play on the radio show *Stardom of Broadway*, broadcast over WEAF.[49]

But then the show unexpectedly went dark on May 14 after 157 New York performances. Decent grosses seemed at odds with the decision to close "suddenly."[50] The problem was allegedly cast members quitting, though there's no evidence that Lugosi was one of them.[51]

In the end, *The Devil in the Cheese* had proven to be an "intermediate success."[52] It bested the runs of *Open House*, *Arabesque*, and *The Red Poppy*, making Lugosi's fourth English-language play (and third on Broadway) the most popular and prosperous of the group.

It had also allowed him to work with Dwight Frye, who would go on to play Renfield in Tod Browning's *Dracula* (1931), with Linda Watkins, who would later appear in such films as *From Hell It Came* (1957), and with Fredric March, who became famous thanks to so many films, among them *Dr. Jekyll and Mr. Hyde* (1931).

March later recalled, "One show I did in New York was called *The Devil in the Cheese*, and in it were Linda Watkins, Bela Lugosi and Dwight Frye. – In fact, Hollywood is Old Home Week for theater productions."[53]

Like its ancient Parmesan, *The Devil in the Cheese* became mummified. Trapped in time, but its fantasies not completely forgotten. As one of its characters declares, "when you're a cheese addict, you see devils.

Endnotes

1   "Tom Cushing." *Variety* 12 Mar. 1941.

2   "New Stage Play to Run Week at Pasadena House." *Los Angeles Times* 15 Nov. 1925; *The Devil in the Cheese* playbill, 1925. A copy of the playbill exists in the Pasadena Playhouse Archives.

3   "Charles Hopkins Plans to Produce Four Plays." *Billboard* 1 May 1926; "Hopkins' Ultra Stock." *Variety* 26 May 1926.

4   "Hopkins Play in Lights Four Months in Advance." *Billboard* 15 May 1926; "What News on the Rialto?" *New York Times* 16 May 1926.

5   "*Tragic 18*." *Variety* 13 Oct. 1926.

6   "*Devil in the Cheese* Ready to Open at Last." *Billboard* 1 Jan. 1927.

7   "Scenic Artists." *Billboard* 13 Nov. 1926.

8   "Theater News." *New York Sun* 4 Nov. 1926.

9   "Scenic Artists."

10 "*Devil in the Cheese* Delayed." *Billboard* 4 Dec. 1926.

11 "Costumers." *Billboard* 4 Dec. 1927.

12 Abel. "*The Devil in the Cheese*." *Variety* 5 Jan. 1927.

13 Zatkin, Nathan. "Hopkins Scores with New Comedy." *The Morning Telegraph* (New York) 31 Dec. 1926.

14 "*The Devil in the Cheese*." *New York Herald-Tribune* 30 Dec. 1926.

15 Gabriel, Gilbert W. "Beggar on Elephant-Back." *New York Sun* 30 Dec. 1926.

16 Garrick. "The New Play." *New York Evening Journal* 30 Dec. 1926.

17 Choate, Edward A. Jr. "Notes on the Theater." *Rye Chronicle* (Rye, NY) 12 Feb. 1927.

18 "Tough On Methuselah." *Abilene Reporter-News* (Abilene, TX) 20 Jan. 1927.

19 Brackett, Charles. "The Theater." *New Yorker* 15 Jan. 1927.

20 Mantle, Burns. "*Devil in the Cheese* Fantastic; *The Padre* with Leo Carillo." *New York Daily News* 31 Dec. 1926.

21 Pollock, Arthur. "Plays and Things." *Brooklyn Eagle* 20 Dec. 1926.

22 Anderson, John. "The Play." *New York Evening Post* 30 Dec. 1926.

23 "The New Plays On Broadway." *Billboard* 8 Jan. 1927.

24 Woollcott, Alexander. "The Stage." *New York World* 30 Dec. 1926.

25 "The Suburbs of Columbia." *Columbia Spectator* (New York) 14 Mar. 1927.

26 Atkinson, J. Brooks. "The Play." *New York Times* 30 Dec. 1926.

27 Dale, Alan. "Alan Dale Appraises *The Devil in the Cheese*." *New York American* 30 Dec. 1926.

28 "Phelps Discusses Drama." *New York Times* 16 Jan. 1927.

29 Cadman, The Rev. Dr. S. Parkes. "The Immigrant Queen." *Brooklyn Eagle* 31 Jan. 1927.

30 "New Yorki Színházi Élet." *Az Ember* 17 Jan. 1927.

31 "*The Devil in the Cheese*."

32 "The New Plays On Broadway."

33 Atkinson, "The Play."

34 Vreeland, Frank. "Rarebit Drama." *New York Telegraph* 30 Dec.1926

35 Mantle, "*Devil in the Cheese* Fantastic."

36 Zatkin, "Hopkins Scores with New Comedy."

37 Woollcott, "The Stage."

38 Halasz, George. "The Curtain Rises." *Brooklyn Eagle* 9 Jan. 1927.

39 Abel, "*The Devil in the Cheese*."

40 "Shows in N.Y. and Comment." *Variety* 19 Jan. 1927.

41 Morehouse, Ward. "Broadway After Dark." *New York Sun* 28 Feb. 1927.

42 On 5 Mar. 1927, the *Brooklyn Eagle* reported that the Hopkins would celebrate Lent by presenting four matinees for the week. This approach was so successful that – except for Easter Week – the policy of four weekly matinees continued into the middle of April 1927 and perhaps beyond.

43 "Wagner Withdraws Closing When Cadman Indorses [sic] Play." *Billboard* 26 Mar. 1927.

44 Bernhard, Arnold. "Forecasts and Postscripts." *New York Evening Post* 26 Feb. 1927.

45 "Shows in N.Y. and Comment." *Variety* 2 Mar. 1927.

46 Morehouse, Ward. "Broadway After Dark – Pleasant Evenings for the Playhouse That Was Once the Punch and Judy." *New York Sun* 22 Feb. 1927.

47 "Hopkins Abandons Play." *New York Times* 15 Apr. 1927.

48 "Shows in N.Y. and Comment." *Variety* 4 May 1927.

49 "Today on the Radio." *New York Times* 6 May 1927.

50 "8 Shows Out." *Variety* 18 May 1927.

51 "Shows in N.Y. and Comment." *Variety* 18 May 1927.

52 "Successes of the Season." *Variety* 1 June 1927.

53 "The Real Life Story of Fredric March." *Screenland* July 1932.

Lugosi in 1927. *(Courtesy of Dennis Phelps)*

Chapter 34

The Magic Lantern

> "All was dark and silent, the black shadows
> thrown by the moonlight seeming full
> of a silent mystery of their own."
> –Bram Stoker, *Dracula*

During the mid-twenties, Lugosi sought work beyond the New York stage, possibly even beyond acting. In 1928, an advertisement for Listerine appeared in the pages of *Photoplay* magazine.[1] Its photo shows a small group of people, and one of them is clearly Lugosi. Had he worked as a model? And if so, are there other long-forgotten ads featuring his face, buried in the musty pages of magazines and newspapers of the Roaring Twenties? Perhaps his face appeared on one or more advertising billposters, flyers, or brochures, all now consigned to the dust and ashes of an era long dead. Perhaps. Photographs and films capture light, but someone has to capture *them*, to save them, to preserve them.

Lugosi's key pursuit outside of the theater was definitely the cinema. In 1926, Famous Lovers Productions hired him to appear in a short film entitled *Punchinello*. In June of that year, the company announced plans to shoot a "series of at least 24 shorts dealing with famous love stories in mythology and history."[2] Duncan Renaldo, a Romanian actor gaining fame in America, would star in all of them.[3] First on the schedule was *Sappho*, to be shot at Tec-Art in New York with help from T. Carlyle Atkins, a producer at the St. Regis Pictures Corporation.[4]

There is no indication that *Sappho* was completed, or that Famous Lovers produced the series. But it is certain that the company finished *Punchinello*, with Renaldo directing as well as starring as the title character, the Italian clown grieving for his lost love Pierrotte (portrayed by Billie Rainsford) while having to listen to his rival's serenade.[5] Lugosi played Pierrot, a harlequin. The reason for making *Punchinello* instead of *Sappho* could well have been the fact that stage versions of *Punchinello* were being produced in 1926, a testament to its recent popularity, and possibly even a route towards obtaining inexpensive costume and prop rentals. For example, the New York Strand presented the story onstage in October 1926 with Edward Albano.[6]

Though Famous Lovers did shoot *Punchinello* at some point during the second half of 1926, there is absolutely no record of it being released that year, or in 1927 or in 1928. *Punchinello* simply disappeared until the autumn of 1929. In September of that year, while Renaldo was in Africa filming scenes for *Trader Horn* (released in 1931), the New York-based company Great Arts Pictures prepared

Above: Published in *Photoplay* in January 1928.

This picture: Lugosi in *Punchinello* (aka *The Mask*), produced in 1926, but not released until 1929. *(Courtesy of John Antosiewicz)*

Duncan Renaldo and Lugosi in *Punchinello* (aka *The Mask*). *(Courtesy of John Antosiewicz)*

Punchinello for release under the title *The Mask*.[7] After edits (or re-edits, possibly) made by Charles Glett, the company printed the one-reel film on Kodak's pre-tinted Sonochrome film stock.[8] The Recording Laboratory of America helped synchronize sound effects, as well as music composed by J. M. Coopersmith. The soundtrack also featured descriptive voiceover.[9]

The old silent became a new talkie, one that Great Arts dubbed a "romantic fantasy."[10] After its release on November 1, 1929, *Film Daily* told readers:

> This is essentially a number for grade audiences, in that it tells a well handled story of Punchinello and Harlequin in love with the same girl. It is done in descriptive dialogue, with rhythmic verse. Duncan Renaldo is the clown who finally wins the girl after he has removed his mask. Bela Lugosi is the Harlequin, and Billie Rainesford [sic] the girl. Very beautifully staged, and with the Sonochrome print that gives delicate tints, it makes a pleasing subject that will go down well with audiences.[11]

Motion Picture Today added, "As a class short, this one rates with the best."[12] And *Motion Picture News* suggested that *The Mask* "should make a pleasant addition to the program" due to its "nice treatment."[13]

Shot in 1926; not seen until 1929. That is one type of outcome, the delayed illumination of a film that finally found its audience. But what of projects that went unmade, or footage that never reached the hands of an editor, let alone a projectionist?

In August of 1927, *Film Daily* described a new movie starring Swedish actress Sigrid Holmquist:

The Silent Witness is in production with Gerald Porter directing. The cast includes Sigrid Holmquist, Arnold Lytton, Bela Lugosi and Josef Swickard. Marcel Le Picard is in charge of photography. The company is now on location, but will use Cosmopolitan for interiors.[14]

"Now on location": such a phrase implies filming had begun, and with Lugosi in the cast.[15]

An article published nearly two weeks earlier referred to *The Silent Witness* as a "dog picture," of the Rin Tin Tin variety, apparently.[16] It also claimed shooting would take place "in the East for Jaklyn Prods."[17] By September of 1927, if not late August, Lugosi would be involved in rehearsals for *Dracula-The Vampire Play*. But presumably he would have been available in terms of schedule and geography for a film shot "in the East," especially in a supporting role that might have taken days, rather than weeks, to complete.

But *The Silent Witness* vanished. Sigrid Holmquist had no film releases during the second half of 1927 or at all in 1928 and 1929, under this title or any other. In fact, her final film, a short subject from Tiffany called *Clothes Make the Woman*, was released in February of 1927.[18] Even more curious is that *Film Daily* of September 4, 1927, claimed that actor Josef Swickard had just finished work on a movie called *In the Silent Witness*.[19] Given his earlier announced casting in *The Silent Witness*, the reference is likely to the same film.

Film captured light, it seems, producing images of an unfinished or an unsold movie, a project never to be projected. Was Lugosi somewhere among those images, in what might have been his final role before Dracula? That is very possible, but the answer is unknown. What is certain is that cinematographer Marcel Le Picard later shot the Lugosi films *Invisible Ghost (1941)*, *Spooks Run Wild* (1941), *Voodoo Man* (1944), *Return of the Ape Man* (1944), and *Scared to Death* (1947).

As for Lugosi in the 1920s, the next curious case is *How to Handle Women* (1928), a film that was not just distributed, but also distributed *twice*, with Lugosi's involvement very much nebulous. On September 29, 1927, *Variety* told readers that Universal Pictures was preparing *The Prince of Peanuts*, a new screen story for its popular young actor Glenn Tryon.[20]

Top: Published in *Motion Picture News* on November 9, 1929. Above: Published in *Film Daily* on November 20, 1929.

Above Left: Published in the *New York Daily News* on June 16, 1928. Above Right: Published in the *Kenosha Evening News* (Kenosha, WI) on September 20, 1928.

Elsewhere in the same issue, the publication referred to the project as *Meet the Prince*.[21] Director William J. Craft was shooting the project under the latter title during October 1927.[22] The studio then considered other titles like *Three Days*, probably because *Meet the Prince* had already been the title of a 1926 movie with Joseph Schildkraut. According to the *Hollywood Vagabond*, the Universal film was in the "cutting" stage by November 3, 1927.[23] Studio boss Carl Laemmle, Sr., promised it would be one of the studio's "outstanding" releases in 1928.[24]

Enter Bela Lugosi, or perhaps not. Lugosi allegedly appeared in the film as a bodyguard. But while it was being shot, he was starring in *Dracula–The Vampire Play* on Broadway (as Chapter 36 will cover). Granted, with the general exception of Wednesday and Saturday matinees, he would have had mornings and some afternoons free. He could also have missed a performance, with an understudy taking his place, though that would have seemingly been unwise given that the play just opened on October 5, 1927.

It is interesting to consider an interview that Lugosi historian Michael J. David conducted with actor Harold Pavey. As a young man, Pavey met Lugosi in New York sometime in the mid-1920s. The two would see each other while working for Universal Pictures. "He used to take my hand and say, 'Harold, would you like to come to the commissary and have a sandwich with me?'" Lugosi would then ask Pavey about colloquial English.[25] Pavey thus acted as something of an informal tutor, with Lugosi signing a photograph to him that expressed his gratitude.

Pavey also told David that he left films about a year before talkies became common, which would likely put this New York anecdote somewhere between 1926 and 1928. As a result of the timing and Pavey's mention of Universal, the only known project that makes sense would be *How to Handle Women*.

How to Handle Women under one of its other titles.

But *Universal Weekly* claimed the movie was being produced at "Universal City," meaning in California.[26] Other trades implied that shooting occurred on the West Coast.[27] That said, it is not impossible that a few scenes could have been filmed in New York, even if the bulk of the shooting occurred in California. After all, the plot of *How to Handle Women* finds Tryon's character working in New York; a foreign prince visits the same city in an effort to borrow money.[28] To shoot a small number of scenes or shots at notable New York locations might have been desirable. Here at least would be a potential explanation not just for Pavey's anecdote, but also for Lugosi's appearance in the film. Otherwise, in terms of his schedule and geography, Lugosi could not have been at Universal City in California.

Unfortunately, no studio files for *How to Handle Women* exist in the Universal archive at the University of Southern California. And the brief, three-minute fragment that survives at the Library of Congress is of no help in solving the mystery. Lugosi does not appear in that footage, but that means nothing in terms of the bulk of the film, which is lost.

Rather than simply being released in 1928, the film went through various evolutions.

Universal previewed it as *The Prince of Peanuts* in January; *Exhibitors Herald and Moving Picture World* reviewed it and gave its running time as seven reels.[29] The *Film Spectator* reviewed it under that same title in March.[30] But Universal copyrighted it as *Fresh Every Hour* on May 14, with *Photoplay* and *Motion Picture News* referring to it by that name.[31] The *New York Times* soon explained: "At the last moment a magazine story turned up [with] that title, and although the company had a right to use it, it would, as the author pointed out, prevent his being able to sell his story for pictures."[32]

In June 1928, Universal officially changed the title to *How to Handle Women*, even copyrighting it again.[33] Some reviews had been poor, which might have been enough to convince the studio to make changes, particularly given their big plans for Glenn Tryon. *Film Daily* derided the movie on June 8, 1928.[34] *Variety* published a poor review on June 20, and claimed its running time was only 60 minutes.[35] That same month, *Harrison's Reports* believed it to be "pretty good," but strangely gave its running time as "65 to 80 min."[36]

How to Handle Women also had a new general distribution date of September 3, 1928.[37] When it received a good notice in *Weekly Film Review*, its running time was listed as only 5,591 feet, meaning approximately 60 minutes.[38] Perhaps the film had been shortened from seven reels. Major cuts could have necessitated shooting a small amount of new transitional footage in order to make the shortened plot understandable. And, even if the running time didn't change, given *Variety*'s contradictory mention of 60 minutes, perhaps some of the content did, to improve the film.

Either way, such changes might explain Lugosi's appearance, meaning that his footage wasn't even shot until the summer of 1928, by which time (as Chapter 37 will explain) Lugosi was in Los Angeles. Or those later changes could have resulted in the reverse, meaning that footage of him filmed in New York fell ungracefully onto the cutting room floor. It is clear that Universal believed the film had changed enough to necessitate a second copyright.

To add to the confusion, the studio pushed the official release date of *How to Handle Women* to October 14, 1928.[39] But an industry trade published exhibitor reports about the film on September 1, reports that specifically referred to it as *How to Handle Women* rather than by one of its earlier titles.[40] Universal had apparently sent one or more prints to some exchanges even before its "new" release date.

Lugosi did not keep a single clipping of *How to Handle Women* in his scrapbook.[41] Perhaps it was because no review mentioned his name. Perhaps it was because his scenes had been cut from the release prints. Or perhaps it was because he was never actually in the movie.

Some films do indeed have a "silent mystery of their own." Lugosi was definitely in *Punchinello*, though audiences didn't see it until it became *The Mask*. He *might* have appeared in footage for *The Silent Witness*, though no one saw it. Viewers definitely watched *How to Handle Women*, but whether or not he was in *any* released version of it is a much greater question than previous historians have realized. And so what can be said of these "dark and silent" mysteries?

Film prints are always either negative or positive. Film history is not.

Endnotes

1 Advertisement. *Photoplay* Jan. 1928.

2 "Plans Famous Lovers Series." *Film Daily* 9 June 1926.

3 Little is known of Famous Lovers Productions. It is possible that Renaldo was involved in the independent company to a greater degree than simply being an actor and director.

4 Harper, Ray W. "Among the Independents." *Movie Monthly* Sept. 1925.

5 The actress in *Punchinello* was named Billie Rainsford, not Ronda Rainsford as some sources claim.

6 "New York Strand." *Exhibitors Herald* 30 Oct. 1926.

7 "Short Shots from New York Studios." *Film Daily* 29 Sept. 1929.

8 "Great Arts Making 13, Three Starring Renaldo." *Film Daily* 25 Aug. 1929.

9 This information appears in a review of *The Mask* published in *Motion Pictures Today* in 1929. Lugosi kept the clipping in one of his personal scrapbooks.

10 Ibid. A copy of *The Mask* is held at the UCLA Film and Television Archive.

11 "Short Subjects." *Film Daily* 3 Nov. 1929.

12 This information appears in a review of *The Mask* published in *Motion Pictures Today* of 1929. Lugosi kept the clipping in one of his personal scrapbooks.

13 "*The Mask.*" *Motion Picture News* 9 Nov. 1929.

14 "Eastern Studios – Gerald Porter Directing." *Film Daily* 21 Aug. 1927.

15 Though it had nothing to do with the Holmquist film, the New York City-based Truart Film Corporation produced a 5,000-foot "novelty series" in 1926 called *The Silent Witness*. See "Truart Film Corporation – Novelty Series." *Moving Picture World* 10 July 1926.

16 "Porter to Direct Dog Picture." *Film Daily* 10 Aug. 1927.

17 Ibid.

18 "*Clothes Make the Woman.*" *Motion Picture News* 25 Feb. 1927.

19 "Eastern Studios." *Film Daily* 4 Sept. 1927.

20 "U's Coming Trio." *Variety* 28 Sept. 1927.

21 "Coast Notes." *Variety* 28 Sept. 1927.

22 "Eight Shooting at U." *Exhibitors Herald* 8 Oct. 1927; "Studio Time-Table." *Hollywood Vagabond* 20 Oct. 1927.

23 "Studio Time-Table." *Hollywood Vagabond* 3 Nov. 1927.

24 "Laemmle Speeds Plans for 1928-29 Season." *Exhibitors Herald* 29 Oct. 1927.

25 David, Michael J. Interview with Harold Pavey. May 1985.

26 "Universal Moviegrams." *Universal Weekly* 15 Oct. 1927.

27 In addition to the trades listed in above citations, see also: "Tryon's Series." *Variety* 21 Sept. 1927; "The Film Mart." *Exhibitors Herald* 15 Oct. 1927. Another article that discussed the production was actually called "In West Coast Studios Production Activities." It was published in *Moving Picture World* on 22 Oct. 1927.

28 "How to Handle Women." *Harrison's Reports* 23 June 1928.

29 "The Studio Preview." *Exhibitors Herald and Moving Picture World* 28 Jan. 1928.

30 Beaton, Donald. "As They Appeal to a Youth." *Film Spectator* 3 Mar. 1928.

31 See, for example, "Laemmle Announces 'U' Lineup." *Motion Picture News* 5 May 1928.

32 "Naming a Film to Win." *New York Times* 17 June 1928.

33 "Title Changes." *Motion Picture News* 30 June 1928.

34 "How to Handle Women." *Film Daily* 8 June 1928.

35 "How to Handle Women." *Variety* 20 June 1928.

36 "How to Handle Women." *Harrison's Reports* 23 June 1928.

37 Ibid.

38 "Capitol Theater." *Weekly Film Review* 1 Sept 1928. With regard to running times, see *"How to Handle Women." Motion Picture News* 14 July 1928.

39 *Harrison's Reports* 20 Oct. 1928.

40 See, for example: "Universal." *Exhibitors World and Moving Picture World* 1 Sept. 1928.

41 Smith, Don G. "The Road to Dracula: The Bela Lugosi Scrapbook." *Scarlet Street* No. 12 (Fall 1993).

Lugosi as Dracula in 1927.

Chapter 35

Vampires

"I saw two red eyes staring at me and a livid
white face looking down on me out of the mist."
– Deane & Balderston, *Dracula–The Vampire Play*

There was not one vampire in America; there were many. On occasion, the term "vampire" referred to nothing more than a criminal, a thief, whether in the nineteenth-century stage play *Invisible Prince! Or, the Island of Tranquil Delights* or in such films as *Vampires of the Coast* (1909), *Vampires of the Night* (1914), *Vasco, the Vampire* (1914), and *The Forest Vampires* (1914), the latter featuring J. Barney Sherry, who later costarred with Lugosi in *Daughters Who Pay* (1925).

Far more prominent was another non-supernatural vampire, the wicked woman who metaphorically bleeds men of their lives and wealth. Philip Burne-Jones' painting *The Vampire* (1897) and Rudyard Kipling's accompanying poem quickly became famous in America, having a major impact on popular culture. By 1899, the *New York Times* wrote, "People nowadays carelessly use the word 'vampire' as a stronger and trifle more loathsome term than 'parasite.'"[1]

Porter Emerson Brown adapted the painting and poem into a 1909 novel and stage play called *A Fool There Was*. The successful play led to an even more successful film of the same name in 1915, starring Theda Bara. She became the most famous of the screen "vamps," but the sheer number of films and actresses associated with this character type forms a long list that began at least as early as Selig's 1910 film *The Vampire* and continued well into the Roaring Twenties.

For many persons in the early twentieth century, the "vampire" and the "vamp" were synonymous. In the *Chicago Tribune* of 1903, a journalist reported the following:

Artwork depicting Philip Burne-Jones while painting *The Vampire* (1897). Published in the *Cleveland Plain-Dealer* on June 26, 1898.

Left: Painting of Robert Campbell Maywood, the first actor to portray a supernatural vampire on the American stage. Above: Cover of the 1856 program for Dion Boucicault's *The Phantom*.

'What is a vampire, anyway?' asked a young woman looking at the Burne-Jones picture now on exhibition.

'A vampire,' [replied] her companion. 'A vampire is the rag and a bone and a hank of hair that Kipling talks about.'

They probably had not spent a portion of their youthful lives in a small town visited occasionally by the 'greatest show on earth' with its sideshow. If they had they would have known all about the 'blood sucking vampire.' They would have dreamed about it....[2]

Exasperated by their lack of knowledge, the journalist proceeded to describe vampires in great detail, both in terms of their folkloric roots and in Bram Stoker's novel *Dracula* (1897).

Top: Horace Liveright. Above: Published in the *New Haven Journal-Courier* (New Haven, CT) on September 17, 1927.

After all, despite shifting and expanding definitions of the term "vampire," the supernatural vampire had long been known in America. Newspaper articles on the subject date to at least as early as 1732 and continued into the twentieth century.[3] Coverage included tales of alleged vampirism in Rhode Island in the 1890s.[4] There was also much discussion of the vampire in fiction, beginning with John Polidori's *The Vampyre, A Tale* in 1819 and returning with Stoker's *Dracula* in 1897.

More than literature, though, the supernatural vampire found a home on the American stage in the nineteenth century. In what was probably the first such performance, the Pavilion Theater in New York staged *The Vampyre* in 1819, an apparently unauthorized and loose adaptation of Polidori's story.[5] Robert Campbell Maywood played the title character, becoming the first in a long line of actors to portray the undead in the United States.

By 1820, James Robinson Planché's *The Vampire, or the Bride of the Isles* appeared at American theaters after having first been presented in London; it was yet another adaptation of Polidori's tale.[6] The *New England Galaxy* reported that an actor named:

> Mr. Brown was the Vampyre, and when we assert that his contortions and distortions of countenance were even more hideous than the author could have conceived of his subject, we believe we do but express the opinion of a majority of the spectators.[7]

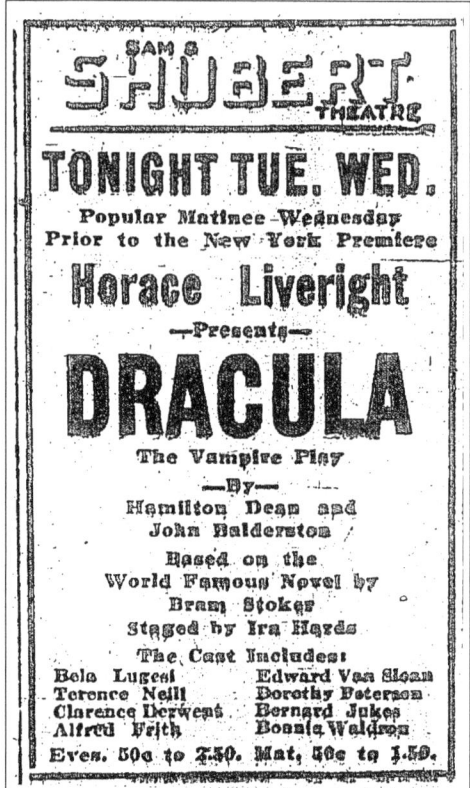

Left: Published in the *New Haven Evening Register* (New Haven, CT) on September 19, 1927. Right: *(Courtesy of the Billy Rose Theater Division of the New York Public Library)*

Versions of *The Vampire, or the Bride of the Isles* continued to be staged for the next several years, making it the most popular vampire play to appear at American theaters in the nineteenth century.[8]

After Planché, the vampire's most notable theatrical appearance came in Dion Boucicault's two-act play *The Phantom*, originally titled *The Vampire* when it premiered in England. At its American debut at Wallack's Theater in New York in 1856, Boucicault portrayed the title role himself. According to one character, within an old castle "dwells a terrible thing – man or fiend." He then describes the fate of travellers who wander into the ruins after sunset. Their corpses are later discovered, "each with a wound in his throat in the right side, from which they have evidently bled to death – but no blood is spilt around, the face is white and fixed, as if it had died of horror."

Over four decades later, newspapers announced a potential stage version of Stoker's *Dracula*. In November of 1899, the *Boston Herald* reported the news: "Since arriving in Boston, Bram Stoker, manager of Sir Henry Irving, has received a proposition to dramatize his latest book, *Dracula*. If it is put on the stage, *Dr. Jekyll and Mr. Hyde* in comparison will, it is said, become a pleasing memory."[9] But discussion of a theatrical version quickly disappeared, at least until the 1920s.

Minor reportage of Hamilton Deane's British stage version of *Dracula* appeared in the American press in 1924, but grew exponentially by 1927. Having played the provinces, Deane's company finally opened in the West End. According to the *New York Times*:

> In London the production met with the same reception from the critics as had been its lot in the provinces – every reviewer literally tore the play to shreds. But the public, as had been its custom in the provinces, reversed the opinion of the critics....[10]

Deane's conception of the Dracula character – portrayed at London's Little Theater by Raymond Huntley – was similar in some respects to Stoker's description, but different in others: Aristocratic bearing, yes; "long, white moustache," no.

American theatrical producer Horace Liveright saw the London play four times during the space of two weeks.[11] He told one journalist, "It is the worst company I have ever seen, but that play can be re-written into a New York success."[12] Liveright was clearly impressed by the large audiences, and may also have been intrigued with the publicity gimmick of having a nurse on hand in the event anyone fainted.[13] Despite warnings from New York producers that the play couldn't succeed on Broadway, he acquired the rights. That alone was perhaps something of a triumph. For one, Stoker's widow disliked him.[14] For another, Deane had already considered an American tour.[15] Liveright then hired John L. Balderston to improve and "Americanize" Deane's text, which led both men to receive authorial credit.[16]

As early as May 18, 1927, the press announced that Liveright would be presenting *Dracula* as his first production of the forthcoming season.[17] It would become one of the latest "novelties"

 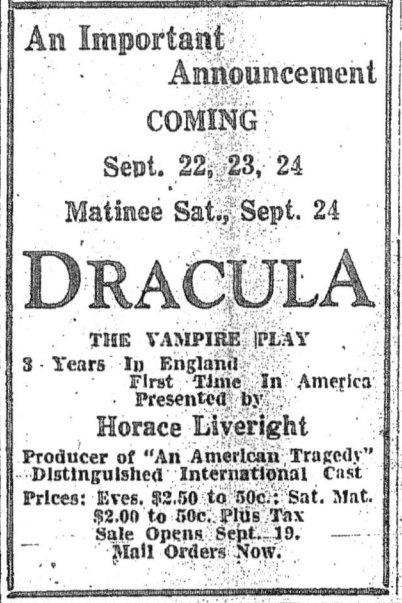

Left: Artwork of Dorothy Peterson published in the *New York Times* on October 30, 1927. Right: Published in the *Hartford Courant* (Hartford, CT) on September 15, 1927.

on Broadway.[18] In June, Bernard Jukes of the London company agreed to reprise his role as Renfield, leaving the British production while it was still being staged.[19] He told journalists that he had visited mental institutions to make a "very careful study of the facial expressions of lunatics. He was careful to observe every movement of the hands and their actions during the conversation."[20]

Liveright began to cast the other roles in July.[21] He selected his lover Dorothy Peterson to play the lead female role of Lucy.[22] For Dracula, he hoped to enlist Raymond Huntley, but the actor turned him down, apparently due to the small salary of only $125 per week.[23] How many other persons Liveright considered is unknown, but he gave Lugosi the role in August.

One account claims that theatrical producer and director John D. Williams recommended Lugosi to Liveright. Williams – who was behind such successful plays as *Rain*, which had a three-year run between 1921 and 1924[24] – had "been particularly impressed by [Lugosi's] expressive hands and how he used them, as much as his voice, in putting over a part."[25] Lugosi later remembered, "it was my hands that won me the part of Dracula on the stage."[26] On another occasion, he said:

> ...a friend of mine urged Liveright to look over the New York field of European trained actors – and particularly me – in hopes of finding one who could make himself a good Dracula. When Liveright asked me to read the part for him, I almost lost it. He was afraid my English wouldn't do. Then he asked me to act a certain scene. I 'put the juice' into it and he gave me the contract.[27]

Was the "friend" that Lugosi mentioned John D. Williams? Presumably it was. At any rate, Lugosi's representatives at Lyons & Lyons helped him work out the agreement.

Ira Hards – who had earlier directed the play *The Cat and the Canary* (1922) – began rehearsals on August 20, 1927, with the New York opening scheduled not in September, as per Liveright's original plans, but instead on October 3.[28] John L. Balderston was present for the rehearsals.[29] Liveright was just recovering from a "severe attack of bronchial pneumonia."[30] Lugosi's fourth wife Lillian later told an interviewer:

> When they were rehearsing, the producers were very disappointed in him because he wasn't acting, so they got him aside and said to him, 'You're not giving us anything.' And he said, 'I'm not acting, I'm learning my part, I'm learning my positions, I'm learning where I stop and where you want me to go. I don't know, do you want me to act?' They said, 'Yeah.' So he took a scene from the first part of the second act where he hypnotizes the maid and studied that the whole night, I suppose, got it letter perfect, knew exactly how he was going to do it and he did it and of course they were 100% sold.[31]

Lugosi himself recalled, "Even though I knew it was all hokum – especially because I knew it – I had to throw all my force into playing it, and make myself believe it. That was the only way I could hold the audience."[32]

Later, Lugosi did admit to actress Marion Shilling's father that one aspect of the play puzzled him. "It is brought out that the only way Dracula can be done away with is for a stake to be driven into his heart while he is sleeping. In his limited English, the only stake he was familiar with was beefsteak. For at least the first six months of the play he simply couldn't figure out how a steak could be driven into his heart, and how that could kill him."[33]

Prior to Broadway, Liveright presented *Dracula–The Vampire Play* at a number of tryout cities, the first being in New Haven, Connecticut. It debuted at Shubert's Theater from September 19 to 21, 1927.[34] Promotion in the local press drew attention to veteran actor Edward Van Sloan, who played Abraham Van Helsing, as well as to Clarence Derwent, who played Dr. Seward.[35] By that time, Derwent had already appeared onstage in *The Ghost Parade* and in an adaptation of *The House of Usher*.[36]

The New Haven show marked *Dracula*'s premiere performance in America.[37] Advance publicity called it the "most weird, thrilling play yet presented to an audience."[38] One newspaper even felt obliged to explain that the play's vampire was not the vamp of the "modern vernacular," but rather a "supernatural demon or ghost who sucks the blood of persons asleep."[39]

After its first performance, the *New Haven Journal-Courier* published the following review:

> ...the net result is a play which kept its audience in suspense from beginning to end. The cast is well selected and Edward Van Sloan's Professor Van Helsing is most convincing. He plays it with calm and cool deliberation bringing out a clear conception of the character. As Lucy Seward, Dorothy Peterson has ample opportunity which she makes the most of. Considerable credit is due Bernard Jukes, who plays the difficult part of Renfield, the

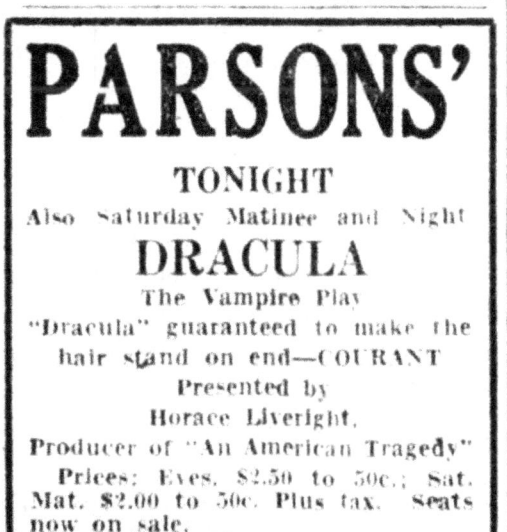

Left: Published in the *Hartford Courant* on September 20, 1927. Right: Published in the *Hartford Courant* on September 24, 1927.

Gary D. Rhodes | Bill Kaffenberger

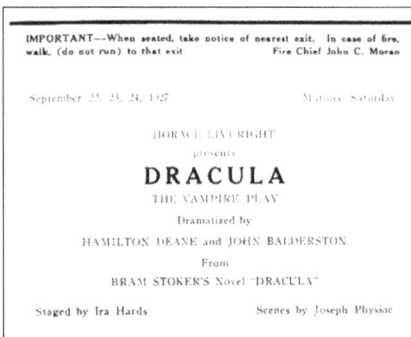

Playbill for *Dracula–The Vampire Play* in Hartford, Connecticut.

lunatic. He earned some well-merited applause on several occasions. Bela Lugosi as Dracula carried the role with conviction, while Terence Neill and Clarence Derwent as Jonathan Harker and Dr. Seward, respectively, give excellent performances.[40]

A critic from *Variety* also saw *Dracula* in New Haven, explaining: "There is no outstanding part in the cast, each being equally forceful, the settings are above average and the lighting in keeping with the production." The critic also predicted that the play would become a "smash with all its superb acting and staging."[41]

More than any review, though, *Dracula* in New Haven spawned wild publicity tales. Dorothy Peterson allegedly "lost her voice for no accountable reason."[42] And the *New York Times* reported that the "stage manager for the show had been fairly driven out of his mind at seeing the ["spine-creeping"] play for the first time."[43] Percy Shostac, the company's stage manager in New Haven, was indeed replaced by Carl Reed by the time of the Broadway opening. The reason is unknown, but it was almost certainly not due to vampire-induced "aphasia."

Dracula then played the Parsons in Hartford from September 22 to 24.[44] A newspaper ad heralded its "Distinguished International Cast."[45] The *Hartford Courant* observed:

> The cast of *Dracula* was admirable; the Hungarian – we suppose him to be Hungarian, certainly he is a native of some picturesque and not too familiar European country – Bela Lugosi, was a portentous figure as Count Dracula, his towering height adding to the effect, and such hands as Mr. Lugosi's are an asset to any artist; they speak, they convey messages of terror and fear. Mr. Lugosi's hands are in a class with those of Mr. A. E. Anson, Mr. H. B. Warner, and even of the great master of them all, Sir Henry Irving.[46]

In another article, the *Courant* told readers, "Lugosi acts the imposing Count Dracula with the assuredness that goes with villainy of the deepest dye.[47] A review in the *New Britain Daily Herald* praised Lugosi for his "convincing manner," but considered Jukes to be the "high spot" of the play.[48]

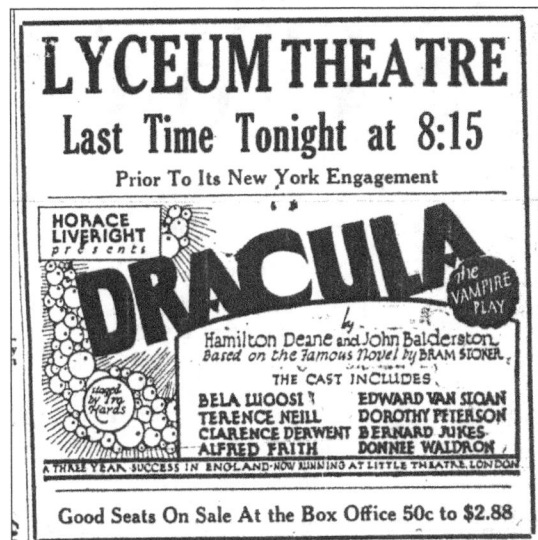
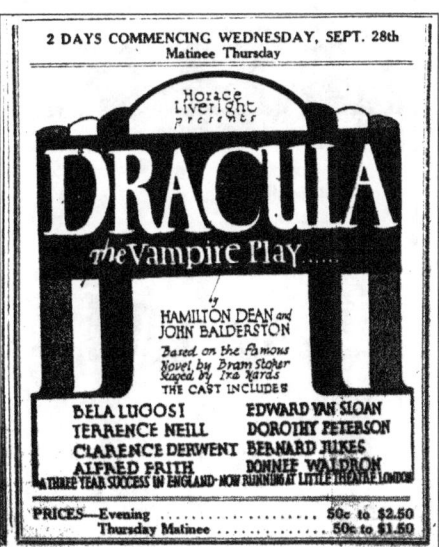

Left: Published in the *New London Evening Day* (New London, CT) on September 27, 1927. Right: Published in the *Stamford Advocate* (Stamford, CT) on September 24, 1927.

NEDDA HARRIGAN, who plays the role of Wells, the English maid, in the exciting vampire play, "Dracula," at the Fulton Theater

Right: Published in the *Cincinnati Enquirer* on December 20, 1928.

Gary D. Rhodes | Bill Kaffenberger

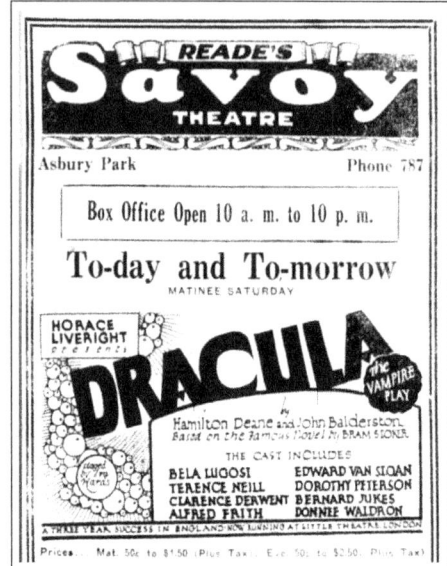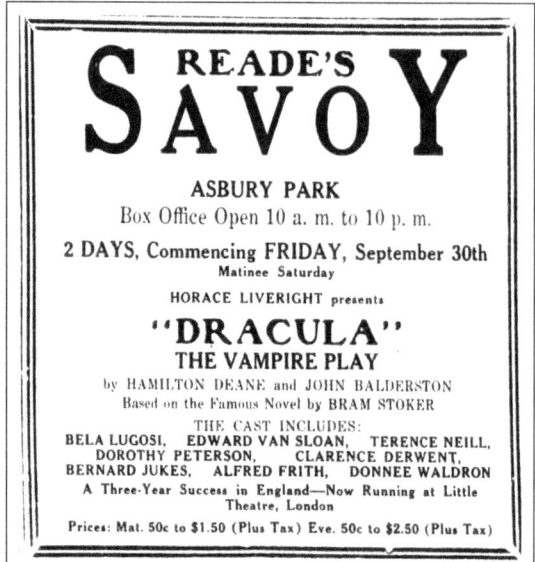

Left: Published in the *Asbury Park Press* (Asbury Park, NJ) on September 30, 1927. Right: Published in the *Spring Lake Gazette* (Spring Lake, NJ) on September 30, 1927.

Actor Clarence Derwent later recalled these performances in his autobiography:

> The tryouts in New Haven and Hartford found the play in bad shape, and the management, as so often happens, began to blame the actors. Each in turn came in for censure from Mr. Liveright, who was in a state of jitters. I am inclined to agree that I was not too well suited to the part of Dr. Seward, but it is a curious fact and typical of the chaos in which they found themselves that five days before the New York opening, they were still debating whether to get rid of me or an unknown actor, Bela Lugosi, playing Dracula. It was indeed fortunate for Mr. Lugosi's subsequent career that the ax fell upon me.[49]

It was actually closer to ten days prior to the Broadway opening that the casting changed, occurring immediately after closing in Hartford. Herbert Bunston replaced Derwent as Dr. Seward, and Nedda Harrigan replaced Donnee Waldron as the Maid, who was listed in playbills by her character name "Wells."

Dracula next appeared at the Lyceum Theater in New London, Connecticut, on September 26-27, and then at the Stamford Theater in Stamford, Connecticut, on September 28-29. The *Stamford Advocate* commended it for being "horror of the first magnitude," placing the audience "on edge from the very start and under a tense strain." The newspaper added that it was "exceedingly well acted," drawing attention to Jukes (who "scored tremendously and repeatedly received recognition of his superior work") and to Lugosi (who was "ideal" as Dracula). The paper also believed that Bunston was "satisfying" in his first performance.[50]

Dracula's final tryouts came on September 30 and October 1 at Reade's Savoy Theater in Asbury Park, New Jersey. For decades, these performances have languished in obscurity, never

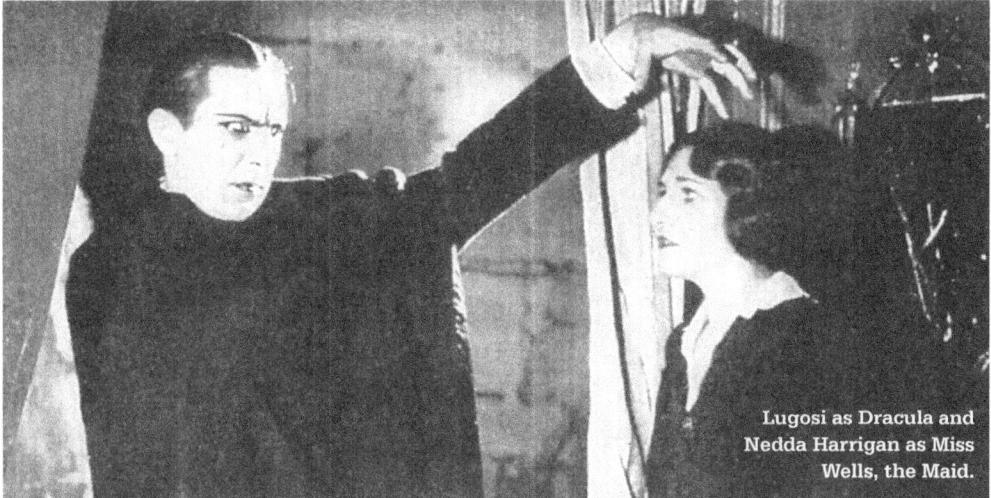

Lugosi as Dracula and Nedda Harrigan as Miss Wells, the Maid.

mentioned in any prior Lugosi book or article. The *Asbury Park Press* reported that audience members' hair "stood on end," adding:

> One has gained nothing by seeing the play *Dracula* except a delightful series of shivers and a slightly haunted feeling for a few hours following.
> Yet for 'that sort of thing' nothing has appeared for a long time to match it.[51]

The local critic praised the cast as "most impressive" and specifically called attention to Jukes and Van Sloan. Asbury Park also spawned yet another "true" publicity story. A photographer paid to take publicity stills "slipped and fell off the stage to the orchestra pit," and the "focusing screen of his camera was smashed without apparently being touched by human hands."[52] Such weird goings-on were allegedly due to the play's subject matter.

On approximately October 2, after what had been a total of 16 tryout performances, the company headed to New York, to Broadway.[53] It is true that Dracula had, to an extent, already entered popular American culture. But thanks to *Dracula–The Vampire Play*, the tale became far more famous. And it greatly assisted the creature of supernatural folklore returning to prominence, displacing the vamp as the most famous type of vampire.

As Van Helsing says in the Deane & Balderston script, "You ask how the Vampire King, during the hours of night, the hours that are his, comes and goes? As the wind, my friend, as he pleases."

Endnotes

1   "Without Prejudice." *New York Times* 5 Mar. 1899.

2   "Vampires." *Chicago Tribune* 25 Jan. 1903.

3   "Medreyga in Hungary." *American Weekly Mercury* (Philadelphia, PA) 15 June 1732.

4   "Believe in Vampires." *Boston Globe* 27 Jan. 1896.

5   "Pavilion Theater." *New York Evening Post* 29 July 1819.

6   James Robinson Planché's *The Vampire, or the Bride of the Isles* was sometimes rendered as *The Vampyre, or the Bride of the Isles*.

7   "The Vampyre." *New England Galaxy* (Boston, MA) 3 Nov. 1820.

8   See, for example: Advertisement. *Charleston Courier* (Charleston, SC) 14 Jan. 1825.

9   Untitled. *Boston Herald* 26 Nov. 1899. Similar information appeared in "Telegraphic News." *New York Dramatic Mirror* 2 Dec. 1899.

10 "Digging Into *Dracula*." *New York Times* 25 Dec. 1927.

11 Dardis, Tom. *Firebrand: The Life of Horace Liveright* (New York: Random House, 1995).

12 Swaffer, Hannen. "London As It Looks." *Variety* 11 May 1927.

13 "Two Plays in London Make Many Faint." *New York Times* 11 Mar. 1927.

14 Dardis, *Firebrand*.

15 "The Legitimate State in London." *Billboard* 2 Apr. 1927.

16 "Digging Into Dracula."

17 "Liveright Tells Plans." *New York Times* 18 May 1927.

18 "Theater." *Chicago Tribune* 1 Aug. 1927.

19 "London Cables." *Billboard* 11 June 1927.

20 "Actor Visited Lunatic Asylums for Grisly Role in *Dracula*." *Cincinnati Enquirer* (Cincinnati, OH) 20 Dec. 1928.

21 "*American Tragedy* Closing." *Billboard* 4 June 1927.

22 "Engagements." *Billboard* 16 July 1927.

23 Dardis, *Firebrand*.

24 "Broadway Successes For Brooklyn Playgoers." *Brooklyn Standard Union* 30 Nov. 1924.

25 "Lugosi Repeats Former Success in Play *Dracula*." *Hartford Courant* (Hartford, CT) 29 April 1943.

26 Lugosi, Bela, as told to Gladys Hall, "Memos of a Madman," *Silver Screen* (July 1941).

27 Quoted in Fried, Alexander. "Those Chilling Horror Roles! Bela Lugosi Loves 'Em." *San Francisco Examiner* 15 Aug. 1943.

28 "Theatrical Notes." *New York Times* 18 Aug. 1927; "Announcing the Shows of the New Theatrical Season." *New York Times* 7 Aug. 1927.

29 "Big Cast for Command to Love." *Brooklyn Daily Eagle* 18 Aug. 1927.

30 "In the Theaters on Broadway." *Brooklyn Daily Star* 13 Aug. 1927.

31 D'Arc, James D. "Oral History Interview Donlevy, Lillian Lugosi, 1912." 20 May 1976. Available at L. Tom Perry Special Collections, Harold B. Lee Library, Brigham Young University, Provo, UT.

32 Coons, Robbin. "Hollywood Sights and Sounds." *Gettysburg Times* (Gettysburg, PA) 24 Apr. 1933.

33 Goldrup, Jim and Tom. *Feature Players: The Stories Behind the Faces.* Vol. 3. (Ben Lomond, CA: J. and T. Goldrup, 1986).

34 "*Dracula* to Open in New Haven." *New York Times* 13 Sept. 1927.

35 "*Dracula* Great London Success Opens at Shubert Tonight." *New Haven Register* (New Haven, CT) 19 Sept. 1927.

36 "Scanning the Stage." *New Haven Register* 18 Sept. 1927.

37 "*Dracula* for New Haven First Time in America." *Billboard* 24 Sept. 1927.

38 "The Local Theaters." *New Haven Journal-Courier* (New Haven, CT) 19 Sept. 1927.

39 "*Dracula* A Play of Intense Moments." *New Haven Journal-Courier* 20 Sept. 1927.

40 Ibid.

41 "*Dracula*." *Variety* 28 Sept. 1927.

42 "Weird Doings Reported by Play Troupe." *Los Angeles Times* 22 June 1928.

43 "A Mystery Play Took to the Road." *New York Times* 2 Mar. 1930.

44 In period articles and advertisements, the Parsons was occasionally rendered with a possessive apostrophe, either before or after the "s" in its name.

45 Advertisement. *Hartford Courant* 15 Sept. 1927.

46 E. N. C. "O' This and O' That." *Hartford Courant* 9 Oct. 1927. Though not published until October, this review specifically discusses a Hartford performance of the play, not one on Broadway.

47 "Bram Stoker Horror Play At Parson's." *Hartford Courant* 23 Sept. 1927.

48 "Theater Reviews of Current Offerings." *New Britain Daily Herald* (New Britain, CT) 23 Sept. 1927.

49 Derwent, Clarence. *The Derwent Story: My First Fifty Years in the Theater in England and America* (New York: Henry Schuman, 1953).

50 "Our Own Broadway and For Diversion." *Stamford Advocate* (Stamford, CT) 29 Sept. 1927.

51 "The Play – Werewolf Legend Modernized." *Asbury Park Press* (Asbury Park, NJ) 1 Oct. 1927.

52 "Weird Doings Reported by Play Troupe."

53 Some historians have catalogued only twelve tryout performances. This is apparently due to being unaware of the three performances in Asbury Park, as well as of the one matinee given in Stamford.

(Courtesy of Richard Sheffield)

Chapter 36

Blood-Curdling

"What a horrible undead thing he is lying there."
–Deane & Balderston, *Dracula–The Vampire Play*

When *Dracula–The Vampire Play* opened on Broadway at the Fulton Theater on October 5, 1927, *Billboard* described it as:

> [A] weird yarn about those legendary 'undead' which are known, not at all in the Theda Bara sense, as vampires. Perhaps werewolf would be a clearer description, the real meaning of vampire having been so confused in common misusage....[1]

Similarly, the *New York American* wrote, "The average New Yorker, asked to define a vampire, would say 'Theda Bara.' And that is as far as his lore goes."[2] This largely forgotten issue of the vamp-versus-vampire terminology remained very much real in 1927, so much so that Van Helsing's dialogue includes a lengthy definition of what supernatural vampires are.

And then there was the issue of how to classify *Dracula*. Many journalists groped for appropriate adjectives and genre identification. Most often they defaulted to calling *Dracula* a "mystery play," a term that conjured such Broadway hits as *Seven Keys to Baldpate* (1913), *The Cat and the Canary* (1922), and *The Gorilla* (1925). To be sure, the characters in *Dracula* are initially at a loss to explain Lucy's mysterious illness, and the Maid does refer to Van Helsing as a "Dutch Sherlock Holmes."

"Nothing more blithely blood-curdling has happened in the Drama since *The Bat* [1920]," the *New York Herald-Tribune* announced.[3] Reference to that particular mystery play and its cloaked villain seemed logical at first, but some critics realized *Dracula* was

Top: (Courtesy of the Billy Rose Theater Division of the New York Public Library). **Middle: Published in the *Daily Worker* (New York) on October 21, 1927. Bottom: Published in the *New Yorker* on November 19, 1927.**

distinctive. *Billboard* also invoked *The Bat* before immediately observing that *Dracula* was not "in any way similar, for it deals with the supernatural – and what a universal appeal there is in that."[4] Old world superstitions had intruded on art deco modernity.

Dracula certainly attempted to create horror in various respects, most notably with Lugosi's character, his makeup having a slightly green cast, and his form sometimes lit with green flood and green spotlights. The play also featured a flying vampire bat, the sound of wolves howling, and the loud echo of the stake driven into Dracula's heart.[5] And then there was the vampire's disappearance via a trap door onstage, followed by a "blackout" that threw the auditorium into complete darkness. Cue shrieks, screams, and faints.

Dracula's only close comparators in the United States dated to seventy or more years earlier, plays like *The Phantom* (1856) and *The Vampire, or the Bride of the Isles* (1820). The American stage had witnessed nothing like *Dracula* in the twentieth century, and it had never seen the likes of Lugosi's performance, one that so expertly melded the attractive with the evil, the romantic with the repulsive. It is difficult to imagine how effective and impactful *Dracula–The Vampire Play* must have been in the Manhattan of 1927.

In an effort to understand, it is important to examine the original critical reviews, something Lugosi, Horace Liveright, and the others in the company must have done themselves the day after the first Broadway curtain fell. They were many, and they varied from favorable to skeptical:

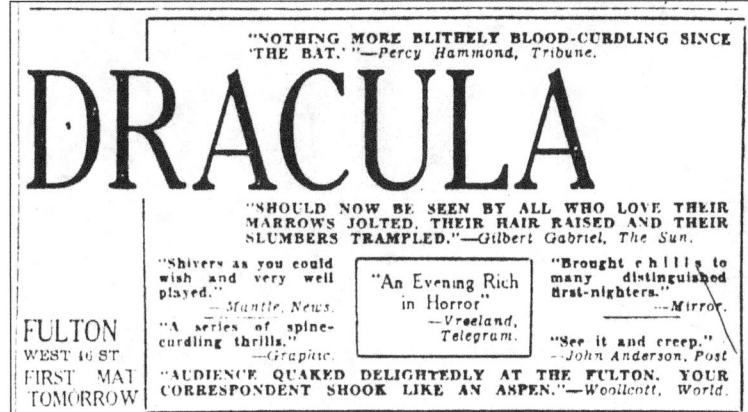

Left: Published in the *New York Herald-Tribune* on October 7, 1927. Right: Published in the *New York Herald-Tribune* on October 5, 1927.

Shuddery but effective.⁶ – *Little Theater Monthly*

Dracula is a good and amusing job in cold-sweats and flesh-creeping. ... It was all extremely harassing in a pleasant way.⁷ – *New York Herald-Tribune*

... an unconditionally excellent play in every acceptance of that term. The dramatization by Messrs. Deane and Balderston has improved, if that is possible, the original diary-form version [in the novel]. ... The loss of effect sustained in omitting the visit to Dracula's castle is amply compensated by the transference of the entire pack of lusty howling bloodhounds to [England].⁸ – *Columbia Spectator*

Being blessed or is it cursed, with a matter-of-fact mind which demands logic and the reason why, this reviewer found no difficulty in agreeing as in a game, to a group of false premises and then getting into the spirit of the play and enjoying every shudder, every quiver, and even every blood-curdling shriek.⁹ – *Wall Street Journal*

The plot, of course, is improbable, but that need not be held against a mystery play if it entertains and thrills without creating a sense of the ridiculous. It must be confessed that it came nearly doing this very thing several times last night, causing a diversion from the illusion on the stage. ... the atmosphere for an evening of creeps is well laid and the audience is in rather an expectant and receptive mood. ... It may reasonably be held, however, that if the play entertains, and it cannot be said that it does not, then it serves its purpose.¹⁰ – *Brooklyn Standard Union*

The show certainly ranks high in the list of what is known in the profession as 'boob catchers.' As a piece of writing it is not so bad either, but it is primarily a shocker of theatrical effects that put audiences into that sublime state of terror with what are

Publicity portrait of Lugosi and Dorothy Peterson in *Dracula–The Vampire Play*.

generally considered to be thoroly [sic] enjoyable chills and creeps. ... Ira Hards has done his best job in some seasons with the staging of it all, and the [Joseph] Physioc settings serve well.[11] – *Billboard*

[T]hough I cared little for it, the signs were favorable. The public that seems to adore the shiver and squeal drama is likely to rise to it in a paying mass. ... A little sickening, some of it. ... But it is as shivery as you could possibly wish and very well played.[12] – *The Daily News*

The play could be even more terrifying without some of the arrant hokum which has been introduced, but it is quite terrifying enough, and supplies that long felt need of the New York stage, a shudder that you can't shake off.[13] – *The New Yorker*

Ira Hards staged the thriller and did a good job. Some of the tricky stuff looked flimsy, but the story held together very well. ... For those who like to mix their evenings in the theater with chills up and down the spine, *Dracula* is quite a dish. And there should be plenty of customers to ensure a profitable engagement.[14] – *Variety*

As a member of this sanguinary public, I found much of *Dracula* terribly entertaining. ... Sometimes I had to grunt like a grown-up over such foolish sights as a bat which joggled around on the backdrop with all the liveliness of a yesterday's washrag. But I was bullied out of noting lacunae like that, not by the gossip, for instance, that in London the bat was a still more dejected object on the end of a six-inch hawser, but by the sheer animal horror of the story. It doesn't do to stick out your tongue at a werewolf. ... The acting is fairly awful, maybe suitably so.[15] – *New York Sun*

Published in *Vanity Fair* in December of 1927.

Plausibly, sentiently, and in one or two cases excellently acted, the piece from time to time slowly conjures up a proper atmosphere of horrid creepiness, only to have the illusion shattered by the clumsiness of the mechanical effects. ... one began to smile at the unexplained black-outs, the untimely lowering of a gauze curtain (while the lights were up) before the blood-sucking scene. Why this spectacle needed to be thus modified for a notoriously sensational-loving public is a mystery. Some, at least, of us could even have endured the sight of red-ink dripping from the vampire's lips.[16] – *The Stage*

It seems to me that they have made a good show of it at the Fulton. But this is not to say that a more practiced hand could not have made it ten times as effective. I thought

Top Left: Published in the *New York Evening Journal* on October 31, 1927. Above and Top Right: Advertisements from a 1928 playbill for *Dracula*. Below: A scene from *Dracula–The Vampire Play*.

that the resorting to a gauze curtain for the vampire's attack on poor Lucy was feeble showmanship and the use of vast outpourings of steam to represent the cloud of midges which entered Lucy's room was too visibly mechanical a trick out of the old melodramas. ... Then I was at a loss to account for the complete collapse of stagecraft which occurred when it was necessary to bring a werewolf out of the darkness. ... I think it was supposed to be a werewolf, but it looked so much like the good old she bear of the Christmas pantomimes that *Dracula* threatened to turn jolly then and there. I suppose the bear was just a friend of kindly Horace Liveright's and needed a job.[17] – *New York World*

The play will probably get by as a curiosity, though it may throw a damper on necking parties.[18] – *New York Telegram*

It is a spectral diversion, inducing the chills of terror and semi-hollow laughter. Though as foolish as the other theatrical creep machines, and often cumbersomely silly, *Dracula* should delight goose-flesh addicts, and cause playgoing teeth to chatter for a good long run.[19] – *New York Post*

When they are treating of this weird force as a mystery they send the customary shivers of apprehension streaming down the back, and *Dracula* holds its audience nervously expectant. When in the next two acts the atmosphere becomes more realistic than occult, the effect is not so horribly fascinating. One begins to protect one's self against the machinations of the 'undead' by watching the stage machinery whirl. One is not so frightened as one had ingenuously hoped to be. Played more swiftly, fiercely and mysteriously, *Dracula* could doubtless scare the skeptics out of several years growth into complete submission.[20] – *New York Times*

Last evening the play was accepted by the first New York audience with mixed feelings. To many in the assembled throng the drama held many thrills and duplicated its London success, but there were those who were inclined to smile at all this strenuous activity. This latter element, let it be said, was in the minority, and *Dracula* weathered its long-anticipated premiere successfully.[21] – *Brooklyn Times*

As a drama it is about on a par with a sword-swallowing act, but it is attractive for exactly the same reason that most people enjoy being made to suffer. ... There are some – and I am one of them – who get no sensual satisfaction out of such self-torture as *Dracula* offers; it leaves me, to tell the gospel truth, quite unmoved, with a normal pulse, an unhurried heart, a brow unspangled by perspiration, and a mind still bored. But all around me I hear the gasps and chuckles of pained delight with which some of Horace Liveright's most famous literary attaches were greeting the hocus-pocus on the stage. I was sorry that I was not so moved, for I should have been the richer by one evening's entertainment.[22] – *The Morning Telegraph*

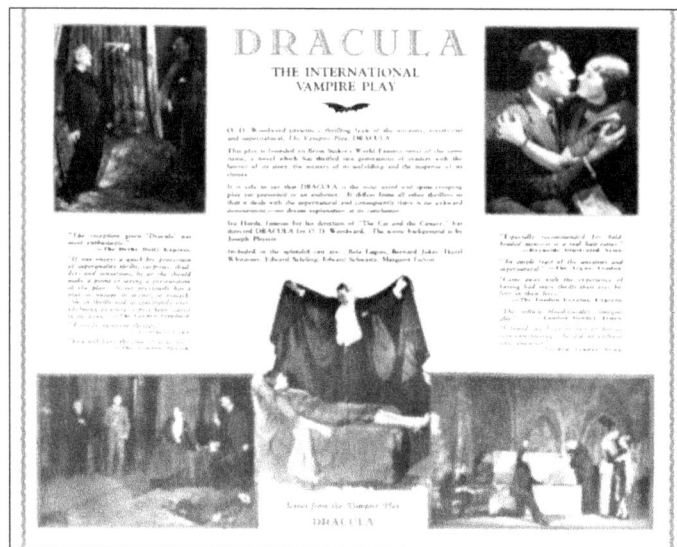 

Left: *(Courtesy of Kristin Dewey).* **Right:** Published in *Az Ember* on November 3, 1927.

This is a novelty in mystery melodramas and proved thrilling until those who watched it grew accustomed to thrills of a kind that repeated themselves.[23] – *Brooklyn Daily Eagle*

Dramatic critics with weak hearts were warned to stay away from *Dracula* or else take a woman along... the bold escort has an opportunity to show his mettle, which should consist of saying to his weaker companion: 'Fear not, I am here.'... If the play is intended as a burlesque on spiritualism, the miraculous powers of sacred wafers and on hokum in general, it is good. But one cannot resist the feeling that the author believed his own hokum, hence the indecision how to take the darned thing.[24] – *The Daily Worker*

Considering how easily audiences laugh in the wrong place, I'll say that at least that didn't happen last night. The piece was well done, and if the play did not exactly bite in vampire style or leave any marks that we could take home with us, it was a respectful theatrization of the novel itself. At times it dragged on in the oodles of 'explanation' – presumably necessary – and one grew anxious to see the thing going instead of prattling. Then again, there were tense moments. ... I am not saying that the show last night proved to be 'good entertainment,' but it followed its origin closely and escaped the ludicrous. ... Nobody laughed, but again, nobody seemed to be hopelessly thrilled.[25] – *New York American*

That it brought chills to the spinal system of many distinguished first nighters must be attested, but that it succeeded in freezing the very marrow of the majority of the local initial test cases is doubtful. To many the eerie suggested horrors of this schocker [sic] suggested but the impotent boos of a child dressed in a bedsheet.[26] – *New York Daily Mirror*

A scene from *Dracula–The Vampire Play*.

The producers have not made it sufficiently clear whether they intended this elaborate hokum to be taken seriously or as a farce.²⁷ – *New York Evening Journal*

It would be more fun were it less shoddily produced and performed. The tempo is terrible. ... The stage effects are crude and musty and appear to take a perverse delight in functioning wrong.²⁸ – *Vogue*

Curiously, a few of the reviews did not specifically mention Lugosi's performance, including those published in the *New York Sun*, the *New York Evening Journal*, and the *New Yorker*. But most critics did discuss him, as the following comments attest:

It is well acted. Edward van Sloan as the doctor, Bela Lugosi as Dracula, Dorothy Peterson as his victim, [and] Bernard Jukes as the crazy one all perform in exemplary fashion in the strange play that Horace Liveright has brought to the stage.²⁹ – *New Yorker Volkszeitung*

Count Dracula also has a remarkable series of effective scenes. Mr. Lugosi took full advantage of his Apollonian figure and Stentorian voice to strike terror in the hearts of his auditors. His appearance in an ingenious Scotch mist, his bloody embraces, his baffling disembodiment, and his subtle animal reincarnations were extremely artful pieces of work. – *Columbia Spectator*

Left: Published in the *New York Sun* on October 24, 1927. Right: Published in the *Brooklyn Eagle* on December 8, 1927.

Bela Lugosi, a massive fellow with just the right cast of countenance and Magyar accent, made the vampire count really sinister.[30] – *The Morning Telegraph.*

Later we met Count Dracula himself, looking a bit like Mephistopheles suddenly released from *Faust*. He had a nice foreign accent and spoke in sepulchral tones. ... the undead Dracula crept on, waving his Hamlet-like cloak, and between hypnotism and vampirism, he had a large and juicy time of it.[31] – *New York American*

Bela Lugosi is first rate as the vampire.[32] – *New York Daily Mirror*

Bela Lugosi, dress suited, used his dialect as the sinister Dracula, a clever conception all around.[33] – *Variety*

...our old friend Bela Lugosi playing Dracula himself, employing that incongruous accent, which American playgoers have come to associate with lovable and threadbare music masters.[34] – *New York World*

Bela Lugosi, a Hungarian, plays Count Dracula with fine authority.[35] – *Brooklyn Daily Eagle*

As the bat seeking this blond canary, Bela Lugosi, Hungarian actor, gave a satisfactory Mephistophelian performance.[36]

Dracula was effectively embodied by Bela Lugosi. No attempt, however, was made to conform with Stoker's description of the Count, Mr. Lugosi's vampire being a massive, cruel-looking, clean-shaven, less-than-middle-aged monster, a sort of cross between a peculiarly bestial man-about-town and a vaudeville magician.[37] – *The Stage*

Sometimes Mr. Lugosi, as Dracula, is, like the performance, a little too deliberate and confident.[38] – *New York Times*

[T]he acting for the most part is all that could be desired, though as Count Dracula, Bela Lugosi hardly suggests the sepulchral being he is supposed to be.[39] – *Brooklyn Life and Activities of Long Island Society*

Mr. Lugosi performs Dracula with funereal decorations suggesting a little more an operatically inclined mortician than a blood-sucking fiend.[40] – *New York Post*

Dracula is played by Bela Lugosi with only fair returns. He seemed to give an over-amount of ponderousness to the difficulties at hand.[41] – *Brooklyn Times*

The torments of the first American performance might have been more alarming had the demon been illustrated less stiffly than he was by Bela Lugosi. It was a rigid hobgoblin presented by Mr. Lugosi, resembling a wax man in a shop window more than a suave ogre bent on nocturnal mischief-making.[42] – *New York Herald-Tribune*

Such varying assessments of Lugosi may not have been surprising, given his otherworldly and methodical performance of such a bizarre character. One of the most favorable notices came in the *Amerikai Magyar Népszava*:

It's a huge acting challenge to play the role of the blood-sucking vampire. It is almost unavoidable for an actor to become exaggerated in such a role, but Lugosi's vast experience in acting helped him out, as he managed to play with his voice in English, too, and use his gestures so that his magical appearance in this creepy role impressed the audience. Every move of his has a special meaning. There is special strength in his tone. The audience welcomed his first appearance on the stage with great applause, and as he left after his first scene. Beside the applause, liberated sighs indicated that Lugosi was able to touch the viewers with the power of his acting of Count Dracula, the vampire. New York dailies received the play with ambivalent feelings, but Lugosi's splendid acting was praised in all cases.[43]

Lugosi might have left Hungarian-American theater for Broadway, but admiration for him in that community continued.

To be sure, the publication *Az Ember* believed that *Dracula* served as his personal and professional redemption:

> Bela Lugosi's sensational and extraordinary success is due to the private affairs of a talented actor, which is now a Hungarian public affair, because the entire American press celebrates the brilliantly talented Hungarian actor. In this way, the emigrant Hungarian artist expelled from his homeland becomes the flagship of Hungarian culture, and thus, Bela Lugosi, chased from the [successful] and talented course [of Budapest] actors, becomes the forerunner of the real Hungarian propaganda in America in the most exposed and upscale position. This is how Hungarian propaganda should be done, and the American Hungarian embassy, which must acknowledge and cable home to Budapest, can learn from this that the only Hungarian actor who gains glory for the Hungarian name on Broadway in the context of true American success is none other than Lugosi.[44]

In another article, the same publication praised Lugosi for playing a "remarkably difficult role brilliantly."[45]

Horace Liveright allegedly spent sixty to seventy percent more money on advertising *Dracula* than producers did on the average non-musical Broadway play.[46] Audience responses must have been largely favorable given its extended success. In December 1927, members of a sorority in Mount Vernon attended the show and held a theater party in honor of it.[47] Then, in January 1928, fifty members of Long Island's South Side High School attended it.[48]

Dracula had quickly became famous, the show to see, so much so that F.W. Murnau might have attended a performance. He was due in New York on October 15, 1927, returning from Europe.[49] Murnau's schedule required him to leave for the West Coast right away, but he might still have had a day or two in Manhattan before doing so. *Dracula* would have likely interested him, given that he directed *Nosferatu* in 1922, as well as Lugosi in the 1920 film *Der Januskopf*.

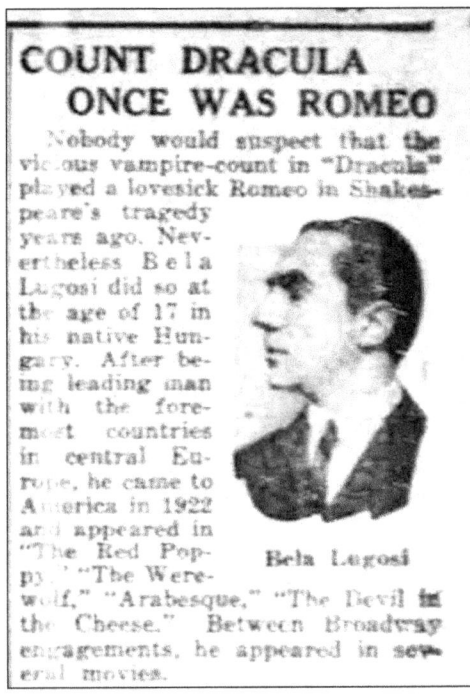

Left: Published in the *New York Daily News* on October 23, 1927. Right: Bernard Jukes.

In terms of audience reactions, separating fact from fiction is sometimes difficult, as the following three accounts make clear:

> During the performance of *Dracula* at the Fulton Saturday matinee, two women in the audience fainted. ... The show management could not convince William Munster, the house manager, that the collapse of the patrons was on the level. Munster insisted they were plants.[50]

> Up to and including the one hundred and fifteenth performance of *Dracula* there were ... 106 casualties [of faintings], which includes people from every walk of life, including one dramatic critic, who passed out in a faint on the night of the premiere of the vampire play last October. ... The Fulton Theater, being especially equipped, has not found it necessary to call for an ambulance.[51]

> Throughout the eight months' run an emergency nurse prowled up and down the aisles of the Fulton Theatre, here and there plucking an 'unconscious' spectator out of his seat and hurrying him out, willy-nilly for treatment. On one happy, record-breaking day there were eight 'faints' at the Fulton, and subsequent rejoicing in the Liveright office.[52]

> **'DRACULA' ON AIR**
> "Dracula" will be broadcast Friday afternoon over WJZ, with Bela Lugosi, Dorothy Peterson, Terrence Neill, Edward Van Sloan.

> A radio version of "Dracula" is scheduled for presentation at 3:30 P. M. on Friday, March 30, over WJZ. Among the actors to face the microphone are Bela Lugosa, Dorothy Peterson, Terrence Neill and Edward Van Sloan.

Left: Published in the *New York Daily News* on March 25, 1928. Right: Published in the *New York Times* on March 22, 1928.

These anecdotes give more insight into publicity gimmicks than they do of specific audience members, indicating that a type of carefully planned drama extended beyond the stage footlights. As the *New York Evening Post* observed, "it is difficult at times for the drama appraisers to tell whether they are reviewing a play or [bogus playgoers]."[53]

As for apparently genuine viewer responses, one journalist recorded the following story:

> Well, next to me, a pretty little thing was sitting. Next to her, a not too handsome gentleman. Now, whenever Bela Lugosi, with lips painted vermillion and a face as ghostly white as only the 'undead dead' Count Dracula could have, entered the stage, she covered her ears to shut out all possible unearthly screams, and hid her face upon what I have previously described as a not too manly bosom. Her escort, like all men under similar circumstances undoubtedly would, enjoyed the whole thing immensely. ... And if you think this girl was the only one in the audience who acted so queerly, you are grossly mistaken. And at least two ladies walked out in the middle of the second act.[54]

Another critic claimed, "Now and then a nervous shriek from the audience paid [the actors] their sincerest compliment."[55]

Professor of Film and English Literature Robert Singer shared an important authentic memory:

> In the winter of 1927, my aunt Sadie saw *Dracula* starring Bela Lugosi when she was an older teenager. According to my family, she was so frightened by the production, its atmospheric and dark setting, as well as Lugosi's menacing performance – in particular, his speech and his advances towards his "prey" – that she could not sleep (at first, not at all) and then later, without having the lights on, for at least two weeks.[56]

Singer added, "When I asked her about this production, by sheer chance, many years ago, I never forgot her mixed reaction of amusement and horror at the recalled memory."

The most extensive account of an audience member comes from horror film producer William Castle. In his autobiography, he wrote:

> When I was 13 years old in 1927, I bought a balcony seat with $1.10 I had taken from my sister's purse.... Enchanted, I watched Dracula suck his victims' blood. Almost every

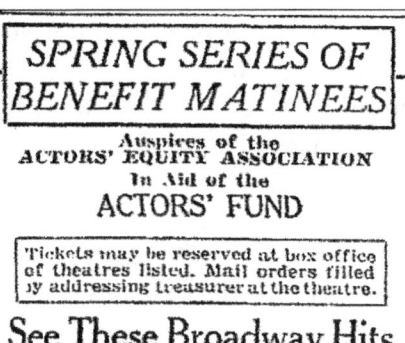

Left: Published in the *New York Times* on April 1, 1928. Right: Published in *Magyarország* on December 29, 1927.

night for the next two weeks, with $1.10 from my sister's purse, I sat in the balcony and listened to frightened audiences scream. Soon I was no longer watching the play; I had more fun watching the audiences.

One night after a performance, I decided to go backstage and meet the great Lugosi. Opening a stage door for the first time I entered the backstage world of make believe. I boldly announced to the old man sitting there that I was a friend of Mr. Lugosi's and that he was expecting me. My bluff worked and the old man said Mr. Lugosi was in dressing room number 1.

Hesitating outside his dressing room, I summoned the courage to knock. A deep, accented voice bade me enter. For a fleeting moment, I thought of escape, but it was too late – I was face to face with Count Dracula.

Luminous piercing eyes looked into mine and I was suddenly struck dumb. 'What can I do for you, young man?' the deep voice inquired. I started to speak, but the words didn't come. Count Dracula smiled and waited patiently. I managed to stammer, 'I've seen the play 12 times ... and I think you're wonderful.'[57]

Lugosi invited Castle to watch the play from backstage the following evening. And Castle realized what he wanted to do with his life, meaning to "scare the pants off audiences."

Dracula–The Vampire Play forged ahead with its own scares, week after week, during the 1927-28 season. The cast presented a condensed version of the play over radio station WJZ's *Stardom of Broadway* program on the afternoon of March 30, 1928.[58] Lugosi later recalled that there was "much indignation among the listeners." One woman "telephoned in demanding that it be stopped, because she had 6 children who had to listen to it."[59]

That broadcast might not have been the only one. On January 5, 1928, station WGBS announced a *Dracula* program at 11:25 p.m., which would have run only five minutes.[60] Its scheduled time would have allowed the cast to appear at the studio after their final stage bows. Even earlier, though, radio listings show that Hugo Gernsback's WRNY would host "Talk, *Dracula*" for several minutes during the 6 p.m. hour on December 14, 1927.[61] Here again, cast members of the company would have been potentially available, as the evening performance didn't begin until 8:30.

Dracula was also represented at a "style show" held to raise money for Actors' Equity in March 1928. Dorothy Peterson modeled, as did one of the stars of *The Silent House* (1928), Helen Chandler, who later played opposite Lugosi in Tod Browning's *Dracula* (1931). A number of other actresses took on the roles of ushers and hostesses, among them Nedda Harrigan.[62]

During its time on Broadway, *Dracula* did change in small respects. By November 12, 1927, actor James Jolley replaced Alfred Frith as the Butterworth, the Attendant, with Frith returning to the cast by December 24.[63] Then, in February 1928, Helen Mack joined the cast; she later starred in such films as *The Son of Kong* (1933) and *She* (1935).[64] Initially, Mack played a second maid character that was added, but at a given point in May she replaced Nedda Harrigan as Miss Wells for the show's final performances.[65]

Other alterations came on March 3, 1928, to help celebrate the 175th performance:

> The first of the thrills is a huge bat which flies through the window and about the stage in the second act, and the other is provided when the body of Dracula the vampire count crumbles to dust at the end of the play, when Professor Van Helsing drives the stake through the heart of the werewolf. Dorothy Peterson, who plays the vampire's victim, displays a new kind of headwear called the vampire hat.[66]

Yet another addition made at some point was a trick coffin that allowed Dracula to disappear into a cloud of fog. William Castle took credit for that idea, as well as for convincing the company to place a black coffin outside the theater to attract attention and to burn exotic incense inside "to get audiences in the mood."[67]

During its run, before and after these changes, *Dracula* held relatively strong at the box office. In November, *Variety* reported grosses for *Dracula*'s fourth week: $13,000, "rather good money and should last through winter."[68] The following week, the trade reported that the play's "standing" was "unquestioned." It was "not in smash class, but drawing substantial trade to good profit."[69] For the rest of 1927, *Dracula* averaged $12,000 or above, its lowest week in mid-December being $10,000.[70] But then the holiday week generated the highest gross to date at over $17,000.[71] Sustained success meant the play forged into the spring of 1928. By April, weekly grosses fell to averages of $10,000, low enough to bring the play to a close on May 19, 1928.[72] In honor of its success, the cast gave Lugosi a "huge bat ring [of green gold] with ruby eyes."[73]

Dracula–The Vampire Play had lasted 33 weeks on Broadway. The *New York Times* reported that the company had staged the play 282 times.[74] While this number has been disputed on occasion, it is correct. There were 16 tryout performances and 266 on Broadway (including three special holiday matinees and one matinee to raise money for the Actors' Fund), which does indeed result in a total of 282.[75]

All the while, Lugosi became somewhat famous in New York. For example, the press reported him being at The Mayfair on October 29, 1927, along with James Gleason, Hope Hampton, and Bert Wheeler.[76] Then, in mid-December, the *New York Post* published an interview with Lugosi. Asked how he mastered the English language, he replied:

> Mastering? You flatter me. I wish that I could feel I have mastered your language. But I am still struggling with it. However, my highest jury is the audience – and if they are satisfied I suppose I should not complain. Would you like to know what I have found is the best way for my work toward perfecting a characterization since I am in New York? I first 'get' my part in my own Hungarian, thinking it out as though I were going to act it in my native tongue, you see? ... when I begin to feel quite at home in it, I begin to concentrate on speaking the part as it should be spoken for the American audience.[77]

Though he was still learning English, his proficiency was far greater in 1927 than many historians have claimed.

Lugosi's accent was of course crucial to his portrayal of the vampire, as were his appearance, his movements, and his hand gestures. Various period journalists took note, which brought even more renewed attention to supernatural vampires. One reporter admitted in 1927 that the "the word 'vampire' can be bought for two cents in the Hollywood coinage," but Dracula was indeed one of the "original vampires."[78] Another wrote, "Dracula is the classic type of fictional human vampire."[79] And *Vanity Fair* declared Dracula to be a "vampire of the old school."[80]

The classic, the original, the old school vampire was new again, embodied in the form of Bela Lugosi. As Edward Van Sloan said in the curtain speech he gave after each performance:

> When you get home tonight and the lights have been turned out and you are afraid to look behind the curtains and you dread to see a face appear at the window – why, just pull yourself together and remember that after all *there are such things*.

Endnotes

1. Leland, Gordon M. "Fulton." *Billboard* 15 Oct. 1927.
2. Dale, Alan. "Dale Finds Stoker Story Well Done in Stage Version." *New York American* 6 Oct. 1927.
3. Hammond, Percy. "The Theaters." *New York Herald-Tribune* 6 Oct. 1927.
4. Leland, "Fulton."
5. The published text of the play refers to the wolves as "dogs."
6. "Theater Guide for New York Plays." *Little Theater Monthly* Feb. 1928.
7. Hammond, "The Theaters."
8. J.M.B. "The Suburbs of Columbia." *Columbia Spectator* (New York) 21 Oct. 1927.
9. R.S. "The Theater." *Wall Street Journal* 7 Oct. 1927.
10. Dobson, Edward. "A Creepy Mystery Play." *Brooklyn Standard Union* 6 Oct. 1927.
11. Leland, "Fulton."
12. Mantle, Burns. "*Dracula* Shivers and Squeals." *The Daily News* (New York) 6 June 1927.
13. "The Theater." *New Yorker* 15 Oct. 1927.
14. "*Dracula*." *Variety* 12 Oct. 1927.
15. Gabriel, Gilbert. "Manhattan Aisles." *New York Sun* 6 Oct. 1927.
16. "The American Stage." *The Stage* 20 Oct. 1927.
17. Woollcott, Alexander. "The Stage." *New York World* 6 Oct. 1927.
18. Vreeland, Frank. "Vampire Play Stages Bats in the Belfry." *New York Telegram* 6 Oct. 1927.
19. Anderson, John. "The Play." *New York Post* 6 Oct. 1927.
20. Atkinson, J. Brooks. "The Play." *New York Times* 6 Oct. 1927.
21. Field, Bowland. "The New Play." *Brooklyn Times* 6 Oct. 1927
22. Davis, Burton. "*Dracula* Opens at the Fulton." *The Morning Telegraph* (New York) 6 Oct. 1927.
23. Pollock, Arthur. "The Other Kind of Vampire." *Brooklyn Daily Eagle* 6 Oct. 1927.
24. T. J. O'F. "A Spooky Farce." *The Daily Worker* (New York) 12 Oct. 1927.
25. Dale, Alan. "Dale Finds Stoker Story Well Done in Stage Version." *New York American* 6 Oct. 1927.
26. Coleman, Robert. "*Dracula* a Thriller." *New York Daily Mirror* 7 Oct. 1927.
27. Stengel, Hans. "*Dracula*, Vampire Play, Opens at the Fulton." *New York Evening Journal* 6 Oct. 1927.
28. Carb, David. "Seen on the Stage." *Vogue* 1 Dec. 1927.

29 "Fulton Theater." *New Yorker Volkszeitung* 9 Oct. 1927.

30 Davis, "*Dracula* Opens at the Fulton."

31 Dale, "Dale Finds Stoker Story Well Done in Stage Version."

32 Coleman, "*Dracula* a Thriller."

33 "*Dracula*," *Variety*.

34 Woollcott, "The Stage." [The reference to music masters presumably is an allusion to the character Svengali.]

35 Pollock, "The Other Kind of Vampire."

36 Vreeland, "Vampire Play Stages Bats in the Belfry."

37 "The American Stage."

38 Atkinson, "The Play."

39 H. H. "Plays Reviewed – *Dracula*." *Brooklyn Life and Activities of Long Island Society* 15 Oct. 1927.

40 Anderson, "The Play."

41 Field, "The New Play."

42 Hammond, "The Theaters."

43 "Színház Művészet." *Amerikai Magyar Népszava* 7 Oct. 1927.

44 "Lugosi Béla." *Az Ember* 13 Oct. 1927.

45 "New Yorki Színházi Élet." *Az Ember* 6 Oct. 1927.

46 "A Mystery Play Took to the Road." *New York Times* 2 Mar. 1930.

47 "In Society." *The Daily Argus* (Mount Vernon, NY) 10 Dec. 1927.

48 "Rockville Centre." *Nassau Daily Review* (Freeport, NY) 12 Jan. 1928.

49 "Murnau Due Oct. 15." *Variety* 28 Sept. 1927.

50 "Fainting Women–Plants?" *Variety* 12 Oct. 1927. A subsequent article claimed that the manager was Warren O'Hara, whose wife was too scared to attend *Dracula*. Here may not be a contradiction, as Munster may have been the manager of the Fulton and O'Hara the manager of the *Dracula* company. See Gebhart, Harriet. "Wife's Afraid of Dark, but Husband Manages Show Packed with Scares." *Brooklyn Daily Star* 27 Jan. 1928.

51 Boyle, Vilas J. "Reflections at Random on Things Theatrical." *Indianapolis Star* (Indianapolis, IN) 18 Feb. 1928.

52 "A Mystery Play Took to the Road."

53 Anderson, John. "Two on the Aisle." *New York Evening Post* 21 Oct. 1927.

54 Halasz, George. "*Dracula* is Good, Exciting Vampire Play." *Cleveland Plain Dealer* 16 Oct. 1927.

55 Gabriel, "Manhattan Aisles."

56 Singer, Robert, Ph.D. Email to Gary D. Rhodes, 7 Mar. 2020.

57 Castle, William. *Step Right Up! I'm Gonna Scare the Pants Off America: Memoirs of a B-Movie Mogul* (New York: Pharos, 1992).

58 "Brooklyn Station Ends Iowa Squeal." *New York Times* 22 Mar. 1928. [The fact Lugosi and fellow cast members performed this condensed version of *Dracula* on the radio was first mentioned in Gary D. Rhodes' book *Lugosi* (Jefferson, NC: McFarland, 1996). The exact date, station identification and other details were first published in Gary D. Rhodes' *Bela Lugosi: Dreams and Nightmares* (Narberth, PA: Collectables, 2007).

59 "*Dracula* Listed as Too Shuddery for Radio Folk." *San Francisco Call and Post* 24 July 1929.

60 "Today on the Radio." *New York Times* 5 Jan. 1928; "Special Features Tonight." *New York Evening Post* 5 Jan. 1928. A listing for this program in the 5 Jan. 1928 issue of the *New Yorker Volkszeitung* calls it "Futuristic broadcast of *Dracula*." The same is true of a radio schedule in the 4 Jan. 1928 issue of the *Albany Times-Union* (Albany, New York). Similarly, a radio schedule in the 4 Jan. 1928 issue of the *Buffalo Evening News* refers to it as "Futuristic of *Dracula*."

61 "Today on the Radio." *New York Times* 14 Dec. 1927.

62 "Crowded Style Show Aids Equity's Fund." *New York Times* 21 Mar. 1928.

63 "Changes in Casts." *Billboard* 12 Nov. 1927; "Changes in Casts." *Billboard* 24 Dec. 1927.

64 "Changes in Casts." *Billboard* 25 Feb. 1927.

65 "Changes in Casts." *Billboard* 19 May 1927.

66 "Few More Faints Put In *Dracula*." *The Daily News* (New York) 4 Mar. 1928.

67 Castle, *Step Right Up!*

68 "Shows in N.Y. and Comment." *Variety* 2 Nov. 1927.

69 "Shows in N.Y. and Comment." *Variety* 9 Nov. 1927.

70 "Shows in N.Y. and Comment." *Variety* 21 Dec. 1927; "Shows in N.Y. and Comment." *Variety* 28 Dec. 1927.

71 "Shows in N.Y. and Comment." *Variety* 11 Jan. 1928.

72 "Shows in N.Y. and Comment." *Variety* 11 Apr. 1928. [During its final month on Broadway, *Dracula* grossed less than $40,000.]

73 Mackey, Joe. "Big Bad Bela." *Picture Play* July 1934.

74 "The Final Reckoning." *New York Times* 3 June 1928. The number has been disputed in the past in large measure because historians had not uncovered all of the tryouts and Broadway performances. But it is also true that, apparently for the sake of publicity, the company skewed the dates of the 150th and 175th performances when celebrating them.

75 *Dracula–The Vampire Play* had eight regularly scheduled performances each week, meaning six evening shows (Monday to Saturday nights) and two matinees (Wednesday and Saturday afternoons). The number of Broadway performances we calculate results from 102 regularly

scheduled performances in 1927 and 160 in 1928, for a total of 262. The only known derivations from the regular schedule came during opening week, which had four evening shows rather than six, due to premiering on Wednesday, 5 October 1927. Several weeks later, the Wednesday matinee for 23 November 1927 was rescheduled for Thursday, 24 November, which was Thanksgiving Day, but this did not affect the overall number of performances for that week. (See Advertisement. *New York Times* 18 Nov. 1927.) In addition, the cast gave four extra matinees to celebrate the holidays, one on Sunday, 25 December 1927, and one on Sunday, 1 January 1928. (See Advertisement *New York Times* 18 Dec. 1927.) The cast also performed an additional holiday matinee on Monday, 26 December 1927. (See "Holiday Matinees – When They'll Be Given." *New York Times* 25 Dec. 1927.) Easter resulted in the fourth holiday matinee, which was presented on Monday, 9 April 1928. (See Advertisement. *New York Evening Post* 5 Apr. 1928.) The Actors' Fund matinee took place on Friday, 13 April 1927. (See "Actors' Fund Matinees Begin Today." *New York Times* 30 Mar. 1928.) Strangely, on 21 April 1928, *Billboard* reported the matinee took place on 14 April 1928. And the *New York Times* of 12 April 1928 claimed the performance would "take place today." However, most primary sources agree that the single Actor's Fund matinee occurred on Friday, 13 April 1928. (See, for example: Advertisement. *New York Times* 1 Apr. 1928; "Other Events." *New York Times* 8 Apr. 1928.) Another newspaper also reported that the matinee would be given on 13 April 1928 at the Republic Theater. ("Broadway Briefs" *The Daily Worker* [New York] 6 Apr. 1928.) That location seems to have been in error, given that all other publicity mentioned the Actors' Fund show would take place at the Fulton. Furthermore, it seems hard to believe the company would have unnecessarily relocated its sets for a single benefit performance.

76 "The Passing Show." *New York Sun* 31 Oct. 1927.

77 "Including the Hungarian." *New York Evening Post* 17 Dec. 1927.

78 "Vampires All." *Boston Transcript* 29 Oct. 1927.

79 "Weird New Facts about Vampires: Winged and Human." *Richmond Times-Dispatch* (Richmond, VA) 20 Nov. 1927.

80 Photo caption. *Vanity Fair* Dec. 1927.

Lugosi and Hazel Whitmore in 1928.

Chapter 37

California

Shortly after *Dracula–The Vampire Play* opened on Broadway, the *New York Herald-Tribune* published a fictional interview with "Count Dracula," all for the sake of a bit of humor. At one point the journalist asked the vampire if he had ever been to Hollywood. "Never," declared Count Dracula firmly, "to my certain knowledge!"[1] His answer was accurate; there had been no film or stage productions of *Dracula* mounted in California. Beginning in 1928, though, all of that began to change.

Orville D. Woodward, usually known as "O.D.," was a well-known head of stock companies in the American west, his career dating to the late nineteenth century.[2] During the spring of 1928, he signed an agreement with Horace Liveright that would let him produce a tour of *Dracula* on the Pacific Coast just weeks after it closed on Broadway.[3]

Originally he planned to hire most of the actors "in the West," some perhaps out of his own companies, but changed his mind after visiting New York.[4] Most of the Broadway cast headed to Los Angeles for a planned eight-week engagement, though Richard Lancaster replaced Herbert Bunston and Hazel Whitmore replaced Dorothy Peterson.[5] Whitmore later mentioned that she had seen the original Broadway production many times, with it holding a "peculiar fascination" for her.[6]

Woodward saw much value in retaining Lugosi, who would star in what became a three-city tour: Los Angeles, San Francisco, and Oakland. As recently as April 5, 1928, Lugosi had declared his intention to become an American citizen. At that time, he was living at 48 West 49th Street in New York. But he may have envisioned California for the next phase of his career, one that would focus on Hollywood.

Dracula arrived at the Biltmore Theater in Los Angeles, opening there on June 25. The *Los Angeles Times* announced that "Vampires – Old Style – Return in *Dracula*."[7] Ads promoted it as "The Season's Best Shudder." The word "best" had particular meaning, as the play faced local

Right: Published in the *Los Angeles Examiner* on June 24, 1928.

competition in the form of *The Spider* with William Courtenay, which opened at the Belasco on June 24. That play promised "thrills," "chills," "screams," and "laughs."[8]

For Lugosi and the rest of the company, *Dracula* in California was different than in New York. Rather than launching a new show, they were presenting a triumphant revival to an audience eager to see what had so captivated Broadway. Local critics seized upon the opportunity, with reviews quickly populating the newspapers:

> The result is much more successful than might be anticipated. ... It is interesting that this play is unrelieved by the comedy of the conventional mystery melodrama. To the contrary, horror is frankly invoked in its most terrible phases by Hamilton Deane and John Balderston. While this may offend some, it will surely bring others under its spell. ... Bela Lugosi ... gives a performance of restrained menace. The play's success lies largely in Lugosi's success in making Count Dracula believable yet sufficiently terrible.[9] – *Los Angeles Evening Herald*

> *Dracula* ... proved satisfying enough to the sensation hunters at the Biltmore last night. Those to whom excitement is not always entertainment, however, found the promised thrills less poignant than they had anticipated. The atmosphere of mystery is fairly well sustained. ... As a play, there is little enough to be said for the offering. [Lugosi's] fine physique and clear-cut features are valuable assets to his portrayal, and his slightly foreign accent is entirely suitable for the part....[10] – *Los Angeles Examiner*

Right: Published in the *Los Angeles Examiner* on June 24, 1928.

Toasts were drunk in blood, you might say, to the art of entertainment at the Biltmore Theater last night. ... *Dracula*, played much in dim light to aid in its grimness, needs the clearest diction and the most skillful spotlighting possible, which it doesn't always have. ... Lugosi ... plays the count with fair authority, but little inspirational force....[11] – *Los Angeles Evening Express*

Bela Lugosi, a giant Hungarian actor plays the title role of Count Dracula in a ghastly and effective make-up with blood-thirsty fervor and fine graveyard manner. He was given a hearty reception.[12] – *Los Angeles Record*

The play has a somber atmosphere, not unlike that of a Poe story. It conjures a dank and unhealthy spell of evil in its stronger moments. ... *Dracula* is essentially a curiosity, demanding much of the imagination. I cannot associate it with the popularity of the familiar mystery thriller, because it is of a different type altogether. Its tempo is slow and measured, and it presents only a very few extraordinary stage effects. It relies more on the ability of the actors and the dialogue for its dramatic intensity. The cumulative effect of what happens, however, is considerable. ... Bela Lugosi ... is admirably sinister in presence. He could not always be heard clearly at crucial moments in the play, but the character as he plays it exerts a peculiar malevolence. Calm, reposed and polished, he is a veritable modern Mephisto, whom you can hardly imagine stepping out of his

Weird Doings Reported by Play Troupe

The original Hamilton Deane dramatization of "Dracula," the Bram Stoker horror-thriller coming to the Biltmore on Monday night, was first presented in Deane's repertory company in Derby, Eng., on a Friday night "just to see what would happen"—to borrow a Stoker phrase.

It is unrecorded as to whether or not anything "happened" that night, but a great deal in the matter and manner of "spooks" has occurred since the first opening. There is a superstition prevalent that actors who have played in "Dracula" have been very successful in a professional way, but have been very unlucky in their private affairs.

In the New York company which will be seen here, many unnatural occurrences are reported to have happened prior to the New York opening. In New Haven, Ct., the stage manager, a man noted for his coolness under fire, became a temporary victim of aphasia. The leading woman lost her voice for no accountable reason. In Asbury Park, N. J., the photographer who was to take the scenes of the play for publicity purposes slipped and fell off the stage to the orchestra pit. The focusing screen of his camera was smashed without apparently being touched by human hands. Light signals from the stage manager to the electrician went "dead" for no seeming reason.

The peculiar part of it is that practically the same identical happenings occurred in England. As yet, nothing of this nature has happened to the company in Los Angeles.

CHILLS--THRILLS!

HAZEL WHITMORE and Bela Lugosi in a scene from "Dracula," now running at the Biltmore Theater, as seen by Artist Flora Smith.

Left: Published in the *Los Angeles Times* on June 22, 1928. Right: Published in the *Los Angeles Examiner* on July 5, 1928.

role even off the stage, his impersonation is so well sustained at every moment.[13] – *Los Angeles Times*

Audiences loved the play; O.D. Woodward confidently proclaimed, "the box office proves it." He hired a "nurse in regulation white costume and an oversupplied first-aid kit, with aromatic spirits of ammonia, smelling salts, and other restoratives" to be given to viewers who couldn't withstand the show's horror.[14] As of August 11, the nurse and the doorman compiled the following statistics:

> Faintings, 110; shrieks, 20 (per performance); left theater (first act), 19; left theater (second act), 150; left theater (third act), 1; returned (after revival), 100; return visits, 10 (per performance); husbands summoned to escort home wives, 10 (per performance); taxicab increase, 500 per cent.[15]

INTERVIEWER DAZED BY HAZE IN EERIE SCENE

BY EDWARD JAMES

A THICK amber light, almost tangible in its murkiness, illumines the lower five-foot stratum of a cavernous cell beneath the pavement near Fifth street and Grand avenue.

In a sort of phosphorescent haze above, two red orbs burn.

A visitor enters upon the eerie scene.

Immediately a book, suspended in the air, is laid upon a shelf.

A chair moves away from a table.

A pause and another chair moves forward to a position advantageous to the visitor.

Another pause and a door to a cupboard in a corner opens. A bottle and two glasses are transported to the table where they go into a huddle.

'BALANCING CAP'

A cap is removed from the bottle and it balances supernaturally above the two glasses.

A pungent odor fills the room. Smells like ginger ale!

The visitor lifts one of the glasses. The other comes up to meet it. They click together. The visitor drinks while the other glass is tilted in the opposite direction and then replaced upon the table.

Presently before a mirror above another table a pot of grease paint is jostled about. A powder puff does a jig. A tiny mascara brush flutters a moment and is replaced upon the table. A lipstick weaves back and forth, its image the only reflection in the glass.

A comb and brush do their usual sister act and then rejoin the other makeup utensils.

WEIRD OCCURENCES

A whisk-broom dances, ghost-like, in mid-air for a spell and lies down again.

A heavy walking stick comes from a corner and leans tipsily upon nothing.

The mystery of the glasses is repeated.

The heavy door into the corridor swings noiselessly. A faint movement of air stirs objects in the room. The door is closed and immediately from all about comes the concerted baying of dogs.

Bela Lugosi, "Dracula," the vampire in the strange play of that name at the Biltmore Theater, has been interviewed by the writer.

* * *

Left: Published in the *Los Angeles Examiner* on July 8, 1928. Above: Published in the *Los Angeles Times* on June 24, 1928.

Another account claimed that the cast members had an ongoing wager about which moments in the play would cause the greatest reaction. Stage manager Carl Reed (who also played Butterworth, the Attendant) decided "where the most responsive reactions occur and who shall buy the after-show malted milks."[16]

During its lengthy run, the press levied a good deal of attention on Lugosi, interviewing him on more than one occasion. One of them wrote:

The Hungarian, in spite of wide screen recognition in his native country, directed his aspirations to the American stage when he arrived in New York City [eight] years ago. Naturally that meant the immediate task of mastering the English language and this is what Lugosi set out to do.

Spare moments were spent in learning the tongue, and subsequent parts became easier to handle while his voice was surely and gradually acquiring faultless pronunciation.

Then came an assignment to his present role – a Hungarian count – and with it orders to affect a south-Hungarian accent. Forty-one weeks Lugosi enacted the part in the original New York company and his contract is certain to keep him at it for several

BELA LUGOSI, as Count Dracula, mastering his victim, BERNARD JUKES, as the maniac, in "Dracula," the current sensation at the Biltmore Theater.

more months. The truth is, he admits, his reversion to accent has affected his natural English-speaking, and figures the part has set him back two years.[17]

Journalist Alma Whitaker reported her own conversation with Lugosi in the form of a transcript:

'I believe you adore the role!' I gasped with a proper shudder.
'Oh, surely, madame, greatly so. It is a marvelous play. We keep nurses and physicians in the theater every night...'
'For the so-to-say blood transfusions? Heavens, is it as realistic as all that?' I faltered.
'No, no. For the people in the audience who faint,' he reassured me, pleasantly. One could see he counted that day lost on which no hysterical fainting humans were carried from the audience during the performance of what he certainly regards as his masterpiece...
'Only one thing I fear,' he confided, with a sly smile. 'That after I play this Dracula some more I become too like him myself... But you understand I am not really a bad character in this role. It is a curse upon me. I am to be pitied, not condemned. I am a vampire because I must....'[18]

Charles Van Sloan and Hazel Whitmore are seen in a tense scene from "Dracula," at the Biltmore, in which the Crucifix is used to cast out the devil spirits which haunt the bodies of the human vampire's victims.

Opposite Page: Published in the *Los Angeles Examiner* on July 1, 1928.
Left: Published in the *Los Angeles Evening Herald* on July 21, 1928.

During its stay in Los Angeles, *Dracula* celebrated what was said to be its 1,500th performance, the number (if accurate) apparently combining numbers from the American and British companies.[19] The successful run lasted nearly two months before closing on August 18, by which time allegedly fifty percent of "Hollywood screen stars" had seen it.[20] Members of the California State Spiritualist Society also attended the show.[21]

At the box office, *Dracula* generated weekly grosses from $10,000 to over $12,000 during June and July before hitting a "slump" in August that dropped to $8,000 and then finally $6,000.[22]

The cast marked the close of *Dracula* with two farewell parties. The first, hosted by Mr. and

Mrs. Eddie Phillips, was held at the Sea Breeze Beach Club, a fashionable location in Santa Monica; the second was held at the nearby private beach home of Mr. and Mrs. Jimmie Fulton.[23] Lugosi then departed for San Francisco on the morning of August 19.[24] The Biltmore followed *Dracula* not with another play, but rather with screenings of Cecil B. DeMille's film *The Godless Girl* (1928).[25]

Dracula opened at San Francisco's Columbia Theater on August 20, drawing "fairly heavy trade" during its first week, despite competition from a local production of *The Spider*.[26] Once again Woodward had a nurse on duty, because "fourteen faints is about the customary matinee tribute to Bram Stoker's eerie drama."[27] Critical reaction in the local press was as follows:

> Listen all ye who crave the nerve-wracking, the blood-curdling, the super-exciting in the theater, you have the greatest thrill of your life in store for you if you have not seen *Dracula*. ... The mere mystery play now becomes passé. It is relegated to the background and pales into insignificance when compared to the stage version of Stoker's wildest of imaginative stories. ... The truly remarkable feature of this thriller is that it could be so capably produced as a play and one that is exceedingly well done. ... Of course there are screams and many of them. In one scene last night a lady cried: 'My god, don't do that.'... Lugosi is the title part and he makes the character a dreaded creature. A monster in human form. His dramatic work is particularly effective.[28] – *San Francisco Bulletin*

> The ordinary mystery thriller has its moments of relieving laughter. Instead of merriment, *Dracula* adds horrors to its thrills. The audience supplies its own relief, if any. Bela Lugosi, noted Hungarian actor, displayed all the uncanniness of a Svengali commanding Trilby to sing as she had never sung before. ... Lugosi is commanding in his height and bearing ... and brings to the role a distinctive polish and suavity. But he will scarcely become a matinee idol.[29] – *San Francisco Call and Post*

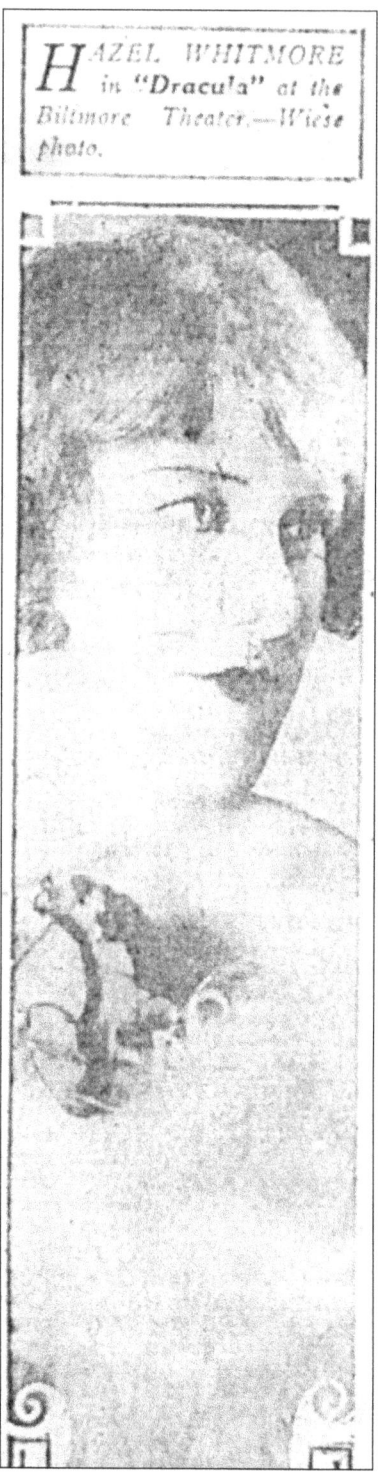

Published in the *Los Angeles Examiner* on June 24, 1928.

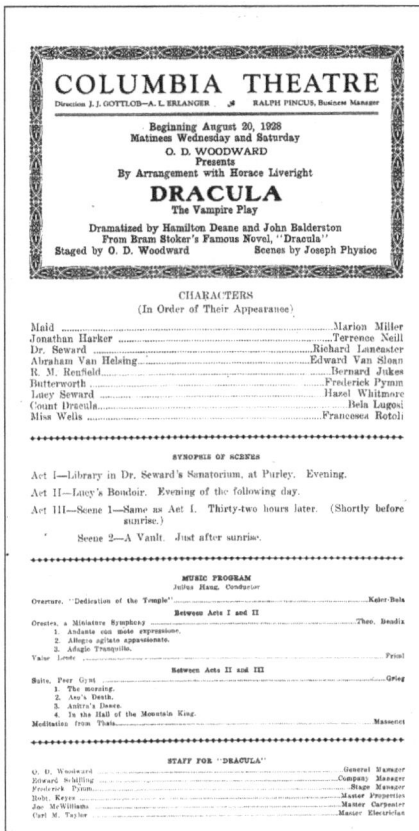
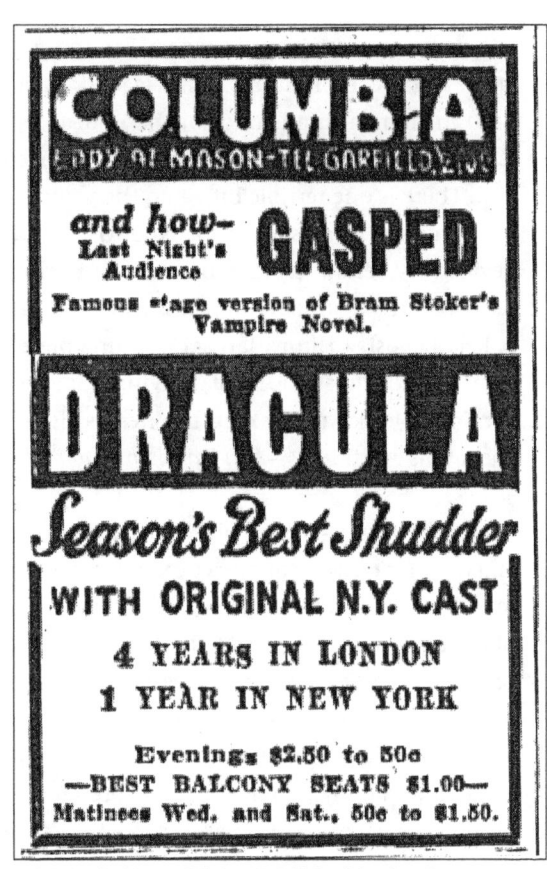

Above Left: *(Courtesy of the Free Library of Philadelphia)*. Above Right: Published in the *San Francisco News* on August 21, 1928. Below Left and Right: Published in the *San Francisco News* on August 28, 1928.

Hazel Whitmore who has leading feminine role in "Dracula" at the Columbia.

Gary D. Rhodes | Bill Kaffenberger

You can laugh at it as a farrago of nonsense, or shudder at the terrible implications of the legend – a belief firmly fixed in human minds once of the undead. And as it is fanciful and horrific, so it must be, and is, played.

... There is one terrible bit when the vampire takes the girl in his arms, bares her throat and with a movement of devilish joy, sets his teeth in her flesh and drains her body of its blood – a shuddering, shivering, horrible episode. ... Bela Lugosi, a Hungarian actor of fine presence, is the ghastly and ghostly Dracula, giving a performance of considerable power, making the nerves tingle when he goes at his evil trade.[30] – *San Francisco Chronicle*

Go see *Dracula* – IF such playful activities appeal to you – and you won't need a chiropractic treatment for months and months. Your nervous system will give the old spine enough of a rub-down to last at least that long. ... [A]s in the case of spook plays that have gone before, last night's audience seemed quite willing to put itself in the right frame of mind, for it screamed at frequent intervals, and yelled warnings every time the mystic forces got too obstreperous. ... Bela Lugosi, Hungarian actor, makes a ghastly Count Dracula, with piercing eyes, hollow voice and sinister manner – just as he should be.[31] – *San Francisco Examiner*

We saw the show. Then, at the theater door, we parted, she to go home – I to come here to my desk to set onto paper my impressions of the play we had just seen. And the bet I have made with myself is that when I have finished and get home, I will find the wife waiting up for me. For *Dracula* is that sort of a play. The vampire – meaning bloodsucker – play. It is horrible – bloodcurdling. ... But *Dracula* is fascinating – terribly so. I wouldn't have missed it for the world. Nor would any of the big, first night audience. We all had a shudderingly good time. ... The portrayal of Bela Lugosi in the part of Count Dracula, the vampire, was startlingly fine, both in makeup and in acting.[32] – *San Francisco News*

While in San Francisco, a journalist referred to Lugosi's Dracula as a "green wraith," his description stemming from

Above: Published in the *San Francisco News* on August 30, 1928. Below: Published in the *San Francisco News* on August 24, 1928.

Published in the *Oakland Tribune* on September 8, 1928.

the ongoing use of green flood and spotlights in the play.[33] In an interview, he sought Lugosi's views about acting in America versus Europe:

> The trouble Lugosi finds in American acting as an institution is in the fact that there are so many actors, and competition is so big and free that the actors as individuals never attain the broad experience of those in Europe.
>
> 'On the continent,' he explains, 'an actor gets no encouragement to proceed with his career unless he is really talented. There he is not chosen as a particular type and doomed to continue as that type for all his professional career. He gains attention because he can create types instead of merely being types. Therefore he is versatile in a variety of dramatic expressions.
>
> 'American acting would be better if it submitted to some such requirements....'[34]

When *Dracula* closed in San Francisco on September 8, 1928, *Variety* called the show's tenure "successful," having gone "neck and neck" with a local production of *The Spider*.[35] The Columbia Theater then reverted to screening roadshow films.[36]

Dracula next descended on Oakland, playing the 12th Street Theater from September 9 to 15, 1928. By that time, Harry Walker replaced Bernard Jukes as Renfield and Maurice Franklin replaced Edward Van Sloan as Van Helsing. The two local newspaper reviews were generally positive:

> Those cold shots will meander up and down your spinal column as never before when you see *Dracula*, famous English horror play – amen, brother, there's a truthful press

Left: Photograph promoting the Oakland performance, as published in the *San Francisco Chronicle* on September 8, 1928. Right: Photograph promoting the Oakland performance, as published in the *San Francisco Chronicle* on September 9, 1928. Below: Photograph promoting the Oakland performance, as published in the *San Francisco Chronicle* on September 6, 1928.

agent – which opened a week's engagement last night. Not in a long, long time has such a company graced the boards of a local playhouse. ... Bela Lugosi ... sets nerves a tingle with a powerful performance.[37] – *Oakland Post Enquirer*

If you learned about vampires from Rud Kipling, go around to the Twelfth street theater and be re-educated. No rag and bone and hank of hair this Dracula. ... Harry Walker's lunatic is splendid, if a looney can be splendid. Maurice Franklin portrays Van Helsing deftly and Bela Lugosi is a nerve-searing Dracula.[38] – *Oakland Tribune*

As for audiences, one critic mentioned, "That woman in back of us screamed every time the vampire dipped his beak in Lucy's blood. She scrambled our nerves with her yelping."[39] Another complained of a "roughneck gang of hoodlums" at the opening night audience who were "noticeably noisy."[40]

Dracula–The Vampire Play was clearly becoming a national phenomenon, no longer restricted to Broadway or even the Pacific

246 BECOMING DRACULA

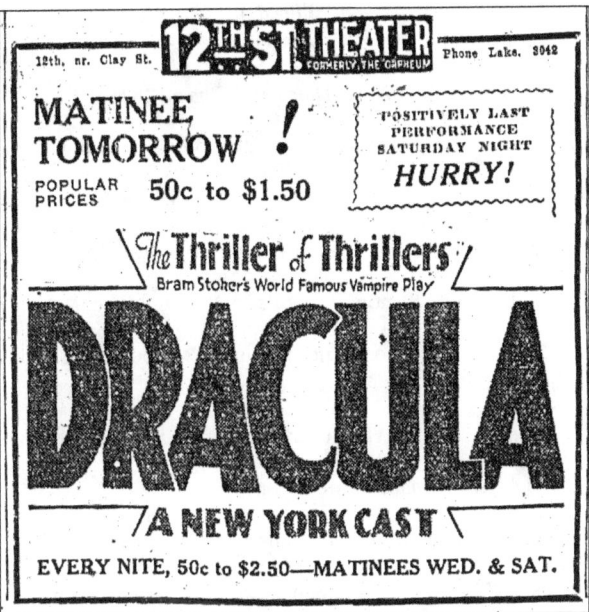

Left: Published in the *Oakland Post-Enquirer* on September 7, 1928. Right: Published in the *Oakland Post-Enquirer* on September 11, 1928.

Coast, as new versions of it were soon being staged elsewhere in America. But those companies did not star Lugosi. In a phone call with famed columnist Louella O. Parsons, he explained his reluctance to be tied to a national tour:

> [H]e would much rather spend a few idle weeks in San Francisco than accompany *Dracula* over the fly-by-night circuit. ... So after the current week in Oakland, the very capable Hungarian actor... will sit down awhile and bask in San Francisco's sun ... to enjoy the feeling of being 'at liberty.'[41]

The green lights temporarily dimmed, but they did not fade. The wraith had visited Hollywood, and it was there that he would return. "The vampire can wait," as Van Helsing explains in the play.

Endnotes

1. Bolton, Whitney. "Count Dracula, Vampire, Admits He Goes on a Bat Every Night." *New York Herald-Tribune* 9 Oct. 1927.

2. "Orville D. Woodward." *New York Times* 10 Jan. 1946. For more information on Woodward, see Ehiers, D. Layne. *American Stock Company Management as Reflected in the Career of O.D. Woodward, 1897-1922*. Ph.D. Dissertation. 1995.

3. "Theatrical Notes." *New York Times* 15 May 1928.

4   "Casting Coast *Dracula*." *Billboard* 12 May 1928. See also "Theatrical and Picture Gossip." *Waterloo Courier* (Waterloo, IA) 19 May 1928.

5   "Woodward Takes Over *Dracula*." *Billboard* 26 May 1928.

6   "Howling Dogs at *Dracula* Are Actors 'Woof-Woofing.'" *Los Angeles Times* 1 July 1928.

7   "Vampires – Old Style – Return in *Dracula*." *Los Angeles Times* 13 June 1928.

8   Advertisement. *Los Angeles Examiner* 24 June 1928.

9   "Audience at Biltmore Under Its Spell." *Los Angeles Evening Herald* 26 June 1928.

10 Lawrence, Florence. "London Vampire Melodrama Has Unusual Setting." *Los Angeles Examiner* 26 June 1928.

11 "*Dracula* No Friend for an Anemic Person." *Los Angeles Evening Express* 20 May 1929.

12 *Los Angeles Record* 26 June 1928.

13 Schallert, Edwin. "*Dracula* Calls Forth Shudder." *Los Angeles Times* 27 June 1928.

14 "Nurse! Please! Smelling Salts!" *Los Angeles Examiner* 5 July 1928.

15 "They Shriek, Faint Daily at *Dracula*." *Los Angeles Times* 11 Aug. 1928.

16 "Wagers Made on Big Thrill by Play Cast." *Los Angeles Times* 10 July 1928.

17 "Return to Native Accent Retards Actor's English." *Los Angeles Times* 29 July 1928.

18 Whitaker, Alma. "Lugosi, Creator Of Dracula Role, Is Courtly Hungarian." *Los Angeles Times* 17 June 1928.

19 "In the Footlight Realm." *Los Angeles Times* 8 July 1928.

20 "Professionals Like Thriller." *Los Angeles Times* 21 July 1928.

21 "Spiritualistic Slant Arouses Interest Here." *Los Angeles Times* 14 July 1928.

22 "L.A. Grosses." *Variety* 4 July 1928; "L.A. Grosses." *Variety* 11 July 1928; "L.A. Grosses." *Variety* 18 July 1928; "L.A. Grosses." *Variety* 25 July 1928; "L.A. Grosses." *Variety* 1 Aug. 1928; "L.A. Grosses." *Variety* 15 Aug. 1928; "L.A. Grosses." *Variety* 22 Aug. 1928.

23 Nye, Myra. "Society of Cinemaland." *Los Angeles Times* 26 Aug. 1928.

24 Ibid.

25 "*Dracula* Out – Film In." *Variety* 8 Aug. 1928.

26 "Frisco Grosses." *Variety* 29 Aug. 1928.

27 "*Dracula*, at Columbia, Eerie Drama." *San Francisco Chronicle* 25 Aug. 1928.

28 Gillaspey, A. Fulton. "Columbia's Weird Play Fascinates." *San Francisco Bulletin* 21 Aug. 1928.

29 Johnson, Fred. "Shivers, Horrors in Stoker Drama." *San Francisco Call and Post* 21 Aug. 1928.

30 Warren, George C. "*Dracula* Shivers and Shudders Through at the Columbia." *San Francisco Chronicle* 21 Aug. 1928.

31 Waite, Edgar. "*Dracula* Has Joyful Load of Horrors." *San Francisco Examiner* 21 Aug. 1928.

32 Swint, Curran D. "*Dracula* at Columbia Is Startling." *San Francisco News* 21 Aug. 1928.

33 "Count Dracula Practices Few Mysteries Off Stage." *San Francisco Examiner* 26 Aug. 1928.

34 Ibid.

35 "Frisco Grosses." *Variety* 12 Sept. 1928; "*Dracula*, $14,000, Frisco." *Variety* 5 Sept. 1928.

36 "Frisco Grosses." *Variety* 12 Sept. 1928.

37 West, Dick. "*Dracula*, Weird Drama Opens at 12th St." *Oakland Post-Enquirer* 10 Sept. 1928.

38 "Blood-Sucking Dracula Roams 12th St. Stage." *Oakland Tribune* 10 Sept. 1928.

39 "Blood-Sucking Dracula Roams 12th St. Stage."

40 West, "*Dracula*, Weird Drama Opens at 12th St."

41 Parsons, Louella O. "Wm. Boyd Has Lead In Big Pathe Picture." *San Francisco Examiner* 13 Sept. 1928.

Lugosi in 1929. *(Courtesy of John Antosiewicz)*

Chapter 38

Broken Battlements

"It's absolute hell …
and of course I can't do any work."
–Deane & Balderston, *Dracula–The Vampire Play*

Some critics applauded the Broadway version of *Dracula* for its bizarre story; others for its acting. At least one praised the settings designed by Joseph Physioc.[1] Mysterious and evocative, particularly when cast in green lighting, the sets were in some respects complicated, necessarily so given special effects that ranged from a flying bat to a trap door that allowed Dracula to vanish.

And then there was the background. Consider the scene in which "Dracula's hand appears from back of couch, then his face. Lucy screams; swoons."[2] With the exception of a red spot thrown through the fireplace, the lights go out, at least until Van Helsing turns them back on. Dracula has disappeared; a bat flies about the room, then out the window. In order to create the effect, Lugosi had to crawl quickly on all fours in the darkness to a bookcase that featured a trick door. Directions for its use were as follows:

> A small bolt at top of the inside of the bookcase door that swings open will assist in keeping this door closed except when in use. It is better to have *Dracula* manipulate the bolt than for a stagehand to handle it. The sliding part of the bookcase, however, *should be* manipulated by a stagehand.[3]

Sometimes actors could do everything they needed to do. But sometimes they needed assistance from others, from those in the background, those behind the scenes.

Just six days after *Dracula* closed on Broadway, Lugosi signed a non-exclusive agreement with

Hungarian-born Dr. Edmond Pauker, an agent and play broker in New York who had also served as representative for the Society of Hungarian Playwrights.[4] The two had been friends since at least 1924. Lugosi wrote him on May 25, 1928:

> Confirming our verbal understanding, I hereby authorize you to act as my personal representative in order to procure a contract for me with one of the American Film companies. It is understood and agreed that if within a year from tonight a contract is made with a film company, it shall be made exclusively through you or through your Hollywood representative.[5]

Pauker's representative was a man they referred to solely by his last name, Lichtig. Presumably this was Harry Lichtig, of the firm of Lichtig and Englander, who represented such notables as Hungarian-born film director Pál Fejős (Paul Fejos) and actor Wyndham Standing, who appeared with Lugosi in *The Rejected Woman* (1924).[6] Lichtig would thus help Lugosi get work at movie studios during and after *Dracula*'s West Coast tour in the summer of 1928.

Lugosi clearly had his eyes set on film roles, but he continued to think about acting in the theater, perhaps as insurance against the travails of Hollywood. On July 4, he sent a telegram to Pauker, asking him about two possibilities: "Try to obtain part of Holbrook Blinn [*The*] *Play is the Thing*. How about [Victor Herbert's] *The Red Mill*?"[7] Pauker replied the next day:

> As to *The Play's the Thing*, nothing will be decided until Gilbert Miller returns from Europe, which will be some time in August. I assure [you] that I will take up the matter with him as soon as he arrives.
>
> As to *Red Mill*, I will have to inquire when Belasco intends to put it on. I do not know whether he has seen you in *Dracula* and whether it would not be necessary for him to use you and have a conversation with you before deciding whether he could give you the part ... please inform me how much longer you intend to be in Los Angeles.[8]

Lugosi's response implied that he was growing worried that film work wasn't forthcoming, even if he did not yet know why:

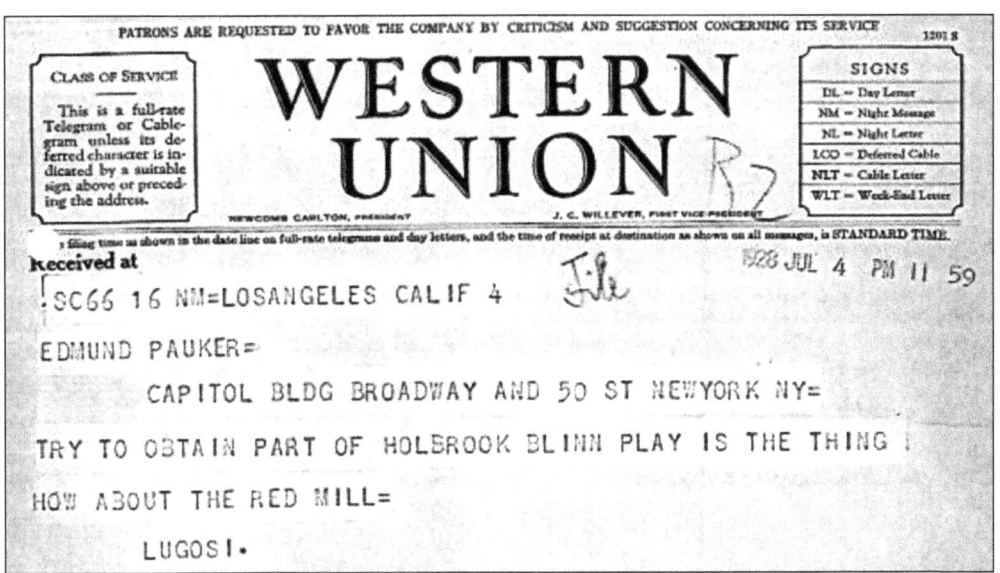

We are going to close *Dracula* in Los Angeles at Aug. 18th and open in San Francisco for four or six weeks. I am at liberty to come to New York if something better is offered. Lichtig will always know where to rich [*sic*] me.⁹

Pauker's office answered Lugosi a couple of weeks later, the delay probably adding to his mounting concerns:

> Dr. Pauker will return from his vacation next week, when he will attend to the matter mentioned in your letter.
> Meanwhile we have given your address to Mrs. Strauss of First National Pictures, who will undoubtedly write you care of Lichtig and Englander....¹⁰

After getting *Dracula*'s West Coast producer O. D. Woodward involved, Lugosi sent Pauker another telegram:

> Since my producer Woodward bought west [coast] rights of *Play is the Thing* on interest kindly see Miller's office re my playing Blinn part Stop This telegram Woodward's suggestion owing to my big personal star success.¹¹

Lugosi apparently believed *Dracula* could land him a major role in a non-horror play. Pauker responded:

> Inasmuch as Gilbert Miller is still in Europe, I got in touch with his office and proposed you for the role. They said that they have already made their arrangements with Mr. Woodward and that as far as they know Blinn's part has already been filled by a star widely known throughout the country…
>
> Should the role not be definitely filled … I shall be pleased to take up the matter with Gilbert Miller after his arrival.[12]

Henry Lichtig (left), pictured with film director Albert S. Rogell in 1926.

What Pauker did immediately thereafter is unknown, but it is evident that Lugosi did not get the roles he wanted. In fact, there were no roles at all, onstage or onscreen.

In October of 1928, Lugosi expressed his anxieties and anger to Pauker in a personal letter:

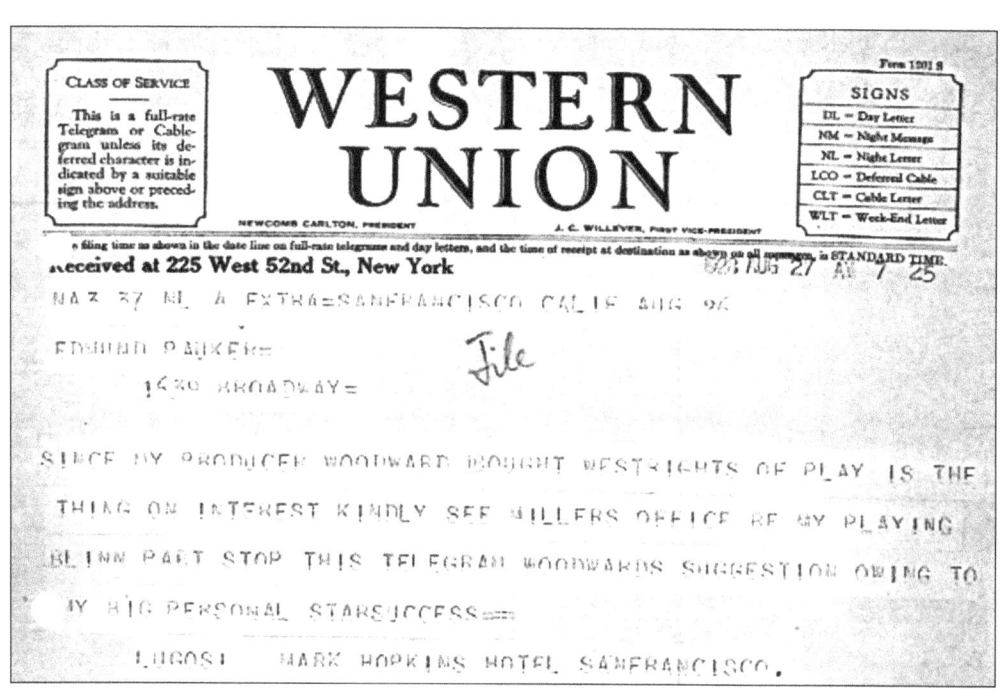

Some time ago, when I arrived in Hollywood, I got in contact with Lichtig. I played *Dracula* rather successfully every evening for two entire months while [Lichtig] did nothing. Only in the fifth month – when I have not been performing anything for two months already – had he got the idea that I should provide him with some photos, which he would show to some *casting directors!*

By now, I have been unemployed for quite some time. Your representative, Lichtig, is incompetent, you are 3000 miles away, and one needs to eat: thus, I am asking you to cancel our current contract (the one with Lichtig), the content of which, in this situation, is not making any sense at all and it lacks any kind of ethical basis.

I am happy for your success. In case you could do something for me in N.Y., I would be grateful.

I already informed Lichtig that I will ask for the cancellation of our contract, which, after all, he accepted naturally.[13]

Pauker responded to Lugosi's complaints with notable speed and diplomacy:

I … regret to note that Mr. Lichtig did not do anything in your behalf. He should have involved some of the film producers to see you while you were playing *Dracula* in Los Angeles. I wrote him to do so when you left New York for Los Angeles and I also wrote him to do his very best for you in every way to get you a film contract.

… I regret that you did not inform me before of Mr. Lichtig's inactivity in this matter. I would have withdrawn this proposition from him and would have referred it to some other agent. Mr. Lichtig is not my general representative in Hollywood. I merely commission him from time to time with certain matters.

I do not want to stand in your way or deprive you of an opportunity to obtain a contract in Hollywood. I therefore agree to dissolve our contract with regard to placing you with the picture companies and you are at liberty to use an agent's services as you may deem best. I wish you success most sincerely.

… Should an opportunity come up for you in New York, I will get in touch with you.[14]

Lichtig had apparently squandered the opportunity of enlisting producers to see Lugosi onstage in Los Angeles. At least that was Lugosi's belief. Perhaps Lichtig and his associates had worked much harder than Lugosi realized.

In *Dracula–The Vampire Play*, Jonathan Harker tells Van Helsing, "This all seems a nightmare." Even with help from others, life was in turmoil, its fortifications crumbling, seemingly broken, at least until daybreak.

Lugosi in 1929.

Endnotes

1 Leland, Gordon M. "Fulton." *Billboard* 15 Oct. 1927.

2 Deane, Hamilton and John L. Balderston. *Dracula: The Vampire Play in Three Acts* (New York: Samuel French, 1933).

3 Ibid. Emphasis in original.

4 "Ernest Vajda." *Motion Picture News* 24 Oct. 1925.

5 Lugosi, Bela. Letter to Dr. Edmond Pauker, 25 May 1928. [Available in the Edmond Pauker Papers, 1910-1957, Box 42, Folder 11 at the New York Public Library for the Performing Arts, Dorothy and Lewis B. Cullman Center.]

6 Advertisement. *Film Daily 1928 Year Book* (New York: Film Daily, 1928); Advertisement. *Wid's Weekly* Jan. 1925.

7 Lugosi, Bela. Telegram to Dr. Edmond Pauker, 4 July 1928. [Available in the Edmond Pauker Papers.]

8 Pauker, Dr. Edmond. Letter to Bela Lugosi, 5 July 1928. [Available in the Pauker Papers.]

9 Lugosi, Bela. Personal note to Dr. Edmond Pauker, 12 Aug. 1928. [Available in the Pauker Papers.]

10 Secretary for Dr. Edmond Pauker. Letter to Bela Lugosi, 22 Aug. 1928. [Available in the Pauker Papers.]

11 Lugosi, Bela. Telegram to Dr. Edmond Pauker, 27 Aug. 1928. [Available in the Pauker Papers.]

12 Pauker, Dr. Edmond. Letter to Bela Lugosi, 29 Aug. 1928. [Available in the Pauker Papers.]

13 Lugosi, Bela. Letter to Dr. Edmond Pauker, 22 Oct. 1928. [Available in the Pauker Papers.]

14 Pauker, Dr. Edmond. Letter to Bela Lugosi, 28 Oct. 1928. [Available in the Pauker Papers.]

Publicity portrait of Lugosi in *Prisoners* (1929).
(Courtesy of John Antosiewicz)

Chapter 39

Talkies

> "If [Lugosi] gives talking pictures a fair trial, I predict
> he will be a strong sensation, as he is one of the
> strongest personalities of the stage."⁶⁴
> – *Detroit Free Press*, 1928

Less than two months after *Dracula–The Vampire Play* opened on Broadway, Hungarian actor Paul Vincenti described "mythic vampires" to an interviewer at the *Los Angeles Times*:

There is no relation, except symbolically ... between the modernized term 'vampire' as used in the picture business, for example, and the old and dread superstition of undead creatures which attacked living beings. However, so potent is the belief in some parts of the old world, that sacred wafers and garlic are used as a protection against the onslaught of vampires.[1]

Vincenti was new to Hollywood films, working at the time as a member of First National's stock company.[2]

When Lugosi's Dracula descended on Los Angeles in 1928, his vampire held many audiences in his thrall, among them the film elite. "He had already impressed Gloria Swanson and Erich Von Stroheim during the Broadway version," one journalist announced. "They dressed him in stalwart, bizarre uniforms and tested him for Gloria's next picture, but he proved so tall that Gloria was submerged beside him."[3]

Being on the West Coast potentially opened the door to more possibilities. "I like your [California], and who knows – I may go into pictures here," he confided in a writer.[4] Another reported that Lugosi regularly socialized with Vilma Banky, Lya de Putti, Ernest Vajda, Victor Varconi (Mihály Várkonyi), Michael Curtiz (Mihály Kertész), Alexander Korda (Sándor Korda), and other Hungarians in Hollywood during the summer of 1928.[5] The press claimed, "Lugosi is accepted, and, in fact, much sought after in the best homes of the movie colony."[6]

Thus, it is hardly surprising that Lugosi suggested adapting *Dracula* for the silver screen. In 1928, the *Los Angeles Evening Herald* reported the following:

> With the talking equipment Lugosi believes the screen version could successfully electrify audiences with almost the same effectiveness of the speaking production. But, he contends, the playgoer's state of mind is different from the picture viewer's.
>
> When living people are on the stage it naturally lends a reality to the movement before them, whereby picture audiences are apt to shake off any alarmed feeling which results when the emotions are excited by reminding themselves they are at a movie, Lugosi believes.[7]

Lugosi would not appear in a film version of *Dracula* in 1928 or 1929. But he may have been shocked to read that Universal Pictures secured the rights to the story.

In October 1928, the *Exhibitors Daily Review* told readers, "The vampire-mystery story will be a 100 percent dialogue and sound picture, with Conrad Veidt slated for the chief role of Count Dracula."[8] The same news appeared elsewhere, including in the pages of a fan magazine called *Motion Picture*.[9] In actual fact, Universal had not obtained the rights. The reports were premature, but they do illustrate the studio's growing interest in a property it had previously eschewed.

Another studio contacted Lugosi, not for a horror role, but instead for a drama about the travails of love: *The Veiled Woman*. At times during its production, the Fox Film Corporation referred to it as *The Veiled Lady*. Perhaps they considered alternate titles given that the Renco Film Company had produced a film with Marguerite Snow called *The Veiled Woman* (1922).

The new Fox film headlined Paul Vincenti, who had spoken so knowledgably about

Bela Lugosi, famous for his interpretation of the weird and fiendish Count Dracula in the stage play, makes his screen debut in the Fox production, "The Veiled Woman."

Published in the *Los Angeles Times* on December 9, 1928.

Lugosi and Lia Tora in *The Veiled Woman* (1928). *(Courtesy of Dennis Phelps)*

Lugosi and Lia Tora in *The Veiled Woman*.

This Page and Opposite: Lugosi and Lia Tora in *The Veiled Woman*.

vampires in 1927, and Lia Tora, a Brazilian actress. It marked their first starring roles. Actor Josef Swickard, who had been cast alongside Lugosi in the unfinished film *The Silent Witness* in 1927, played a supporting character.[10] Ivan Lebedeff, known for his work in *The Sorrows of Satan* (1926), also appeared in *The Veiled Woman*, as did Lupita Tovar, who would later play Eva in Universal's Spanish-language film *Drácula* (1931).

Together with her husband Julio De Moraes, Lia Tora wrote the script for *The Veiled Woman*. Set in Paris, its plot revolves around the beautiful woman Nanon, who wears a veil and rescues

From the pressbook for *The Veiled Woman*.

a young lady from the designs of a nefarious man. Nanon relates memories about the terrible men from her own past. She also describes her great love, Pierre, who went to prison in her place after she killed a villain. Nanon then takes the young woman home in a cab. Pierre is the driver, and the two reunite.

Emmett J. Flynn, known for such movies as *East Lynne* (1925) with Alma Rubens, directed *The Veiled Woman*.[11] *Variety* claimed it would be a "sound picture."[12] The production was supposed to begin on August 28, 1928, though there might have been a short delay.[13] As of September 20, the *Exhibitors Daily Review* reported that *The Veiled Woman* was "nearing completion."[14] By October 10, the same publication wrote that the film had been "newly finished."[15] Ten days later, *Exhibitors Herald and Moving Picture World* also reported that it was "completed."[16]

But strangely, on October 16, 1928, another trade announced that Byron Douglas had been "added" to the cast.[17] At roughly the same time (and certainly prior to November 1), Lugosi was contracted.[18] *Variety* even told readers that Lugosi would be "featured" in *The Veiled Woman*, having "attracted the attention of film producers when he appeared in a local legit presentation of *Dracula*."[19] *Exhibitors Daily Review* provided further details:

> *The Veiled Lady*, which Emmett Flynn is directing, will have Bela Lugosi in the role of [a] heavy. Mr. Lugosi is a Hungarian and a newcomer to the screen. ... This will be a talkie production.[20]

The trade was not alone in stating that the film would mark Lugosi's screen debut; the *Los Angeles Times* twice printed the same inaccurate information.[21] However, the most curious detail that both publications mentioned was that the movie would not just feature sound (which could have just been synchronized music and sound effects), but would actually be a talkie.[22]

On November 24, 1928, the *Hollywood Filmograph*'s critic responded to a preview of *The Veiled Woman* held at the Uptown Theater. "This picture did not click," he wrote, due to the "lack of a good screen story."[23] On December 8, the *Motion Picture News* told readers that director Flynn was "out" at Fox, even though he was originally slated to make another film for them.[24]

Had Fox fired Flynn because of *The Veiled Woman*'s troubles? Had these troubles necessitated reshoots and changes that led to Douglas and Lugosi being cast? Answers to both questions are likely yes.

On December 19, the *Exhibitors Daily Review* published a review, referring to the film as *Veiled Lady* (without the word *The*). The verdict: "The story is nothing new and the production drags very often." However, it does continue to say, "Kenneth Thompson and Lu Gosi [sic] give capable support."

What role did Lugosi play? One article claimed that he played the suitor who Nanon kills, which was probably the case, given action depicted in surviving publicity stills, including one that shows Lugosi in agony, as if he has been injured. Another article claimed he played a diplomat, though it seems Walter McGrail played that character.[25] Unfortunately, the film's pressbook doesn't mention Lugosi at all.[26]

Adding to the confusion is a newspaper article from 1929 that announced, "Walter MacGrail [sic], who has done such sterling work in many Fox productions, has replaced Bela Lugosi in the prologue and epilogue of *The Veiled Woman*, the Emmett Flynn production now nearing completion...."[27]

Perhaps Lugosi's role had changed. Perhaps he was originally to speak at the beginning and end of the film, but for some reason that did not come to pass. When Fox released *The Veiled Woman* under that title on April 14, 1929, it did feature synchronized sound, but no dialogue. But even if the overall soundtrack was music-only, the film still could have featured a spoken prologue and epilogue.

In any event, a critic for the fan magazine *Photoplay* was distinctly unimpressed:

> Not good, not bad; the most interesting feature being its array of foreign faces. ... The captivating Lia's husband wrote the script but he didn't do right by the 'little woman,' for it's a trite tale.[28]

Industry trades didn't generally review release prints until June of 1929, presumably because *The Veiled Woman* didn't play a major New York City theater until that summer. *Variety* strangely claimed the film was "French Made," an error apparently caused by the film's Parisian setting.[29]

Harrison's Reports complained the film was "not only 'rotten,' but also unsuitable to be shown to the family circle," given its "sordid" content.[30] Importantly, the trade published differing lengths for the silent and synchronized versions, which might be another indication that the sound version did have a prologue and epilogue. At any rate, on September 21, 1929, the same publication judged that *The Veiled Woman* was "poor as sound and worse as silent."[31]

Billboard's review offered the following details, which refers only to music:

> [T]his Fox production is offered with [a] synchronized score. ... Rothafel (Roxy) created the music in New York. ... The picture may be played in silent houses, as it is complete without the score, titles telling the story. A fair effort only....[32]

Spoken prologue and epilogue or not, some exhibitors advertised the film using words and phrases like "Movietone," "sound," "see and hear," and even "talking," thus implying that the film's narrative featured spoken dialogue.[33] Such misrepresentations were hardly unknown at the dawn of the talkie.

Given the major changes underway in the film industry, everyone in Hollywood was talking about talkies in 1928. Lugosi himself said the following in October of that year:

> Talking films will educate the public into expecting good actors in the smallest speaking parts on the stage. ... It will no longer be possible for a stage producer to engage a few artists for the principal roles and use 'fill-ins' for the minor parts. The American stage will in time adopt the European system, where the players are like the musicians in a symphony orchestra, all artists, and one yielding the center of public attention to the other as the character of the work requires.
>
> Experience in talking pictures will help the stage actor immensely. I know from personal experience, having appeared in a silent picture in Europe, how studying one's appearances on the screen helps to increase the effectiveness of the performance. The study of the voice on the screen will help the actor just so much more.
>
> Talking pictures are still in an elemental form and do not yet do justice to the stage artist. But in time they will.[34]

Lugosi and Corinne Griffith in *Prisoners*.

Lugosi told another interviewer that talkies would become a "fruitful field for stage talent."[35]

He was hoping to enjoy fruit from that very field. Whatever the truth of the prologue and epilogue in *The Veiled Woman*, Lugosi's first talkie became *Prisoners* (1929), which First National originally titled *Paid For*.[36] The film was based on Ferenc Molnár's 1908 novel *Rabok* (*Prisoners*), with the story set in Budapest and Vienna. In 1928, the same studio had released Alexander (Sándor) Korda's *The Yellow Lily*, a film version of another Hungarian classic, Lajos Bíró's *A sárga liliom*.

Forrest Halsey adapted the Molnár novel and wrote the film's dialogue; he had earlier written the screenplay for *The Sorrows of Satan* (1927).[37] William A. Seiter directed the story of Riza (Corinne Griffith), who steals money from a café. Nicholas (Ian Keith), her attorney, soon learns that she stole in order to buy better clothes in order to attract his attention. The two love each other. Nicholas decides to marry Riza in eight months' time, once she is released from prison.

Publicity for the film claimed that Griffith went to Hungary to learn more about the culture:

> ... she traveled all through Hungary studying the manners and customs of the people, taking photographs of houses and inns and farms she thought would be of value to the technical department. She talked with the women and sat in several cheap restaurants to watch the waitresses, because that was what she had to play in *Prisoners*.[38]

Corinne Griffith in *Prisoners* (1929).

There is in fact no proof whatsoever that Griffith went to Hungary. Rather, shooting began when Griffith and her husband, producer Walter Morosco, returned from a trip to the Grand Canyon.[39]

Griffith opened a bottle of champagne on the set to celebrate the fact that *Prisoners* would inaugurate First National's new sound recording system.[40] *Variety* also touted the fact that *Prisoners* would be the first time Shakespearean dialogue would be heard in a talkie, given that one sequence included a scene from *A Midsummer Night's Dream*.[41]

On February 9, 1929, *Billboard* announced that "Bela Logusi" [sic] would appear in *Prisoners*.[42] It was Dr. Edmond Pauker, Lugosi's friend and New York agent, who brokered the film rights to the Molnár novel; he was quite likely involved in Lugosi's contract as well.[43] The press noted Lugosi's pride at appearing in a movie written by Molnár.[44] One newspaper even claimed that he would wear onscreen a pair of trousers he purchased in Hungary eighteen years earlier.[45]

Lugosi played "Brottos," a character initially referred to simply as "The Man." One critic described his role as "the suave and sinister proprietor of a boisterous Vienna night club."[46] Another wrote, "As the proprietor of a nightclub in Vienna... [Lugosi] is again surrounded by an atmosphere of mystery.[47] The only known production anecdote involving him is as follows:

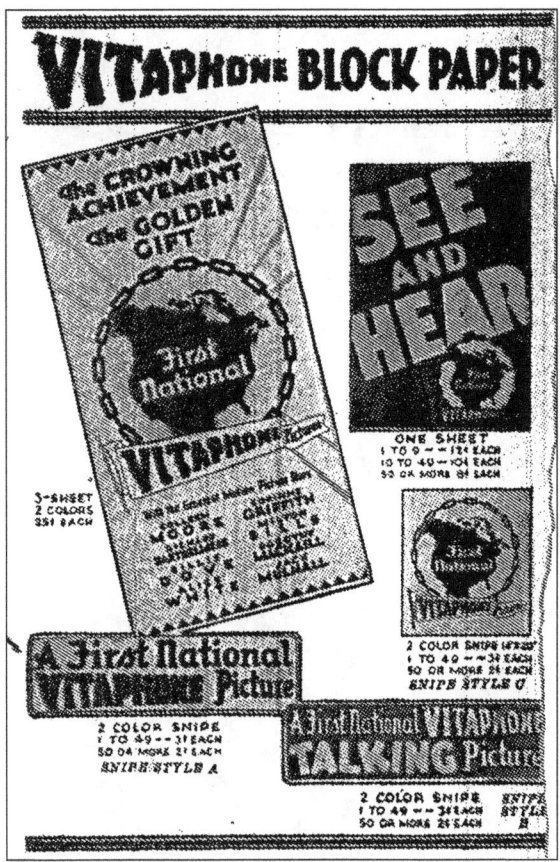

Above: From the pressbook for *Prisoners*.

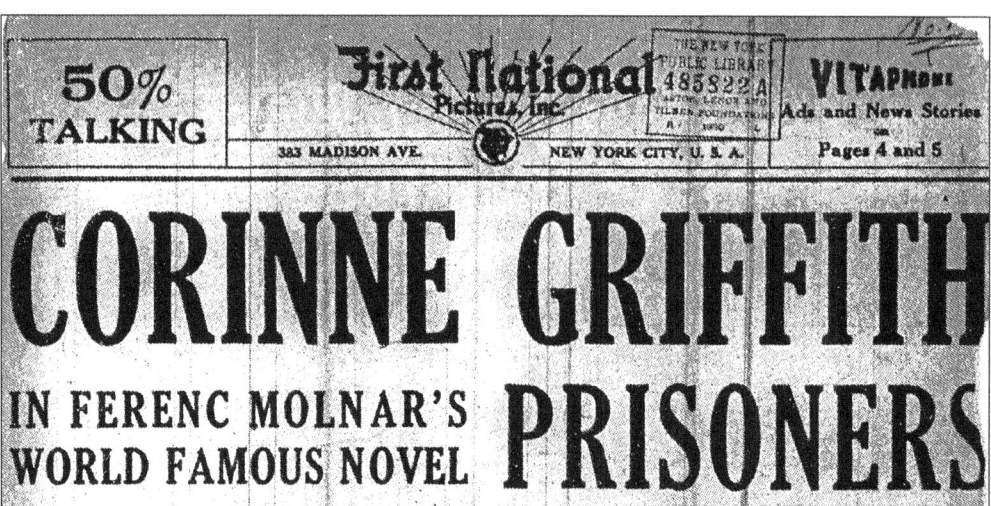

Above: From the pressbook for *Prisoners*. Below: A scene from *Prisoners*.

In *Prisoners*, Lugosi has a fiery fistal [*sic*] encounter with [actor] James Ford. [William] A. Seiter, who wielded the megaphone for this ... story, had all he could do to keep the intense Hungarian from putting so much realism into the fight that Ford was in danger of waking up in a hospital.[48]

The *Los Angeles Times* incorrectly told readers that *Prisoners* was Lugosi's "American film debut."[49] The film's pressbook made the same claim.

Left: From the pressbook for *Prisoners*. Above: Advertisement for the Hungarian release of *Prisoners*, as published in *Pécsi Napló* on March 20, 1930.

Seiter completed shooting *Prisoners* in March.[50] The Vitaphone Symphony Orchestra recorded the synchronized score. A review in *Variety* noted that the film was only ten percent dialogue, heard in its final minutes.[51] By contrast, a few primary sources reported something different. In two press articles and in the film's pressbook, First National claimed that *Prisoners* was "fifty percent dialog."[52] And its Vitaphone trailer was all-talking. In it, Ian Keith introduced the cast members, with Lugosi presumably among them.[53]

Once released in May 1929, industry trades decried *Prisoners* as much as they had *The Veiled Woman*:

> Not worth anyone's time. For intelligent adults: Mediocre.[54] – *The Educational Screen*

> The picture is rather weak, there being insufficient action in the story plot, which is stretched almost to the breaking point.[55] – *Weekly Film Review*

> The story is artificial, unconvincing and rambles along drearily till you are ready to call quits on it after the middle of the third reel.[56] – *Film Daily*

It is the poorest picture that has ever been released by First National with Corinne Griffith. There is not a spot where the emotions of the spectator are appealed to. And the action is uninteresting and draggy.[57] – *Harrison's Reports*

By contrast, the movie magazine *Photoplay* assured readers that the Molnár novel "becomes effective screen entertainment and Corinne Griffith is quite adorable," adding that Lugosi played an "important" role.[58]

Exhibitors used various ballyhoo stunts to attract moviegoers to *Prisoners*, including "Vitaphone streamers" made of cardboard musical notes.[59] The pressbook suggested that theaters hold a "Hungarian Bread Eating Contest." And Grosset and Dunlap released a "photoplay" edition of the Molnár novel that included stills from the film.

Some exhibitors devised their own gimmicks. For example, the manager of the State Theater in Dayton, Ohio, decorated his lobby like an actual prison, with bars "made out of wood and painted a drab grey." Behind them, he placed a cut-out of the six-sheet with glittered letters proclaiming, "Corinne Griffith in Prison."[60]

Above: From the pressbook for *Prisoners*.

Publicity wasn't enough to make all viewers happy, though, as the following two exhibitor reports reveal:

> Lay off this one. It's rotten and then some. They will walk out on this show. About the rottenest piece of junk First National ever forced on an exhibitor.[61]

> Oh, oh, hum! Another one of those foreign things. Why waste a good star on nothing? Recording fair.[62]

Though it seemingly performed better than *The Veiled Woman*, *Prisoners* was certainly not a hit.

It is evident that *Prisoners* played in Hungary. On October 10, 1929, the film magazine *A Hét* featured a full page spread on it that mentioned Lugosi more than once. Hungarian newspapers such as *Nyírvidék* printed reviews and quarter page advertisements. Lugosi himself had not and would not return to Hungary, not even for a visit. But many of those who knew him in Budapest and elsewhere likely saw his face flickering onscreen in 1929.

As for Lugosi, perhaps he was sought after at the "best homes of the movie colony," but not so much at the studios. His first two sound films – one apparently without spoken dialogue, and the other a "part-talkie" – did little to raise his screen profile. Neither movie was well received, which could be the reason that Lugosi revised his views on the merits of the talking picture.

In July 1929, just weeks after *Prisoners* was released, the *San Francisco Call and Post* published an article entitled "*Dracula* Sees No 'Talkie' Future." In it, Lugosi declared:

> We will continue to have pictures – silent ones, likely – and the radio will carry the dialogue of the world's best actors in broadcasting of plays. If this doesn't satisfy, those who are within reach of legitimate theaters will have the enjoyment of the best drama.[63]

Endnotes

1 "Actor Discusses Europe's Fear of Mythic Vampires." *Los Angeles Times* 27 Nov. 1927.

2 Ibid.

3 Whitaker, Alma. "Lugosi, Creator of Dracula Role, Is Courtly Hungarian." *Los Angeles Times* 17 June 1928.

4 Johnson, Fred. "*Dracula* Escapes Coffin, Reveals in S.F." *San Francisco Call* 26 Aug. 1928.

5 "Lugosi Complains of Shortness of Life." *Los Angeles Times* 28 June 1928.

6 "Hollywood Likes Vampire Actor." *Los Angeles Record* 29 June 1928.

7 "*Dracula* on Stage and Screen Being Discussed." *Los Angeles Evening Herald* 26 July 1928. The *Los Angeles Times* had published the same text in "*Dracula* Is Discussed as Picture" on 22 July 1928.

8 "*Dracula* Bought by 'U' for Talkie." *Exhibitors Daily Review* 22 Oct. 1928.

9 "Whispering Wires." *Motion Picture* Dec. 1928.

10 For more information on *The Silent Witness*, see Chapter 34 of this book.

11 "Complete Fox Production Plans for 1929 Announced." *Exhibitors Daily Review* 29 Dec. 1928.

12 "Emmett Flynn Back." *Variety* 26 Sept. 1928.

13 "*Exhibitors Herald and Moving Picture World* Production Directory." *Exhibitors Herald and Moving Picture World* 15 Sept. 1928.

14 "Fox Busiest Lot on W.C." *Exhibitors Daily Review* 20 Sept. 1928.

15 "Fox Completes Three." *Exhibitors Daily Review* 10 Oct. 1928.

16 "Season Under Way for Five Big Time Artists in Coast Studios." *Exhibitors Herald and Moving Picture World* 20 Oct. 1928.

17 "Douglas at Fox's." *Exhibitors Daily Review* 16 Oct. 1928.

18 Shaffer, George. "Griffith Film, Supposed Done, on Grid Again." *New York Daily News* 1 Nov. 1928.

19 "Hungarian Lands." *Variety* 7 Nov. 1928.

20 "*Veiled Lady* Cast." *Exhibitors Daily Review* 19 Nov. 1928.

21 "Bela Lugosi in Talkers." *Los Angeles Times* 21 Nov. 1928; "Dracula!!" *Los Angeles Times* 9 Dec. 1928.

22 "*Veiled Lady* Cast"; "Bela Lugosi in Talkers."

23 George, Wilbur. "Preview: *The Veiled Woman*." *Hollywood Filmograph* 24 Nov. 1928.

24 "Flynn, Newmeyer, Reed Are Reported Out at Fox." *Motion Picture News* 8 Dec. 1928.

25 "Veiled Woman, The." *Photoplay Magazine* Feb. 1929.

26 The pressbook for *The Veiled Woman* is archived at the New York Public Library for the Performing Arts, Dorothy and Lewis B. Cullman Center.

27 "Coming Fox Pictures." *Derry Journal* (Derry, Northern Ireland) 8 May 1929.

28 "The Shadow Stage." *Photoplay Magazine* Feb. 1929.

29 "*The Veiled Woman*." *Variety* 26 June 1929.

30 "*The Veiled Woman* (SF) Lia Tora." *Harrison's Reports* 29 June 1929.

31 "Again About Silent Pictures." *Harrison's Reports* 21 Sept. 1929.

32 "*The Veiled Woman*." *Billboard* 13 July 1929.

33 See, for example: Advertisement. *Rockford Register-Gazette* (Rockford, IL) 1 June 1929; Advertisement. *Pittsburgh Press* (Pittsburgh, PA) 28 Apr. 1929; Advertisement. *Springfield Republican* (Springfield, MA) 11 May 1929.

34 "Talkies Will Aid Stage." *Los Angeles Times* 14 Oct. 1928.

35 "Return to Native Accent Retards Actor's English." *Los Angeles Times* 29 July 1928.

36 "*Prisoners*." *Harrison's Reports* 15 June 1929.

37 "Views and Reviews." *Film Mercury* 15 Feb. 1929.

38 "Getting into Character." *Screenland* Mar. 1929.

39 "Corinne Completes First Talk Film." *The Times-Picayune* (New Orleans, LA) 3 Feb. 1929. By contrast, Corinne Griffith and Walter Morosco traveled to Europe after finishing *Prisoners*. See "Pictorial Section." *Exhibitors Herald-World* 6 Apr. 1929.

40 "F.N.'s Own Sound." *Variety* 30 Jan. 1929.

41 "The Bard in Sound." *Variety* 20 Feb. 1929.

42 "Film Notes." *Billboard* 9 Feb. 1929. One newspaper article claimed that Loretta Young would appear in *Prisoners*, but there is no evidence that she did. See "Corinne Completes First Talk Film."

43 Advertisement for Dr. Edmond Pauker. *The Film Daily 1929 Year Book* (New York: Film Daily, 1929).

44 "Erstwhile Dracula at First National." *Los Angeles Times* 13 Feb. 1929. See also *Hollywood Daily Citizen* 12 Feb. 1929.

45 *Toledo Blade* (Toledo, OH) 8 Mar. 1929.

46 "Corrine Griffith In *Prisoners*." *Jefferson City Post-Tribune* (Jefferson City, MI) 6 July 1929.

47 "Hungarian Actor Enters Talking Picture Field." *San Diego Union* 5 May 1929.

48 "Too Much Realism Almost Ruins Film." *The Courier-Post* (Camden, NJ) 14 Sept. 1929.

49 "Hungarian Actor Engaged." *Los Angeles Times* 21 Apr. 1929.

50 "Directors Get Credit Only if Contract Terms Are Kept." *Motion Picture News* 16 Mar. 1929.

51 "*Prisoners*." *Variety* 21 Aug. 1929.

52 "F.N. Advising Exhibs of Exact Dialog Percentage, in Advance." *Variety* 17 Apr. 1929; "Exhibs to Know Amount of Dialog in F.N. Pictures." *Billboard* 4 May 1929. The pressbook for *Prisoners* is archived at the New York Public Library for the Performing Arts, Dorothy and Lewis B. Cullman Center.

53 Liebman, Roy. *Vitaphone Films: A Catalogue of the Features and Shorts* (Jefferson, NC: McFarland, 2003).

54 "*Prisoners*." *Educational Screen* Sept. 1929.

55 "Metropolitan." *Weekly Film Review* 29 June 1929.

56 "*Prisoners*." *Film Daily* 18 Aug. 1929.

57 "*Prisoners*." *Harrison's Reports*.

58 "The Shadow Stage." *Photoplay* Aug. 1929.

59 These publicity "accessories" are described in the film's pressbook.

60 "Managers' Round Table Club." *Motion Picture News* 7 Sept. 1929.

61 "What The Picture Did For Me." *Exhibitors Herald-World* 26 Oct. 1929.

62 "What The Picture Did For Me." *Exhibitors Herald-World* 30 Nov. 1929.

63 Johnson, Fred. "*Dracula* Sees No 'Talkie' Future." *San Francisco Call & Post* 24 July 1929.

64 "*The Veiled Woman*." *Detroit Free Press* (Detroit, MI) 18 Nov. 1928.

The Kiss That Kills

No matter how lonesome you are, young ladies, never do any necking with *Dracula*. He is the vampire in human form whose kiss, at once horrible and irresistible, brings about both the death of the body and the perdition of the soul. This is not the kid himself, it's Bela Lugosi impersonating him. But the resemblance is close enough to aid you in identification if the need arises. There is a rumor that Lugosi may repeat on the screen his stage success in "Dracula." At present he's playing in "The Thirteenth Chair"

Published in *Motion Picture Classic* in October 1929.

Chapter 40

The Kiss That Kills

"Red, you see, made the Hungarian simply wild."[56]
– Harriet George, 1929

"Dracula! He Eats 'Em Alive!"[57]
– *Los Angeles Examiner*, 1929

In the spring of 1929, E.P. Dutton published Montague Summers' book *The Vampire*, which chronicled the origins and histories of vampire folklore.[1] It also discussed Bram Stoker's novel and the resulting Broadway play. Summers mentioned Lugosi playing Dracula, marking the first time the two names were connected in any book. But Summers mistakenly spelled his name "Lugoni." Lugosi had fame, but was not yet famous.

That same year, O.D. Woodward formed a new Pacific Coast company to return *Dracula–The Vampire Play* to Los Angeles, San Francisco, and a number of other cities. Lugosi would star, the press announced, leaving a version of *Dracula* in Chicago to head west.[2] That report was inaccurate. Raymond Huntley – who had earlier appeared in *Dracula* in England – successfully portrayed the vampire in Chicago.

Lugosi was himself living in Los Angeles during the first half of 1929.

He appeared at a gathering in February of that year given in honor of Camilla Horn, star of F.W. Murnau's *Faust* (1926).[3] He also attended a tea party at the Hollywood Athletic Club. Also present was Lila Lee, with whom he appeared in *The Midnight Girl* (1925).[4]

The following month, Lugosi acted in a version of Ferenc Molnár's drama *Az ördög* (*The Devil*) at the Capitol Theater. The play, performed in the Hungarian language, was a benefit for disabled artists. After the performance, Lugosi hosted a "box party" attended by famed columnist Louella O. Parsons.[5] He was actively attempting to ingratiate himself with Hollywood players, including journalists.

Then, at the beginning of May, *Variety* reported that Horace Liveright had filed a lawsuit against O.D. Woodward in Los Angeles for over $2,000 in royalties owed him from the 1928 West Coast tour of *Dracula*.[6] Lugosi had been the star of that production, just as he would be again, once Liveright and Woodward quickly came to a settlement.

The 1929 production of *Dracula* opened at the Hollywood Music Box on May 19. Its cast featured Harriet George as Lucy, Harry Walker as Renfield, J. Raymond Brown as Van Helsing, Donald Woods as Harker, Richard Lancaster as Dr. Seward, Frederick Pymm as Butterworth, the Attendant, and Francesca Rotoli as Wells, the Maid.[7] Woodward also had a nurse on duty in the theater lobby, as well as a female "audience member" paid to faint each night.[8]

A day before the show opened, Lugosi explained to the *Los Angeles Record* how much "confusion" still existed over the "exact meaning" of the term "vampire":

> The word has generally been associated with motion picture stars whose so-called 'sex-appeal' is often more obvious than convincing. According to Webster, 'In the superstition of Eastern Europe, a vampire is a ghost which sucks the blood of its sleeping victim. One who lives upon others.'[9]

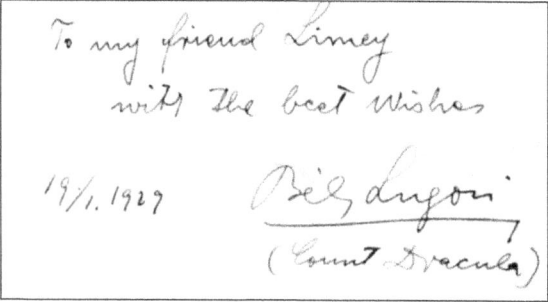

Top Left: Published in the *Los Angeles Examiner* of May 19, 1929. Top Right: Published in the *Los Angeles Evening Express* on May 20, 1929. Above: *(Courtesy of Dennis Phelps)*

Top: Published in the *Los Angeles Times* on May 20, 1929. Above Left: Lugosi with Hazel Whitmore and Bernard Jukes. *(Courtesy of George Chastain).* Above Right: Published in the *Los Angeles Evening Herald* on May 20, 1929.

During the show's run, Lugosi described the "Dracula Kiss" to the same newspaper. It was the "kiss of the villains… too evil ever to become popular for heroes."[10]

But Lugosi was popular, at least locally. After the company opened at the Music Box, costume designer Katinka de Justh and danseuse Selma Rita threw a party in Lugosi's honor.[11] And the Music Box lobby displayed a three-quarter-length painting of Lugosi created by his friend, fellow Hungarian Géza Kende.[12] Newspaper critics also drew attention to Lugosi:

> The bloodthirsty Count Dracula lifted his cadaverous head last night at the Music Box and chilled a large slice of the Hollywood population into panting submission. They came to 'Pshaw!' but stayed to shudder. … [Lugosi] puts strange life into the character of the 'undead.' Outré gestures and queer intonations come from him as devastatingly as a hollow voice from the tomb. … This second viewing gave me as many hot and cold waves as the first. The enthusiasm which greeted its return last night indicated that Hollywood is all set to entertain it for a nice run.[13] – *Los Angeles Evening Herald*

People go to *Dracula* just as they go to see exhibits of horror executed in wax. The human psyche craves at times to curdle. The capacity audience last night congealed in

Above Left: Published in the *San Diego Sun* on June 10, 1929. Above Right: Published in the *San Diego Evening Tribune* of June 6, 1929. Below Left: Published in the *San Diego Sun* on June 6, 1929. Below Right: Published in the *Santa Barbara Morning Press* on June 13, 1929.

great content. To be sure, one customer fainted, but she probably got her money back. She should have had a bonus. These things are great for atmosphere. Bela Lugosi ... is theatrical in a big way, which is well.[14] – *Los Angeles Examiner*

To a rising crescendo of shrieks and half-suppressed ejaculations, Bram Stoker's thriller *Dracula* noised its way into the Hollywood Music Box Theater last night. Bela Lugosi portrays his original role of Dracula with sinister suavity. He does easily the outstanding work of the play and seems ever more malevolently predatory with his ghastly, phosphorescent makeup and Satanic mannerisms than he did last summer.[15] – *Los Angeles Times*

Bela Lugosi's magnificent figure dominates the play as before. As the blood-sucking Count Dracula ... Lugosi has achieved a great characterization. ... In its present form, it is more effective than the average mystery thriller of clutching hands and muffled screams because it gives the imagination a free rein.[16] – *Los Angeles Record*

It is extremely difficult to realize that Bela Lugosi is not all that he is supposed to be as he appears on the stage as the vampire. His hands and his very stature seems [sic] to grow huge and out of proportion as he goes about his horrible business. He seems something horribly unreal and inhuman–a distorted soul manifested. Such acting as Lugosi's is not often found and when it is, it is difficult to find words to pay tribute to the man's artistry.[17] – *Hollywood Daily Citizen*

Despite Lugosi's local popularity, the play's Los Angeles revival was not particularly successful. *Variety* reported its first week gross as a decent $2,400, but later added that the play "just could not get them" during its second week, generating a poor $1,800.[18] In fact, *Dracula* would have closed after two weeks, but Woodward kept it going because the rented theater would otherwise have been dark. Final verdict: *Dracula*'s three-week stay in Los Angeles was "lean."[19]

The company then rapidly began haunting city after city, thus calling to mind Bram Stoker's declaration, "For the dead travel fast." *Dracula* first moved to San Diego, playing the Spreckels Theater from June 10 through 12. "Those inclined to be fearful should make their reservations for the Wednesday matinee," warned one journalist.[20] Reviews were as follows:

Let it be said at once that it supplies an evening of exceptionally good entertainment. That is, if you care for mystery plays. It is excellently done and the audience last evening got two hours of solid, intense enjoyment and interest from it. It is gripping. It holds you tense and alert from start to finish. ... Tall, slender, deliberate in movement and graceful in gesture, [Lugosi] is well fitted to suggest the vampire-like character of the count who has been dead for five centuries but still lives.[21] – *San Diego Union*

Most San Diegans were 'shaken out of their boots' last night when *Dracula* ... was produced by a most excellent company of stage artists headed by Bela Lugosi, who impersonates a Hungarian possessed of vampire spirit, with all the excellencies, perhaps, with which it is possible to excel. ... Bela Lugosi handles the Count Dracula role with a virtuosity born of native talent and long practice.[22] – *San Diego Tribune*

It's as unconvincing as all get-out, and what the play is for I haven't the least idea. ... The talent of the actors was too good for a play of this sort. ... Bela Lugosi is the billboarded member of this party of woman-frighteners. As a boy, I just know he used to jump out of trees at passersby.[23] – *San Diego Sun*

Dracula next played Santa Barbara's Lobero Theater from June 13 to 15, for three nights and a matinee.[24] By this time, Anna Spanier had replaced Francesca Rotoli as Wells, the Maid.

Local publicity drew attention to the fact that Lugosi broke a mirror every day onstage, shattering not only looking glasses, but also longstanding superstition.[25] In response to *Dracula*, the *Morning Press* wrote:

As for the show, it is just what it is advertised – and if you don't care to listen to and view the unfolding of such an impossible plot, you don't have to go. If you do care for that sort of thing, the plot is in good hands and is well acted. ... As a matter of fact, the play is in excellent hands throughout.[26]

The company then played the Nile Theater in Bakersfield for one day, June 17, the city's first roadshow in "many moons."[27] A local critic told readers:

Count Dracula [is] excellently done by the noted Hungarian actor Bela Lugosi, smooth, suave, sleek, with all the finish for which Hungarians are known.... [It] was an excellent show and it was produced by a fine cast.[28]

From there, the company staged *Dracula* at the Pantages in Fresno from June 18 through 20. Critical response was more negative than usual:

As to the performance last night, it cannot be said to have been more than fair ... the cast on the whole is inferior to the one that played in [San Francisco] ... one fails to see how any amount of acting could make the piece more than mildly amusing. However, two individual performances stood out, and merit praise. Bela Lugosi was, as might have been expected, excellent as Count Dracula the vampire. And Harry Walker as the lunatic Renfield, contributed several very effective scenes. The worst fault of nearly all the players was bad diction, and the result was that about a quarter of what they said could not be understood.[29] – *Fresno Bee*

Left: Published in the *Fresno Morning Republican* on June 17, 1929. Top Right: Published in the *Fresno Morning Republican* on June 16, 1929. Bottom Right: Published in the *Fresno Morning Republican* on June 12, 1929.

Its plot is transparent, which is a crime in these days. Modern audiences want to be thrilled and at the same time left in doubt as to the villain's identity until the final scream has ceased to echo. ... *Dracula* offers a cast which is excellent under any standards.[30] – *Fresno Morning Republican*

The first of these two critics drew attention to the artificiality of the prop bat, the second to the lonely nurse in the lobby who treated no patients.

For June 21 and 22, *Dracula* descended on Sacramento's Sutter Theater. The *Bee* was distinctly unimpressed:

The play is very uneven in character. A fine atmosphere of the mysteriously horrible is built up in the first act, and one thinks that *Dracula* is going to provide as many thrills as such sterling shockers as *The Cat and the Canary* and *The Bat*. But the second act is rather draggy. ... If the story, however, fails to quite ring the bell, there is some acting that must be given its due. Bela Lugosi, who has the title role, is just such a creature as imagination would concoct for one who must spend his days wrapped in a shroud in a coffin and his nights prowling about seeking whom he may devour. He contributes several effective

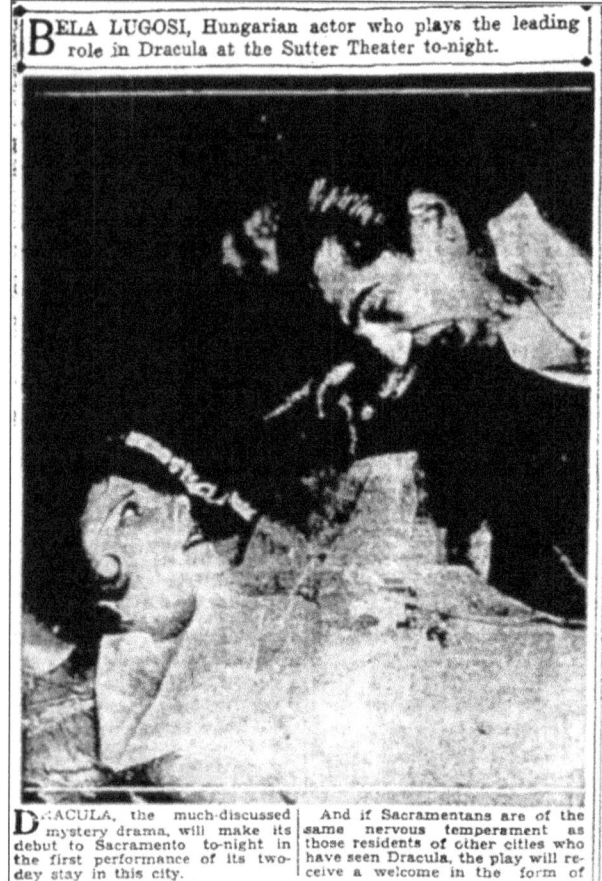 

Left: Published in the *Sacramento Bee* on June 21, 1929. Right: Published in the *San Francisco Chronicle* on July 29, 1929.

scenes and in make-up, tone of voice, and particularly in the use of his hands, creates an illusion of the existency [*sic*] of just a fearful individual....[31]

After Sacramento, Lugosi took a break from *Dracula* from June 23 to July 21 in order to appear in Tod Browning's film *The Thirteenth Chair* (1929), which will be discussed in Chapter 41.

During the same time frame, O.D. Woodward opened *Dracula* at the Pantages in Portland, Oregon, with Frederick Pymm playing the vampire.[32] But Woodward faced troubles when Horace Liveright sued him for copyright infringement in the amount of $10,000.[33] A San Francisco judge temporarily restrained Woodward from continuing the show.[34] As of July 6, the order was "dissolved," Woodward and Liveright having come to some sort of settlement.[35] *Dracula* resumed, moving on to Seattle and Tacoma with Pymm still playing the title role.[36]

Plans for a San Francisco run also proceeded. By July 13, if not sooner, Woodward arrived in the city to prepare for the play's "readvent."[37] Here Lugosi would return as Dracula, as would the cast members from earlier in the summer, save for two. Hazel Whitmore took Harriet George's place as Lucy, and Henry Hall – later to play opposite Lugosi in *Murder by Television* (1935), *Shadow of Chinatown* (1936), *The Ape Man* (1943), and *Voodoo Man* (1944) – replaced Richard Lancaster as Dr. Seward.

City newspapers heralded the return engagement, as well as "San Francisco girl" Anna Spanier as Wells.[38] The press also mentioned that a former candidate for Senator bought a block of thirty tickets to *Dracula*.[39] As for the show itself, one journalist claimed:

> Thousands of spectators have viewed *Dracula* with widely variant emotions during its two runs at the Columbia Theater, with the formidable Bela Lugosi in the title role ... And while many were disappointed, a far larger number succumbed without a struggle to the weird titillations it induces on the spine and flesh of the beholder.
>
> Yet the revolutionary importance of *Dracula* as a stage production has been overlooked. We have had dramatic 'shockers' by the score in the last ten years, but *Dracula* alone turns frankly to the supernatural in evoking an atmosphere of terror. ...
>
> Those who see the play ... either abandon themselves to its outré spell and enjoy *Dracula*; or, poor matter-of-fact mortals, they squirm uneasily in their seats and wish they had gone across the street to see Clara Bow... Shudders are tonic no less than laughs. *Dracula* is a courageous attempt to bring this vogue to the stage....[40]

Left: Published in the *San Francisco Chronicle* on July 21, 1929. Right: Published in the *San Francisco Chronicle* on July 21, 1929.

San Francisco area critics gave the 1929 revival of the play overwhelmingly positive reviews:

Dracula has its quota of thrills. Its plot is built largely upon suspense and legendary myth and as such it is bound to click with many San Francisco audiences. Essentially this presentation of O.D. Woodward is not good drama, but it provides entertainment of the variety that should prove lucrative.[41] – *San Francisco Chronicle*

Lugosi's long service in the role of a despicable denizen of the dark affords the audience three acts of rare artistry.[42] – *San Francisco Call and Post*

Published in the *San Francisco Examiner* on August 4, 1929.

An outstanding performance was presented by each of the actors. It is hard to choose which was the best. ... [*Dracula*] sounds absurd and yet it won't seem absurd when you see it – in truth when you see his thin white hands, his pointed, rather emaciated face, blooded, red lips, and pointed teeth, you will go home and shut your windows tight....[43] – *San Francisco Bulletin*

The months that have passed since *Dracula*'s last appearance here have not reduced any of the thrills nor lessened any of its terrible appeal. ... And the gasps and shrieks that greet [the vampire] have nothing of laughter in them. No sir! The folks out in the house are just plainly scared. It is all very adroitly done. ... *Dracula* is splendidly enacted entirely after the manner of the old school by an exceptionally good cast. Bela Lugosi in the part of Count Dracula is startlingly fine, both in makeup and in acting.[44] – *San Francisco News*

Bela Lugosi moves through the drama with sinister suavity. He endows his portrait of the unmortal [sic] man who rises from earth at night to live on the blood of the living, with imagination and an authority born of traditional lore. His make-up is an achievement.[45] – *San Francisco Examiner*

Bela Lugosi in the leading part of "Dracula" gave many thrills to the audience at the Columbia last night. Hazel Whitmore is the girl of the play.

Above: Published in the *San Francisco Bulletin* on July 23, 1929. Right Top: Published in the *San Francisco Chronicle* on July 23, 1929. Right Bottom: Published in the *San Francisco Chronicle* on July 22, 1929.

Bela Lugosi was just what a vampire should be. Handsome, yet sinister, very much a stage presence yet seemingly unreal, he commanded the respect and fear to which a Count Dracula would naturally be accustomed. It must be admitted that Mr. Lugosi loved to dwell over his words and revel in his role, but what vampire wouldn't?[46] – *Stanford Daily*

Variety reported that *Dracula*'s first week received "fair attention"; its second week generated a "satisfactory" gross.[47]

In addition to reviews, the local press recounted a performance in which the "most important mechanical effect

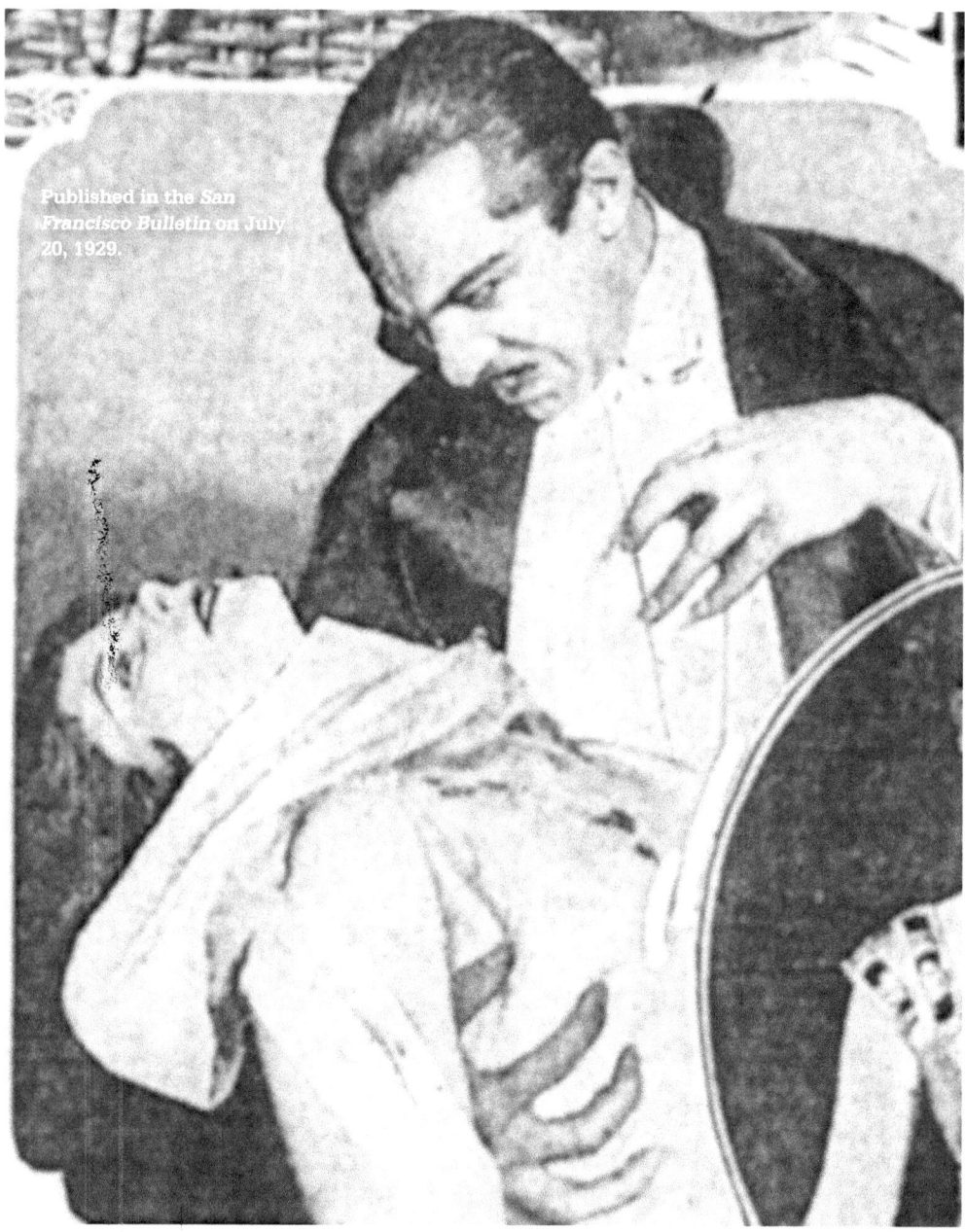

Published in the *San Francisco Bulletin* on July 20, 1929.

... failed to function." The trap door that allows Dracula to "disappear" did not work, causing the befuddled actors to stare at each other. Lugosi immediately "saved the scene." Keeping in character, he "hissed a message to the electrician off-stage." Thus the scene "was swathed in darkness," allowing Dracula to disappear by means other than the norm.[48]

While in San Francisco, Lugosi gave more than one interview, but the most fascinating was with Ada Hanifin of the *Examiner*:

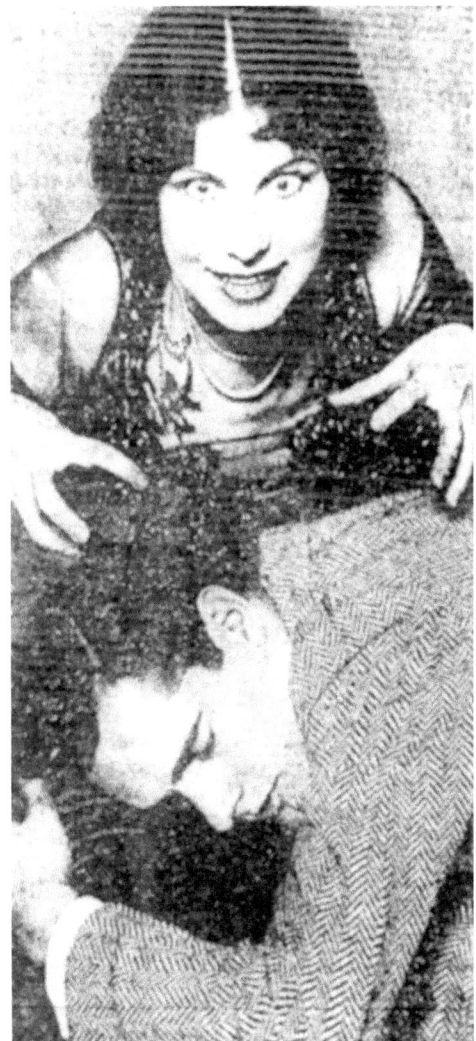

Left: Published in the *San Francisco Examiner* on July 28, 1929. Above: Lugosi and J. Raymond Brown.

Bela Lugosi's reflection in the mirror was taking on a Mephistophelean cunning. With deft touches of grease, chalk, and paint, he was fast evoking the likeness of Dracula. In a few moments, he would doff his smile and ingenious manner. Werewolves move with a sinister suavity....

It was after 8 when the man reputed to be Hungary's greatest actor entered his dressing room backstage at the Columbia. Mystery had cloaked his movements during the day. He had disappeared with Dracula-like proclivity. No one could find him. Now that he was late, he offered no explanation.

As he donned his mask with urgent rapidity, he talked volubly. He would be entertaining at any cost. There was a charm in his accent, but in his eyes...! Conflicting emotions welled in their depths.[49]

After finishing the final San Francisco show on August 10, the company moved to the Fulton Theater in Oakland for August 11 through 24. Harriet George resumed the role of Lucy. According to the *Oakland Tribune*:

It is a well-constructed play, as mystery thrillers go, and unlike all of its fellows. ... Yesterday's crowd was a friendly and eager gathering content to accept anything from vampires to bad acting and they were given both in abundance. Bela Lugosi the original Count Dracula, was on hand to give his eerie reading of the vicious Transylvanian....

But acting or no acting, *Dracula* dashes along on its own momentum. It is as close to an actor-proof play as may be imagined, differs materially from the accepted school of mystery melodrama, and was greeted with huzzahs by a house filled from cellar to attic with enthusiastic thrill fans.[50]

The *Oakland Post-Enquirer* also reviewed the play, responding that Lugosi "makes the Count as ghastly a shriek-getter as one could possibly desire. If we could believe in ghost stories, we would not be satisfied with any ghost other than [him]."[51]

Many audiences appreciated Lugosi's Dracula, though his fame was still limited. In an advertisement for *Dracula*'s run at the Music Box, the *Hollywood Filmograph* – which would become one of Lugosi's great supporters – misspelled his name not as "Lugoni," as Montague Summers had, but rather as "Logosi."[52]

But those who did recall his appearance remembered him clearly. Frederick Pymm called Lugosi "ideal for the part."[53] And Harriet George – the actress who played Lucy Seward during most of the 1929 tour – spoke to a journalist about the indelible impression Lugosi made on her:

> Harriet George, ingénue, or the flapper role girl ... likes to be mauled on a sofa. In the past several months she has had her dress torn off a few times doing that very thing. 'It's thrilling,' she said. 'For four months I had the most wonderful man maul me. His name was Bela Lugosi, a Hungarian. I just paid $25 to have a flaming red dress fixed up after having been ripped several times during the mauling process. Red, you see, made the Hungarian simply wild.'[54]

Even wilder tales appeared in Gladys Hall's article "The Case of the Man Who Dares Not Fall Asleep," published in *Motion Picture* in August 1929. She described the vampire woman who bit Lugosi in Europe. And she offered such prose as:

> Moldering graveyards and shrieks in the night. The drip-drip-drip of blood. The odor of Death that comes from the secret places. A man with a pale green face and stretching hands. Ghouls. Unspeakable things. The worm that never dies.[55]

Then, in October of the same year, *Motion Picture Classic* printed a full-page photograph of Lugosi as Dracula that illuminated only his face and claw-like hands, the rest of his body engulfed by darkness. Its caption: "The Kiss that Kills."

Endnotes

1 "Origin and History of the Strange Vampire." *New York Times* 24 Mar. 1929.

2 "Vampire Play Coming Back." *Los Angeles Times* 19 Apr. 1929.

3 "Miss Livingston Concert Hostess." *Los Angeles Examiner* 24 Feb. 1929.

4 "Contest Winners Honored at Tea." *Los Angeles Examiner* 24 Feb. 1929. [The dinner party cited in endnote 4 apparently happened on 18 Feb. 1929, but was not reported until the Sunday edition of the *Examiner* on 24 Feb. The tea party at the Hollywood Athletic Club was mentioned in the same Sunday edition, but was indeed a separate event. The newspaper notes it had happened "recently," but presumably after the previous Sunday edition published on 17 Feb. 1929.]

5 Nye, Myra. "Society of Cinemaland." *Los Angeles Times* 17 Mar. 1929.

6 "Los Angeles." *Variety* 1 May 1929.

7 "Mystery Thriller at Hollywood Box Office." *Los Angeles Times* 19 May 1929.

8 "Vampire and Bats in Foray." *Los Angeles Times* 20 May 1929; "Hollywood Chatter." *Variety* 12 June 1929.

9 "*Dracula* Comes to Music Box." *Los Angeles Record* 18 May 1929.

10 "'Dracula Kiss' to Be Popular Among Villains." *Los Angeles Record* 1 June 1929.

11 "For *Dracula*." *Los Angeles Times* 26 May 1929.

12 "Portrait at Theater." *Los Angeles Times* 21 July 1929.

13 Oliver, W.E. "Bela Lugosi Is Prince of Ghouls." *Los Angeles Evening Herald* 20 May 1929.

14 Greene, Patterson. "*Dracula* Weird 'Thrill' Drama at Music Box." *Los Angeles Examiner* 20 May 1929.

15 "Vampires and Bats in Foray." *Los Angeles Times* 20 May 1929.

16 Bradford, Sax. "*Dracula* as Blood-Chilling as Ever." *Los Angeles Record* 20 May 1929.

17 Denbo, Doris. "*Dracula* Affords Thrills." *Hollywood Daily Citizen* 20 May 1929.

18 "L.A. Shows Stay Down; Fear Shriners No Aid." *Variety* 29 May 1929; "Parties, Shriner's Cut Rates, All Help L.A." *Variety* 5 June 1929.

19 "Still Struggling in L.A.; *Bach Father*, $12,000." *Variety* 12 June 1929.

20 Johnson, T. T. "*Dracula* Here Soon." *San Diego Sun* 4 June 1930.

21 Hubbard, Havrah. "*Dracula* Gives Evening of Good Entertainment." *San Diego Union* 11 June 1929.

22 Short, Don. "*Dracula*, Play of Extreme Soul Thrills." *San Diego Evening Tribune* 11 June 1929.

23 Miller, Max. "*Dracula*." *San Diego Sun* 11 June 1929.

24 "Mystery Rules Famous Play." *The Morning Press* (Santa Barbara, CA) 12 June 1929.

25 "Breaks Mirror Once Every Day." *The Morning Press* 13 June 1929.

26 "*Dracula* Is Spooky Play in Hands of Good Actors." *The Morning Press* 14 June 1929.

27 "Mystery Drama Proves Thriller." *Bakersfield Californian* (Bakersfield, CA) 18 June 1929.

28 Ibid.

29 Elliot, William Foster. "*Dracula* Fails to Measure Up to Expectations." *Fresno Bee* (Fresno, CA) 19 June 1929.

30 Lee, John. "*Dracula*, Stage Thriller, Makes Good with Fresno Audience; Excellent Cast." *Fresno Morning Republican* (Fresno, CA) 19 June 1929.

31 Bailey, Roy B. "*Dracula* Tells All About Vampires." *Sacramento Bee* (Sacramento, CA) 22 June 1929.

32 "*Dracula* Is Enjoined." *The Oregonian* (Portland, OR) 1 July 1929.

33 "Sued for $10,000 on *Dracula* Rights." *San Diego Union* 26 June 1929; "O.D. Woodward Sued for Using *Dracula*." *Billboard* 6 July 1929.

34 "*Dracula* Is Enjoined."

35 "*Dracula* Resumes West Coast Tour." *Billboard* 13 July 1929.

36 "*Dracula* to Open at Pantages Today." *Seattle Times* (Seattle, WA) 7 July 1929; "*Dracula* on Pan Stage." *Tacoma News Tribune* (Tacoma, WA) 16 July 1929.

37 "O.D. Woodward to Produce *Holiday* in San Francisco." *Billboard* 20 July 1929.

38 "First Nighters Get Hysteria Over *Dracula*." *San Francisco Bulletin* 23 July 1929.

39 Waite, Edgar. "Cat and Curtain Calls." *San Francisco Examiner* 26 July 1929.

40 Jimerson, Royal W. "*Dracula* Advised for 'Pleasantly Horrific Night.'" *San Francisco Examiner* 4 Aug. 1929.

41 J.V.H. "Shudders Fill Tale of Old, Wicked Count." *San Francisco Chronicle* 23 July 1929.

42 *San Francisco Call and Post* 23 July 1929.

43 "First Nighters Get Hysteria Over *Dracula*."

44 Massey, Charles F. "*Dracula* Has Old Thrills at Columbia." *San Francisco News* 23 July 1929.

45 Hanifin, Ada. "*Dracula*, Playing Return Engagement." *San Francisco Examiner* 23 July 1929.

46 Gould, Burnell. "The Reviewer." *Stanford Daily* (Stanford, CA) 25 July 1929.

47 "Frisco Grosses." *Variety* 31 July 1929; "Frisco Grosses." *Variety* 14 Aug. 1929.

48 "Dracula Has Narrow Escape." *San Francisco Bulletin* 29 July 1929.

49 Hanifin, Ada. "Dracula! Found Out; Secret of Lugosi Revealed." *San Francisco Examiner* 28 July 1929.

50 Soanes, Wood. "Bills at Theaters Diversified." *Oakland Tribune* 12 Aug. 1929.

51 Grattan, W.H. "Oh! Horrors! *Dracula* at Fulton." *Oakland Post-Enquirer* 12 Aug. 1929.

52 Advertisement. *Hollywood Filmograph* 1 June 1929.

53 Warren, George C. "Frederick Pymm, Stage Villain, Sketches Career." *San Francisco Chronicle* 9 Nov. 1930.

54 "Likes to Be Mauled on a Sofa." *El Paso Evening Post* (El Paso, TX) 17 Oct. 1929.

55 Hall, Gladys. "The Case of the Man Who Dares Not Fall Asleep." *Motion Picture* Aug. 1929.

56 "Likes to Be Mauled on a Sofa."

57 Creedon, Richard. "Lovely Girl in Dire Peril." *Los Angeles Examiner* 19 May 1929.

Publicity photo of Lugosi in *The Thirteenth Chair* (1929).

Chapter 41

Two Helens

"If you don't thrill over [*The Thirteenth Chair*],
try reading *Dracula* in a graveyard at midnight."
– *Photoplay*, November 1929

In 1928, *Motion Picture Classic* published a lengthy article on Tod Browning, director of such films as *The Mystic* (1925), *The Unholy Three* (1925), *The Show* (1927), *The Unknown* (1927), and *London After Midnight* (1927). The journalist declared:

He is a stylist among stylists. Almost a specialist. The murky, the grotesque, the gruesome, the mystifying, is his stock in trade. Give this man a Lon Chaney characterization, a mystery concoction of his own weaving, and he can tell a story as masterly as one of Poe's. With every chill. With every nerve-racking swing of the pendulum.[1]

Later that same year, Browning continued bringing the bizarre to the silver screen, directing *West of Zanzibar* (1928) with Lon Chaney.

Then, in 1929, Browning made his first talkie, *The Thirteenth Chair*, based on one of the most famous of the "old dark house" stage plays. He told the *New York Times*:

Such plays ... were hitherto mostly for the stage. Shrieks were the most important adjuncts to a successful thriller, but the silent films could have none of it. Now, with the addition of sound, we can almost lend dimensional proportions to the spooky atmosphere.[2]

Opposite Page and Above: Publicity photos of Lugosi in *The Thirteenth Chair*.
Right: Published in *Motion Picture News* on February 8, 1929.

Browning understood the potential for sound in amplifying, even creating, horrifying situations.

Bayard Veiller's *The Thirteenth Chair* debuted at the Fulton Theatre on Broadway on November 20, 1916. Running for 328 performances, the show starred Veiller's wife Margaret Wycherly as medium Rosalie La Grange. The *New York Times* believed the play had brought something new to Broadway. Certainly, there had been book after book in which murder spurred the action of detection and solution. But the *Times* believed such plots had resulted in only a few plays, and "none written for the American stage quite so thoroughly as in *The Thirteenth Chair*."[3] The *Evening World* promised, "It will give you chills and thrills."[4]

The successful play led to a silent film adaptation. Léonce Peret directed *The Thirteenth Chair* (1919), which featured Creighton Hale as Willy Crosby and Mary Shotwell as La Grange. Peret, who also wrote the scenario for the film, made important changes to Veiller's play, particularly

Gary D. Rhodes | Bill Kaffenberger

Lugosi as Inspector Delzante.
(Courtesy of John Antosiewicz)

Lugosi and Margaret Wycherly stand in this scene from *The Thirteenth Chair*. *(Courtesy of John Antosiewicz)*

in reworking the La Grange character. He also included a good deal of footage of actor Marc McDermott portraying the first murder victim in an effort to show how horrible he was; by contrast, at the beginning of the Veiller play, the first victim is already dead. Peret also appended a humorous epilogue in which the young male and female leads are shown after their marriage with a new baby who sits in a "fourteenth chair."⁵ *Motion Picture News* complained, "To those who have seen the stage play, it will suffer in comparison because it is not so compact with mystifying action nor is it so endowed with electrifying suspense."⁶

(Courtesy of Buddy Barnett)

Tod Browning rightly believed he could make a better version of the play. On May 3, 1929, Louella O. Parsons told readers:

> Tod Browning will alone direct *The Thirteenth Chair*, and Elliott Clawson will write the scenario instead of co-direct. My error. Tod Browning has never needed assistance in any of his pictures, but these days of talkies, there is often a man put on the directorial force to aid with the dialogue. It did not seem anything out of the way when my pals at MGM wired to tell me news of *The Thirteenth Chair*. We will blame the wire for the mistake. And hope it won't happen again.⁷

Parsons' mistake was just that. Clawson was a writer and producer, never a director; he had earlier worked on Browning's films *The Road to Mandalay* (1926) and *West of Zanzibar* (1928). (She was correct that some studios in 1929 considered using two directors to helm talkies, one devoted to dialogue.⁸)

In late May of 1929, MGM hired Margaret Wycherly to reprise her stage role as La Grange.⁹ Just over a week later, the press reported Leila Hyams had been cast.¹⁰ Publicity for the film would maintain that Hyams actually regarded the number thirteen as lucky.¹¹

As for the lead male role of Richard Crosby, the press claimed that Lon Chaney was offered the role, but turned it down.¹² The *Hollywood Filmograph* told readers that Joel McCrea would play Crosby, but Conrad Nagel replaced him before production began.¹³ Also in the cast was Lal Chand Mehra, who had voiced roles on radio station KHJ during broadcasts of "weird

Lugosi's Inspector Delzante interrogates other characters in this scene from *The Thirteenth Chair*. (Courtesy of John Antosiewicz).

A scene from *The Thirteenth Chair*. (Courtesy of John Antosiewicz)

melodies of India."[14] In addition to playing a small role in *The Thirteenth Chair*, Mehra acted as a "technical adviser in its production."[15]

And then there was Bela Lugosi as the film's inspector; *Film Daily* mistakenly announced him as "Bola."[16] Not long before shooting began, he replaced the original choice for the role, William "Stage" Boyd. The character's name from the stage play would be changed to better suit Lugosi's persona and accent.

Elliott Clawson's "First Temporary Incomplete" script (dated May 8, 1929) changed the play's setting from New York to Calcutta, India, perhaps at Browning's behest. The change was not tied to the casting of Lugosi, however, as the next script draft (also set in India) still used the name "Inspector Donahue," which was the character's name in the play. But Donahue's name is marked through with pencil and replaced with handwriting that says "Inspector Delzand" and "Bela Lugosi." A synopsis continuity dated June 11, 1929, also used the name Donahue, so the change to "Delzand" – and finally "Delzante" – probably happened after that date.

However, surviving drafts of the script do not otherwise indicate much in the way of changes to Delzante's character or his dialogue, suggesting that the character was not particularly written or rewritten for Lugosi. As for cuts, Delzante's most intriguing deleted dialogue – marked through with pencil, suggesting it might not have even been filmed – is as follows: "Funny how these old superstitions cling to us. One of the first tests for guilt invented by detectives was to ask the supposed murderer to touch the body of his victim."

On June 25, 1929, Colonel Jason S. Joy of the Motion Picture Producers and Distributors of America (MPPDA) wrote to MGM after reading the shooting script, approving it for production, save for the "occasional use of profanity which I am sure you are looking out for."[17]

Whether to distinguish his own film from the silent version or whether to be faithful to Veiller (or both), Browning largely followed the story of the stage play. Edward Wales (John Davidson), friend of murder victim Spencer Lee, holds a séance at the home of Sir Roscoe Crosby (Holmes Herbert) in hopes of scaring the murderer into a confession. But the murderer uses the darkness of the séance room to stab Wales and hide the knife. That leads to a police investigation and another séance, at which a phony medium named Rosalie La Grange (Wycherly) makes it seem as if Wales's corpse moves its arm and points its finger toward the location of the murder weapon, which is stuck in the ceiling. Out of fear of the supernatural, the murderer breaks down into a confession.

Browning knew that at least some moviegoers would remember the Veiller play. They might have seen it staged, or they might even have access to the Samuel French publication of it and could quickly thumb to the back of it and learn the murderer's identity. So instead of having Dr. Philip Mason (Charles Quatermaine, credited on-screen as "Quartermaine") be the killer as Veiller did, Browning did make a crucial change; in his film, Mary Eastwood (Helen Millard) confesses to the murder. The shift to Eastwood within a film that is otherwise largely faithful to its source material suggests that Browning was playing a trick on any viewer who thought he or she already knew "whodunit."

The murderer's identity is further obscured thanks to the device of including two characters with the same first name. As Inspector Delzante's famous dialogue suggests, there are *"Two

Lugosi's Inspector Delzante confronts Madame La Grange (Margaret Wycherly) and Helen "Nellie" O'Neill (Leila Hyams) in *The Thirteenth Chair*. *(Courtesy of John Antosiewicz)*

Helens ... two Helens." Here is a key reason the first séance goes awry and Edward Wales is murdered. Wales wrongly believed that Helen Trent (Moon Carroll) was the murderer and intended to expose her at the first séance. Later, when Delzante learns that Wales suspected a woman named Helen, he believes it must have been Helen O'Neill (Leila Hyams), who goes by the name "Nellie."

What nationality is Delzante supposed to be? Strangely, there aren't really any narrative clues; at most, Grimshaw says Delzante "has arrived," but from where? Certainly, he isn't meant to be British, even though the British – given the colonial setting and even the British Grimshaw – are in charge of the police. That being said, Delzante is most likely supposed to be Indian; any other nationality doesn't make sense, as why would someone come from, say, France or Italy to work on a single murder case in British-ruled India? One newspaper article did note that he was a "Calcutta detective."[18] And the fact that the studio publicized the imported Indian linen bought for Lugosi's white suit is another reason to believe that Delzante was supposed to be Indian.[19]

At least one member of the press believed the casting of Lugosi was surprising:

Above: Published in *Picture Play* magazine in November of 1929. Right Top: Artwork of Lugosi in the pressbook for *The Thirteenth Chair*.

When Tod Browning, who has spent several profitable years directing Lon Chaney's pictures, was casting his mystery thriller *The Thirteenth Chair*, he chose the Hungarian player to enact a ... detective who solves the mystery. For a talking picture such a step was almost revolutionary, but Browning is elated over what he considers a discovery for the screen.[20]

After interviewing Lugosi, another journalist learned about the "intense study" he undertook before playing given roles. "You have to have the mental slant of a doctor to play a doctor, for instance, and to get it you have to study the doctor's work," Lugosi claimed.[21]

Browning certainly knew of Lugosi's work in *Dracula–The Vampire Play* and had perhaps seen it in Los Angeles in 1928 and/or 1929. But there is no reason to believe that Browning considered Lugosi's work in *The Thirteenth Chair* to be a tryout for a future film adaptation of *Dracula*. After all, Lugosi is playing a man of the law, a "good guy," one who is initially dressed in white. No visual cues depict him as villainous, such as the close-up of his staring eyes in *The Silent Command* (1923). Lugosi himself understood this in 1929, as he told the

Hollywood Daily Citizen that he was fearful of becoming typed for roles of the Lon Chaney style. He was thus happy that *The Thirteenth Chair* allowed him to play what he considered to be a "straight role."[22]

It was also a role that faced one notable obstacle. In the summer of 1929, just as he was playing *Dracula* onstage, a major issue arose between the Actors' Equity Association, Hollywood producers, and film actors. On June 5, Actors' Equity – which previously represented only stage actors – declared jurisdiction over the talkies.[23] Producers like Cecil B. DeMille responded that they would continue to issue their own standard contracts. At least 164 actors and actresses, many of them prominent in Hollywood, deserted Actors' Equity by signing unapproved contracts.[24] Actors Equity thus suspended a number of them for not following the union rules:

> In setting the [June 5] date, Frank Gillmore, president of the association, bound the members not only to affix their signatures to nothing but the Equity form of contract, but also to refrain from signing at all unless for productions the entire casts of which consisted of Equity members in good standing.[25]

Lugosi ignored this edict, signing a non-Equity contract for *The Thirteenth Chair*. So did his costar John Davidson, with Equity vowing to take up Davidson's case "in the immediate future."[26] After siding against Equity, Conrad Nagel was even threatened by person or persons unknown with disfigurement; MGM provided him with a bodyguard during at least part of the *Thirteenth Chair* shoot.[27]

Many other actors joined the stand against Equity, including some of Lugosi's past or future costars, among them Helen Chandler, Ivan Lebedeff, Edmund Lowe, and Wheeler Oakman.[28] Though exempting contract players, Actors' Equity called for a strike, but it ended unsuccessfully in August 1929. Conrad Nagel even held a large dinner at the Hollywood Roosevelt for screen actors who felt "ostracized by their brethren for not taking the 100% stand with [Equity]."[29]

The battle might account for why production on *The Thirteenth Chair* didn't start on June 3, 1929, as planned, but rather on June 10.[30] After visiting the film set, columnist Robbin Coons wrote:

> Herewith nominated for the Hollywood hall of fame is Bela Lugosi. You know him better, perhaps, as 'Dracula' – so fixedly has the Hungarian stage actor become associated with the gruesome vampire role.
>
> Well, most Hollywood actors, no matter how sincerely modest they are ... somehow, they expect people to know them. But Bela Lugosi, when a mere reporter was presented to him, said: 'My name's Lugosi. How are you?'
>
> As if that were really news! So, clear out a niche. But more –
>
> 'Interlock!' drawls Director Tod Browning. 'Everybody quiet!'
>
> Lugosi begins his lines in that pronounced foreign accent of his. Cold cutting interrogation – Bela is a detective ... He is quizzing Moon Carroll, fresh from the stage. She

replies. The dialog waxes warm. Then Browning waves his arms. For the third time the scene is spoiled. Someone has slipped on the lines. 'Tis Moon,' accuses Tod, impersonally, patiently, inoffensively, Moon acknowledges guilt, prettily, laughing. 'But it was my fault!' insists Lugosi, unperturbed, suave, gallant.

Quick – carve the niche wider![31]

The niche was indeed carved widely, as Lugosi was surprisingly paid at least $2,000 for his work on the film, meaning the same amount originally allotted for William Boyd.[32]

Few other details have emerged about the shoot. Browning did place a camera on a pedestal that vibrated during the filming of the séance sequences, the slight movements creating what he hoped to be a ghostly and "weird diffused effect."[33] *Variety* explained that Browning "had to invent the device after the technical department failed to give him what he wanted."[34] That said, the effect is barely noticeable when watching the film.

Published in the *Los Angeles Times* on October 30, 1929.

Rehearsals and shooting totaled 36 days, with principal photography ending on July 15, 1929.[35] On August 10, the *Hollywood Filmograph* reported that Browning was in post-production, apparently near completion.[36] *The Thirteenth Chair*'s final negative cost was $262,270.56.

On August 24, the *Hollywood Filmograph* described a preview screening:

> The reaction of the preview audience ... indicated only too clearly that picturegoers have had their fill of this sort of entertainment. Really alert and interested spectators do not snicker during séances or giggle while murders are being committed.[37]

Did Browning and MGM make changes to *The Thirteenth Chair* as a result of the preview? That is certainly possible, given that the formal release date was not until October 19, 1929.

Soon thereafter, MGM released a silent version of *The Thirteenth Chair*, standard practice at that time given that many movie theaters had not wired for sound. In the "Cutting Continuity" prepared on October 25, 1929, Lugosi's most famous dialogue was represented with onscreen emphasis: "So there are two Helens." More curious is that throughout the document his character's name is consistently spelled "Delante," without the "z." The sheer repetition in the continuity suggests that onscreen intertitles also spelled it that way.

Critical response to *The Thirteenth Chair* varied, including with regard to its use of sound:

> ... Several scenes, as it happens, depend entirely upon sound for their effect. The lights on the settings are turned off and the screen is a glimmering grayness. One hears shrieks, screams, thuds and the effect is a sense of uncanniness and irritation, to which the audience did not react favorably.[38] – *Hollywood Filmograph*

> The talkies, of course, add many thrills to the mystery story which were unknown to the silent film. We can have a perfectly dark screen with eerie sounds and shots and cries issuing forth which send the shivers up and down our spines.[39] – *National Board of Review Magazine*

Browning's grasp of sound can be seen and heard as of *Thirteenth Chair*'s very first scene, one of only two that

Published in the *Hollywood Daily Citizen* on November 29, 1929.

takes place outside the Crosby home. Scene One – which doesn't exist in Veiller's play – establishes an exotic locale, due in part to the beating of drums accompanied by a quiet flute and a stringed instrument, perhaps a sitar.

Shot 1 of Scene One is a long shot of the interior of Spencer Lee's home. It is dark; the only illumination is moonlight beaming through the blinds. Edward Wales enters the room surreptitiously. As Wales's darkened figure approaches the camera in Shot 6, the loud squawk of a parrot (seen in closeup in Shot 7) jars him, the household, and the viewer. Browning's first talkie thus begins without dialogue, opting instead for exotic background music and a particularly jarring sound effect.

Published in the *Hollywood Daily Citizen* on November 30, 1929.

Consider also the first séance, which takes place in near-complete darkness, as only part of a lampshade can be seen. The single shot lasts for approximately two minutes and twenty seconds, save for a very brief insert of two servants in the hallway. Sound takes center stage. A bloodcurdling scream interrupts La Grange's faked trance. Much the same could be said of the second séance, which causes Mary Eastwood to confess her crime. Once the lights go out, blackness fills the screen for approximately two minutes, this time without a break. This is all in addition to Browning's surprising use of overlapping dialogue in more than one scene.

As for the overall film, major industry trade publications had a range of different reactions:

Tense and gripping murder mystery, skillfully picturized, well acted ... Above average.[40]
– *The Educational Screen*

... this latest of the murder stories is rattling good entertainment. Fortunate in possessing at the start a theme of sustained plot and suspense, it moves steadily toward its murderer's confession climax with the slick skill and interest that Tod Browning is noted for giving his better efforts, and leaves the picturegoer completely satisfied. ... Should prove a popular film for general consumption.[41] – *Billboard*

A mystery thriller which will keep them hanging on until the end trying to guess who the guilty party is. ... Finish itself is weak, after two killings, with the second murder left unexplained. Still because of its mysterious murders, false accusations and séances, it should satisfy the taste for melodrama of the customers.[42] – *Variety*

Another added to the already long and still growing list of murder mysteries. It has nothing outstanding to recommend it beyond the capable direction of Tod Browning and a neat performance by that stage veteran, Margaret Wycherly. For one thing, there is entirely too much left unexplained in the final solution. The result will be [a] rather skeptical and perhaps, unsatisfied audience.[43] – *Motion Picture News*

The picture is rather jerky in spots and leaves one with the feeling it just misses being good entertainment.[44] – *Weekly Film Review*

Mediocre! The story is thin, the action is slow and the slightly interwoven romance is not interesting. It has some suspense and mystery, well enough, and the disclosure of the real murderer is a surprise, but there are only two scenes that hold the spectator's attention. These are the two séances by the fake medium.... The rest is jumpy and disconnected. ... Tod Browning directed it in a disjointed manner.[45] – *Harrison's Reports*

Despite some negative reviews, viewing the film makes clear that Browning was adept at far more than film sound.

Visually, he reserves his most elaborate tracking shot for the arrival of La Grange at the Crosby home. As the audience hears the offscreen Chotee (Lal Chand Mehra) announce La Grange's name, the film cuts to her and the camera swiftly tracks inward. In the same continuous shot, the camera tracks backwards to show La Grange shaking hands with Lady Crosby (Mary Forbes). Then it tracks back and left to show her greeting Wales. Then it moves back and to the right to show La Grange in another two-shot with Lady Crosby. And then, it moves backwards again to show her with Lady Crosby and Wales.

But the film's single crane shot creates the most fascinating image. The camera starts near the ceiling of a large room at the Crosby home and moves downward and inward to Inspector Delzante and the others. Not only is the shot another attempt to instill motion into the confines of the main set, it is also one of Browning's key visual tricks in the film. The shot begins with the camera already moving downward. Something is visible in the top of the frame, but it quickly falls out of view. What is it? Only a careful viewer will notice this crucial clue, which eludes even La Grange until later in the film. It is the murder knife, stuck into the ceiling.

Of the actors, Margaret Wycherly is superlative. She delivers a particularly subtle performance for the emergent talkie era. "One of the finest performances so far flashed upon the screen," the *Hollywood Daily Citizen* declared.[46]

As for Lugosi, the *New Movie Magazine* called him "excellent."[47] The *Times-Picayne* of New Orleans told readers, "The real acting is given over chiefly to Bela Lugosi."[48] But the most extensive response came from W.F. Willis of the MPPDA. He wrote:

From the pressbook for *The Thirteenth Chair*.

Another point which startled me was the characterization of the Inspector and his relationship to the whole story. ... His accent betrays him as Continental, and not British, and to me this aggravates his offence. I cannot imagine that a Continental could have risen to an inspectorship without a better sense of the deportment expected in the drawing room of a gentleman in Sir Roscoe's position.

This difficulty with the characterization of the Inspector at once creates further difficulties, for it falsifies all of the other characters. ... Incidentally, I enjoyed the picture immensely until the advent of the Inspector, and even then the work of Margaret Wycherly held the picture together for me. But I could have enjoyed her work much more if she had been opposed by a purely intellectual menace instead of a menace so largely brutally physical.[49]

Despite these somewhat spurious complaints, Lugosi dominates the scenes in which he appears, not only physically, but also verbally. His intense performance is – along with Browning's direction and Wycherly's acting – the key reason the film remains captivating. Of his surviving films of the 1920s, *The Thirteenth Chair* is the best, just as it is the best of his pre-1931 talkies.

MGM's press sheet for the film suggested that theaters hold local contests about superstitions and unlucky omens. Ballyhoo ideas included carrying a prop chair around town that heralded the film's title; the same could be placed in the lobby.[50] Some exhibitors implemented these ideas, while others devised their own unique gimmicks.[51] One turned "13" into a "lucky number" by repeatedly giving away that number of free passes to *The Thirteenth Chair*.[52] Others did tie-ups with local furniture stores.[53] But perhaps the most fascinating ballyhoo came at the Loew's Rochester Theater in Rochester, New York, where the theater manager presented an actual séance onstage.[54]

After a screening in Atlanta, one journalist wrote, "audience opinion [was] divided."[55] Varying judgments appeared in exhibitor reports from across the country:

> To my surprise it did the best Friday and Saturday business for weeks. Not only that, but it gave excellent satisfaction. Some patrons came two nights in succession.[56]

> Very good were the comments from the patrons who came.[57]

> If you want a hair-raising mystery picture, buy this one.[58]

> Will please the mystery fan.[59]

> Left patrons wondering what it was all about.[60]

> This one is terrible. I don't think it pleased over 20 percent.[61]

> This is a mystery picture so mysterious that it is about as complete a piece of literary junk as you could put on your screen. Nobody understood it, not even the kids, who are invariably more alert than older people in catching on.[62]

Had audiences in urban America responded to *The Thirteenth Chair* better than those in small towns? Perhaps. Two Helens, two murders, two séances, and one hidden knife might have been a bit too complex for some viewers, wherever they lived. Nevertheless, the film was relatively successful, generating a net profit of $148,000.

Perhaps its most memorable screening came at Grauman's Egyptian Theater on December 4, 1929. Bela Lugosi made a personal appearance; Tod Browning was slated to appear alongside him.[63]

Whether they spoke or not is unknown, but during the late twenties, Lugosi's views on sound cinema evolved, becoming ever the more positive. Only weeks after working with Browning, the man sometimes known as the "Edgar Allan Poe of Hollywood," Lugosi confidently predicted:

> The screen will learn to draw on the vast fund of stage technique perfected through the centuries, and when it has learned this, talking pictures will become as great a medium as the stage.[64]

Working together on *The Thirteenth Chair*, Lugosi and Browning had expertly explored that very potential.

Endnotes

1 Dickey, Joan. "A Maker of Mystery." *Motion Picture Classic* Mar. 1928.

2 "Mystery Film Director." *New York Times* 24 Nov. 1929.

3 "A Detective Play by Bayard Veiller." *New York Times* 21 Nov. 1916.

4 Darnton, Charles. "The New Plays." *The Evening World* (New York) 21 Nov. 1916.

5 "Bayard Veiller's Famous Melodrama Filmed with Fair Force." *Wid's Daily* 24 Aug. 1919.

6 "*The Thirteenth Chair*." *Motion Picture News* 23 Aug. 1919.

7 Parsons, Louella O. *Los Angeles Examiner* 13 May 1929.

8 For a discussion of this practice, see: "Favor One Director for Talking Films." *Film Daily* 29 May 1929.

9 Denbo, Doris. *Hollywood Daily Citizen* 30 May 1929.

10 Binckley, Elena. *Hollywood Daily Citizen* 9 July 1929.

11 "Odd Number Brings Luck." *Los Angeles Times* 2 Nov. 1929.

12 Parsons, Louella O. *Los Angeles Examiner* 3 May 1929.

13 "Talking Up." *Hollywood Filmograph* 22 June 1929.

14 Power, Ralph L. "Broadcast India's Lure." *Radio Digest* May 1930.

15 "Hollywood Notes." *Close Up* Sept. 1929.

16 "*Thirteenth Chair* Cast." *Film Daily* 17 June 1929.

17 Joy, Jason. Letter to Robert Harris, MGM, 25 June 1929. [Available in the file for *The Thirteenth Chair* in the Motion Picture Association of America, Production Code Administration collection at the Margaret Herrick Library in Beverly Hills, CA.]

18 "True Indian Mystic in *13th Chair*." *Syracuse American* (Syracuse, NY) 8 Dec. 1929.

19 "Acting Ability Declared Need." *Los Angeles Times* 14 July 1929.

20 Shaffer, Rosalind. "Foreign Actor Hurdles Talkie Language Bar." *Chicago Tribune* 28 July 1929.

21 "*Thirteenth Chair* at Loew's Theater." *Daily Argus* (Mount Vernon, NY) 16 Jan. 1930.

22 Denbo, Doris. "Bela Lugosi Hails Chance at 'Straight' Roles." *Hollywood Daily Citizen* 4 Dec. 1929.

23 "Equity Timeline 100 Years." Available at https://www.actorsequity.org/timeline/timeline_1920.html. Accessed 11 Dec. 2018.

24 "Producers Charge 164 Equity Actors Have Deserted Ranks." *Hollywood Filmograph* 22 June 1929.

25 "Actors Ignore Equity's Edict." *Los Angeles Times* 21 June 1929.

26 "Producers Will Fight Demands." *Variety* 12 June 1929.

27 "Studio Noises When Suspended Actors on Stage." *Variety* 3 July 1929.

28 "Producers Charge 164 Equity Actors Have Deserted Ranks"; "The Passing Week." *Hollywood Filmograph* 22 June 1929.

29 "Nagel's Screen Credit Group Ask Turner Lots of Questions During Private Dinner Called for Discussion." *Variety* 14 Aug. 1929.

30 "Browning Directs *13th Chair*." *Film Daily* 10 July 1929.

31 Coons, Robbin. "Flashes From Hollywood." *Appleton Post-Crescent* (Appleton, WI) 24 July 1929.

32 *Estimated Cost Director and Cast; Production No. 434 – Thirteenth Chair; Director – Tod Browning* 29 May 1929, featuring subsequent, handwritten additions. This document shows Boyd's salary would be $2,000. A handwritten note suggests Lugosi would make $1,000 per week, but whether that cumulatively exceeded a total of $2,000 is unknown.

33 "Vibrating Camera Gives Movie Ghostly Effect." *San Diego Union* 2 June 1929; "Film Stars In First Talkies Mike Conscious." *Stamford Advocate* (Stamford, CT) 18 June 1929.

34 "Inside Stuff–Pictures." *Variety* 12 June 1929.

35 *Estimated Cost Director and Cast; Production No. 434 – Thirteenth Chair; Director – Tod Browning* 29 May 1929, featuring subsequent, handwritten additions.

36 "M-G-M Lot Hums with Production Activity." *Hollywood Filmograph* 10 Aug. 1929.

37 Graham, Fanya. "Preview: *The Thirteenth Chair*." *Hollywood Filmograph* 24 Aug. 1929.

38 Ibid.

39 "The Thirteenth Chair." *National Board of Review Magazine* Nov. 1929.

40 "The Film Estimates." *The Educational Screen* Jan. 1930.

41 "*The Thirteenth Chair*." *Billboard* 21 Dec. 1929.

42 "*The Thirteenth Chair*." *Variety* 22 Jan. 1930.

43 Meyers, Al. "*The Thirteenth Chair*." *Motion Picture News* 9 Nov. 1929.

44 "Pictures Playing Atlanta This Week." *Weekly Film Review* 2 Nov. 1929.

45 "*The Thirteenth Chair*." *Harrison's Reports* 21 Dec. 1929.

46 Denbo, Doris. "Egyptian Offers Excellent Show Full of Novelty." 29 Nov. 1929.

47 "All You Want to Know." *New Movie Magazine* Jan. 1930.

48 "Asbestos." *The Times-Picayune* (New Orleans, LA) 21 Dec. 1929.

49 Willis, W.F. "*The Thirteenth Chair*." 1 Oct. 1929. [Available in the file for *The Thirteenth Chair* in the Motion Picture Association of America, Production Code Administration collection at the Margaret Herrick Library in Beverly Hills, CA.]

50 The press sheet for *The Thirteenth Chair* is archived at the New York Public Library for the Performing Arts, Dorothy and Lewis B. Cullman Center.

51 For example, an exhibitor in Illinois arranged a "superstition contest" with a local newspaper. See "*The Thirteenth Chair*." *Billboard* 7 June 1930.

52 "Lucky '13' Gag a Corker for Mgr. Barnett Lazarus." *Motion Picture News* 8 Mar. 1930.

53 "Thirteenth Chair Revolves in Lobby in Hookup with Furniture Firm." *Exhibitors Herald-World* 22 Feb. 1930; "Thirteen Ads for *Thirteenth Chair*." *Film Daily* 13 Mar. 1930.

54 "That Man Addison Arranges Séance on Theater Stage." *Exhibitors Herald-World* 1 Feb. 1930; "Exploitation Tips." *Billboard* 1 Feb. 1930.

55 "Pictures Playing Atlanta This Week."

56 "*The Thirteenth Chair*." *Exhibitors Herald-World* 18 Jan. 1930.

57 "*The Thirteenth Chair*." *Exhibitors Herald-World* 15 Feb. 1930.

58 "*The Thirteenth Chair*." *Exhibitors Herald-World* 15 Mar. 1930.

59 "*The Thirteenth Chair*." *Exhibitors Herald-World* 17 May 1930.

60 "*The Thirteenth Chair*." *Exhibitors Herald-World* 7 Dec. 1929.

61 "*The Thirteenth Chair*." *Exhibitors Herald-World* 4 Jan. 1930.

62 "*The Thirteenth Chair*." *Exhibitors Herald-World* 21 June 1930.

63 *Hollywood Daily Citizen* 4 Dec. 1929.

64 Shaffer, "Foreign Actor Hurdles Talkie Language Bar."

Lugosi as Dracula, as photographed in 1929 by *Theatre Magazine*.

Chapter 42

Open for Business

> "[H]e began pouring out a perfect torrent
> of love-making, laying his very
> heart and soul at my feet."
> Bram Stoker, *Dracula*

Gladys Hall was an extremely notable journalist during the teens, twenties, and thirties. *Flair* magazine dubbed her "one of the principal architects of the wondrous Hollywood myth."[1] Hall's work appeared in *Photoplay*, *Modern Screen*, *Motion Picture Classic*, and various others. And she would write about Lugosi in movie fan magazines more than anyone else: four articles, all published at key moments in his career.[2]

"The Case of the Man Who Dares Not Fall Asleep" of August 1929 was the first. A two-page article in *Motion Picture* magazine, it featured three photographs of Lugosi, all costumed as Dracula. Hall mentioned *Prisoners* (1929), advising readers to "Watch for him. Scrutinize his eyes."[3] But cinema was not the focus of her article.

Instead, she concentrated on Lugosi's biggest stage success. "Are they each other?", she asked. "*Dracula* is Bela Lugosi. Is Bela Lugosi *Dracula*?"[4] Here was the story of the woman who had allegedly haunted Lugosi since his days in Hungary, since before the war, the woman who never let him out of her grasp, even after he fled to America. During their mad affair, he lost much weight, apparently due to her "tiny pointed teeth, like fangs." She had to feed; she had to. Hall explained:

> [Lugosi] can never love again. He told me this, too. The person of a beautiful woman, the usual thing called sex-appeal is nil to him. He cannot get a reaction as other men

do. He can only love the love some woman bears for him. He can love the emotion she feels. The separate emotion. The instant that emotion dies, his feeling dies with it.[5]

Yes, Lugosi had "touched the charnel houses of the Plutonian shores," but nevertheless, he dared not fall asleep, at least not at night, for he knew the "secrets we dare not listen to."[6] And he could not love. Allegedly.

Whatever bit of truth existed in the story of this woman who haunted Lugosi, the retellings in the fan press nearly rivalled the fiction of Stoker's *Dracula*. And as for Lugosi, he did fall asleep, and he did allow himself to love, again and again, blatantly telling one reporter in 1928 that he was single and "open for business."[7]

Among the women he admired was Clara Bow, one of the biggest box-office stars of the era. Consider Jack Oakie's memory of a night in late June or perhaps July of 1928:

> Suddenly [Clare Bow] came running out. 'Come on, everybody! We've got tickets!' she said. 'We're going down to the Biltmore to see *Dracula.*' She was so excited that she didn't stop to dress. She just threw a great long mink over her swimsuit and we all got into her chauffeur-driven black Packard limousine.

Above Top: Clara Bow. Above: Published in *The Daily Mirror* (New York) in 1929.

> ... Bow kept her mink coat on, and we watched Bela Lugosi in his monstrous makeup with his teeth sticking out, chewing on gals' necks all evening. Then we went backstage.
>
> He couldn't speak English, but no language barrier could hide his thrill at meeting Clara Bow. He was overwhelmed with the Redhead. ... Bow invited him to her home and they became very good friends.[8]

Clara Bow's Engagement To Count Surprise to Kin

News of Clara Bow's reported engagement to Count Bela Lugosi, the Hungarian actor, who took the leading role in "Dracula," came as a surprise today to the screen actress' relatives in Brooklyn.

Mrs. Eurilla Bow Decker of 37 Halsey st., an aunt, was inclined to consider the rumor as "just another story."

"Of course you can't tell what or from our relatives who are on the coast with her.

"I never believed Clara would marry Harry Richman, but the most she would say about it was 'Wait and see,'" she added.

The red-haired actress, who grew up in Brooklyn with her aunt, will go to Europe some time this month for a rest, Mrs. Decker said.

Left: Lugosi in 1929. Above: Published in the *Brooklyn Eagle* on November 5, 1929.

Lugosi did of course speak English when he met Bow. Perhaps Oakie was referring to his limited skills with the language. Perhaps Lugosi even gave the appearance of being less adept at English than he was in order to impress Bow; she was in awe of the notion that Lugosi spoke dialogue he didn't understand.

Little is known of Lugosi and Bow's relationship, but it perhaps went beyond simply being "good friends." Marion Shilling, whose father had invested money in the 1928 West Coast version of *Dracula*, recalled:

> Clara Bow, then at the peak of her fame, attended at least two performances a week during the two months run. She'd sometimes come directly from her beach house wearing a fur coat over her bathing suit. The play's attraction for her? Bela Lugosi! She had a terrific crush on him.
>
> Bela liked to tell my father that if I were a bit older, without question he'd marry me. I'm certain this was a bit of blarney. In competition with the scintillating Clara, what chance would poor, green, little Marion have had![9]

The story of Bow wearing nothing but a swimming suit under her fur coat fueled the imagination of later writers, suggesting as it did frisson and ecstasy between the Vampire and the It Girl. Lugosi did not need to sleep at night; fireworks between the two lovers lit up the darkness.

But the reality might well have been less exciting, less scandalous. Certainly Lugosi's name became romantically linked with Bow's in newspapers, ranging from the New York *Daily Mirror* to the *Los Angeles Times*, which told readers, "Morley Drury and Bela Lugosi each had a brief

Above: Lugosi's painting of Clara Bow. Right: Artist Géza Kende. Below Right: Published in the *New York Daily News* on October 5, 1930.

Bela Lugosi was Clara's playmate for a while last year.

inning in Clara's affections."[10] Journalists likely heard these tales from Bow's secretary, Daisy DeVoe.

Another key memory of Lugosi and Bow comes from Tui Lorraine Bow, who recalled the two staying at Bow's Malibu cottage. Three bedrooms and full occupancy, but it was Tui, *not* Lugosi, who shared Clara's bedroom.[11] House guests might have prevented more amorous arrangements, but it does seem that the torrid details of their relationship came from fairly spurious accounts.

Nevertheless, the duo certainly parted with fond feelings, keeping mementos of one another until their deaths. Bow kept several signed photographs of Lugosi, including images from *Arabesque* and *The Devil in the Cheese*. And he owned a large painting of her in the nude, which – given Bow's attitude towards such things – was almost certainly painted by artist Géza Kende's imagination in 1929, rather than with Bow as the model.

The next woman in Lugosi's life was in some ways different from Clara Bow and Ilona Montagh: Beatrice Woodruff Weeks. Born in 1897, she claimed to be a direct descendant of John and Priscilla Alden.[12] Her father was Commodore John S. Woodruff.[13] Beatrice didn't work, and came from a family wealthier than Lugosi's; in those respects, she was similar to Ilona Szmik.[14] But like Bow, she was American, a modern and independent woman of the Roaring Twenties.

And like Bow, Beatrice met Lugosi as a result of his West Coast version of *Dracula*. A newspaper article described their "whirlwind" romance.[15]

Bela Lugosi ... will become leading man in the affairs of Mrs. Beatrice Woodruff Weeks, society woman and widow of Charles Peter Weeks, former wealthy architect, next Saturday after a courtship which has set something of a record for speed.

Lugosi met his bride-to-be a year ago at a reception given at Mare Island by Captain and Mrs. George B. Landenberger. The acquaintance was continued but nothing "serious" came of it until yesterday morning.

Then Lugosi proposed the question, was accepted, and followed right through with a trip to Redwood City, where the couple applied for a marriage license. They plan to be married Saturday morning at Redwood City.[16]

Luigi Stilliti, an Italian Consul-General, introduced Lugosi to Weeks at that 1928 reception.[17] Party host Captain Landenberger, a hero of the Great War, commanded numerous ships during his illustrious naval career.[18] As for Lugosi, he quickly learned that Beatrice was a widow. Only five months earlier, her husband Charles Peter Weeks had died, leaving her an estate allegedly worth $2,500,000.[19]

Weeks was a noted architect who studied in Paris. He designed buildings in San Francisco, Sacramento, and San Jose; he even drew up the plans for the Loew's State Theatre in Los Angeles, where the Lugosi film *The Thirteenth Chair* played in 1929. Weeks was also twenty years older than Beatrice, but neither were strangers to romance. Both had been married before, Beatrice to New York stockbroker James Mills, Jr.[20] In fact, Beatrice had only been legally divorced from her first husband for one day when she and Weeks took their vows.[21]

By the time Beatrice met Lugosi, though, she was a widow. That fifteen years separated their ages was hardly a worry. A wider age gap had separated Beatrice from Weeks, just as it had in reverse for Lugosi and both Ilonas. And Lugosi would have seemed even more worldly than Beatrice's recently deceased

Above Top: Coverage of Lugosi's divorce in the Hungarian press. Published in the *Pécsi Napló* on February 2, 1930. Above: Lugosi and Beatrice Woodruff Weeks.

husband. Perhaps she was fascinated by his role in *Dracula*; presumably she saw the play at least once in 1928.

By the autumn of 1928, Lugosi left Beatrice in San Francisco and returned to Los Angeles. The two wrote to each other, but it is impossible to know how close of a relationship they had developed, or how frequently they corresponded.[22] It would seem logical that she told Lugosi about her father's death in January 1929.[23] John S. Woodruff – an attorney, naval commander, and member of the U.S. Shipping Board – had died after a relapse of influenza; he was only 58 years old. Whether Beatrice made it to his burial at Arlington Cemetery two days after his death is unknown.[24]

What is certain is the fact that Beatrice was alone. Her husband and father were dead. She had no siblings, and her mother lived thousands of miles away in Washington, D.C.[25] Then Lugosi returned to her. *Dracula-The Vampire Play* was staged in San Francisco almost a year after the 1928 production. A newspaper journalist wrote about how the two of them conquered that vampire woman who kept Lugosi from sleeping at night:

Above: Charles Peter Weeks designed the Loew's State Theater in Los Angeles. This ad was published in the *Los Angeles Times* on October 31, 1929.
Below: Published in *The Daily Mirror* (New York) on November 5, 1929.

the foreign actor, the latest Mrs. Lugosi expressed no animosity to the youthful screen actress, whom she charges now holds the key to her husband's heart.

BATTLE STARTS EARLY.

Lugosi fought the second day of their married life, his wife declared yesterday. "He slapped me in the face because I ate a lamb chop which he had hidden in the ing the nuptials, when Lugosi demanded her checkbook and key to her safe deposit vaults, Mrs. Lugosi explained.

"He told me that he was King; that in Hungary a wife and all she possessed were placed at the husband's disposal; that, in effect, she was nothing but a servant.

"Of course, I objected to this, and we quarreled.

"His table manners were terrible. He would break an apple

Years ago, before Bela left his native Hungary, he says he met and was adored by a beautiful actress with pale, brown hair and ghostly pale skin. This woman loved the handsome young actor inordinately – perhaps because he, too, had something of the bizarre in his appearance. He fled to America to escape the uncanny mental net she was weaving about him, only to have her dark, piercing glances haunt his sleep.

'I dare not love anyone,' he said then. 'I could not love while she lives. She would send her wordless command to me and I cannot contend with the agencies of darkness...'

But he did not know that he was destined to meet the fascinating Beatrice Weeks, wealthy San Francisco society matron ... the mysterious siren of Lugosi's past was forgotten.

This time the actor wanted to make sure it was true love. He wanted to be sure that the spell of the pale woman of his past had been eradicated from his life. He went away for a year to discover whether the flame of his love for Mrs. Weeks would burn on; and it did.

'That was the longest, dreariest year of my life,' he confessed. 'On my return we both felt that we could not wait any longer.'[26]

Talking to a reporter in 1929, Lugosi added, "I fell in love with Beatrice Weeks at first sight." But he claimed not to know whether she was a blonde or brunette: "You see, it is like this. The eyes got in the way. You understand."[27]

On July 26, 1929, a mere four days after *Dracula*'s opening in San Francisco, the couple married in a Redwood City courtroom.[28] Strangely, Lugosi would later tell one reporter that he had "only known her but a few days" prior to the wedding.[29]

They could not take a honeymoon: Lugosi had to keep working in the San Francisco *Dracula* for another two weeks.[30] Unless he allowed an understudy to take his place, he even appeared in matinee and evening performances of *Dracula* on the very day after the wedding. In the short-term, the newlyweds stayed in a group of rooms on the top floor of the Hotel Mark Hopkins in San Francisco; it had been designed and partly owned by Charles Peter Weeks.[31]

The Lugosis originally intended to move to Los Angeles together, but that was not to be. In fact, it seems apparent they didn't even survive as a couple for the duration of *Dracula*'s run in San Francisco. Lugosi once said the marriage survived only three days; on another occasion, he said it was a week.[32] Beatrice claimed it had lasted four and a half days.[33] What could have gone so horribly wrong in such a short amount of time? Lugosi later complained about Beatrice dancing with other men, her smoking, and her lack of help with his hangovers.[34] He was also distressed by the fact that she drank gin in the morning.[35]

Beatrice gave a very different account of their life together. She argued that Lugosi began fighting on the second day of their marriage.[36] He was "sullen and morose and inhospitable to their guests."[37] He was "vicious" and "irascible."[38] Beatrice's statement to the court added that Lugosi was unable to "cast aside entirely his said role [as Dracula] and to conform to the ordinary, usual and accepted life of the human being, especially as applied in a domestic sense."[39]

The *Daily Mirror* quoted Beatrice as saying:

> [Lugosi] slapped me in the face because I ate a lamb chop which he [had] hidden in the icebox for his after-theatre, midnight lunch. ... His table manners were terrible. ... He constantly used his fingers in place of a fork and was addicted to similar habits that simply frayed my nerves.
>
> He told me that he was King, that in Hungary a wife and all she possessed were placed at the husband's disposal, that, in effect, she was nothing but a servant.
>
> Of course I objected to this, and we quarreled.
>
> His table manners were terrible. He would break an apple in half and crowd one of the portions in his mouth, unable to speak or swallow, until he had chewed it up fine.[40]

On the third day of their marriage, Lugosi allegedly demanded her checkbook and the key to her safe deposit box.[41] But the breaking point came when Lugosi furnished his own bedroom, "afterward informing her if she didn't care to equip her own, she could sleep on the floor."[42] The latter tale was likely an invention, as the two were indeed staying in a hotel.

According to one fan magazine, Beatrice had asked Lugosi for a particular wedding present: "A life-sized portrait of you in oils, darling."[43] Whether Lugosi already owned his nude portrait of Clara Bow is unknown, but Beatrice certainly blamed Bow for some of her marital troubles.

"I don't know when they will be married," she said. "But before I left my husband he told me he and Clara had been engaged; that they had agreed to remain away from each other a year to test their love."[44] The implication was that Lugosi had married Beatrice for her money, while waiting for the right moment to reunite with Bow. And so Beatrice filed for divorce on August 20, 1929.

But the story became more confused when the *Daily Mirror* suggested that Lugosi – whom they referred to as "Count Lugosi" – had "jilted" Bow to marry Beatrice. Did Beatrice say any of this? The *Daily Mirror* reported that the information was made public when Beatrice filed for divorce. Even if that's true, though, it is possible that some or most or even all of what she said was invented to show proper grounds for a divorce. Or, given that the bar for obtaining a divorce in Reno was relatively low, perhaps she was speaking out of anger.

"I wish Miss Bow all the luck in the world," Beatrice said. "However, I cannot see any happiness for her if she marries my husband, unless he improves his manners."[45] In the fall of 1929, Walter Winchell told readers, "Clara Bow's current pash is Bela Lugosi."[46] He published the news prior to the *Daily Mirror*'s article and the divorce, but that still doesn't mean Lugosi and Bow were involved in a heated romance. Nor does it mean the two were engaged, as another publication claimed. Bow's aunt Eurilla Bow Decker of Brooklyn told the press she hadn't "heard anything about the Lugosi engagement," claiming it was probably "just another story."[47] By the time the divorce was final, it's possible Lugosi was no longer even in contact with Bow.

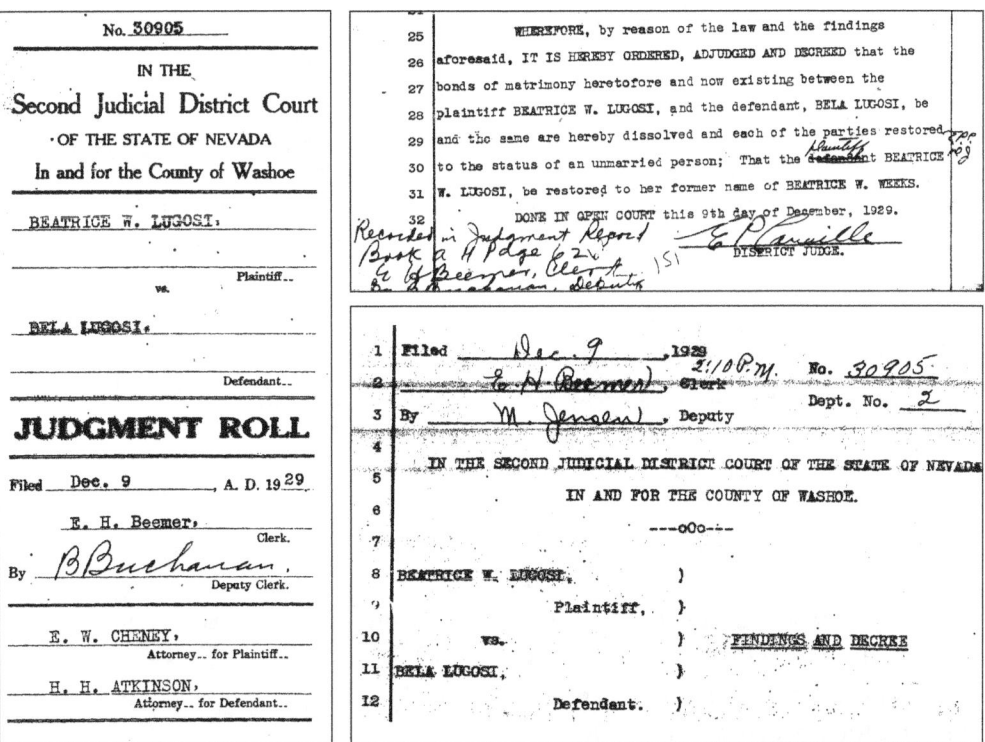

As with the court proceedings with both Ilonas, Lugosi didn't appear in person to challenge the divorce. Beatrice charged him with "extreme cruelty" and the divorce was granted in Reno on December 9, 1929. That same month, a reporter for the *Hollywood Daily Citizen* "timidly" asked Lugosi, "You were married recently for just a few days, weren't you?" He responded affirmatively, adding:

> I cannot accustom myself to the modern girl. She is a creature of impulse. She has found a new liberty in thinking for herself. She has discovered all things are possible for her, and she is forgetting there is a greater happiness in consulting and thinking things over with friends, husband, family. She will never be completely happy until she once again takes her place by the side of man as his companion and helpmate. It is her natural place and she will be unhappy, restless, and doing things she is sorry for until she adjusts herself to this place.[48]

On another occasion, Lugosi spoke at greater length about the divide that separated the couple, explaining, "Beatrice wanted to have a good time in the American style – parties, theaters, cabarets; a ceaseless succession of trivial amusements. There is my art – I have not the time and I do not approve."[49] He went on to say:

> Of course, I'll admit I'm old-fashioned and conservative, with European ideas about womanhood. Home life has long been denied me; it seems to me very much worthwhile. Four days after our marriage, Beatrice and I decided that our mental attitudes, inculcated by home atmospheres, could never be made compatible. We parted.
>
> Beatrice had the modern American attitude toward married life. Not, you understand, the attitude of the original Americans, the Indians, among whom the men fought the wars of the tribe and brought home the food, while his wife did the work at home. Not that. But the jazz idea, the 'speed passion.'
>
> I wanted a wife who would share pleasures and burdens with me. Fifty-fifty, as they say. Beatrice could not see that....

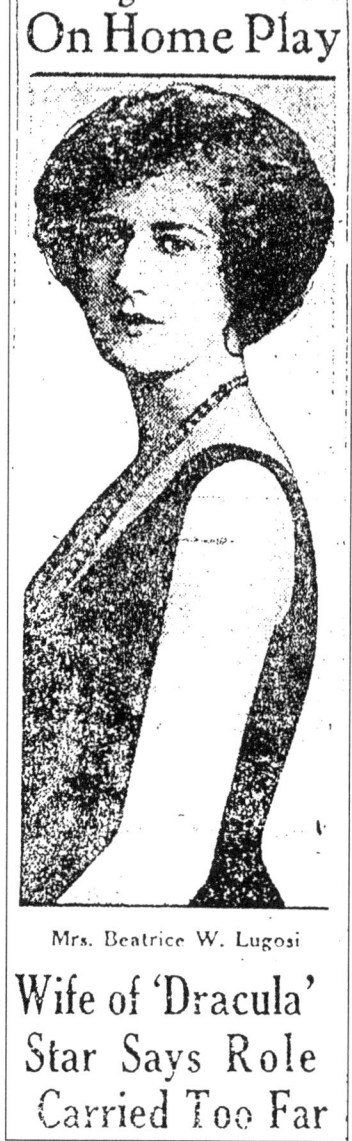

Mrs. Beatrice W. Lugosi

Rings Curtain On Home Play

Wife of 'Dracula' Star Says Role Carried Too Far

Published in the *San Francisco Chronicle* on December 10, 1929.

I believed that it was the husband's duty to take full charge of all affairs and provide for the wife's happiness as he deemed best. My wife insisted upon finding happiness in her own way.⁵⁰

To another interviewer, Lugosi said, "She is so independent and seems to demand liberties I simply cannot seem to accept. It is too bad. I loved her."⁵¹

Lugosi later added that he did see Beatrice after the divorce. "And why not?" he questioned. "Two people who failed at marriage may still find each other enjoyable and entertaining persons."⁵²

For reasons that aren't entirely clear, Beatrice became increasingly unhappy. Perhaps it was because of alcohol, perhaps it was because of the loss of her father and husbands. At a given point, Beatrice even reached out in vain to Lugosi, asking him to

Published in the *Victoria Daily Times* on September 26, 1936.

take her back.⁵³ Along with whatever depression she experienced, Beatrice also had increasing medical problems. She moved to Colon, Panama, where she died of pulmonary disease in May 1931 at the age of 34. Her ashes were inurned beside those of Charles Peter Weeks.⁵⁴ The *New York Times* obituary didn't mention Lugosi, who later said that he regretted the divorce.⁵⁵

Their marriage had clearly been a mistake. Whatever the actual reasons, it had nothing to do with Lugosi being haunted by a vampire woman. But that didn't keep yet another fan magazine from claiming it did, quoting Lugosi as saying:

> Two nights after my marriage when the curtain rose [in San Francisco], it seemed as if the world crashed at my feet, for there, just as it had been in Budapest, just as in New York, two yellow eyes held mine from the front row. To me it is all a blur. The moment I saw Hedy, I knew that she still held me and that my marriage was again doomed. I shuddered for I remembered that this time she had promised to strike harder! This time I did not struggle against the inevitable.

Lugosi at home in the 1930s. The painting of Clara Bow hangs on his wall.

Heartbroken, scarcely wanting to live, I told Beatrice, my wife, that it was all over. There is no use probing the wound of that night, for what explanation could I offer that would be acceptable or understandable to Beatrice? My first two wives had been Hungarian, and we are a mystic people, a psychic race who feel. They at least had understood, if only that it was something I could not explain. Beatrice could not.[56]

As Gladys Hall wrote in 1929, Lugosi suffered from the "ghastly two-pronged mark of the vampire on his throat." His was the "strange tale of the man who never sleeps and cannot love." [57] Hall was indeed an architect of myths, every bit as much as Charles Peter Weeks was of buildings.

Endnotes

1   "Gladys Hall, 86; Writer for Film-Fan Magazines." *New York Times* 22 Sept. 1977.

2   The four articles are: Hall, Gladys. "True Hollywood Ghost Stories II: The Case of the Man Who Dares Not Fall Asleep." *Motion Picture* Aug. 1929; Hall, Gladys. "The Feminine Love of Horror." *Motion Picture Classic* Jan. 1931; Hall, Gladys. "Do You Believe This Story?" *Modern Screen* June 1935; Lugosi, Bela, as told to Gladys Hall. "Memos of a Madman!" *Silver Screen* July 1941.

3   Hall, "True Hollywood Ghost Stories II."

4   Ibid. Emphasis in original.

5   Ibid.

6   Ibid.

7   Whitaker, Alma. "Lugosi, Creator of Dracula Role, Is Courtly Hungarian." *Los Angeles Times* 17 June 1928.

8   Oakie, Jack. *Jack Oakie's Double Takes* (Portland, OR: Strawberry Hill, 1980).

9   Goldrup, Jim and Tom. *Feature Players: The Stories Behind the Faces*. Vol. 3. (Ben Lomond, CA: J. and T. Goldrup, 1986).

10 Whitaker, Alma. "Flamboyant Clara Bow Now Emerges as Lady." *Los Angeles Times* 25 Sept. 1932.

11 Stenn, David. *Clara Bow: Runnin' Wild* (New York: Doubleday, 1988). At the time, Tui Lorraine was married to Clara's father Robert, even though she was roughly the same age as Clara.

12 "Widow of Noted S. F. Architect Dead in Panama." *Hanford Sentinel* (Hanford, CA) 23 May 1931.

13 "Descendant of Puritan Lovers Dies in Panama." *Fresno Bee* (Fresno, CA) 25 May 1931.

14 "C.P. Weeks, Bay City Architect, Expires." *Los Angeles Times* 26 May 1928.

15 The term "whirlwind" appears in "Affairs of the Heart." *Talking Screen* Jan. 1930.

16 "Hungarian Actor To Wed S. F. Widow." *Oakland Tribune* 24 July 1929.

17 Nye, Myra. "Society of Cinemaland." *Los Angeles Times* 4 Aug. 1929.

18 Ibid.

19 "C.P. Weeks, Bay City Architect, Expires." *Los Angeles Times* 26 May 1928; Mefford, Arthur. "Lugosi Wins Heart of Clara Bow, Says Second Wife, Seeking Divorce." *The Daily Mirror* (New York) 5 Nov. 1929.

20 Ibid. See also "Descendant of Puritan Lovers Dies in Panama." See also Woods, Virginia. "Society." *Los Angeles Times* 1 Sept. 1920.

21 "New York Divorcee Bride of San Francisco Man Day after Decree is Final." *San Francisco Chronicle* 31 Jan. 1923.

22 "S.F. Widow to Wed Star of *Dracula* Play." *San Francisco Chronicle* 24 July 1929.

23 "Comdr. Woodruff Dies of Influenza." *Washington Post* 14 Jan. 1929.

24 "John S. Woodruff Dies in Washington." *New York Times* 14 Jan. 1929.

25 Ibid.

26 "Haunted Honeymoon of the 'Vampire Man's' Society Bride." *Hamilton Evening Journal* (Hamilton, OH) 12 Oct. 1929.

27 Hanifin, Ada. "*Dracula* Found Out; Secret of Lugosi Revealed." *San Francisco Examiner* 28 July 1929.

28 "Hungarian Stage Star Weds Widow of S.F. Architect." *San Francisco Examiner* 28 July 1929.

29 Denbo, Doris. "Bela Lugosi Hails Chance at 'Straight' Film Roles." *Hollywood Daily Citizen* 4 Dec. 1929.

30 For a lengthy discussion of Lugosi in *Dracula-The Vampire Play* in 1929, see Chapter 40.

31 "Mrs. Weeks to Wed Bela Lugosi Today." *San Francisco Examiner* 27 July 1929. Also, "Charles Peter Weeks, S.F. Architect, Found Dead." *San Francisco Chronicle* 25 Mar. 1928. Also, Rhodes, Gary D. Interview with Ruth Sheffield, 17 Mar. 1996. [Lugosi told Ruth and Richard Sheffield about having all the rooms on the top floor of the hotel.]

32 Chrisman, J. Eugene. "Masters of Horror – Karloff and Lugosi." *Modern Screen* (Apr. 1932).

33 Mefford, "Lugosi Wins Heart of Clara Bow."

34 Cremer, Robert. *Lugosi: The Man Behind the Cape* (Chicago: Henry Regnery, 1976).

35 Sheffield, Richard. Letter to Gary D. Rhodes, 27 June 1989.

36 Mefford, "Lugosi Wins Heart of Clara Bow."

37 "*Dracula* Star Divorced Here." *Reno Evening Gazette* (Reno, NV) 9 Dec. 1929.

38 "Rings Curtain on Home Play." *San Francisco Chronicle* 10 Dec. 1929.

39 *Beatrice W. Lugosi, Plaintiff, vs. Bela Lugosi, Defendant.* Complaint No. 30905 Filed in the Second Judicial District Court of the State of Nevada, in and for the County of Washoe. 9 Dec. 1929.

40 Mefford, "Lugosi Wins Heart of Clara Bow."

41 Ibid.

42 Ibid.

43 "Gossip of the Studios." *New Movie Magazine* Dec. 1929.

44 "Wife of *Dracula* Star Says Role Carried Too Far." *The Daily Mirror* (New York) 5 Nov. 1929.

45 Mefford, "Lugosi Wins Heart of Clara Bow."

46 Winchell, Walter. "On Broadway." *Wisconsin State Journal* (Madison, WI) 21 Oct. 1929.

47 "Clara Bow's Engagement to Count Surprise to Kin." *Brooklyn Eagle* 5 Nov. 1929.

48 Denbo, Doris. "Bela Lugosi Hails Chance at 'Straight' Film Roles." *Hollywood Daily Citizen* 4 Dec. 1929.

49 "Haunted Honeymoon of the "Vampire Man's Society Bride."

50 "Bela Lugosi, Spouse Part After 4 Days – Hungarian Actor and S. F. Widow Agree to Separate When Marriage Views Conflict." *San Francisco Examiner* 24 Aug. 1929.

51 Denbo, "Bela Lugosi Hails Chance at 'Straight' Film Roles."

52 Sinclair, John. "Master of Horrors!" *Silver Screen* Jan. 1932.

53 Sheffield, Richard. Email to Gary D. Rhodes, 16 June 2006.

54 "Mrs. Beatrice Weeks Is Dead in Panama." *Oakland Tribune* 23 May 1931.

55 "Deaths." *New York Times* 24 May 1931. Also, Sheffield, email to Rhodes. [In the 1950s, Lugosi told Sheffield that he regretted not staying married to Weeks, given that he would have become wealthy at the time of her death.]

56 Chrisman, "Masters of Horror – Karloff and Lugosi."

57 Hall, "True Hollywood Ghost Stories II."

Lugosi in 1929.

Chapter 43

Doppelgänger

In late October of 1929, Bela Lugosi attended a Los Angeles party honoring Fern Andra, an actress known for such movies as Robert Wiene's *Genuine* (1920, aka *Genuine: A Tale of a Vampire*). Lugosi and Andra might well have met in Berlin. From his days in Hungary, Lugosi definitely knew Michael Curtiz (Mihály Kertész), and Alexander Korda (Sándor Korda), who were also present. Other party guests included directors Ernst Lubitsch and Sidney Olcott, and actors James Gleason, Charles Bickford, Lew Cody, and Marie Prevost.[1]

A trio of major players from Universal Pictures also attended: Edward Laemmle (director, and nephew of founder Carl Laemmle, Sr.), Paul Kohner (who would later produce the Spanish-language film *Drácula* in 1931), and Pál Fejős (aka Paul Fejos, director of such Universal movies as *Lonesome* in 1928 and *Broadway* in 1929).

Only a few weeks later, in mid-November of 1929, the *Los Angeles Times* reported:

> We learn on good authority that the very first talking picture made in the Hungarian tongue has just been completed by Universal.
>
> It is a Hungarian talking version of *The Last Performance*, done in the English and German versions by Conrad Veidt and Mary Philbin.
>
> Bela Lugosi is the star of the Hungarian version, the translation of which was in the hands of John Auer. Dr. Paul Fejos, who directed, also appears in the prologue.[2]

Hungarian-born János Auer (John Auer) later became the writer-director-producer of *The Crime of Doctor Crespi* (1935) with Eric Von Stroheim.

Earlier that same year, *Photoplay* described dubbing, which was often termed "voice doubling" at the time: "There are voice doubles in Hollywood today just as there are stunt doubles."[3] Studios used voice doubles for actors on numerous occasions in 1929; for example,

Lugosi shaking hands with Paul Fejos (Pál Fejós) at Universal on the set of *Captain of the Guard* (1930).

Eva Olivotti's singing came out of Laura LaPlante's mouth in Universal's *Show Boat* (1929). And then there was the Hungarian Pál Lukács, who became popular in Hollywood as Paul Lukas. *Photoplay* reported, "Mr. Lukas, an exceptionally fine actor, is handicapped for American pictures by a foreign accent. For that reason, therefore, it is necessary for someone else to speak his lines."[4]

By contrast, Lugosi became the voice double for Conrad Veidt in *The Last Performance* (1929). The two had earlier worked together on F. W. Murnau's *Der Januskopf: eine Tragödie am Rande der Wirklichkeit* (*The Head of Janus: A Tragedy on the Border of Reality,* 1920), a loose adaptation of one of the greatest stories of duality, Robert Louis Stevenson's *Strange Case of Dr. Jekyll and Mr. Hyde* (1886). A Hungarian publication reported:

> They have been doing talkies in Hollywood for two years, but it happened for the first time that the picture was talking in Hungarian. The farther people are blown from their home, the closer they get to it – useless to deny it. Here, ten thousand miles away from home, most people miss the Hungarian atmosphere and the warmth of the land as one misses embracing their mother. And this was best conveyed by our emotions, our loud heartthrobs when we heard the first Hungarian words of the movie: 'Mr. Chairman...'
>
> It was such a pleasure to hear. Everyone got into a festive mood. We heard the sweet and warm melodies of the Hungarian language, which sounded like music to our ears

Publicity photographs of Conrad Veidt in *The Last Performance* (1929). *(Courtesy of John Soister)*

and to our souls, like a bell ringing for a mass. And we remembered all the beautifully sore memories of our Hungarian roots: parents, siblings, unforgettable graves. Loyal friends and disloyal lovers. Everything that was beautiful in our life in Hungary and that we had to leave once. And on the screen the first sentence was finished: 'Mr. Chairman, I can explain everything...'

The voice was that of Bela Lugosi, who interpreted in Hungarian what Conrad Veidt was communicating silently, with mimics and gestures on the screen, in the forensic scene of the Pál Fejős movie entitled *The Last Performance*. When the first Hungarian phrase ended, Fejős exclaimed in delight: 'Finally, a Hungarian talkie exists...'

Lugosi jumped up from his seat and shouted into the darkness of the movie theatre: 'Kids, finally, we, Hungarians can have a word, too!'

And we all shook hands congratulating each other. We were as happy as only children can really be. We were so happy because the picture was talking in Hungarian...

I think it is worth capturing how the first Hungarian talkie was born in Hollywood.

The supervisor, Paul Kohner, is the Head of the Foreign [Language] Department of Universal Studios, and he has been helping many Hungarian endeavors in Hollywood. He turned the film entitled *Love Me and the World Is Mine* [1927], by Imre Fazekas, into a success, among others. Kohner's deputy is a talented young Hungarian, János

> # UNIVERSAL WEEKLY — MARCH 8, 1930
>
> ## UNIVERSAL TAKES LEAD IN FOREIGN VERSION FILMS
>
> "Last Performance" in German and Hungarian First Picture to be Made in Foreign Languages—Followed by Spanish and German Versions of "Broadway," "Show Boat," "Shanghai Lady," "Mississippi Gambler," "Skinner Steps Out," "Hell's Heroes" and Latest Schildkraut Film
>
> UNDER the program and supervision of Carl Laemmle, Jr., general manager of Universal west coast studios, an all dialogue picture of feature length entirely in Spanish, with an exclusive Spanish cast, has been projected at Universal City.
>
> The picture, which is unnamed at this time, will also be the starring vehicle of Joseph Schildkraut in English, with an English speaking supporting cast. Schildkraut will work during the day, and at night the Spanish players will occupy the same set and enact the same scenes made a few hours before in English.
>
> Universal was the first company to make foreign versions of its pictures, having produced several as late as last spring under the supervision of Paul Kohner, who is in charge of this department. The first foreign language version was that of "The Last Performance," starring Conrad Veidt and Mary Philbin, which was made in German and Hungarian.
>
> Then followed versions of "Broadway" and Show Boat" in Spanish and German. Versions of Universal's more recent pictures, "The Shanghai Lady," starring Nolan; "The Mississippi Gambler," starring Joseph Schildkraut; "Skinner Steps Out," starring Glenn Tryon and Merna Kennedy, are being made in Spanish, and "Hell's Heroes" in Spanish and German.
>
> Foreign language experts read the complete dialog script of a completed picture and count the syllables used in each sentence. They then translate the dialogue to match the lip movement and facial expressions of the players. The picture is run in a sound-proof theatre with the language cast seated at microphone. As the picture is run they speak their lines which are recorded by movietone system, and the sound track thus provided replaces the English version.
>
> This system comes as close as humanly possible to a perfect "translation." It was used solely for the reason that there are not more than fifty theatres in the world wired for sound that use Spanish spoken pictures.

Auer, who had already had considerable acting success before he signed a contract with Universal. Kohner and Auer have been planning a Hungarian sound movie for weeks, but Universal's management did not find the Hungarian market firm enough, and they did not know whether those few Hungarian cinemas, which were set up for the release of talkies, could provide sufficient income or not.

One morning Paul Kohner and Bela Lugosi showed up at the Universal Studios' *La Marseillaise* set, where Fejős was directing the battle scenes of the French Revolution using Movietone [for the 1930 film *Captain of the Guard*]. When they reached the end of the scene, Fejős climbed off the three-story-high shooting crane, from where he was conducting the movements of the crowd. Kohner and Lugosi shook hands with Fejős and with Hal Mohr, the cameraman in chief. Lugosi turned to Fejős and said:

> **Hungarian Talker Made**
>
> We learn on good authority that the very first talking picture made in the Hungarian tongue has just been completed by Universal.
>
> It is a Hungarian talking verison of "The Last Performance," done in the English and German versions by Conrad Veidt and Mary Philbin.
>
> Bela Lugosi is the star of the Hungarian version, the translation of which was in the hands of John Auer. Dr. Paul Fejos, who directed, also appears in the prologue.
>
> Carl Laemmle, Jr., is responsible for the tremendous enterprise recorded by Universal in the production of foreign language talking pictures, while we hear that Paul Kohner is supervising.

BELA LUGOSI

Published in the *Los Angeles Times* on November 16, 1929.

'Hello, my dear Pali. I've just seen *The Last Performance* in English. It was beautiful. Congratulations. And my pleasure was doubled by the fact that the director of the film, whom I consider to be Hollywood's greatest director, is Hungarian. I only need to know one thing: Why don't you do it in Hungarian, too?'

'Because there is no suitable actor who would dub it in Hungarian,' replied Fejős. 'But, for example, if you would volunteer for it, I suppose we could do it...'

'Please,' said Lugosi, 'you know that dubbing other actors is not my business, but if it is about creating the first Hungarian talkie, I'll happily volunteer to take on the assignment.'

They shook hands and said goodbye. Kohner informed Mr. Laemmle about the agreement, and he in turn decided to experimentally make the first Hungarian talkie. *The Last Performance* was chosen – the original title of which had been *Erik the Great* – because the director was Hungarian and most parts of the film took place in Hungary. The direction of the Hungarian scenes was assigned to János Auer, who chose Lugosi for the main role. By now, Lugosi has acquired a 'big name.' There was only one threatening sign on the horizon: Lugosi's $1,000 weekly payment. This experiment was by all means very expensive for Universal and it was feared that this high sum would hinder the creation of the first Hungarian 'talkie.'

Therefore, keeping in mind the good cause for Hungary, Lugosi offered to take the role free of charge. Thus, Lugosi eschewed $1,000 with a generous gesture, to promote the birth of the Hungarian talkie. Other roles were recited by Károly Darvas [who had appeared in a few plays with Lugosi in New York in 1921 and 1922] and Mihály Mezei. The role of Mary Philbin was assigned to Aranka Krajnyák née Balkányi, a young actress from Igló. The author of this article, who had been sent to the Universal as a correspondent, received a role, too: he roared the protest of the court attorney in the microphone...

It turned out not long ago that, following Paul Kohner's orders, a hidden film camera recorded the scene between Fejős and Lugosi by the shooting crane, with the 'revolting actors' in the background, and the microphone recorded the whole dialogue, too, so even the inception of the

Published in the *Nemzeti Újság* on February 27, 1930.

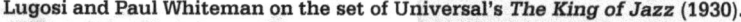

Lugosi and Paul Whiteman on the set of Universal's *The King of Jazz* (1930).

first Hungarian talkie is preserved in sound film. And, of course, this will also be shown in Hungary ...[5]

And so Lugosi appeared onscreen in a prologue as well as being heard in *The Last Performance*, a film that features extreme closeups of Veidt's hypnotic eyes, imagery similar to what would appear in such Lugosi movies as *Dracula* (1931) and *White Zombie* (1932).[6]

The Last Performance was released in Budapest on approximately February 27, 1930 under the title *Féltékenység* (*Jealousy*). How well it resonated with Hungarian audiences is unknown.

But Universal remained committed to "foreign version films," describing the process at length in 1930:

> Foreign language experts read the complete dialogue script of a completed picture and count the syllables used in each sentence. They then translate the dialogue to match the lip movement and facial expressions of the players. The picture is run in a soundproof theater with the language cast seated at the microphone. As the picture is run, they speak their lines which are recorded by [the] Movietone system, and the sound track thus replaces the English version.[7]

The studio proclaimed its voice double system to be "as close as humanly possible to a perfect 'translation.'"

In 1930, Lugosi worked once again with Paul Kohner at Universal, on a foreign-language version of the studio's *The King of Jazz* (1930). Directed by John Murray Anderson, the Technicolor musical featured jazz orchestra leader Paul Whiteman and a number of celebrities, including Jeanette Loff, Universal's original choice to play Mina in Tod Browning's *Dracula* (1931).[8] According to a Budapest newspaper:

> In reality, Mr. Laemmle only wanted to make foreign-language versions of Whiteman's revue for some countries which seemed to be important from the point of view of business, but Paul Kohner persuaded him to make a Hungarian version, too, in recognition of the outstanding Hungarian culture, even if it doesn't guarantee serious business ... that's how the Hungarian version of *The King of Jazz* was born, and the Czech, Swedish and Japanese versions of the revue followed suit....[9]

The studio proceeded to make nine foreign versions of *The King of Jazz*, each with a "master of ceremonies" speaking onscreen in the appropriate language.[10] For example, Lia Tora, who costarred with Lugosi in *The Veiled Woman* (1928), acted in that capacity for the Portuguese version.

Lugosi – together with fellow Hungarians János Auer and Lucy Doraine, who had once been married to Michael Curtiz (Mihály Kertész) – appeared as hosts in scenes added to the Hungarian version. Lugosi's particular task was reportedly to explain the onscreen action for a culture somewhat unfamiliar with jazz and Whiteman. Under the title *A jazzkirály*, this version played Budapest in September 1930. One Hungarian newspaper explained:

> Lugosi starts announcing in Hungarian and he introduces Whiteman. The King of Jazz bows and says in Hungarian: '*Whiteman Pál vagyok...*' (which means: I am Paul Whiteman). However, the revue must be given a diverse frame, so, for each variant on a foreign language more than one performer was assigned.[11]

Another article described a particular "Hungarian scene" that featured folk music arranged by Kálmán Kovács.[12] And a trade publication claimed that Lugosi, Doraine, and Auer spoke in Hungarian during the "whole length" of the film.[13]

At least nine Budapest newspapers and magazines promoted *A jazzkirály* in September of 1930, but not all audiences enjoyed the onscreen hosts.[14] *Variety* published a report from Hungary:

> Hungarian dialog was placed in [*The King of Jazz*] by Lucy Doraine and two men, lesser lights of Hollywood. They are not known here and evidently having resided in America for years, their Hungarian was spoken with such a strong foreign accent it was hardly intelligible and rather ridiculous. Nevertheless, [*The King of Jazz*] had a fairly good run of three weeks at the Decsi, though it was far from being the smashing hit previous publicity made people expect.[15]

Published in the *Budapesti Hírlap* on September 5, 1930.

Hardly intelligible, in his native language: On Hungarian theater screens, Lugosi had become something of his own double, or at least a dark reflection of himself. Stoker's Dracula cared not for mirrors, but in a "strange intonation" he voiced his affection for the "shade and the shadow."

Endnotes

1   Nye, Myra. "Society of Cinemaland." *Los Angeles Times* 27 Oct. 1929.

2   "Hungarian Talker Made." *Los Angeles Times* 16 Nov. 1929.

3   Larkin, Mark. "The Truth about Voice Doubling." *Photoplay* July 1929.

4   Ibid.

5   "Magyarul beszélt a mozivászon Hollywoodon." *Pesti Napló* (Budapest, Hungary) 29 Dec. 1929.

6   It is not our contention that close-ups of Lugosi's eyes in *Dracula* (1931) and *White Zombie* (1932) intentionally duplicated shots of Veidt in *The Last Performance*. Rather, we are drawing a visual parallel between them.

7   "Universal Takes Lead in Foreign Version Films." *Universal Weekly* 8 Mar. 1930.

8   Lugosi and Jeanette Loff were together at a dinner given by the Women's Association of Film Publicists in February of 1930. Also present was Gladys Hall. See "Film Publicists Dinner." *Los Angeles Examiner* 23 Feb. 1930.

9   "Paul Whiteman meséskönyve." *Pesti Napló* 20 July 1930.

10 "*King of Jazz* Filmed in 9 Foreign Tongues." *Motion Picture News* 20 Sept. 1930.

11 "Paul Whiteman meséskönyve." *Pesti Napló* 20 July 1930.

12 "Hollywoodból jelentik." *Budapesti Hírlap* 31 July 1930.

13 *Színházi Élet* (Budapest, Hungary) 7-13 Sept. 1930.

14 During the month of September 1930, advertisements, references, and reviews appeared in the following Budapest publications: *Pesti Napló, Budapesti Hírlap, Népszava, Pesti Hírlap, Sporthírlap, Újság, Színházi Élet, Nemzeti Sport*, and *A Hét*.

15 "10 Germans to 1 U.S. Talker." *Variety* 15 Oct. 1930.

Lugosi in 1930.
(Courtesy of David Wentink)

Chapter 44

Indecision

At the beginning of 1930, Lugosi was at a crossroads, considering whether to focus on the stage or the screen, particularly given that his success in Hollywood had been limited. He thought for some time about trying to produce plays himself, as is evident in a letter he sent to Dr. Edmund Pauker in October of 1928:

> I have a chance to have Kelemen's play entitled *A fejedelem* [*The Prince*] played here, in English. Most probably it would be a success, and then we could take it to New York. I know that Bohém translated it for you. – I wonder whether you have already sold the rights of the play for the stage and for the screen? In case you have not, please send me a copy straightaway.[1]

Pauker's responses were not encouraging, but Lugosi persisted. If others would not cast him appropriately or frequently, he would do so himself in his own productions. On December 30, 1929, he wrote to Pauker again:

> Will you please ascertain for me whether or not *A Kek Róka* was produced in New York. If not please send it to me. Also *Doumont* which was produced in Berlin in 1929 at the Folks Buhne Theater. *Petroleuminseln* by Lion Feuchtwanger, *Kalcutta in May*, *Anarchie in Silian* by Arnold Bronnen, *Happy End* by Bert Brecht, *Királynőm, Meghalok Érted* by Villányi, and any other plays that you think would be of interest to me as a starring or co-starring vehicle.
>
> Please send with each play the details regarding the stage and screen rights, as the field here for motion picture production of any play produced is unlimited. However, if a play promised great stage success it would be produced in New York after being tried out here. Best wishes for a Happy New Year and a prosperous one.[2]

In early 1930, Pauker finally sent Lugosi a copy of *A fejedelem*, along with a few other scripts, to review for a possible English-language stage versions. But Lugosi's plans to produce and star in them came to naught.

The same was true of some of his film opportunities. In February of 1930, Warner Bros. announced Lugosi would costar in *Playboy* along with Flora Finch and Beryl Mercer.[3] It would have starred famed comedian Frank Fay in his first film, and – most excitingly – Lugosi's old colleague Michael Curtiz (Mihály Kertész) would direct.[4] Their planned reunion even made news in Hungary.[5] But something happened. Lugosi and several others were dropped from the cast before production began. The finished movie was released as *The Matrimonial Bed* (1930).

Mention of *Playboy* in the Hungarian press. Published in the *Székely Nép* on April 10, 1930.

```
FORM 129  10-M  11-29  KP-260
                        IMPORTANT
                WARNER BROTHERS PICTURES, INC.
                        WEST COAST STUDIOS
                    INTER-OFFICE COMMUNICATION

TO          JOE MARKS                        DATE JAN. 14, 1930

SUBJECT:    VIENNESE NIGHTS

    Sign BERT ROACH to play the part of GUS in "VIENNESE NIGHTS" to
    start on or about February 1st. Get a working schedule from Gordon
    Hollingshead, the assistant on this production, and sign the follow-
    ing people for the correct starting date as per the breakdown:

    FREDDIE FREDERICKS.....THE CHILD
    VON BRINCKEN..........LIEUT. OF GUARDS
    LUCIEN PRIVAL.........HUGO
    PETER LUGOSIA.........COUNT VON RATZ

                                    DARRYL ZANUCK
```

Lugosi did appear in Warners' film *Viennese Nights* (1930), directed by Alan Crosland, who had famously helmed *The Jazz Singer* (1927). The brainchild of Sigmund Romberg and Oscar Hammerstein II, it became the very first operetta written specifically for the screen.

Harvey Thew – who later coauthored such films as *Supernatural* (1933) and *Terror Aboard* (1933) – worked on the adaptation.[6] Unfolding over a period of many years in Vienna, the story features Otto and Franz, who both love Elsa. She weds Franz, but after encountering Otto years later, she realizes her mistake. Reunion is impossible because Otto has a child. As an old woman, the impoverished Elsa encourages her granddaughter to marry a wealthy man, but the granddaughter falls in love with a young composer. He turns out to be Otto's grandson. Elsa dies in a garden, dreaming that Otto sings to her.

The film headlined musical star Vivienne Segal. The cast also included Walter Pidgeon, who had appeared in both the 1927 and 1930 versions of *The Gorilla*, as well as Jean Hersholt, who would costar with Lugosi in *Mark of the Vampire* (1935).

On January 14, 1930, Darryl F. Zanuck sent a memo asking that five actors be signed for the movie, one of them being Lugosi – whose name Zanuck mangled into "Peter Lugosia" – for the role of Count von Ratz, an Ambassador.[7] Also appearing in the film was Louis Silvers, the studio's musical director, playing a conductor.[8]

Mr. and Mrs. Coolidge Visit the
One of our foremost realists in the land of make-believe. Here Calvin Coolidge and Mrs. Coolidge are shown watching the filming of a scene for "Viennese Nights," at the Warner Brothers studio. At left is Jack Warner, production head.

Left: Published in *Exhibitors Herald* on March 8, 1930.
Above: Published in *Exhibitors Herald* on August 16, 1930.
Below: Lugosi in a scene from *Viennese Nights* (1930).

BECOMING DRACULA

A scene from *Viennese Nights*.

Shooting began on February 12 and continued until March 8.⁹ As of February 20, Zanuck told Crosland that:

> The rushes are excellent. ... The musical numbers are fine. ... However, I still cannot understand why in the scenes at the tea party at the girl's home, there should be any excuse for camera noise, especially in a small set like this, unless of course you used too many cameras.¹⁰

Zanuck also chided Crosland for his choice of shot composition in one scene, another indicator of how closely the producer was monitoring the director.

During the shoot, former President Calvin Coolidge and his wife visited the set and watched a scene being filmed.¹¹ *Screenland* reported:

> After the Coolidges had met Alexander Gray and Vivienne Segal ... they were introduced to Jean Hersholt, Bert Roach, Dick Winslow, and Norwood Penzer, the last two being children. Then they asked to meet Louise Fazenda, whose work they both admire, and fortunately she happened to be working on the lot.¹²

Fazenda – who had the distinction of yelling the very first scream in a talking picture, the movie being *The Terror* (1928) – was also in the cast of *Viennese Nights*.¹³

Above Left: Published in *Film Daily* on October 12, 1930. **Above Right:** Sheet music for *Viennese Nights*.

Whether Lugosi met President Coolidge that day is unknown. His role of Count von Ratz featured very limited footage and dialogue. If nothing else, though, *Viennese Nights* provided Lugosi his first opportunity to appear in a Technicolor movie.

Originally *Viennese Nights* was just a working title that the studio initially intended to change, but it stuck. Ads heralded the film as "The greatest love story ever told." For added promotion, sheet music of its original songs was published.[14] Leo Reisman recorded two of them for Victor Records.[15] And Warner Bros. booked Vivienne Segal on a personal appearance tour.[16]

A special "News Reel Trailer" featured behind-the-scenes footage. Though it does not seem to survive, the script for its narration does:

> Here we have a scene taken in Warner Bros. Hollywood, Theater, Hollywood, California. The director, Alan Crosland, is the gentleman in the center with the megaphone. ... The camera is being panned around the auditorium, finally to center on Miss Vivienne Segal, the prima donna in a box at the upper right, which is not visible in this particular shot.[17]

The trailer featured other shots inside the theater set as well. There is certainly a possibility that Lugosi was seen in this unique footage.

Viennese Nights had its world premiere in New York on November 26, 1930.[18] It was held at Warners' theater on Broadway, returning Lugosi's face to the Great White Way, but not his

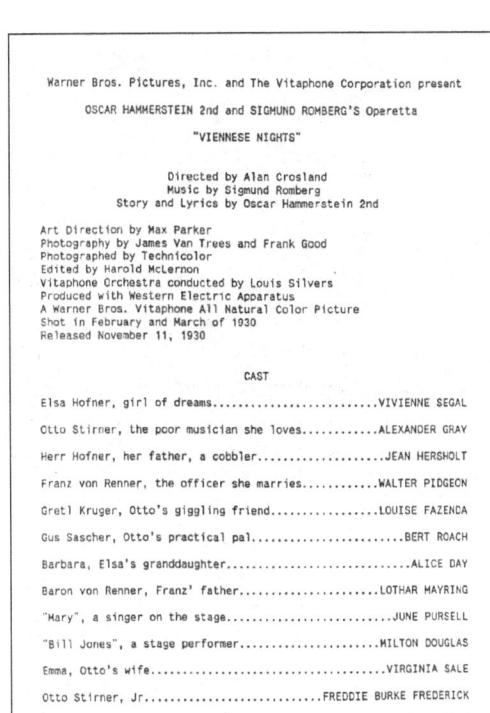 

Above Left: From the program distributed at the premiere of *Viennese Nights*. Above Right: Published in *The Democrat and Chronicle* (Rochester, NY) on December 28, 1930.

person. The film had actually been finished for months, but the studio delayed its release, fearing the public had become too inundated with musicals.[19] *Harrison's Reports* later observed that was a major obstacle to its success.[20]

Industry reviews were largely positive. *Film Daily* was an outlier, but its response might well have been the same that many Depression-era viewers had, particularly in smaller towns and rural areas: "Pretentious operetta with good music and colorful background, but mixed story and slow action."[21]

During the shoot, Warners had filmed two "German numbers" specifically for foreign-release prints, one of them sung by the German-Hungarian Lotti Loder.[22] When released in Hungary in January 1932, *Viennese Nights* was retitled *Kék Duna mentén (Csákó és hegedű)*, which translates as *Along the Blue Danube (Shako and Violin)*. But its biggest international success surprisingly came from playing 550 screenings over 23 straight weeks in Sydney, Australia.[23]

As for Lugosi, he could hardly have appreciated the brevity of his role, or the fact that Warner Bros. did not credit him on the film or in publicity materials.[24] In early March 1930, just after appearing in *Viennese Nights* – or perhaps while still working on it – Lugosi attended a Hollywood party. Also present was Wilfred Lucas, who had appeared in films since 1908 and

Left: Published in *Milwaukee Journal* (Milwaukee, WI) on December 28, 1930.

would continue to do so until 1941.[25] Steady work came for him in the talkies, but most of his roles were small and unbilled. Here was not the future Lugosi desired.

During the lengthy period from finishing the film to its release, Lugosi continued to think about returning to the stage. In March 1930, he signed a contract to appear in Marguerite Drennen's play *The Second Cup*.[26] Nothing came of it. In a 1930 letter to New York literary agent Harold Freedman, Lugosi made the same request he had so often made to Dr. Pauker:

> If you have plays in which there are great character parts suitable to my kind of ability, I would appreciate it if you would send me copies… [27]

Endnotes

1. Lugosi, Bela. Letter to Dr. Edmund Pauker, 16 Oct. 1928. [Available in the Edmund Pauker Papers, 1910-1957, Box 42, Folder 11 at the New York Public Library/Lincoln Center for the Performing Arts.]

2. Lugosi, Bela. Letter to Dr. Edmund Pauker, 30 Dec. 1929. [Available in the Edmund Pauker Papers, 1910-1957, Box 42, Folder 11.]

3. "Coast Notes." *Variety* 12 Feb. 1930.

4. "Switching Post." *Motion Picture News* 15 Feb. 1930.

5. "Hollywoodi Magyar Egyveleg." *Magyarország* (Budapest, Hungary) 1 Mar. 1930.

6. "Color *Viennese Nights*." *Variety* 25 Dec. 1929.

7. Zanuck, Darryl F. Memo to Joe Marks, 14 Jan. 1930. [Available in the file for *Viennese Nights*, 2347B, at the Warner Bros. Archives housed at the University of Southern California.]

8   "Up and Down the Alley." *Exhibitors Herald-World* 20 Sept. 1930.

9   "Warner Studio Resumes; Three Specials Started." *Film Daily* 15 Jan. 1930.

10 Zanuck, Darryl F. Memo to Alan Crosland, 20 Feb. 1930. [Available in the file for *Viennese Nights*, 2347B.]

11 "Pictorial Section." *Exhibitors Herald-World* 8 Mar. 1930.

12 "Hot from Hollywood." *Screenland* May 1930.

13 May McAvoy's scream became the most famous heard in *The Terror* (1928), but in terms of the film's running time, Fazenda's scream was heard first.

14 "Harms to Publish Film Score." *Film Daily* 19 June 1930.

15 "*Viennese Nights* Tunes Recorded." *Film Daily* 3 Dec. 1930.

16 "Vivienne Segal in Person with *Viennese Nights*." *Film Daily* 30 Dec. 1930.

17 *Viennese Nights *** Special News Reel Trailer B.T. 459*. [Available in the file for *Viennese Nights*, 2704B, at the Warner Bros. Archives.]

18 "*Viennese Nights* Premiere." *Film Daily* 9 Nov. 1930.

19 "*Viennese Nights*." *International Photographer* Apr. 1931.

20 "*Viennese Nights*." *Harrison's Reports* 13 May 1933.

21 "*Viennese Nights*." *Film Daily* 20 Nov. 1930.

22 "Composing for Europe." *Variety* 19 Feb. 1930.

23 "Foreign Markets." *Film Daily* 1 Nov. 1931.

24 The program given out at the New York premiere did credit Lugosi, the last name out of thirteen.

25 Nye, Myra. "Society of Cinemaland." *Los Angeles Times* 9 Mar. 1930.

26 Whitaker, Alma. "Sugar and Spice." *Los Angeles Times* 23 Mar. 1930.

27 Lugosi, Bela. Letter to Harold Freedman, 12 July 1930.

Lugosi in 1929.

Chapter 45

Movietone City

"[Bela Lugosi is] capable, commanding,
and a trouper who knows his stuff."[54]
–*Inside Facts of Stage and Screen*,
January 1930

It was Warner Bros., with its sound-on-disc Vitaphone system, that ushered in the talkie revolution. But it was William Fox, producer and studio mogul, who adopted Movietone, the sound-on-film system that became the preferred technology.

In the spring of 1930, *Film Daily* told readers: "Fox Movietone City is based on sound's future."[1] Major construction work in 1928 led to the creation of Movietone City, a group of twelve soundstages, an acoustical laboratory, a music library, and much more. Three more buildings were erected in 1929, including the Hall of Music and the Laboratory of Engineering Research.[2] Winfield Sheehan, the studio's vice-president in charge of production, also focused on improving Movietone cameras and sound equipment to allow for more outdoor shoots.[3]

With all of its advances, though, the studio was plagued with one major difficulty: Due to financial troubles, William Fox's presidency of his own company was threatened. In March 1930, it temporarily looked like he would remain in place.[4] As of April, though, Fox was out for good, paid handsomely to retire from studio leadership.[5] One of the major figures of film became the subject of film history, the studio forging ahead without him as an industry leader, renowned for its movies and its movie theaters.

During a turbulent era, the Fox Film Corporation hired Lugosi to appear in at least four films, thus becoming the closest he had to a home studio in America prior to starring in *Dracula* (1931).

The Plastic Surgeon

In May of 1929, Fox announced it would adapt Elinor Glyn's short story *Such Men Are Dangerous*, based on the real-life suicide of a German financier.[6] Alfred Santell was set to direct, though Kenneth Hawks, brother of Howard, later replaced him. From the start, the studio planned to star Warner Baxter as the wealthy Ludwig Kranz, who fakes his own death and undergoes plastic surgery in an effort to make his unhappy wife fall in love with him. To play her, Fox originally selected Mary Duncan, who was replaced first by Kay Johnson, and then by Catherine Dale Owen.[7]

As of November 1929, Hungarian author and screenwriter Ernest Vadja had signed a contract to adapt Glyn's story.[8] Perhaps it was Vadja who suggested Lugosi to the powers that be at Fox. Or perhaps Fox himself, being Hungarian-American, took an interest in Lugosi, even remembering him from *The Silent Command* (1923). At any rate, production began by mid-December 1929.[9]

Disaster struck on January 2, 1930.[10] While filming aerial footage, the plane

Above: Published in the *Los Angeles Times* on January 10, 1930. Below: Warner Baxter and Bela Lugosi in a scene from *Such Men Are Dangerous* (1930). Published in the *Brooklyn Eagle* on March 30, 1930.

Left: Published in the *Exhibitors Herald-World* on February 8, 1930. Right: From the pressbook for *Such Men Are Dangerous*.

carrying Kenneth Hawks and cinematographer George Eastman crashed into another plane.[11] *Talking Screen* described what had happened:

> A lazy, languorous day on the Pacific shore. Ten boys with scant years of life behind them, welcome an air jaunt as relief from studio routine. They fly to film a sequence for *Such Men Are Dangerous*. A sequence that was never made. Three thousand feet up the planes collide. With death as pilot the ten fall in flames, screaming through a half-mile of horror to the solace of the sea's still depths. So passed director Kenneth Hawks and his crew.[12]

There were ten casualties. Three men were thrown to their deaths from the planes, spiraling into the waters below.[13] The hunt for human remains began, with the event receiving wide coverage in the press.[14] Even Charles Lindbergh commented on the "unfortunate" tragedy.

Nevertheless, shooting continued in early January.[15] Then, at the end of that month, Fox previewed the film as *The Mask of Love*.[16] The studio reverted to the title *Such Men Are Dangerous* by the time they showed it to the Motion Picture Producers and Distributors of America (MPPDA) in early February. The MPPDA approved the film, claiming it was "good entertainment for the entire family, although beyond the understanding of children."[17]

Released on March 9, 1930, *Such Men Are Dangerous* received various reactions:

Left: From the pressbook for *Such Men Are Dangerous*. Right: Window card for *Such Men Are Dangerous*.

[The film] is geared to do much better than average business.[18] – *Motion Picture News*

The opus has been given excellent direction and Warner Baxter wins new laurels in a difficult part.[19] – *Weekly Film Review*

It's a swell plot and Kenneth Hawks has done very well by the direction.[20] – *Film Daily*

A few more like this and [Warner] Baxter will be stealing Lon Chaney's thunder, and the billing, *A Man of a Thousand Faces*, will become applicable to the Fox star. ... [Kenneth Hawks'] last work is a credit to his name.[21] – *Billboard*

This may be rated as above average for a program picture.[22] – *The Film Spectator*

The story is an improbable society drama, but it is so expertly executed that it is very diverting.²³ – *Motion Picture Reviews*

The story is not of the kind that can be believed, but good direction and acting have made the picture interesting.²⁴ – *Harrison's Reports*

No one ever accused Elinor Glyn of writing art for film's sake, so *Such Men Are Dangerous* is an average, not overly subtle, film.²⁵ – *Exhibitors Herald*

Published in *Motion Picture News* on April 26, 1930.

With all of its exploitation possibilities and newspaper hookups, it remains mediocre fare for the better first runs.²⁶ – *Variety*

Perhaps the most notable praise for the film came from columnist H. David Strauss, who incorrectly predicted that the Academy of Motion Picture Arts and Sciences would award Warner Baxter's performance in *Such Men Are Dangerous*.²⁷

The film's pressbook and – following from it – most critical reviews name Lugosi's character "Dr. Erdmann," but characters onscreen audibly refer to him instead as "Dr. Goodman" (or perhaps "Dr. Guttmann").²⁸ Lugosi portrays a German plastic surgeon, and even briefly speaks in German with his onscreen nurse. He seems polished and at ease in the role of a kindly doctor, a very different approach from his subsequent portrayal of the sadistic plastic surgeon in *The Raven* (1935). And he was excited about the role, reassuring an interviewer, "I can be kindly and human."²⁹

The pressbook claimed Lugosi spoke English "fluently," but twice in the film he speaks dialogue that probably varied slightly from the script. "I can do too much good with this money," he says to Kranz. Later, he tells the same character, "Just a little minute." Both lines are nonstandard English phrases, not dissimilar to how he spoke particular dialogue in such later films as *Black Friday* (1940) and *Bride of the Monster* (1955).

Attempting to invest as much realism as possible into his role, Lugosi reportedly took lessons from a real-life expert:

Inasmuch as Lugosi portrays a plastic surgeon… he visited Dr. Joseph Ginsburg [sic], a Viennese plastic surgeon now in town, to learn a few tricks. Ginsburg has promised to appear on the … set and offer advice in person should this be advisable.³⁰

Ginsberg (as his name was actually spelled) also wrote an article for the film's pressbook, assuring readers that the dramatic transformation of Kranz's face was scientifically "feasible."

The industry press generally ignored Lugosi's performance, though *Film Spectator* praised him for doing "some capital work."³¹ A small number of newspaper reviews mentioned him as well.³² And, perhaps not surprisingly, a Hungarian newspaper drew attention to his role when *Such Men Are Dangerous* played Budapest under the title *Veszedelmes emberek* (*Dangerous People*).³³

The Nightclub Owner

As of January 22, 1930, Fox announced it would "talkerize" its 1928 silent movie *Road House* (aka *Roadhouse*), which had starred Lionel Barrymore, Warren Burke, and Maria Alba (who would play opposite Lugosi in *The Return of Chandu* in 1934).³⁴ The studio hired Bradley King to adapt Philip Hurn's story and Leo McCarey to direct.³⁵ McCarey had begun his illustrious career as an assistant director for Tod Browning.³⁶

In early May, Fox retitled the film *Wild Company*, probably to distinguish it from Paramount's *Roadhouse Nights*, which had been released in February of 1930.³⁷ Then, on May 10, the *Hollywood Filmograph* reported that Lugosi had joined the cast.³⁸ That seems to have necessitated some other minor script changes, as his character Felix Brown was, in a surviving script dated April 9, 1930, referred to as Joe Brown. And some of Joe's dialogue in that script isn't heard in the final film, perhaps being cut because it wasn't suited to Lugosi's accent and persona.

The film's story is rather simple. Larry (Frank Albertson) is the wild and reckless son of the wealthy Henry Grayson (H.B. Warner). His "undisciplined whoopee" (as the *San Francisco Chronicle* described it) causes him to be duped by gangster Joe Hardy (Kenneth Thomson) and his moll (Sharon Lynne, aka Sharon Lynn).³⁹ When Joe murders nightclub owner Felix Brown (Lugosi), Larry gets the blame. A judge sentences him to the care of his father.

Wild Company became one of the last films on Fox's production schedule for its 1929-30 season. After it was released on July 5, 1930, industry trades gave mixed responses:

> The feature picture, *Wild Company*, is certainly a good lesson for parents who allow their offspring entirely too much latitude.⁴⁰ – *Hollywood Filmograph*

From the pressbook for *Wild Company* (1930).

It's positively amazing how those movie boys and girls simply can't seem to behave like the people you and I know as next-door neighbors.... Even so, though, it's pretty exciting and makes good entertainment for those who like melodrama.[41] – *Talking Screen*

Good family picture showing evils of wild company worked out in interesting plot. Nice summer number.[42] – *Film Daily*

It's a familiar, but always intensely interesting theme, and will register as excellent entertainment.[43] – *Film Curb*

Pretty good program picture. ... There is some human interest, and the attention is held pretty well all the way.[44] – *Harrison's Reports*

Light enough at the start, but increasingly heavy as it unfolds, this, nevertheless, is good program material.[45] – *Motion Picture News*

From the pressbook for *Wild Company* (1930).

Leo McCarey directed and, except for a few sequences that are inclined to a lethargic pace, has done a good job.[46] – *Billboard*

Fox's *Wild Company* loses considerable through the fact that it is another in the cycle of racketeer pictures. ... The picture is entertainment, but not outstanding.[47] – *Exhibitors Herald-World*

Supposedly a moral lesson, but even fine acting fails to make it convincing.[48] – *The Educational Screen*

Wild Company holds nothing worthy of attention, save for a newcomer-juvenile's performance, that of Frank Albertson.[49] – *Variety*

Top Left: From the pressbook for *Wild Company*. Top Right: Published in *The Oregonian* (Portland, OR) on July 26, 1930. Above Left: Published in the *Rockford Republican* (Rockford, IL) on August 24, 1930. Above Right: Published in the *Newark Advocate* (Newark, OH) on October 7, 1930.

Those hoping for greater morality in the cinema appreciated it most of all. Columnist J.C. Jenkins wrote, "Pictures like *Wild Company* are what builds public confidence in the industry."[50] And the Atlanta Better Films Committee gave it a "high recommendation."[51]

Wild Company's basic formula, showing teenagers running wild and then having a judge sermonize at the conclusion, was venerable, so often repeated in exploitation films during the years to come. *Screenland* magazine wrote, "Reckless youth at play – only this time it's all the fault of the older generation."[52] And poster taglines announced, "Jazz speeds a son towards prison bars and family disgrace."

Reviews ignored Lugosi, who played the small role of Felix Brown, owner of the Skyrocket nightclub. In his key scene, he had to plead for his life after discovering a gangster robbing his office safe:

> Wait a minute, Joe. Don't get rough with the gunplay. I won't tell. I know you should bump me off, but… I'd rather stay alive and keep my mouth shut. You know me. I'm not dumb. I'm Felix Brown. I've been in the same racket myself. Now, keep the money and run right along with it. I won't squawk.

With his hands in the air, Lugosi uses his elbow to turn out the office lights. That earns him a bullet. And an onscreen credit, even though he was billed last.

Nevertheless, one newspaper mistakenly referred to him as "Dela Lugosi."[53] Lugosi was still learning about English; Americans were still learning about him.

Endnotes

1. "Fox Movietone City Is Based on Sound's Future." *Film Daily* 27 May 1930.
2. Ibid.
3. Denbo, Doris. "What Trend Pictures in 1931?" *Screenland* Dec. 1930.
4. "Biggest Year in Pictures Coming." *Inside Facts of Stage and Screen* 15 Mar. 1930.
5. "The Fox Reorganization." *Variety* 9 Apr. 1930.
6. "Los Angeles." *Variety* 1 May 1929.
7. Advertisement. *Variety* 19 June 1929; "Vajda to Adapt Glyn Tale." *Film Daily* 9 Dec. 1929.
8. "Coast Notes." *Variety* 27 Nov. 1929.
9. "Hawks' Unit on Retakes When Air Crash Kills 10 – 'Overloading' Probe; Total Film Aviation Fatalities Now 24." *Variety* 8 Jan. 1930.
10. "Baxter Film in Production." *Film Daily* 15 Dec. 1929.
11. "Hawks and Nine Others Killed in Plane Crash." *Film Daily* 3 Jan. 1930.
12. Cruikshank, Herbert. "The Risks They Take." *Talking Screen* Aug. 1930.

13 "Hawks' Unit on Retakes When Air Crash Kills 10 – 'Overloading' Probe; Total Film Aviation Fatalities Now 24."

14 See, for example: "Parts of Death Planes Dragged Out of Depths." *Los Angeles Times* 4 Jan. 1930; "Film-Plane Hunt Delayed." *Los Angeles Times* 14 Jan. 1930.

15 "Sedan in Fox Film." *Film Daily* 20 Jan. 1930.

16 "The Mask of Love." *Motion Picture News* 1 Feb. 1930.

17 Fisher, James B. M. *Such Men Are Dangerous* 19 Feb. 1930. [Available in the Motion Picture Association of America, Production Code Administration collection at the Margaret Herrick Library in Beverly Hills, CA.]

18 Ibid.

19 "Such Men Are Dangerous." *Weekly Film Review* 4 Mar. 1930.

20 "Such Men Are Dangerous." *Film Daily* 9 Mar. 1930.

21 "Such Men Are Dangerous." *Billboard* 15 Mar. 1930.

22 "Such Men Are Dangerous." *The Film Spectator* 15 Feb. 1930.

23 "Such Men Are Dangerous." *Monthly Film Reviews* Mar. 1930.

24 "Such Men Are Dangerous." *Harrison's Reports* 15 Mar. 1930.

25 "Such Men Are Dangerous." *Exhibitors Herald* 15 Mar. 1930.

26 "Such Men Are Dangerous." *Variety* 12 Mar. 1930.

27 Strauss, H. David. "Long Shots and Flashbacks." *Billboard* 26 Apr. 1930.

28 The pressbook for *Such Men Are Dangerous* is archived at the New York Public Library for the Performing Arts, Dorothy and Lewis B. Cullman Center.

29 Denbo, Doris. "Bela Lugosi Hails Chance at 'Straight' Film Roles." *Hollywood Daily Citizen* 4 Dec. 1929.

30 "Behind the Scenes in Hollywood." *Logansport Pharos-Tribune* (Logansport, IN) 23 Dec. 1929.

31 "Such Men Are Dangerous," *The Film Spectator*.

32 See, for example: Keats, Emma. "The New Films." *Richmond Times-Dispatch* (Richmond, VA) 22 Apr. 1930; E.L.H. "The Screen." *Boston Herald* (Boston, MA) 2 June 1930.

33 "Veszedelmes emberek." *Pesti Hírlap* (Budapest, Hungary) 12 Apr. 1930.

34 "Talkerizing." *Variety* 22 Jan. 1930.

35 "Bradley King Gets Assignment." *Film Daily* 28 Jan. 1930; "Di-a-log." *Exhibitors Herald-World* 22 Feb. 1930. [King ended up receiving coauthor credit along with John Stone.]

36 Wilk, Ralph. "A Little from 'Lots.'" *Film Daily* 1 May 1930.

37 "Wild Company." *Hollywood Filmograph* 10 May 1930.

38 "Now in *Road House.*" *Hollywood Filmograph* 10 May 1930.

39 "Whoopee Fun Offered at Grand Lake." *San Francisco Chronicle* 28 Sept. 1930.

40 "Review: *Wild Company.*" *Hollywood Filmograph* 2 Aug. 1930.

41 "*Wild Company* (Fox)." *Talking Screen* August 1930.

42 "*Wild Company.*" *Film Daily* 20 July 1930.

43 "*Wild Company.*" *Film Curb* 26 July 1930.

44 "*Wild Company.*" *Harrison's Reports* 12 July 1930.

45 "*Wild Company.*" *Motion Picture News* 19 July 1930.

46 "*Wild Company.*" *Billboard* 26 July 1930.

47 "*Wild Company.*" *Exhibitors Herald-World* 26 July 1930.

48 "The Theatrical Field." *The Educational Screen* Sept. 1930.

49 "*Wild Company.*" *Variety* 23 July 1930.

50 Jenkins, J.C. "J.C. Jenkins – *His Colyum.*" *Exhibitors Herald-World* 13 Sept. 1930.

51 "Better Films Forum." *National Board of Review Magazine* Sept. 1930.

52 "Critical Comment on Current Films." *Screenland* Oct. 1930.

53 "Amusements Now Playing." *Rushville Republican* (Rushville, IN) 10 Sept. 1930.

54 "Name-by-Name Estimate." *Inside Facts of Stage and Screen* 11 Jan. 1930.

Lugosi in a publicity still for *Women Everywhere* (1930). *(Courtesy of Dennis Phelps and John Ellis)*

Chapter 46

Variety

> "You know, ever since I played all over
> the country in such roles as *Dracula*, I have been
> stamped as a regular Lon Chaney, a real bad fellow.
> I am so tired of being a menace, I would like to be
> a kindly chap, or be permitted to act as a natural
> human being would act."
> – Bela Lugosi, 1929[52]

The year 1930 was good for Hungarians in Hollywood. MGM released a short subject featuring one of Lugosi's friends, violinist Duci de Kerékjártó.[1] Lajos Bíró – famed author of *A sárga liliom* (*The Yellow Lily*) and the man who had so praised Lugosi in 1911 – was working as a screenwriter.[2] Count Michael Karolyi (Mihály Károlyi), in whose government Lugosi served in 1919, visited Universal Pictures in May.[3] And Michael Curtiz (Mihály Kertész) was directing films at Warner Bros.

Lugosi remained connected to Hungary in many respects, not least of which is the fact that in the spring of 1930 he lived next door to Géza Kende, the artist who painted his nude portrait of Clara Bow. Kende also painted the likeness of Lugosi that hung at the Hollywood Music Box during the 1929 run of *Dracula–The Vampire Play*.

During his tenure at Fox, Lugosi encountered not only Ernest Vajda, who worked on *Such Men Are Dangerous*, but also Alexander (Sándor) Korda, who directed films for the studio in 1930. In fact, Korda may well have directed Lugosi in *Women Everywhere* (1930), a Fox movie about the French Foreign Legion and cabaret singers in Morocco. Released in June 1930, *Women Everywhere* had four writers, two being Lajos Bíró and Sándor's brother Zoltán Korda.[4] A publicity still shows Lugosi dressed as an Arab with the film's star, J. Harold Murray.

Publicity stills for *Women Everywhere*.

However, Lugosi does not appear in the surviving print of the film preserved at UCLA, unless it is in a shot showing a number of Arab characters at such a distance that their faces are not distinguishable. Perhaps Lugosi had one or more scenes that were cut, or perhaps he appeared in nothing more than the publicity still. Here is yet another mystery in his filmography.

Fox definitely announced Lugosi for a supporting role in *Luxury*, which was to star H.B. Warner and Claire Luce. Shooting was to begin in August, but Fox postponed due to a subpar script.[5] When the film was released in 1931 under the title *Once a Sinner*, it did not feature Warner, Luce, or Lugosi.[6]

By contrast, Lugosi was never slated to appear in Frank Borzage's *Liliom*, produced and released by Fox in 1930. Given his contacts with the studio, it is not at all difficult to imagine that he lobbied for a role in the film, based as it was on the famed Ferenc Molnár play. But such were the vagaries of Hollywood logic. Alexander Korda didn't work on *Liliom* either, even though he was under contract at Fox.

Inside Facts of Stage and Screen reported on Lugosi's return to Hollywood in late July 1930. The trade mentioned that he was set to make "two pictures for Fox."[7] These became *Renegades* (1930) and *Oh, for a Man!* (1930), which further expanded the range and type of performances he played at Movietone City.

The Marabout

Renegades (1930) was a "lusty *Beau Geste*," *Variety* explained.[8] As of April 1930, Fox had acquired the rights to André Armandy's novel *Le renégat* (*The Renegades*).[9] It tells the story of Deucalion (Warner Baxter), who deserts the French Foreign Legion with three of his friends. They join a band of thieves after Eleanor (Myrna Loy) breaks Deucalion's heart. She then becomes involved with a Marabout named Sheik Muhammed Halid (Lugosi).

As of May 1930, the studio announced that Victor Fleming would direct; he would later gain fame as the director of *Gone with the Wind* (1939) and *The Wizard of Oz* (1939). Warner Baxter of *Such Men Are Dangerous* was set to star, along with Luana Alcañiz, Kenneth MacKenna, J.M. Kerrigan, and Mitchell Harris.[10] Of that group, only Baxter appeared in the film, the others being replaced by Myrna Loy, Noah Beery, Gregory Gaye, and George Cooper.

Production began in August 1930.[11] Fox's "Outdoor Romance Department" crewed the film, having to some degree overcome the problems of recording sound on location. In May 1930, *Film Daily* described how they achieved such success:

> Special apparatus was designed and constructed by sound and motion picture engineers. Cameras were wrapped in sound proof coverings; special trucks to carry generating apparatus for electricity in the event the location might be miles from civilization; sound recording apparatus was constructed to fit in portable trucks so that it could be moved with ease and set in position anywhere.[12]

For locations, Fleming used the "sand dunes near Point Hueneme, and on barren spots in the San Jacintos and the Sierras."[13] To help instill accuracy, he relied on technical director

Above: Lugosi (far right) with Warner Baxter (far left) in *Renegades* (1930).
(Courtesy of John Antosiewicz)

Louis Van Den Ecker, who spent six years in the French Foreign Legion.[14] Fleming also hired over 100 extras for a desert battle scene.[15]

Fox went to unusual lengths to ensure the comfort of the production crew and the cast:

> Despite the ominous warnings of the weather prophets, director Victor Fleming and his *Renegades* company ... selected the Mojave Desert, near Victorville, to film many of the thrilling scenes of this talkie of the French Foreign Legion.
>
> Special arrangements to keep the players and technicians cool in the intense heat were made through electric refrigerators, specially wired to use the voltage supplied by the big studio generators....
>
> The tents were all equipped with water-sprays which maintained the interiors at a livable degree through evaporation, and with those and other devices for artificial coolness, director Fleming managed to keep his company from melting away before the scenes were completed.[16]

Lugosi and Myrna Loy in *Renegades*. (Courtesy of John Antosiewicz)

Fleming wrapped by September 10, if not earlier.[17] After returning to Hollywood, the cast humorously asked for "ice water in plenty and not a sign of sand anywhere."[18] By September 12, Harold Schuster was editing the film.[19] More than anything else, perhaps, the studio was excited by Myrna Loy's performance, signing her to a long-term contract in October.[20]

The studio released *Renegades* theatrically on October 26, 1930. Critics gave the film mixed reviews:

> A very American interpretation of the French Foreign Legion which utterly fails to be convincing.[21] – *Motion Picture Reviews*

> [*Renegades*] develops into a rather monotonous, long-drawn-out story of the French Foreign Legion....[22] – *Billboard*

Above Left: Published in *Exhibitors Herald-World* on September 27, 1930. Top Right: Published in *The Bioscope* on November 12, 1930. Above Right: Published in *Film Daily* on May 27, 1930.

Super-violent picture glorifying sheer nerve, heroic agonies, and crass depravities of four tough pals.... Particularly vulgar vamp has leading role.[23] – *Educational Screen*

The interest of the spectator is held pretty tight by what is unfolded, but there are no scenes with deep human appeal.[24] – *Harrison's Reports*

With some excellent fight scenes and good performances, *Renegades*, because of involved adaptation and highly implausible theme, even for another Hollywood version of French Legionnaires, hasn't the edge to make it real money in the big weekly change houses.[25] – *Variety*

The picture was well received in preview form and looks like good box-office.[26] – *Motion Picture News*

Above: (Courtesy of Russell McGee)

Foreign Legion story packs wallop with gripping action, ace acting, and excellent direction.[27] – *Film Daily*

The Fox Corporation should be cited for achievement of first quality for assembling the units that are responsible for *Renegades*. Are all the laws of good entertainment observed? I'm not asking you, I'm telling you.[28] – *Inside Facts of Stage and Screen*

Bela Lugosi ... gives a fine performance in the role of the egotistical Arab ruler on whom the girl exerts sufficient influence to exact her revenge against Baxter.[29] – *Exhibitors Herald-World*

[Lugosi] shone brilliantly as the Marabout.[30] – *Hollywood Filmograph*

According to *The Denver Post*, "Lugosi distinguishes himself as the Arab chief."[31] The *San Diego Tribune* called him "a suave and intriguing oriental commander."[32] Perhaps Lugosi's most favorable review came from *The Evening Telegram* in Dundee, Scotland:

> ... you will laugh at the sayings of a tall and bearded Marabout, delicately played by Bela Lugosi. [Señor] Lugosi, of whom I confess I have not heard before, has a little comedy effect of raising his voice to a high pitch as a sentence finishes, a trick that may one day be as well known as Buster Keaton's absent smile. He ends his suggestion[s] of torture, such as burying in anthills or slow roasting, with a little phrase, 'What you think, hey?' The effect is funny.[33]

The review is apt. *Renegades* not only gave Lugosi his biggest role of any of the Fox films of 1930, but also his best, as he plays the "uncrowned king of the region," a sheik with far more pomp and circumstance than intelligence and courage. His banter with Myrna Loy is particularly enjoyable, and the overall role was as rewarding as it was humorous.

The Impressario

Fox borrowed Viola Brothers Shore from Paramount to adapt Mary F. Watkins' short story *Stolen Thunder*, which had just been published in *The Saturday Evening Post* on June 7, 1930. From the start, Fox saw the project as a vehicle for Jeanette MacDonald.[34] The studio originally thought of Edmund Lowe as her costar, but ended up replacing him with Reginald Denny.[35]

The plot revolves around opera diva Carlotta Manson (MacDonald), who rejects several suitors in order to concentrate on her career. She soon befriends a crook trying to rob her home (Denny), because he admires her singing. Manson demands that the crook, an amateur singer, be given a job with her opera company. They fall in love, marry, have a falling out, and then eventually reunite.

Hamilton MacFadden (who would later direct Lugosi in the 1931 film *The Black Camel*) replaced Sidney Lanfield as director of *Stolen Thunder*. The production was supposed to begin in mid-August 1930, but apparently didn't get underway until September 2.[36] By that time, William Kernell had composed two original songs for the movie, *On a Summer Night* and *I'm Just Nuts About You*.[37]

In October, Fox had decided to change the film's title to *Heart Breaker*.[38] By the time the Fox previewed it on October 9, it was called *Her Kind of Man*. Response was favorable, with one representative of the MPPDA calling it a "very amusing and sophisticated romance ... It is first rate entertainment for adults, for the story is splendid and has been handled most intelligently." Nevertheless, the same representative suggested the word "wop" should be removed, along with offensive references to an Italian tenor's habit of eating garlic.[39]

Another member of the MPPDA described favorable audience response at the preview, but drew attention to potential violations of the Motion Picture Production Code, most notably Carlotta's dialogue, "Won't you take off your things and stay awhile?", as well as Barney's line, "I might have taken a lot more than a kiss." These were in addition to a number of lesser concerns, including use of the word "pansy."[40]

By October 14, Fox changed the title yet again, this time to *Oh, for a Man!*, which was usually rendered with an exclamation point.[41] The studio's pressbook included a very short article on Lugosi "bridg[ing] the gap" between playing Dracula onstage and an opera impresario

A scene from *Oh, for a Man!* (1930). *(Courtesy of John Antosiewicz)*

Lugosi and Jeanette MacDonald in *Oh, for a Man!*

onscreen. Along with various ideas for ballyhoo, the pressbook offered a film trailer from National Screen Service, as well as a 16" transcription disc that exhibitors could use as a pre-recorded trailer for radio stations.[42]

Prior to the film's premiere at the end of November 1930 and its theatrical release beginning December 14, censor boards in Massachusetts, New York, and Ohio required that the line, "I might have taken a lot more than a kiss" be removed.[43] Critics for the industry trades generally reacted less favorably than the preview audience had in October:

> The pleasing singing and acting of Miss MacDonald save a trite story.[44] – *National Board of Review Magazine*

> It is a silly and ridiculous affair, saved only by the characterizations of the principal actors and the direction.[45] – *Billboard*

> An excellent cast works hard to put over this frothy yarn, but lack of material proves almost too much for them.[46] – *Film Daily*

> Picture is hardly of deluxe house calibre, but in the neighborhood spots with some judicious cutting of the draggy opening sequence it should get by nicely.[47]
> – *Variety*

> A load of laughs in this. Which makes it well worth a boost. *Oh, for a Man* is not big, but is amusing and sexy in a manner which can prove offensive to nobody.[48] – *Motion Picture News*

> The picture has been produced well; therefore, it should hold the interest of cultured picture-goers. But it is doubtful if those of the rank and file will enjoy it. There is some pathos, and excellent singing, and the interest is held fairly tight all the way through.[49] – *Harrison's Reports*

Lugosi and Jeanette MacDonald in *Oh, for a Man*

Fox was pleased enough with the result to place Jeanette MacDonald under contract.[50]

Of all of Lugosi's Fox films, *Oh, for a Man!* gave him the least interesting role. Though dapper as opera impresario Frescatti, Lugosi has little to do other than fawn, sometimes humorously, over MacDonald's character. He doesn't even have a scene as strong as the death of Felix Brown in *Wild Company* (1930).

Characters

During 1930, Lugosi played four roles at Fox (if not five, given by the possibility of footage cut from *Women Everywhere*). Within mere months, he became a German surgeon, an American gangster, an Arab sheik, and an Italian impresario. Here was diversity. Here was an experience akin to what he so often recalled fondly about his days in Hungarian theater, playing different kinds of roles on a regular basis, not being tied to any particular type.

And yet, as he worked on these films, particularly the last two, Lugosi became increasingly dedicated towards winning the title role of *Dracula* at Universal Pictures. In an interview from the period, he described the potential value of the American entertainment industry:

> [I]n America a young actor can make a single hit and obtain what you call a 'break.' Some say it's a matter of luck – and perhaps it is – but there are opportunities in this country the European aspirant to the stage never sees.[51]

Above: From the pressbook for *Oh, for a Man!*

Lugosi's break in America would come in 1930, not at Fox, but at another studio, and it would forever limit the variety of roles he would play.

Endnotes

1 "*Duci de Kerekjarto.*" *Variety* 9 Apr. 1930.

2 Wilk, Ralph. "A Little from 'Lots.'" *Film Daily* 1 June 1930.

3 "Seccion Espanol." *Hollywood Filmograph* 24 May 1930.

4 "*Women Everywhere.*" *Film Daily* 1 June 1930.

5 "Three Pictures Are Started at Fox Studio This Week." *Film Daily* 21 Aug. 1930; "No Fox *Luxury*." *Variety* 27 Aug. 1930.

6 "Two Fox Title Changes." *Film Daily* 16 Sept. 1930.

7 "Oakland Pickups." *Inside Facts of Stage and Screen* 26 July 1930.

8 "Perfect Lady Menace." *Variety* 12 Nov. 1930.

9 "Sheehan's Unique Record." *Variety* 16 Apr. 1930.

10 "$25,000,000 for 48 Fox Pictures in 1930-31." *Film Daily* 21 May 1930; "Outdoor Romance Department to Produce 10 of 48 Features." *Film Daily* 27 May 1930; "Things Have Changed Since." *Variety* 28 May 1930.

11 Murray, Ray. "Hollywood Gossip." *Exhibitors Daily Review and Motion Pictures Today* 25 July 1930.

12 "Outdoor Romance Department to Produce 10 of 48 Features." *Film Daily* 27 May 1930.

13 Wilk, Ralph. "A Little from 'Lots.'" *Film Daily* 1 Aug. 1930.

14 Wilk, Ralph. "A Little from 'Lots.'" *Film Daily* 27 Aug. 1930.

15 "Extras' Heyday." *Variety* 20 Aug. 1930.

16 "Warner Baxter Fears No Desert Heat Wave." *The News Journal* (Wilmington, DE) 10 Dec. 1930.

17 "19 New Fox Pictures to be Finished by Sept. 10." *Film Daily* 2 Sept. 1930.

18 Wilk, Ralph. "A Little from 'Lots.'" *Film Daily* 15 Sept. 1930.

19 Wilk, Ralph. "A Little from 'Lots.'" *Film Daily* 12 Sept. 1930.

20 "Loy Gets New Contract." *Billboard* 18 Oct. 1930.

21 "Renegades." *Motion Picture Reviews* Nov. 1930.

22 "Renegades." *Billboard* 15 Nov. 1930.

23 "Renegades." *Educational Screen* Nov. 1930.

24 "The [sic] Renegades." *Harrison's Reports* 25 Oct. 1930.

25 "Renegades." *Variety* 12 Nov. 1930.

26 "Renegades." *Motion Picture News* 4 Oct. 1930.

27 "Renegades." *Film Daily* 9 Nov. 1930.

28 "Renegades." *Inside Facts of Stage and Screen* 29 Nov. 1930.

29 "Renegades." *Exhibitors Herald-World* 15 Nov. 1930.

30 "As Seen and Heard By." *Hollywood Filmograph* 22 Nov. 1930.

31 "*Renegades* at Aladdin, Film of Unusual Merit." *Denver Post* (Denver, CO) 22 Nov. 1930.

32 "Baxter Stars in Orpheum Picture." *San Diego Evening Tribune* (San Diego, CA) 22 Nov. 1920.

33 "Renegades." *The Evening Telegraph* (Dundee, Scotland) 5 Dec. 1930.

34 "*Variety*'s Bulletin Condensed." *Variety* 30 July 1930.

35 "*Stolen Thunder* Lowe's Next Film." *Exhibitors Daily Review and Motion Pictures Today* 26 Aug. 1930. Denny was in fact the fifth choice for the role in *Oh, for a Man!* See "Hollywood Bulletins." *Variety* 10 Sept. 1930.

36 "To Play Lead in Big Fox Film." *Exhibitors Daily Review and Motion Pictures Today* 21 July 1930; "Four Assignments Made at Fox Studios." *Film Daily* 2 Aug. 1930; "Six Fox Productions Going in Work Soon." *Film Daily* 5 Aug. 1930; "Seven Fox Features Now in Cutting Room." *Exhibitors Daily Review and Motion Pictures Today* 14 Aug. 1930; "Work Prospect Now Brighter." *Inside Facts of Stage and Screen* 30 Aug. 1930.

37 See the pressbook for *Oh, for a Man!*, which is archived at the New York Public Library for the Performing Arts, Dorothy and Lewis B. Cullman Center.

38 "*Heart Breaker* is Final Title." *Film Daily* 8 Oct. 1930.

39 Fisher, James. *Her Kind of Man* 14 Oct. 1930. [Available in the Motion Picture Association of America, Production Code Administration collection at the Margaret Herrick Library in Beverly Hills, CA.]

40 Wilson, John V. Letter to Robert M. Yost, 10 Oct. 1930. [Available in the Motion Picture Association of America, Production Code Administration collection.]

41 Wilk, Ralph. "Hollywood Flashes." *Film Daily* 14 Oct. 1930.

42 See the pressbook for *Oh, for a Man!*

43 See the file on *Oh, for a Man!* in the Motion Picture Association of America, Production Code Administration collection.

44 "*Oh, for a Man!*" *National Board of Review Magazine* Jan. 1931.

45 "*Oh, for a Man!*" *Billboard* 13 Dec. 1930.

46 "*Oh, for a Man!*" *Film Daily* 9 Nov. 1930.

47 "*Oh, for a Man.*" *Variety* 3 Dec. 1930.

48 "*Oh, For a Man.*" *Motion Picture News* 8 Nov. 1930.

49 "*Oh, for a Man!*" *Harrison's Reports* 6 Dec. 1930.

50 "Fox Signs Jeannette [*sic*] MacDonald." *Billboard* 22 Nov. 1930.

51 "This American Scene." *The Evening Star* (Washington, D.C.) 20 Oct. 1929.

52 Denbo, Doris. "Bela Lugosi Hails Chance at 'Straight' Film Roles." *Hollywood Daily Citizen* 4 Dec. 1929.

Raymond Huntley as Dracula.

Chapter 47

The Un-Dead

> "It is that we become as him; that we henceforward
> become foul things of the night like him–without
> heart or conscience, preying on the bodies
> and the souls of those we love best."
> –Bram Stoker, *Dracula*

Bram Stoker's novel *Dracula* describes its title character as the "King-Vampire." But there were others, even if they were of less regal stature, that formed the "ghastly ranks."

However much Lugosi became associated with Dracula in the late twenties, he was not yet as famous as the vampire character. That meant Dracula could return from the grave, over and over again throughout America without him. One didn't have to be Lugosi or even European to play the role.

On March 2, 1930, the *New York Times* announced that, thanks to a production in Jackson Heights, "*Dracula* will play its one thousand, two hundred and fifty-seventh performance, and still looks ahead to solid months of booking." The vampire was a triumph on the road, a "strolling success."[1] Between 1928 and 1930, a number of companies toured America, with no less than six notable actors temporarily becoming Dracula. As Stoker wrote, "it is thus that in old times one vampire meant many."

Of all of these Lugosi imitators, the best known was not really an imitator at all. Raymond Huntley – who first played Dracula in provincial England in 1924 before becoming a sensation in London in 1927 – had turned down the role on Broadway, thus paving the way for Lugosi. But Huntley was soon lured to America to play Dracula again and again.

PLAYS OF THE YEAR.

"DRACULA" AT THE LITTLE.
Mr. SAM LIVESEY, Mr. BERNARD JUKES, Mr. RAYMOND HUNTLEY, Mr. STRINGER DAVIS, Miss DOROTHY VERNON, Mr. PETER JACKSON, and Miss BEATRICE DE HOLTHOIR.

(Courtesy of George Chastain)

Between 1928 and 1930, Huntley starred as the vampire in Baltimore, Boston, Chicago, Minneapolis, Newark, Philadelphia, Rochester, and Washington, D.C., as well as in Battle Creek, Michigan, and Columbus, Ohio. Huntley's performances generally received positive reviews; a critic in Newark called his Dracula "superb."[2] Perhaps his most successful run in America came at Chicago's Blackstone Theater, where *Dracula-The Vampire Play* was grossed a respectable $7,500 in the fifteenth and final week of its long run.[3]

After portraying the attendant Butterworth in Lugosi's West Coast *Dracula* tour in 1928, the English actor Frederick Pymm graduated to the title role for a number of performances. He became Dracula in San Francisco in 1928, and then in San Jose, Tacoma, and Seattle in 1929, and then again in San Francisco in 1930. The *Seattle Post-Intelligencer* called him "acceptable."[4] Aside from portraying Dracula, Pymm also served as the stage manager for one of the road company tours.[5] "A most agreeable gentleman," one journalist reported in 1930, who didn't "seem at all the evil demon one might expect," given the vampire role.[6]

Courtney White, who played Dracula primarily in 1930, had originally worked on the technical side of the play before being promoted. When he described *Dracula* to a journalist in April 1930, White made clear that it really was not a mystery, but rather a "weird" tale that relied on "trickery" to scare the audience. As for the title role, he explained it was "so exacting, so wearing" that he and another actor alternated the title role in the same company, week by week.[7]

The other actor was Howard Sinclair (aka Howard St. Clair), who became the vampire in such cities as Cleveland, Indianapolis, Milwaukee, and St. Louis.[8] In April 1930, while Courtney White was on vacation, the *Lansing State Journal* called Sinclair's portrayal "excellent."[9] The next month, the *Des Moines Register* told readers, "Sinclair is perfectly cast in his role, with the stature, bearing, and most of all the voice and manner of speech that accomplishes every bit required."[10]

Published in the *Cleveland Plain-Dealer* (Cleveland, OH) on March 31, 1929. *(Courtesy of George Chastain)*

Victor Jory, the Canadian-American actor who appeared alongside Lugosi in the Fox films *Renegades* (1930) and *The Devil's in Love* (1933), played Dracula on more than a few occasions in 1929 and 1930, including in Minneapolis and in Pasadena. The *Hollywood Filmograph* believed Jory did an "excellent job" at causing "young ladies to grasp their escorts' arms fiercely."[11]

Perhaps the most unexpected Dracula was popular American tennis player William Tatem Tilden II (aka "Big Bill" Tilden). He had dominated the tennis world during the first half of the 1920s and had been ranked the number one male player for six years. Then, as Stoker wrote, he became "one more to swell the grim and grisly ranks of the Un-Dead." Tilden's 1928 tour in *Dracula* played such cities as Allentown, Knoxville, Louisville, and Nashville. The *Atlanta Constitution* reported: "It was surprising to see a man whose entire career has been devoted to athletics step out on the stage and make a real and genuine hit on his own merits as an actor."[12]

"Dracula" in Boston For a Fourth Time

As Boston usually takes mystery or "horror" plays, they depart after a first stay, never to return. "Dracula," however, is making its fourth visit in three seasons and rounding out a grand total of twelve weeks as though it were the regular thing in the regular way.

There are habitues who have seen it almost as many times and still get their gooseflesh. They say, also, that the present werewolf baron, Courtney White, outdoes his predecessors. All of which is respectfully submitted as a note on the habits and customs of this hinterland with the theater.

The Hayden Players at the Showhouse in Dallas will produce "Dracula" Sunday.

Above Left: Frederick Pymm as Dracula in 1930. Above Right: Published in the *Seattle Post-Intelligencer* (Seattle, WA) on June 24, 1929. Far Left: Published in the *Dallas Morning News* (Dallas, TX) in 1930. Left: Courtney White as Dracula, as published in the *Pittsburgh Press* (Pittsburgh, PA) on September 17, 1930.

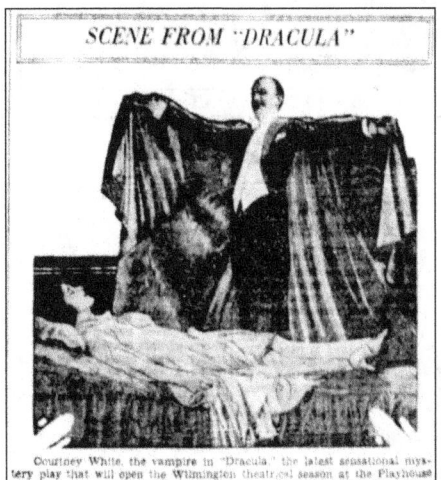

Courtney White, the vampire in "Dracula," the latest sensational mystery play that will open the Wilmington theatrical season at the Playhouse tomorrow night. The engagement is for three nights and Saturday afternoon. The picture is a scene from the play.

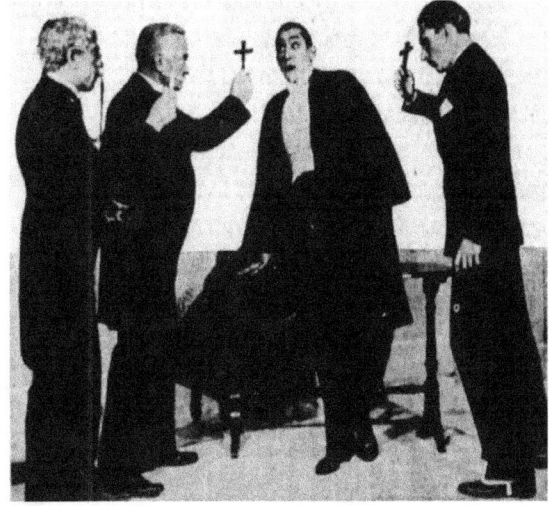

ABOUT THE PLAYERS IN "DRACULA"

VICTOR JORY returns to the Playhouse in the title role of this play after an absence of nearly two years in which he has gathered many dramatic honors

and earned a prominent place in the professional theatre in the East. As the creator of Caligula, the insane

Howard St. Claire
He is "Dracula" at the Davidson.

Top Left: Published in the *Wilmington Evening Journal* (Wilmington, DE) on September 17, 1930. Top Right: Victor Jory as Dracula. Published in the *Minneapolis Star* (Minneapolis, MN) on September 21, 1929. *(Courtesy of George Chastain)* Bottom Left: From the playbill for *Dracula* in Pasadena in 1930. Bottom Right: Published in the *Milwaukee Journal* (Milwaukee, WI) on April 6, 1930.

And the *Springfield Republican* reported, "The tennis champion becomes a menacing figure as he glides about in the shroud of Dracula. His voice, too, takes on the metallic quality of an unearthly being, and he succeeded last night in eliciting several shrieks of horror from the more impressionable members of the audience."[13]

In many cases, these Draculas appeared in major successes. In Boston in the autumn of 1928, *Dracula–The Vampire Play* generated the "biggest grosses" of the season.[14] At roughly the same time, the show became a "smash" in Philadelphia.[15] And its ongoing "freak" success led Horace Liveright to form a company specifically to play Brooklyn in 1929.[16]

City after city thus encountered the itinerant vampire. As the *New York Times* said, "The list could go on and on until it would seem to be indefinite and, for all a layman knows, it may be."[17] And on March 1, 1930, *Billboard* reported that *Dracula*, the "perennial mystery play," would stay on the road for another 41 weeks.[18]

Published in *The Morning Call* (Allentown, PA) on November 9, 1928.

As for the horde of stage vampires whose names were not Lugosi, perhaps it does make sense that, in the curtain speech to *Dracula–The Vampire Play*, Van Helsing states, "*there are such things*," distinctly using the plural. The vampire count was not singular. The king of his kind would suffer many challenges to his unearthly throne, a veritable procession of the Un-Dead.

Endnotes

1 "A Mystery Play Took to the Road." *New York Times* 2 Mar. 1930.

2 "*Dracula* Delights at Broad Theater." *Jersey Journal* (Newark, NJ) 20 Feb. 1929.

3 "Only Four Shows Left to Fight the Loop." *Variety* 17 July 1929.

4 Armstrong, Everhardt. "Eerie Drama Centers about Wise Vampire's Battle with Scientist." *Seattle Post-Intelligencer* (Seattle, WA) 25 June 1929.

5 "Fred Pymm Goes To Henry Duffy." *Inside Facts of Stage and Screen* 1 Nov. 1930.

6 Warren, George C. "Frederick Pymm, Stage Villain, Sketches Career." *San Francisco Chronicle* 9 Nov. 1930.

7 "The Stage and Motion Picture Are Distinct, Will Never Meet, Says Courtney White." *Escanaba Daily Press* (Escanaba, MI) 19 Apr. 1930.

8 "*Dracula* Has Mighty Good Cast." *Indianapolis Times* (Indianapolis, IN) 9 May 1930; "The Screams Have It." *Kansas City Times* (Kansas City, MO) 28 Apr. 1930; "You Can Yell If You Insist." *Milwaukee Journal* (Milwaukee, WI) 7 Apr. 1930; "*Dracula* Coming to the American Tomorrow Night." *St. Louis Star and Times* (St. Louis, MO) 19 Apr. 1930.

9 "Spine-Tickling Thrills Provided in Spooky Mystery Play, *Dracula*." *Lansing State Journal* (Lansing, MI) 1 Apr. 1930.

10 Churchill, G.W. "*Dracula* Has Its Horrors." *Des Moines Register* (Des Moines, IA) 5 May 1930.

11 "Stage Review: *Dracula*." *Hollywood Filmograph* 23 Aug. 1930.

12 Stevenson, Paul. "Tilden Proves Strong Actor In Eerie Play at Erlanger." *Atlanta Constitution* (Atlanta, GA) 20 Nov. 1928.

13 "News of the Theaters." *Springfield Republican* (Springfield, MA) 26 Oct. 1928.

14 "*Americana* $18,000, Sole Hub Prospect." *Variety* 17 Oct. 1928.

15 "*Rosalie* Big in Phila." *Variety* 21 Nov. 1928.

16 "*Dracula*, Werba's Special." *Variety* 20 Feb. 1929.

17 "A Mystery Play Took to the Road."

18 "Perennial Mystery Play, *Dracula*, Booked 41 Weeks." *Billboard* 1 Mar. 1930.

(Courtesy of Dennis Payne)

Chapter 48

I am... Dracula

> "Once there appeared a strange optical effect:
> when he stood between me and the flame
> he did not obstruct it, for I could see its
> ghostly flicker all the same."
> –Bram Stoker, *Dracula*

In *Dracula–The Vampire Play*, the title character angrily hurls a vase and shatters a mirror that does not show his reflection. Dracula is simultaneously present and absent, not unlike the cinema itself. After all, film is spooled around a reel, but that is not where the audience sees it. Rather, light passes through the frames, pulsing temporally and temporarily onto a screen.

But even the screen is not a film's permanent home, not in the way that a picture frame provides to a painting. The location of film is in flux. A film is most alive while it is being projected, materialized in the darkness, existing between two worlds, the reel and the screen. The same is true of a vampire, its status is difficult to locate, let alone comprehend. To be undead is to be neither alive nor dead, but rather to exist in a twilight world between the two, unreal and corporeal at the same time.

As of 1929, film vampires achieved new prominence in America, with F.W. Murnau's film *Nosferatu* (1922) screened in New York and various other cities. It had returned from the cinematic grave, probably due to the success of *Dracula–The Vampire Play* on Broadway and across America. In June of that year, the *New Yorker Volkszeitung* called *Nosferatu* an "extremely dramatic story," adding that Max Schreck as the title character played his role "magnificently."[1] Then, in December 1929, *Motion Picture News* wrote:

Lugosi circa 1930.

The program states that [*Nosferatu*] was 'inspired by motives from *Dracula*.' The word 'Dracula' is played up as strongly as the title, and in the advertising in front of the house the same general scheme is carried out. The picture itself is a most morbid and depressing affair without entertainment value. It will not be acceptable anywhere except in the 'arty' houses. For the regular picture houses it is a 'bust' before it starts.[2]

Nosferatu held little appeal for most Americans in 1929, but the same could not be said of the character Dracula.

Whether Lugosi ever saw *Nosferatu* is unknown, but he definitely heard rumors about Hollywood's growing interest in adapting Bram Stoker's vampire. In 1939, the *New York Post* quoted him as follows, complete with an unfortunate effort to reproduce his accent:

Den de movies wanted to do it. De Bram Stoker heirs asked $200,000 for de film reidts but Uniwersal didn't like to pay dat much. Zo dey asked me would I correspond wid Mrs. Stoker, de widow, and get it maybe a liddle cheaper.

I wreidt and wreidt until I get cramps, and after aboudt two mondts, Mrs. Stoker says O.K., we can haff it for $60,000.[3]

Lugosi's involvement is difficult to verify. While some persons at Universal Pictures knew him, he was hardly in the habit of acquiring stories for any studio. There is some evidence that he was writing to Florence Stoker in April 1930 to broker a deal that would include himself as star of the film. In a surviving telegram to New York literary agent Harold Freedman, Lugosi claimed he had an "excellent reputable director with biggest studio here willing to buy and do *Dracula* with me as star through my manager Harry Weber."[4] The studio in question was apparently MGM rather than Universal.[5]

As for the latter, Universal studio boss Carl Laemmle, Jr. (aka "Junior Laemmle") sent a telegram on March 27, 1930, that stated, "Not interested Bela Lugosi Present Time."[6] But the context of the telegram is unknown: whether Laemmle was referring specifically to *Dracula* is in question, as the studio had not yet even acquired the rights to the novel or play.

It is certainly clear that, once Universal could legally proceed with the project, the studio considered casting numerous other actors. In 1931, the *New York Times* wrote, "[Director Tod] Browning had hoped to have Mr. Chaney play the part of Stoker's human vampire, but this was not to be...."[7] Here is the stuff of legend. One of the great Hollywood myths is that Chaney was to portray Dracula, but the casting was disrupted due to the actor's death on August 26, 1930. The tale is simultaneously true and false. False, given that Chaney was never cast as

Left: Carl Laemmle and Carl Laemmle, Jr. Right: Published in the *Film Daily* in 1926.

Gary D. Rhodes | Bill Kaffenberger

Dracula. Indeed, he was not under contract to Universal in 1930. He was ill prior to his death, which preceded *Dracula*'s production and even the studio's acquisition of the rights to it. Chaney was not Dracula, and due to his health problems and demise, he could never have been, certainly not when the film was finally produced in the autumn of 1930.

Conversely, it probably is true that Tod Browning had wanted Chaney to play the role. Chaney's fame could have greatly contributed to the success of the talkie version of *Dracula*, particularly in the eyes of those who viewed the story as too risky to adapt. Chaney successfully made the transition to sound in *The Unholy Three* (1930). His continued box-office appeal seemed assured, but he died of throat cancer on August 26, 1930, at which time Universal was considering different actors for the role of Dracula.[8]

If Chaney had lived, it would have been theoretically possible for him to star in *Dracula*. Loans of major stars did occur occasionally; for example, Universal loaned Lew Ayres to Warner Brothers right after he appeared in *All Quiet on the Western Front* (1930).[9] However, in the case of Lon Chaney, such a loan would have been unlikely. After all, Chaney brought suit against Universal in March 1930 over publicity for the sound reissue of *The Phantom of the Opera* (1925) that gave audiences the false impression that they would hear him speak in it.[10] Such a disagreement probably made Chaney at least temporarily unhappy with Universal.

Furthermore, Chaney's name was never mentioned publicly in conjunction with *Dracula*'s casting during the summer of 1930.[11] For example, at the beginning of July 1930, Tod Browning noted his own "definite ideas of how *Dracula* should be produced on the screen," arguing that a famous star should not be cast. "I favor getting a stranger from Europe," he said, "and not giving his name. It takes away from the thrilling effects of the story."[12] Browning's conception of the character had changed even before Chaney's death.

What names did appear in the press? During the third week of June 1930, Universal touted John Wray as its choice for the "neck-biter."[13] *Film Daily* described his portrayal in *All Quiet on the Western Front* as "one of the screen's acting achievements."[14] Not only was Wray associated with Junior Laemmle's hit film, he was also under a long-term studio contract, one that he signed shortly after appearing in Universal's *The Czar of Broadway* (1930).[15] When Universal announced he would star as Dracula, the 43-year-old Wray was receiving acclaim for his latest role. It is difficult to know why Junior Laemmle decided against Wray, save for the fact that the studio

Lon Chaney.

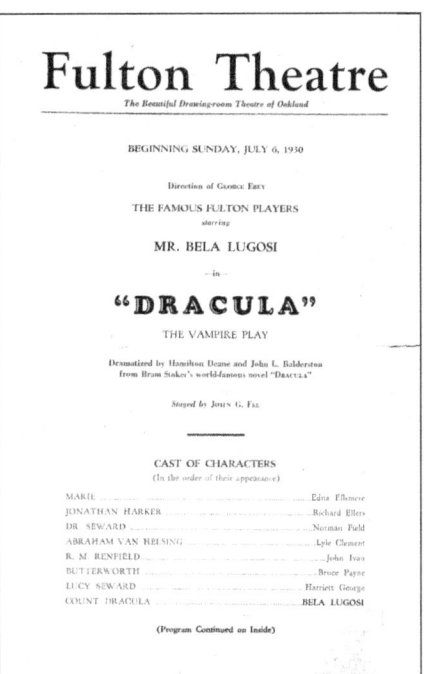

MUSIC PROGRAM

JOHN WHARRY LEWIS, *Conductor*

1. Overture, "RAYMOND" .... Thomas
2. "DREAM RIVER" .... Bowers
3. "HUNGARIAN FANTASIE" .... Friedman

ACT I.
4. "THE PASSING OF SALOME" .... Joyce
5. VEIL DANCE .... Chaminade

ACT II.
6. "ZEGUENERLIEBE" .... Lehar

ACT III.
7. "CORTEGE DU SARDARE" .... Ipolitow-Iffanoff

Above Right: Playbill for *Dracula–The Vampire Play* in Oakland in 1930. **Left:** Music credits for *Dracula–The Vampire Play* in Oakland in 1930.

was simultaneously crafting a starring role for him in *Saint Johnson* (aka *St. Johnson*), which would have been shot in the autumn had it not been shelved.[16] Similarly, in early August, *Motion Picture News* reported that Wray would costar with Lew Ayres in an "air picture to be directed by Howard Hawks."[17]

Rumors in late June 1930 also suggested Bela Lugosi's name. As the *Los Angeles Times* wrote on June 21, 1930, "one cannot imagine anyone else doing it as well as he."[18] It could be that Browning was already considering Lugosi, that he was the "stranger from Europe" that Browning mentioned. Despite his stage successes, Lugosi remained largely unknown to the everyday American filmgoer in 1930. Casting him would add further risk to an already risky production.

At any rate, Lugosi appeared onstage when *Dracula–The Vampire Play* returned to Oakland's Fulton Theater for two weeks beginning July 6, 1930. He likely signed the contract as part of his effort to win the film role. And certainly it didn't hurt that his film *The Thirteenth Chair* (1929) played at Oakland's Century Theater during part of *Dracula*'s run.[19]

Harriett George reprised her role of Lucy, with the rest of the cast comprised of Oakland-based actors. Large crowds packed the auditorium on opening night.[20] The *Oakland Post-Enquirer* told readers:

> The drama, of course, belongs to the star, Lugosi. He is master of the play in reality as well as in the leading role. Through the scores of times he has portrayed the ghoulish hero, he has developed a remarkable smoothness in presentation of the character which makes it fascinating and not altogether too overwhelming.[21]

The *Oakland Tribune* added that Lugosi "once again dominated the scene with his eerie presence, his hypnotic gestures, his becoming voice, and his courtly Continental manners."[22]

During the play, Lugosi had breakfast with theatrical columnist and critic Wood Soanes at the Ambassador Hotel.[23] He shared several observations about the vampire onscreen:

> I am looking forward to the screen production which is being planned by Universal. ... There is one scene in particular that cannot be presented on the stage but would be most effective on the screen. I refer to that episode describing Dracula's voyage by sea to England. He starts on a vessel containing a full complement of sailors. Each night the vampire, in order to retain his earthly form, must drink the blood of one human. Each morning there is a dead sailor. Finally, the vessel comes within view of the coast of England. Only one sailor remains and Dracula takes his hideous toll.
>
> As the vessel comes onto the rock-bound coast, Dracula is at the wheel of the charnel vessel but the countryside has been aroused. The Britons are awaiting him, prepared to drive the stake through his heart that will stop him from further walkings on the

Top: Published in the *Oakland Post-Enquirer* on July 12, 1930. Above: Published in the *Oakland Tribune* on July 17, 1930.

earth. Dracula runs the ship on the rocks, wrecks it and turns himself into a wolf. As they shoot at him, he changes to a bat, flies away and escapes. It should make a most stirring picture.[24]

Lugosi also told Soanes that the role of Dracula required "time and meditation to catch the mood of the character; each performance must be approached with some care."

The play ran two weeks at the Fulton, with Lugosi indicating that he might return to Oakland in September and star in a different play.[25] But he remained focused on the cinematic undead. While in Oakland, Lugosi wrote to Harold Freedman:

[I] wish to thank you very much for your kind effort in suggesting I play the part in *Dracula* when it is filmed. I am sure the success of this enterprise will be largely due to your endeavors, which I very much appreciate."[26]

Here Lugosi was staying in touch with someone that he knew had been involved in the sale of the film rights to *Dracula*, perhaps hoping that Freedman would mention him to Universal.

At some point during the Fulton run, at least three persons involved in *Dracula*'s pre-production at Universal attended a performance: associate producer E. M. Asher, and writers Louis Bromfield and Dudley Murphy. Curiously absent from the delegation was Junior Laemmle, though he may well have already seen the play on one or more occasions. Laemmle later told film historian Rick Atkins, "After seeing Bela Lugosi successfully do the character on stage, in New York, Browning and I eventually went with Bela."[27] Either the two attended the play in 1927 and/or 1928 when it was still on Broadway, or – more likely if they actually saw the play together – the two attended the play on the West Coast.

Tod Browning.

On August 2, 1930, the *Hollywood Filmograph* quoted the *Oakland Post-Enquirer* as saying: "According to studio announcement following [the Asher/Bromfield/Murphy 'visit' to the Fulton Theater], Bela Lugosi, who is playing the title role here, will play for the screen the part he has made famous on the stage."[28] The *Filmograph* may have reprinted the quotation from the newspaper because its editor had not yet heard the same directly from Universal. Indeed, it seems to have been a premature announcement, one that Lugosi might have even encouraged the *Post-Enquirer* to publish.

Then, on August 16, the *Hollywood Filmograph* reiterated what became its regular refrain that summer: Lugosi was the "greatest living portrayer" of Dracula, and thus should win the role.[29] Three days later, Elizabeth Yeaman at the *Hollywood Daily Citizen* declared that it was "hard to picture anyone [other than Lugosi] in the part." She added, "I suspect that Universal feels that way about Mr. Lugosi, although no definite announcement in this connection has come from the studio."[30]

Given *Dracula*'s importance on Universal's studio schedule for 1930-31, Junior Laemmle and others labored over the decision of who would play the title role. By August 30, the *Hollywood Filmograph* told readers that the studio had made a screen test of Lugosi. It consisted of two scenes shot in the space of a few hours. The publication added, "right now Bela Lugosi and a number of others are awaiting the final O K of Carl Laemmle."[31] As Lugosi himself claimed in 1939 (in a quotation that tried to preserve his accent):

> And who was tested? De cousins and brodder-in-laws of de Laemmles – all deir pets and de pets of DEIR pets! Dis goes on for a longk time and den oldt man Laemmle says, 'Dere's nobody in de family dat can play it, zo why don't you hire an egdor![32]

Who were these other persons? An agent proposed Joseph Schildkraut, though there is no evidence that Junior Laemmle seriously considered him.[33] John Carradine later claimed that he was considered as well, but – like Schildkraut – his name never formally appeared in conjunction with *Dracula* in the press of 1930.[34]

Had Junior Laemmle wanted to do so, he could have chosen from an array of Draculas populating stages across America: Courtney White, Raymond Huntley, William Tilden, Victor Jory, and others. To be sure, the only one of them to receive serious consideration was Frederick Pymm.[35] But collectively they did prove one thing: more than one person could play the role and receive applause for so doing.

Paul Muni in *Seven Faces* (1930).

Who else did Universal seriously consider? On August 11, 1930, E. M. Asher contacted director Roland West about Chester Morris, an actor who had just starred in *The Bat Whispers* (1930). Though *The Bat Whispers* would not be released until after *Dracula*'s production began, Asher had likely seen Morris' work in other films, including *Alibi* (1929) and *The Big House*

William Courtenay (right) with Erich von Stroheim in *Three Faces East* (1930).

(1930). Casting Morris would have meant casting a famous film actor, and it also meant a chance to connect the film directly to the mystery genre. But Roland West – who had Morris under contract – turned Asher down on August 12, mentioning that he was trying to find a romantic story for the actor.[36] At age 29, Morris was likely the youngest actor the studio considered as a possible Dracula.[37]

By late August 1930, Universal moved on to at least two more possibilities, one being Paul Muni, who remains famous for his work in such films as *Scarface* (1932). Muni made a great deal of sense in the summer of 1930, as the press described him as a "new" Lon Chaney thanks to his performance in *Seven Faces* (1930).[38] Like Chaney, he would have brought a unique quality to the role, one that would have probably been much less romantic and more dependent on heavy makeup.[39] Universal did shoot a test of Muni as Dracula, though it does not seem to survive.[40]

At roughly the same time, Universal also made a screen test of William Courtenay, who had played a magician in the stage version of *The Spider*.[41] While that role may have been one reason the studio thought of him, another was the film *Three Faces East*, which was released in August 1930. In it, Courtenay's tall slender body, large eyes, receding hairline, and commanding presence made him seem like a suitable candidate for the role. Universal's "New York offices" actually issued a "demand" that he portray Dracula.[42] Given that fact, his screen test (which also does not survive) may have been little more than an effort to placate some executives. At any rate, Courtenay – who was 55 years old in 1930 – was the oldest Dracula of those considered.

Even as the number of would-be Draculas grew, various persons in the press continued to support Lugosi, perhaps because he intentionally ingratiated himself to journalists, but also because they had presumably seen him in one of the stage versions. "It seems like everybody that is anybody is pulling for Bela Lugosi to play Dracula," the *Hollywood Filmograph* wrote on September 6, adding that the "story is made to order for him, since he has the voice along with the appearance that is necessary for the part."[43]

One week later, however, the same trade published news that Lugosi would have found disappointing: "Dame Rumor has it that Universal has selected Ian Keith [to be Dracula], who just finished a picture on their lot."[44] The film in question was *The Boudoir Diplomat* (1930), in which Keith played the male lead. Immediately prior, Keith played a supporting role in Raoul Walsh's *The Big Trail* (1930) at Fox; he had also portrayed John Wilkes Booth in D. W. Griffith's *Abraham Lincoln* (1930). The 31-year-old actor cut an impressive figure, and would probably have created a romantic Dracula; in *The Boudoir Diplomat*, he played a ladies man who flirts with other men's wives.

> There has been so much said and done about who will play Dracula for Universal, that everybody has sort of watched with interest who the powers that be will select.
>
> Dame Rumor has it that Universal has selected Ian Keith, who just finished a picture on their lot. Prior to this he appeared in "The Big Trail" for Fox Films and is right now working at the RKO in "Sheeps' Clothing." directed by Louis Wolheim.
>
> For some time it has been rumored that Bela Lugosi was to have the leading role, since he played it so well on the stage, both here and abroad. Then William Courtney was mentioned as the man who was liable to gain the part on demand from the New York offices of the firm.
>
> Maybe we are a bit premature with our announcement, but we have every reason to believe that Ian Keith has been selected and unless some un-

Published in the *Hollywood Filmograph* in September 1930.

"Maybe we are a bit premature with our announcement," the *Filmograph* admitted, "but we have every reason to believe that Ian Keith has been selected and unless some unforeseen thing happens will play Dracula."[45] At roughly the same time, however, *Film Daily* told readers that Junior Laemmle was "very favorably impressed" with Lugosi's screen test.[46] Contradictions, apparent or real, abounded.

The *Hollywood Filmograph* called Count Dracula the "prize role of the season," adding that the mystery of who would play him was "the burning question right now in the film industry."[47] Subsequently, the same publication reported, "[T]here has been so much said about who will play Dracula for Universal that everybody has sort of watched with interest who the powers that be will select."[48] And in her newspaper column, Louella O. Parsons wrote, "Seems to me I never heard so many people mentioned for a part in my life."[49]

Finally, after nearly three months, Universal made its decision. On September 15, *Film Daily* announced that Lugosi would indeed play Dracula; he had signed a contract on September 11.[50] Various other publications reported the news over the days that followed. Discussing the choice, the *Los Angeles Times* wrote, "Sometimes certain players who please the dramatic writers really are chosen for certain roles, and that is just what has happened, so far as this writer is concerned, to Universal's production of *Dracula*."[51]

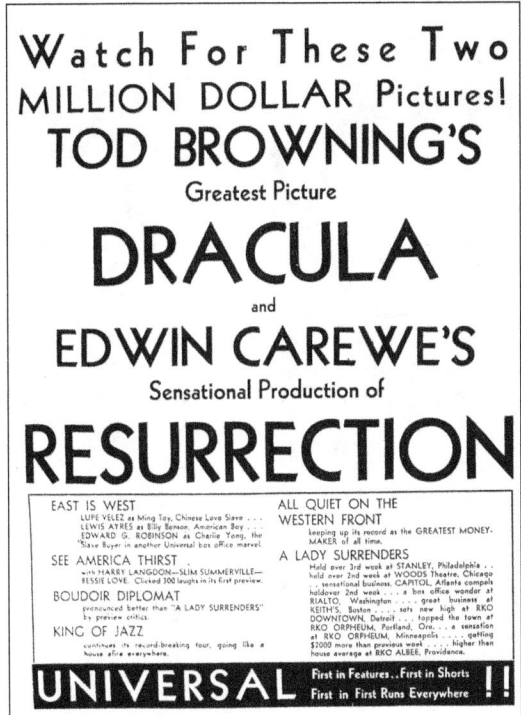 

Left: Published in *Motion Picture News* on October 25, 1930. Right: Published in the *Los Angeles Times* on September 13, 1930.

Despite all of the others under consideration, Lugosi's name kept surfacing repeatedly throughout the entire process, at Universal and in the press, far more than anyone else's. Perhaps the fact he lobbied so hard for it helped, or perhaps it did not. Perhaps some persons at Universal expressed opposition to Lugosi, or perhaps not. Lugosi himself claimed:

> [Universal] tested five other actors – each executive having a favorite actor for the role. But Mr. Laemmle said, 'As we cannot decide on who shall play it, let us use the original Dracula and make the film without even testing him.'[52]

Lugosi was incorrect in recalling he did not undergo a screen test. But it is extremely clear that Junior Laemmle – in conjunction with Tod Browning, as Laemmle himself claimed – cast Lugosi in the role, thus expressing confidence in him.

In late 1930, *Picture Play* magazine reported on Lugosi's quest to win the role:

> Rewards sometimes come to those who wait. ... About two years ago Lugosi took the part in a Coast production of [*Dracula*], and there was talk of its being done in pictures. So he decided to stay on and wait, fighting his way along in small roles in a variety of films, but doing nothing outstanding. Between times he would play on the stage again in revivals of *Dracula*.

Publicity shot of Lugosi applying makeup in 1930.

Lugosi with his *Dracula* costars. From left to right, they are David Manners, Helen Chandler, Dwight Frye, and Edward Van Sloan.

Finally when it came to the making of the picture, things began to look rather dismal. Other actors were mentioned for the role, and it is said that tests were made of some of them.[53]

But "waiting around in Hollywood paid this time," as Lugosi had bested the competition. Director Tod Browning began production on *Dracula* on September 29, 1930. In an American interview, translated during the production of *Dracula* for his Hungarian compatriots by Budapest's *Az Est* newspaper, Lugosi said:

I played Dracula. In this mysterious great role – although I have played it more than a thousand times – I can still find something new and something for improvement. A role, an actor or a person is never complete.[54]

Universal's *Dracula* premiered at New York's Roxy Theater on February 12, 1931.[55] On that day, and ever since, Lugosi introduced himself as Dracula. 'Midst the wild Carpathians, he bid us welcome. He invited us to listen to the children of the night.

By that time, Lugosi was 48 years old. He had lived in four countries and had been an actor for three decades. The sheer breadth of his life and career – as well as the variety of roles

Lugosi on the set of Universal's *Dracula* (1931).

he played – hardly dictated this outcome. It was not inevitable, not ineluctable. His was a circuitous and unexpected journey into the realm of the undead. But that perhaps makes the result even more remarkable.

Bela Lugosi became Dracula, and vice versa. Since Lugosi's death in 1956, Dracula has dressed as Lugosi, the vampire forever remade in Lugosi's own image. And so Lugosi exists forever in the twilight world of cinema, caught between man and legend, between actor and icon, between film reel and film screen. We have seen, and always shall see, his ghostly flicker.

As Jonathan Harker explains in Bram Stoker's novel, "I thought it was some trick of the moonlight, some weird effect of shadow; but I kept looking, and it could be no delusion."

AFRAID OF HIMSELF

By LILLIAN SHIRLEY

Mr. Lugosi hates the character of Dracula. But his fascinating portrayal of it dooms him to go on playing it despite this hate.

Bela Lugosi is haunted by the horrible character he has created on the stage and screen—Count Dracula

IMAGINE the feelings of a man who for more than one thousand times has played a part which he hates with all his soul and yet is compelled to go on playing because his very hatred of the rôle makes it so convincing that no other man can give a satisfactory portrayal of it!

Bela Lugosi is the man and "Count Dracula" is the rôle in the play of that name. On the streets, men who don't know Lugosi stare unpleasantly when they recognize him, and women experience anticipatory shivers. Say "vampire" to almost anyone in Hollywood and they will reply, "Lugosi."

At this writing "Dracula" is being filmed into a talking picture at Universal City. You may remember "The Phantom of the Opera" with its mystery, gruesomeness and the horrible make-up of Lon Chaney. It was a trifling bug-a-boo tale to frighten infants compared to this "Dracula." It gives me a crawling spine just to think of it, and it produces shudders and backward looks over the shoulder in everyone connected with the making of it. So—I went off to Universal City, and carefully chose a terrifically hot day with plenty of bright sunlight to talk with Bela Lugosi, the mystery man of Hollywood.

I AM a Hungarian by birth and education," he told me very quietly, almost sombrely. "I was reared in the town of Lugos, named for my family. I began stage work at the age of twenty, entirely by accident, and until after the war I had never been more than a few kilometers away from my native land. Most of the time I spent in Budapesth. Then I left—suddenly, to avoid being shot or hanged."

"In heaven's name—why?" I gasped, for young leading men do not usually make that kind of confession.

"It was the post-war penalty for being on the wrong side of politics," he replied with a faint smile. "I'm told they use the same method in Chicago occasionally. Well, I didn't wish to be 'taken for a ride.'"

Without doubt Bela Lugosi is Hollywood's prime mystery, but behind the mystery lies something that first attracts women to him before it makes them gasp and shiver. And looking at him in his make-up for the part of Dracula I wouldn't doubt it for a moment. To begin with, the story of Bram Stoker's gruesome novel which was first made into a stage play and is now being made into a moving picture is a terrible, supernatural story. It it a tale of vampires—the "undead"—who lived on human blood—an incredible tale for this twentieth century. No need to go deeply into it for this is not the story of the story, but of the man who for several years has lived the story, week in and week out.

Dracula is a blood curdling being with a dreadful fascination. Bela Lugosi has played the part so often he is afraid he is permanently absorbing the horrible creature's personality.

AS I understand it, an actor is a man who tries to make you believe that the character he shows you on the stage or screen is a real character. If he makes you believe it he is called a good actor. Sometimes he lives his part so thoroughly that he becomes the character he portrays—that is, if he plays it long enough and intensely enough. There was Joseph Jefferson in "Rip Van Winkle," and here in Hollywood is an old man who played one rôle for forty years—typifying a man who limped with his left leg—and now he needs no make-up and cannot help limping though there is nothing wrong with his leg.

This Count Dracula is a horrible, unnatural, repulsive super-fiend. Bela Lugosi, underneath the make-up and between scenes, is a gentlemanly, quiet, studious, courteous person. But we shiver—we women—because he's the kind of actor who can't do a trifling job of acting, and—here's the unpleasantness again—he comes from that part of Hungary where they believe in human vampires; resurrected creatures able to transform themselves into huge bats. Mr. Lugosi was brought up on those vampire tales, and he has made such a terrible success of the part because he has *(Continued on page 106)*

61

Published in *Modern Screen* in March 1931.

Above: Lugosi and Helen Chandler in *Dracula* (1931). Right: One of many advertisements that publicized *Dracula* (1931) in Hungary. Published in *Pécsi Napló* on February 25, 1932.

Endnotes

1. "*Nosferatu, the Vampire* im Film Guild Cinema." *New Yorker Volkszeitung* 3 June 1929.

2. "*Nosferatu, the Vampire*." *Motion Picture News* 21 Dec. 1929.

3. Mok, Michael. "Horror Man at Home." *New York Post* 19 Oct. 1939.

4. Lugosi, Bela. Telegram to Harold Freedman, 8 Apr. 1930.

5. Skal, David J. *Hollywood Gothic: The Tangled Web of* Dracula *from Novel to Stage to Screen* (New York: W. W. Norton, 1990).

6. Skal, David J. *The Monster Show: A Cultural History of Horror* (New York: W. W. Norton, 1993).

7. "*Dracula* as a Film." *New York Times* 22 Feb. 1931.

8. For more information on Lon Chaney, see Blake, Michael F. *Lon Chaney: The Man Behind the Thousand Faces* (New York: Vestal Press, 1990), and Blake, Michael F. *A Thousand Faces: Lon Chaney's Unique Artistry in Motion Pictures* (New York: Vestal Press, 1995).

9. "Lewis Ayres Loaned by Universal to Warners." *Exhibitors Herald-World* 2 May 1930.

10. "Chaney's U Suit." *Variety* 5 Mar. 1930.

11. See, for example: "Lon Chaney Better." *Variety* 30 July 1930: 4; "Lon Chaney Recovering." *Film Daily* 5 Aug. 1930.

12. Parsons, Louella O. *Los Angeles Examiner* 2 July 1930.

13. "Wray, the Neck-Biter." *Variety* 25 June 1930.

14. "John Wray Signed for Long Term." *Film Daily* 20 Apr. 1930.

15. "John Wray for U Cast." *Film Daily* 10 Feb. 1930.

16. "U Shelves Pictures." *Motion Picture News* 27 Sept. 1930.

17. "U Plans Air Special." *Motion Picture News* 9 Aug. 1930.

18. Kingsley, Grace. "Fox Picks Story for Wayne." *Los Angeles Times* 21 June 1930.

19. "*13th Chair* Tops Program at Century." *Oakland Post-Enquirer* 9 July 1930.

20. "*Dracula* Thrills with Story of Vampire." *Oakland Post-Enquirer* 7 July 1930.

21. Ibid.

22. Soanes, Wood. "*Dracula* Again Thrills Crowd at the Fulton." *Oakland Tribune* 7 July 1930.

23. Soanes, Wood. "Jane Fooshee Will Open Special Fulton Season Following Lugosi Week." *Oakland Tribune* 6 July 1930.

24. Ibid.

25. "Oakland Pickups." *Inside Facts of Stage and Screen* 26 July 1930.

26. Lugosi, Bela. Letter to Harold Freedman, 12 July 1930.

27 Atkins, Rick. *Let's Scare 'Em: Grand Interviews and a Filmography of Horrific Proportions, 1930-1961* (Jefferson, NC: McFarland, 1997).

28 "Producers Have Their Eyes on Him." *Hollywood Filmograph* 2 Aug. 1930.

29 "Bela Lugosi." *Hollywood Filmograph* 16 Aug. 1930.

30 Yeaman, Elizabeth. *Hollywood Daily Citizen* 19 Aug. 1930.

31 "Universal Has Made Test of Bela Lugosi for *Dracula* Talkie." *Hollywood Filmograph* 30 Aug. 1930.

32 "Horror Man at Home."

33 Skal, *Hollywood Gothic*.

34 Weaver, Tom. "*Dracula* (1931)." In Brunas, Micheal, John Brunas, and Tom Weaver. *Universal Horrors* (Jefferson, NC: McFarland, 1990).

35 "*Dracula* Cast." *Inside Facts of Stage and Screen* 16 Aug. 1930.

36 Asher, E. M. Letter to Roland West. 11 Aug. 1930; West, Roland. Letter to E. M. Asher. 12 Aug. 1930. [Available in the Roland West Papers, Correspondence 1930, at the Margaret Herrick Library, Academy of Motion Picture Arts and Sciences, Beverly Hills, CA.]

37 If John Carradine's story is true, he would have been – at age 24 –the youngest actor that Universal considered. In any event, Chester Morris was certainly the youngest actor under serious consideration.

38 "6 New Universal Films Start Work This Month." *Film Daily* 12 Sept. 1930.

39 Burton, Stanley. "Don't Call Me Lon Chaney." *Photoplay* Jan. 1930.

40 On 3 Sept. 1930, *Variety* mentioned that "tests of a number of actors have been made in the part [of Dracula]" before claiming that the selection was "now down" to William Courtenay, Bela Lugosi, or Paul Muni, the implication being that tests would have been shot of all three actors, if not others.

41 Courtenay's screen test is mentioned in: "Behind the Scenes in Hollywood." *Logansport Pharos-Tribune* (Logansport, IN) 18 Sept. 1930.

42 "Ian Keith to Play *Dracula* For U–Rumored." *Hollywood Filmograph* 13 Sept. 1930.

43 "Pulling for Him." *Hollywood Filmograph* 6 Sept. 1930.

44 "Ian Keith to Play *Dracula* For U–Rumored."

45 Ibid.

46 Wilk, Ralph. "A Little from 'Lots.'" *Film Daily* 11 Sept. 1930.

47 "Universal Has Made Test of Bela Lugosi for *Dracula* Talkie."

48 "Ian Keith to Play *Dracula* for U–Rumored."

49 Parsons, Louella O. *Los Angeles Examiner* 17 Sept. 1930.

50 "To Start *Dracula* Next Week." *Film Daily* 15 Sept. 1930.

51 Kingsley, Grace. "Star and Executive to Travel." *Los Angeles Times* 16 Sept. 1930.

52 Wallace, Inez. "Dracula's Castle is in Hollywood." *Cleveland Plain-Dealer* 26 Dec. 1937.

53 "Waiting Wins Reward." *Picture Play* Dec. 1930.

54 "A Chat with Dracula." *Az Est* (Budapest, Hungary) 19 Nov. 1930. Lugosi's claim that he had played Dracula over 1000 times was an overestimate.

55 For more information on the film, see: Rhodes, Gary D. *Tod Browning's Dracula* (London: Tomahawk Press, 2014).

Epilogue

"[Lugosi] hopes, when the talkie *Dracula* is completed, to escape the shackles of the role and essay other characterizations. He will never again play Dracula on the stage, he says." – Robbin Coons, 1930

"When I finish this picture [*Dracula* (1931)], if it is possible to avoid it, I shall play Dracula no more. No. Never!" – Bela Lugosi, 1931

Lugosi in a publicity portrait for *The Red Poppy* (1922).
(Courtesy of David Wentink)

Appendix C

American Stageography 1921-1930

Researched and compiled by Gary D. Rhodes and Bill Kaffenberger

This catalogue of Lugosi's stage work covers his American period from 1921 through 1930. His stage work prior to that time is chronicled in Volume I of this book.

We gratefully acknowledge the groundbreaking work of Robert Cremer, the first biographer to catalogue Lugosi's stageography in any depth. Our own work has been conducted with important assistance from him, as well as from Robert Singer and Mirjam Dénes.

Importantly, we have relied whenever possible on primary sources, including but not limited to playbills, critical reviews, and published reports. The result is the most accurate and comprehensive stageography of Lugosi's career in America in the 1920s that has ever been compiled.

Dealing with gaps in the timeline as well as misinformation are two of the hurdles we had to overcome. This was particularly the case for Lugosi's Hungarian and German-language theatrical activities in the United States. For example, previous biographies have assumed that Lugosi's American tours in Hungarian-language plays were limited and largely unsuccessful. By contrast, exhaustive research using surviving Hungarian-language newspapers published in America reveals a different picture.

We include not only legitimate theater productions, but also other known live performances as well, including cabaret shows. We do not include *A fejedelem* (*The Prince*), a play that Lugosi had hoped to stage in Los Angeles in 1928, as no production of it took place.[1] Nor do we include *The Second Cup*; according to the *Los Angeles Times*, Lugosi signed a contract to appear in that three-act play in March of 1930.[2] However, there is absolutely no evidence that a version with Lugosi was ever staged.

English translations of the play titles are given in parentheticals. Where no parenthetical appears, it is because the play title needs no translation, as in the case of Ferenc Molnár's *Liliom*. In addition, when known, the genre of the productions – for example, "drama," "comedy," "tragedy," "operetta," etc. – has been provided in parentheticals.

We would stress that the "opening night" dates we give are for the *particular* productions catalogued; "opening night" does not refer to a play's premiere, meaning the first time it was ever staged anywhere.

1921

Boldogság (Happiness) (Comedy)
Tour Dates: January 30 at the People's House Theater (aka the Rand School Theater) in New York City; January 31 at the Mercantile Hall in Philadelphia, Pennsylvania; February 1 at the Magyar Házban in South Bethlehem, Pennsylvania; February 5 at the Rákóczi Hall in Bridgeport, Connecticut; February 6 at the Munkás Otthon in Newark, New Jersey; February 10 at the Szent László Hall in New Brunswick, New Jersey; February 11 at the Magyar Otthon in Trenton, New Jersey.

Author: John Hartley Manners.
Role: Unknown.

Note: This play may have been Lugosi's first professional work with Ilona Montagh. Also in the cast were Kornélia Lőrincz (aka Cornelia Lőrinc) and István Papp (aka Stefan Papp). Produced by the Modern Magyar Színpad (Modern Hungarian Stage), a theatrical troupe organized at the beginning of 1921 under the direction of László Schwartz. Also reportedly staged in June 1921 at an undetermined location with Lugosi directing the production. Sometimes the title was rendered as *A boldogság*.

A kisasszony férje (A Young Lady's Husband) (Comedy)
Tour Dates: February 18 in Bridgeport, Connecticut; February 19 in Passaic, New Jersey; February 20 at the Thirty-Ninth Street Theater in New York City; February 21 in South Bethlehem, Pennsylvania; February 22 in Philadelphia, Pennsylvania; February 25 in Perth Amboy, New Jersey; March 5 at the Turn Hall in Elizabeth, New Jersey; March 6, at the Belmont Theater in Newark, New Jersey (afternoon performance only); March 6 at the Belmont Theater, New York City (evening performance); April 14 (likely date) in Trenton, New Jersey; April 15 (likely date) in New Brunswick, New Jersey.

Author: Gábor Drégely.
Director: Béla Lugosi.
Role: Lugosi had the leading role as The Husband.

Note: Lugosi's name was spelled "Lugossi" on at least one advertisement. Sometimes rendered as *Kisasszony férje*, the title could be a play-on-words, as the literal translation of "kisasszony" is an "unmarried woman." Some newspapers, such as the *New York Evening Telegram*, the *New York Tribune*, the *New York Evening World*, and the *New York Daily Call*, referred to the play as *Almost Married*. It was originally scheduled to open in New York City at the People's House, but the premiere was delayed until February 2, when it was staged for the benefit of the Hoover Fund for Suffering Hungarian Children. Along with Lugosi, the cast included Ilona Montagh, Lajos Horváth, Kornélia Lőrincz (aka Cornelia Lőrinc), Gyula Szalai (aka Gyula Szalay), Klári Winton, Ferencz Kálnay, and István Papp (aka Stefan Papp). It is possible Lugosi appeared in this play again in June of 1921. Avery Hopwood subsequently adapted this play into English; under the title *Little Miss Bluebeard*, it played Broadway from August 1923 to February 1924.

A kaméliás hölgy (Lady of the Camellias, aka Camille) (Drama)
Tour Dates: February 27 at the Belmont Theater in New York City; March 3 at the Szent László Hall in New Brunswick, New Jersey; March 4 at the Magyar Otthon in Trenton, New Jersey; March 7 at the Rákóczi Hall in Bridgeport, Connecticut.

Author: Alexander Dumas.
Director: Béla Lugosi.
Role: Armand Duval.

Note: This play was sometimes rendered simply as *Kaméliás hölgy*. Produced by the Modern Magyar Színpad (Modern Hungarian Stage). Included in the cast were Kornélia Lőrincz (aka Cornelia Lőrinc), Lajos Horváth, József Kenessei (aka József Kenessey), Ilona Montagh, Gyula Szalai (aka Gyula Szalay), and Arisztid Latensen.

Fiú-e vagy leány? (A Boy or a Girl?) (Comedy)
Tour Dates: March 9 in Perth Amboy, New Jersey; March 12 in Passaic, New Jersey; March 13 at The People's House Theater in New York City; March 15 in South Bethlehem, Pennsylvania; March 16 in Philadelphia, Pennsylvania; March 17 in Trenton, New Jersey; March 18 in New Brunswick, New Jersey; March 19 at the Bohemian Auditorium in Newark, New Jersey.

Author: Jenő Heltai.
Director: Béla Lugosi.

Note: Produced by the Modern Magyar Színpad (Modern Hungarian Stage). Lugosi directed, but did not appear in the play. The cast included Kornélia Lőrincz (aka Cornelia Lőrinc), Ilona Montagh, Zoltán Nyikos, Lajos Horváth, Boriska Bozóky (aka Boriska Bozóki), and József Kenessei (aka József Kenessey).

Halló (Hello) (Comedy)
Tour Dates: April 7 at the Columbia Hall in Perth Amboy, New Jersey; April 8 at the Rákóczi Hall in Bridgeport, Connecticut; April 9 at the Mokrai Hall in Passaic, New Jersey; April 10 at the Yorkville Casino in Yorkville, New York City; April 11 at the Magyar Házban in South Bethlehem, Pennsylvania; April 12 at the Mercantile Hall in Philadelphia, Pennsylvania; April 13 at the Magyar Otthon in Trenton, New Jersey; April 14 at the Szent László Hall in New Brunswick, New Jersey; April 15 (likely date) in Detroit, Michigan; April 16 at the Kossuth Hall in Youngstown, Ohio.

Author: Imre Földes.
Directed by: Béla Lugosi.
Role: Unknown.

Note: Produced by the Modern Magyar Színpad (Modern Hungarian Stage). The title was sometimes rendered with an exclamation point as *Halló!* Along with Lugosi, the cast included Ilona Montagh, Kornélia Lőrincz (aka Cornelia Lőrinc), Klári Winton, Zsigmond Nyikos, Lajos Horváth, and Gyula Szalai (aka Gyula Szalay). On April 6, the *Amerikai Magyar Népszava* stated, "after its performance in New York, the company will hit the road to Detroit and on their way, they will visit all places inhabited by Hungarians." Thus, it is likely additional performances were scheduled and probably staged in other cities both before and after the listed Philadelphia and Youngstown appearances.

Magyar művészek előadása (A Performance by Hungarian Actors)
Opening Night: June 5 at the Yorkville Casino in Yorkville, New York City.

Director: Béla Lugosi.
Role: Unknown.

Note: This was an evening of Hungarian variety entertainment, with Lugosi apparently directing the entire program. The evening consisted of a performance by Lajos Rózsa from the Metropolitan Opera House, a recital of Hungarian Operetta and Folk songs by József Diskai (aka József Diskay) and accompanist Béla Rózsa, music by pianist Olga Bíbor, and Tamás Emőd's one-act play, *Lotharingia*, starring Lugosi and Ilona Montagh.

Béla Lugosi Recital
Opening Night: June 30 at the Mazaret Hall in Trenton, New Jersey.
Note: The piano player for Lugosi failed to show up. Information not available as to how the evening proceeded without him.

One-Act Play
Opening Night: September 4 at the Lexington Theater, as part of a musical concert by Hungarian folk singer Ernő Király.

Author: Unknown.
Role: Unknown.

Note: Despite Király's opposition, this one-act play apparently was staged. The play was likely *Törvény (The Law)*, which Lugosi performed later that month at a different venue. A September 10 concert by Király also featured the play but likely without Lugosi's participation.

Törvény (The Law)
Opening Night: September 8 at Rákóczi Hall in Bridgeport, Connecticut.

Author: Unknown.
Director: Béla Lugosi.

Note: This was a one-act play, also featuring Ilona Montagh. It may have been under the auspices of the Amerikai Magyar Színtársulat (American Hungarian Theater Company).

Liliom
Opening Night: September, location unknown.

Author: Ferenc Molnár.
Role: Liliom.

Note: Lugosi directed this play and starred as the title character; Ilona Montagh was featured in the role of Juli. Ilona Fülöp was probably the producer. Based on two primary sources, it seems this production was in fact staged once, but Lugosi's hopes to stage it in New York did not come to fruition.

1922

A sárga liliom (The Yellow Lily)
Opening Night: January 1 at the Washington Irving High School in New York City.

Author: Lajos Bíró.
Director: Béla Lugosi.
Role: The Archduke.

Note: This play was sometimes rendered simply as *Sárga liliom*. Based on the advertisements, this production appears to have been produced and directed by Lugosi. It was a charity event sponsored by Az Amerikai Polgári és Munkás Kultur Közös Bizottsága (The American Hungarian Citizen and Munkás Joint Committee on Culture). The production may have also toured other nearby cities during the month of January. The New York production included a cast of 27, including Kornélia Lőrincz (aka Cornelia Lőrinc), Károly Darvas, and Aladár Zsandányi.

Királynőm, meghalok érted (My Queen, I Will Die For You) (Romantic Drama)
Opening Night: January 22 at the Yorkville Casino in Yorkville, New York City.

Role: Unknown.

Note: Produced under the auspices of the Amerikai Magyar Színtársulat (American Hungarian

Theater Company). Lugosi directed and starred. Also in the cast were Erzsi Torday (aka Erzsi Tordai), Frida P. Tábory (aka Frida P. Tábori), Sándor Palásthy, Károly Darvas, and Aladár Zsandányi.

Kossuth-Egylet házi hangversenye (Kossuth Society Home Concert)
Opening Night: February 19 at the Public High School Auditorium at 421 East 88th Street in New York City.

Role: While billed in advertisements, the nature of Lugosi's performance is unclear. The event started at 2:30 pm.

Az élet a jövő társadalmában (Life in a Future Society)
Opening Night: February 19 at the Munkás Lyceum in New York City.

Role: The nature of Lugosi's performance at this lecture event given by the Matild Zala Society is unclear. The start time of the event was 3:00 pm. Lugosi was indeed present at both February 19 events, as published reviews make clear. The venues were only a ten-minute walk from each other.

Gettó (Ghetto)
Opening Night: February 26 at the Central Opera House in New York City.

Author: Herman Heyersman.
Director: Béla Lugosi.
Role: Rafael.

Note: Lugosi produced, directed, and starred in this play. Also in the cast were Károly Darvas, Ilona Thury, Márton Lukács, Mária Elek, Gyula Szalai (aka Gyula Szalay), Erzsi Torday (aka Erzsi Tordai), József Balala, Sándor Heller, and Jenő Schlinger.

A new yorki magyar munkásifjuságtánc - és kabare-estótys (New York Hungarian Workers Evening of Dance and Cabaret)
Opening Night: March 18 at the Liberty Hall on 257 East Huston Street in New York City.

Role: Lugosi sang a song called *Vén cigány* (*The Old Gypsy*).

Balala József búcsúja (József Balala Celebration)
Opening Night: April 1 at the Munkás Lyceum in New York City.

Role: Unknown.

Note: In honor of Balala's departure for California, three one-act plays were staged. Lugosi acted in at least one of them.

Az ember tragédiája (The Tragedy of Man) (Poetic Drama)
Opening Night: April 8 at the Lexington Theater in New York City. Also staged on April 9.

Author: Imre Madách.
Role: Adam.

Note: Actress Bella Pogány played Eve, Károly Darvas played Lucifer, and Ilona Montagh played Hippia. Along with playing the lead role, Lugosi co-produced and directed the production. Hungarian language newspapers indicate that major rehearsals were held on March 20 and 27 and on April 3 and 5.

A demarkáció (Demarcation) (Drama)
Opening Night: April 16 at the People's House Theater (aka the Rand School Theater)

Author: Unknown.
Director: Béla Lugosi
Role: Unknown.

Note: Actors included Bella Pogány, Károly Davas and Aladár Zsandányi. It is unknown as to whether Lugosi acted in the play, or whether he just directed it.

Lugossy Film
Opening Night: October 8 at the Washington Irving High School in New York City.

Note: Presented twice on the same day, at 5pm and at 8pm. Apparently organized, promoted and possibly directed by Lugosi, the "grand theatrical program" consisted of:

Jaj, a feleségem (Oh, My Wife!), a comedy in one act.
Kisasszony (The Miss), a drama in one act.
Dániel, ne bőgj! (Daniel, Don't Be a Crybaby!), a comedy in one act.
With performers: Bella Pogány, Paula Csáki, István Papp (aka Stefan Papp), and Károly Hatvári (a member of the Schubert Theater). György Adorján acted as the "master of ceremonies."

Asszonyszívek kalandora (The Adventurer of Women's Hearts)
A Hungarian film in two acts with English and Hungarian intertitles that starred Béla Lugosi.

Commemoration of the Russian Revolution
Opening Night: November 5 at the Lyceum Theater in New York City.

Role: Lugosi recited poetry.

Note: Lugosi likely performed his recitation early in the day, given that he had two other events in the late afternoon and evening.

Lugossy Film
Opening Night: November 5 at the Washington Irving High School in New York City.
Note: The program consisted of Lugosi and Ferike Boros starring in a one-act play written especially for Lugosi, *A Gyászruhás nő (The Woman in Mourning Dress)*, followed by songs from Irma Bráver and Ferenc Zsolt. After the live performances, the Hungarian film *Játék az esküvővel (The Wedding Game)* was screened.

The Red Poppy
Tryouts: The Apollo Theater in Atlantic City, New Jersey, November 27 through December 2; The Orpheum Theater in Harrisburg, Pennsylvania on December 4 and 5; The Grand Theater in Wilkes-Barre, Pennsylvania on December 6 and 7; and The Playhouse, Wilmington, Delaware on December 8 and 9.
Opening Night: December 20, 1922 at the Greenwich Village Theater in New York City. Closed on December 30 after 13 performances.

Author: André Picard and Francis Carco.
Producer: Iden Payne.
Director: Henry Baron.
Role: Fernando the Apache.

1923
A bagoly (The Owl)
Opening Night: May 5 at the Yorkville Casino in New York City.

Author: Unkown.
Role: Unknown.

Note: While one announcement claimed Lugosi would appear in this play, a review of it did not mention Lugosi's name or any of the cast. As a result, this entry should be treated with caution.

Táncmulatsággal egybekötött művészi – estély (An Evening of Dance and Art)
Opening Night: May 26 at the Munkás Lyceum in New York City.

Role: Poetry recitations.

Note: Lugosi read selections from "masterpieces of modern poetry" (*Új Előre* [New York City] 20 May 1923).

Die Sorina (The Sorina)
Opening Night: December 19 at the Brinckerhoff Theater, Columbia University in New York City. Also staged on December 20, 21 and 22 (matinee and evening performances that day).

Author: Georg Kaiser.
Director: Béla Lugosi.

Note: Presented by the Deutscher Verein (German Society). Tryouts were held on October 16. Lugosi held a script reading at his home on October 21. Rehearsals were held daily from October 22 to 26, and then regularly thereafter until the final dress rehearsal on December 18. Originally hired primarily as an "acting coach," Lugosi eventually became director of the production.

1924
Fata Morgana
Opening Night: April 14 at the Lyceum Theater in New York City.

Author: Ernest Vajda.
Role: Master of Ceremonies.

Note: Although Lugosi did not have a role in the play, he appeared onstage to "compere" the performance. In addition, he gave a speech during a break in the production. On April 13, *Új Előre* reported that Lugosi had originally been contracted to act in it.

Szántós Gáspár bucsuhangversenyé (Gáspár Szántós Farewell Concert)
Opening Night: May 25 at the Stuyvesant High School in New York City.

Role: While listed on the bill, the nature of Lugosi's participation is uncertain.

Note: Presented by the Victoria Sports Club.

The Werewolf
Tryouts: May 27 at the Stamford Theater in Stamford, Connecticut; May 29-31 at the Shubert Teck Theater in Buffalo, New York.
Opening Night: June 1 at the Adelphi Theater in Chicago, Illinois.

Author: Rudolf Lothar.
Role: Vincente, the butler.

Producer: George McClellan.
Staged by: Clifford Brooke.

Note: Lugosi signed his standard Actors Equity Association contract for *The Werewolf* on May 9. The contract calls for up to the first four weeks of rehearsal to be without pay. Lugosi apparently left the cast after June 4. However, on June 27, the *Daily Northwestern* (Evanston, Illinois) listed Lugosi in the cast for its review of the prior evening's performance. This suggests the small possibility that Lugosi remained with the cast as an understudy until the play moved to New York City, stepping back into the role of Vincente on June 26. That said, an advertisement for the play in the October issue of *Motion Picture Classic* still incorrectly listed Lugosi in the cast, so references to him after June 7 might be nothing more than errors based on publicity materials prepared prior to that date.

1925
Forradalmi nász (The Revolutionary Wedding)
Tour Dates: January 30 at the Magyar Hall in Northhampton, Connecticut;
January 31 at the Rákóczi Hall in Bridgeport, Connecticut; February 1 at the Mokrai Hall in Passaic, New Jersey; February 2 at the Magyar Hall at Lyons Farm, New Jersey;
February 3 at the Mercantile Hall in Philadelphia, Pennsylvania; February 4 at the Magyar Hall in Trenton, New Jersey; February 5 at the Workmans Circle in New Brunswick, New Jersey; February 6 at the Bohemian Hall in Newark, New Jersey;
February 7 at St. Mary's Lyceum in Perth Amboy, New Jersey; February 8 at the Cort Theater in New York City.

Author: Sophus Michaëlis.
Director: Béla Lugosi.
Role: Marc-Arrán.

Note: Artistic director József R. Tóth presented this production. Jenő Vass was the director, and Jenő Siposs the producer.

Ady-est (Poetry Reading)
Opening Night: May 23 at the People's House Theater (aka the Rand School Theater)

Note: Hungarian poetry readings in honor of Endre Ady.

Arabesque
Tryouts: October 5-10 at the Schubert Teck Theater in Buffalo, New York; October 12-14 at the Wieting Theater in Syracuse, New York.
Opening Night: October 20 at the National Theater in New York City. Closed November 7.

Author: Cloyd Head and Eunice Tietjens.
Producer: Norman Bel Geddes and Richard Herndon.
Director: Norman Bel Geddes.
Role: The Sheik of Hammam, a Minor Official.

Note: Rehearsals started in September and lasted for five weeks.

Az Arábiai éjszaka cabaret (The Arabian Night Cabaret)
Opening Night: December 12 at the Yorkville Casino in New York City.

Role: Lugosi was co-director of the event.

Note: The event featured guest artists in Arabian-style costumes, presumably influenced by Lugosi's short-lived performances in *Arabesque*.

Open House
Tryouts: December 7 at the Windsor Theater in the Bronx, New York.
Opening Night: December 14 at Daly's Theater in New York City. Closed on February 10, 1926.

Author: Samuel R. Golding.
Producer: Samuel R. Golding.
Director: Henry Stillman and Robert W. Lawrence.
Role: Sergius Chernoff.

Note: Rehearsals were held in Fordham, New York in November and December. Numerous tryout performances came prior to December 7, but Lugosi was not in the cast for any of them.

1926
Thury Ilona jubileuma (Ilona Thury Jubilee Celebration)
Opening Night: October 3 at the Al Jolson Theater in New York City.

Role: Unknown.

Note: Advertisements listed Lugosi as one of the major performers, but the nature of his contribution was not specified.

The Devil in the Cheese
Opening Night: December 29 at the Charles Hopkins Theater in New York City. Moved to the Plymouth Theater in late April of 1927. Closed on approximately May 14, 1927 after approximately 157 performances.

Author: Tom Cushing.
Settings: Norman Bel Geddes.
Producer and Director: Charles Hopkins.
Role: Father Petros.

Note: Rehearsals began in New York City in September, but were soon suspended until November.

1927
Hungarian Bohemians Sensational Summer Costume Ball
Opening Night: June 18 at the Ritz-Carlton Hotel in New York City.

Role: Special guest.

Note: Advertisements listed Lugosi as one of the major performers/guests, but the nature of his contribution was not specified. Others in attendance included Vilma Bánky, Lajos Bíró, Mihály Kertész (Michael Curtiz), Sándor (Alexander) Korda, and Mihály Várkonyi (Victor Varconi).

Dracula
Tryouts: September 19-21 at Sam Shubert's Theater in New Haven, Connecticut; September 22-24 at the Parsons Theater (sometimes rendered as Parson's or Parsons') in Hartford, Connecticut; September 26-27 at the Lyceum Theater in New London, Connecticut; September 28-29 at the Stamford Theater in Stamford, Connecticut; September 30-October 1 at Reade's Savoy Theater in Asbury Park, New Jersey.
Opening Night: October 5 at the Fulton Theater in New York City. Closed May 19, 1928.

Author: Hamilton Deane and John L. Balderston, based on the novel by Bram Stoker.
Producer: Horace Liveright.
Director: Ira Hards.
Role: Count Dracula.

Gyula Rudnyánszky Memorial Service
Opening Night: December 4 at the Julia Richmond High School, New York City.

Role: Guest performer.

Note: Rudnyánsky was a newspaperman and poet, originally from Budapest, who had lived and worked in New York City before going blind and returning to his native country prior to his death in 1913. Performing at this memorial event along with Lugosi were Mária Sámson, prima donna, Juliska Keleti (aka Juliska Kelety), the singer, Lola Grill, a ballerina, and other singers and musicians.

1928
Baptism Ceremony and Feast
Date: On or about April 2 at the Rockville Center, New York home of John Rieger.

Role: Honored guest.

Note: John Rieger was a noted Hungarian painter. The baptism of his child, James Victor Rieger, had been delayed due to the illness of the parish priest. According to the *Amerikai Magyar Népszava* (April 3, 1928), "The house, as it should be, was filled with an upscale number of guests on the occasion of this holiday...." Lugosi attended along with such Hungarian luminaries as János Horvai (creator of the Kossuth statue), Dr. János Varga (a toast master), J. Rónai (painter), József Szabó (painter), and others.

Dracula
Tour Dates: June 25-August 18 at the Biltmore Theater in Los Angeles; August 20-September 8 at the Columbia Theater in San Francisco; September 9-15 at the 12th Street Theater in Oakland, California.

Producer and Director: O. D. Woodward.
Role: Count Dracula.

1929
Az ördög (The Devil) (Drama)
Opening Night: March 16 at the Capitol Theater in Los Angeles.

Author: Ferenc Molnár.
Role: Unknown.

Note: The March 17 edition of the *Los Angeles Times* reported that Lugosi was "starring in a special performance ... The presentation was given in Hungarian by guest players for the benefit of their disabled fellow-artists." A "box party" at the theater followed the performance.

Dracula
Tour Dates: May 19-June 9 at the Music Box Theater in Los Angeles; June 10-12 at the Spreckels Theater in San Diego, California; June 13-15 at the Lobero Theater in Santa Barbara, California; June 17 at the Nile Theater in Bakersfield, California; June 18-20 at the Pantages Theater in Fresno, California; June 21-22 at the Sutter Theater in Sacramento, California; July 22-August 10 at the Columbia Theater in San Francisco; August 11-24 at the Fulton Theater in Oakland, California.

Producer and Director: O. D. Woodward.
Role: Count Dracula.

1930

Dracula

Tour Dates: July 6-July 18 at the Fulton Theater in Oakland, California.

Producer and Director: O. D. Woodward.
Role: Count Dracula.

Endnotes

1 See Chapter 44 for more information on this play.

2 Whitaker, Alma. "Sugar and Spice." *Los Angeles Times* 23 Mar. 1930.

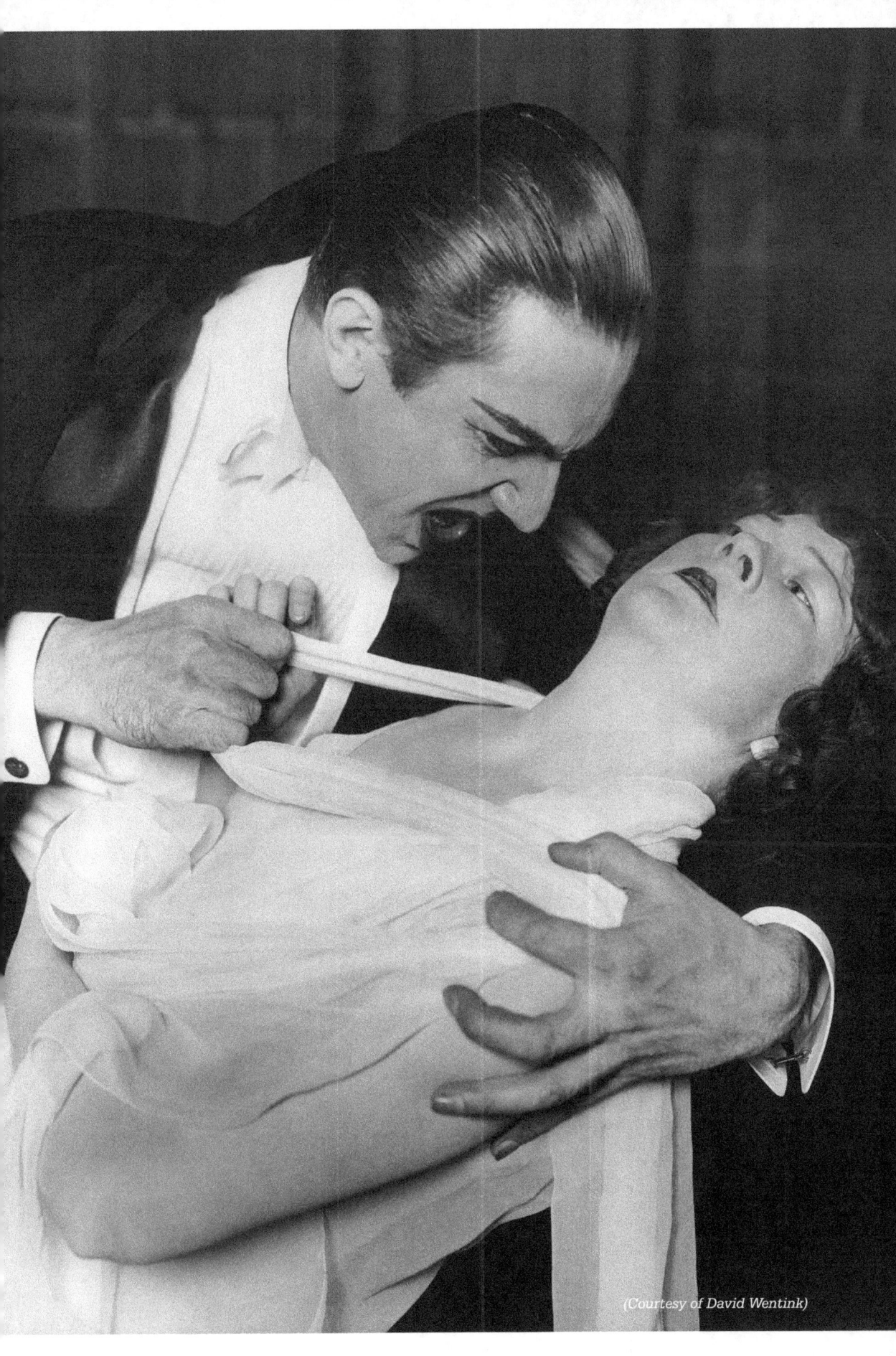

(Courtesy of David Wentink)

Lugosi in a publicity portrait for *The Thirteenth Chair* (1929). *(Courtesy of John Antosiewicz)*

Appendix D

American Filmography 1923-1930

Researched and compiled by Gary D. Rhodes and Bill Kaffenberger

The following filmography is the most complete and accurate catalogue of Lugosi's output based on the best available primary sources. The films are listed in chronological order and include all of Lugosi's films from 1923 through 1930.

Though we list *How to Handle Women* (1928), we have serious doubts as to whether Lugosi appeared in the final release prints. Universal Pictures apparently shot the movie in California while Lugosi was still appearing in *Dracula–The Vampire Play* on Broadway. After some screenings, the studio apparently retooled *How to Handle Women* in the summer of 1928, by which time Lugosi was in Los Angeles. That might have been when Lugosi's footage was shot. He is not seen in the surviving fragment that exists at the Library of Congress, but it constitutes only five percent of the final running time. We have decided to include *How to Handle Women* at present due in part to memories of actor Harold Pavey and in part due to conflicting data in primary sources.[1]

He Who Gets Slapped (MGM, 1924) represents a much greater question mark. In Lugosi's own files, Richard Sheffield believed he saw a photograph from that movie showing what appeared to be Lugosi as a clown alongside star Lon Chaney, Sr. He also saw a second photograph of a large group of clowns, one of which resembled Lugosi. But Lugosi's name does not appear in any known primary sources. And, of course, Lugosi appearing in a publicity photo with Chaney does not necessarily mean he appeared in the running time of the released movie. At this time, it is certainly not possible to include *He Who Gets Slapped* in a Lugosi filmography.[2]

Nor do we include MGM's *Lady of Scandal* (1930); rumors that Lugosi appeared in the film are definitely false. Likewise, unless he is in a long shot where facial recognition is impossible, Lugosi did not appear in the final edit of Fox's *Women Everywhere* (1930). He is definitely visible in a publicity still for the film, which implies he was probably in the cast, but if so, his footage was not used. As a result, *Women Everywhere* cannot be catalogued herein.[3]

The films that are listed below have been checked and double-checked for accuracy against existing copyright records, censorship records, and surviving film trade publications. Any variances from previous filmographies are intentional and should be seen as corrections.

The Silent Command
Fox Film Corporation, 1923
Role: Benedict Hisston.
Note: Released on 20 Aug. 1923.

The Rejected Woman
Distinctive Pictures, 1924
Role: Jean Gagnon.
Note: Released on 4 May 1924.

The Midnight Girl
Chadwick Pictures, 1925
Role: Nicholas Harmon.
Note: Released on 15 Feb. 1925.

Daughters Who Pay
Banner Productions, 1925
Role: Serge Romonsky.
Note: Released on 10 May 1925.

How to Handle Women
Universal Pictures, 1928
Role: A Bodyguard.
Note: Released on 14 Oct. 1928.

The Veiled Woman
Fox Film Corporation, 1929
Role: A Suitor to Nanon.
Note: It is possible that Lugosi's role changed prior to or during the production. Released on 14 Apr. 1929.

Prisoners
First National Pictures, 1929
Role: Brottos, "The Man."
Note: *Prisoners* was Lugosi's first talkie, though it was only a part-talkie. Released on 19 May 1929.

The Thirteenth Chair
Metro-Goldwyn-Mayer, 1929
Role: Inspector Delzante.
Note: Released on 19 Oct. 1929.

The Mask
Famous Lovers Productions, 1929
Role: Pierrot, a harlequin
Note: Fictional short subject. Originally titled *Punchinello*. Though produced in 1926, there is absolutely no evidence it was screened that year. It does not seem to have been released until 1 Nov. 1929.

Féltékenység (The Last Performance)
Universal Pictures, 1929
Role: Erik the Great
Note: Lugosi dubbed Conrad Veidt's English-speaking character into Hungarian. Additionally, the studio filmed a prologue showing Lugosi and the dubbing process. The Hungarian title translates as *Jealousy*. Released in Hungary on approximately 27 Feb. 1930.

Such Men Are Dangerous
Fox Film Corporation, 1930
Role: Dr. Goodman.
Note: Most contemporary credits refer to Lugosi's character as "Dr. Erdmann," but characters onscreen clearly articulate the name "Dr. Goodman" (or perhaps "Dr. Guttmann"). Released on 9 Mar. 1930.

Wild Company
Fox Film Corporation, 1930
Role: Felix Brown.
Note: Released on 5 July 1930.

A jazzkirály (The King of Jazz)
Universal Pictures, 1930
Role: Himself
Note: Along with Lucy Doraine and János Auer, Lugosi appeared as a Hungarian-language host. Released in Hungary on 6 Sept. 1930.

Renegades
Fox Film Corporation, 1930
Role: Sheik Muhammed Halid, the Marabout.
Note: Released on 26 Oct. 1930.

Viennese Nights
Warner Bros., 1930
Role: Count von Ratz, an Ambassador.
Note: Released on 26 Nov. 1930.

Oh, for a Man!
Fox Film Corporation, 1930
Role: Frescatti.
Note: The film's title was sometimes rendered without an exclamation point. Released on 14 Dec. 1930.

Endnotes

1 For more information on *How to Handle Women* (1928), see Chapter 34.

2 For more information on *He Who Gets Slapped* (1924), see Chapter 28.

3 For more information on *Women Everywhere* (1930), see Chapter 46.

Index

Abbott and Costello Meet Frankenstein (1948) (film) 49
Abraham Lincoln (1930) (film) 394
Actors' Equity Association 85-86, 108, 160, 163, 228, 304, 416
Adelphi Theater (Chicago) 110, 415
Ady, Endre 167, 173-174, 416
Ady-est (poetry reading) 173, 416
Álarcosbál (*The Masked Ball*) (1917) (film) 54
Alba, Maria 356
Albertson, Frank 356-357
Alden, Hortense 141, 151, 153-154
Alcañiz, Luana 365
Alibi (1929) (film) 392
Amerikai Magyar Színtársulat (American Hungarian Theater Company) 14, 16, 19, 39, 411
Amberg, Gustave 59
Anderson, John Murray 337
Andra, Fern 331
Andruss, Albert 159
Ape Man, The (1943) (film) 49, 285
Apollo Theater (Atlantic City) 74, 414
Arábiai éjszaka cabaret, Az (*The Arabian Night Cabaret*) 173, 417
Armandy, André 365
Armetta, Henry 93
Arabesque (play) 140, 141-157, 160, 164, 173, 178, 182, 184, 185, 318, 416-417
Asher, E. M. 391-393
Asszonyszívek Kalandora (*The Adventurer of Women's Hearts*) (film) 51-54, 413
Atkins, Rick 391
Atkins, T. Carlyle 189
Auer, János (John Auer) 331, 333, 335, 337, 425
Ayers, Lew 388-389

Balderston, John L. 199, 203-204, 209, 213, 215, 236, 251, 418

Balogh, Gyöngyi 52
Banky, Vilma 173, 260, 418
Banner Productions 127, 129-130, 424
Bara, Theda 93, 108, 199, 213
Baron, Henry 71-72, 8, 85-86, 414
Barrymore, John 93, 124, 141, 154
Barrymore, Lionel 356
Barton, Charles 49
Bat, The (play) 213-214, 283
Bat Whispers, The (1930) (film) 392
Baxter, Warner 352, 354-355, 365-366, 369
Beery, Noah 365
Bel Geddes, Norman 141-143, 150-151, 178, 181, 417, 418
Belmont Theater (New York) 17, 19, 408, 409
Bennison, Louis 112
Best Man Wins, The (1935) (film) 93
Bickford, Charles 331
Big House, The (1930) (film) 392
Big Trail, The (1930) (film) 394
Biltmore Theater (Los Angeles) 235, 237, 419
Bíró, Lajos 39, 106, 173, 267, 363, 411, 418
Bitzer, G. W. "Billy" 132
Black Camel, The (1931) (film) 370
Black Cat, The (1934) (film) 36, 38
Black Friday (1940) (film) 74, 355
Blackstone Theater (Chicago) 378
Blinn, Holbrook 252-254
Boldogság (*Happiness*) (play) 14-15, 408
Boros, Feríke 50, 414
Borzage, Frank 365
Boucicault, Dion 200, 202
Boudoir Diplomat, The (1930) (film) 394
Bow, Clara 285, 316-318, 322-323, 327, 363
Bow, Tui Lorraine 318
Bowers, John 129, 130
Bowery at Midnight (1942) (film) 167, 169
Boyd, William "Stage" 301, 305
Bráver, Irma 50, 414

Brecher, Egon 36, 38
Bride of the Monster (1955) (film) 94, 355
Briquet, Jean 135
Briskin, Samuel J. 129
Broadway (1929) (film) 331
Bromfield, Louis 391
Brooke, Clifford 109, 416
Brown, J. Raymond 278, 289
Brown, Porter Emerson 199
Browning, Tod 123, 185, 228, 284, 295, 297, 299, 301, 303, 304-308, 310, 311, 337, 356, 387-389, 391, 395, 397
Bruder Straubinger (*Brother Straubinger*) (operetta) 61
Bunston, Herbert 208, 235
Burke, Warren 356
Burne-Jones, Philip 199-200

Cadman, Reverend Doctor S. Parkes 182
Camille (1917) (film) 93
Capitol Theater (Los Angeles) 277, 419
Capitol Theater (New York) 126
Captain of the Guard (1930) (film) 332, 334
Carew, Arthur Edmund 123
Carradine, John 392
Carroll, Moon 302, 304-305
Cassinelli, Dolores 132, 136
Castle, William 226-228
Cat and the Canary, The (play) 204, 213, 283
Central Opera House (New York) 412
Central Park Opera House (New York) 61
Central Theater (New York) 95
Chandler, Helen 228, 304, 397, 400
Chadwick Pictures 132, 134-136, 424
Chandu the Magician (1932) (film) 93
Chaney, Lon 115, 117-118, 129, 177, 295, 299, 303, 304, 354, 363, 387-388, 393, 423
Charles Hopkins Theater (New York) 179, 180, 417
Clarke, Betsy Ross 77, 78
Clawson, Elliot 299, 301

Cleopatra (1917) (film) 93
Clothes Make the Woman (1927) (short subject) 192
Cody, Lew 331
Columbia University (New York) 105, 415
Cooksey, Curtis 141, 142, 143, 144, 154
Coolidge, Calvin 345-346
Coons, Robbin 304, 405
Cooper, George 365
Coopersmith, J. M. 191
Cort, John 160
Cort Theater (New York) 171, 416
Courtenay, William 236, 393-394
Craft, William J. 193
Crews, Laura Hope 109
Crime of Doctor Crespi, The (1935) (film) 331
Crosland, Alan 343, 345-346
Csanak, Gézáné 66
Currie, Louise 133
Cushing, Tom 177-181, 418
Czar of Broadway, The (1930) (film) 388

Dale, Alan 85
Daly's 63rd Street Theater (New York) 160, 163, 417
Darvas, Károly 335, 411, 412, 413
Daughters Who Pay (1925) (film) 127-132
Davidson, John 301, 304
Davis, George H. 129
Davis, Irving 105
Davis, Károly 41
DeMille, Cecil B. 242, 304
De Justh, Katinka 279
De Kerékjártó, Duci 12, 363
De La Motte, Marguerite 129-131
De Moreas, Julio 262
De Putti, Lya 260
De Voe, Daisy 318
Deane, Hamilton 123, 199, 203, 209, 213, 215, 236, 251, 418
Debrecen, Hungary 41, 168

Decker, Eurilla Bow 323
Denny, Reginald 370
Derwent, Clarence 205, 206, 208
Devil, The (1915) (film) 129
Devil in the Cheese, The (play) 176-187
Deutscher Verein (German Society) 105, 415
Distinctive Pictures 124-126, 424
Doraine, Lucy 337-338, 425
Doucet, H. Paul 159-160
Douglas, Byron 265
Dr. Jekyll and Mr. Hyde (1920) (film) 93
Dr. Jekyll and Mr. Hyde (1931) (film) 185
Dracula (character) 11, 49, 50, 117, 123, 124, 192, 203, 204, 205, 206, 260, 273, 277, 304, 315, 316, 363, 370, 376, 385, 386, 387-388, 390-391, 392, 393-395, 397-398, 405
Dracula (1931) (film) 94, 132, 185, 303, 336, 337, 351, 373, 385-403, 405
Drácula (1931) (film, Spanish version) 262, 331
Dracula (1897) (novel) 23, 24, 32, 65, 123, 189, 201, 202, 295, 315, 338, 376, 377
Dracula–The Vampire Play (play) 11, 192, 194, 198, 199, 205-209, 213-233, 235-249, 251, 253-256, 259, 260, 265, 277-293, 303, 304, 316, 317, 318, 320, 322, 363, 377-383, 385, 386, 389-390, 418-420
Dracula of the Hills (1923) (poem) 123
Dracula's Daughter (1936) (film) 132
Dream of a Rarebit Fiend (1906) (film) 177
Drennen, Marguerite 348
Drury, Morley 317

East Lynne (1925) (film) 264
Eastman, George 137, 353
Edwards, J. Gordon 92-93
ember tragédiája, Az (*The Tragedy of Man*) (play) 11, 41-47, 63, 72, 92, 413
Erkel, Ferenc 41

Fairbanks, Douglas 129
Falusi Menyecskék (*Village Brides*) (operetta) 61
Famous Lovers Productions 189-190, 425
Famous Players-Lasky Corporation 164, 168-169
Fata Morgana (play) 106-107, 415
Faust (1926) (film) 222, 277
Fay, Frank 342
Fazenda, Louise 345
Fehér báránykák (*Little White Sheep*) (play) 57
Fejős, Pál (Paul Fejos) 252, 331-335
Fészek Club 107-108, 114, 173
Finch, Flora 342
First Hungarian Literary Society of New York 23, 31
First National Pictures 253, 259, 267, 269, 271-272, 424
Fiú-e vagy leány? (*A Boy or a Girl?*) (play) 18, 409
Fleming, Victor 365-366
Florey, Robert 49
Flynn, Emmett J. 264-265
Fool There Was, A (play) 199
Forbes, Mary 308
Forest Vampires, The (1914) (film) 129, 199
Forradalmi nász (*The Revolutionary Wedding*) (play) 168-171, 173, 416
Fort, Garrett 132
Fox, Sidney 55
Fox, William 92, 351
Fox Film Corporation 260, 351, 424, 425, 426
Fox Movietone City 351
Frankenstein (1932) (film) 132
Franklin, Maurice 245, 246
Freedman, Harold 348, 387
Frith, Alfred 228
From Hell It Came (1957) (film) 185
Frye, Dwight 178, 179, 183, 184, 185, 397
Fulton, Mr. and Mrs. Jimmie 242

Fulton Theater (New York) 213, 225, 418
Fulton Theater (Oakland) 289, 390, 391, 419, 420
Fülöp, Ilona 13, 37, 411

Gaye, Gregory 365
Genuine (1920) (film) 331
George, Harriet 277-278, 285, 289-290
Gettó (*Ghetto*) (play) 35, 41, 412
Ghost Parade, The (play) 205
Gift of Gab (1934) (film) 93
Gillmore, Frank 304
Ginsberg, Dr. Joseph 355
Gleason, James 229, 331
Glett, Charles 191
Go and Get It (1920) (film) 129
Godless Girl, The (1928) (film) 242
Golding, Samuel Ruskin 159
Goldwyn Cosmopolitan 126
Gone With the Wind (1939) (film) 365
Gorilla, The (play) 213, 343
Goudal, Jetta 124
Grand Theater (Wilkes-Barre) 78, 414
Great Arts Pictures 190
Greenwich Village Theater (New York) 78-81, 85, 414
Glyn, Elinor 352, 355
Griffith, Corrine 267, 268
Grill, Lola 168, 418
grófnő betörői, A (*The Countess' Burglars*, 1916) (film) 57
Griffith, D. W. 44, 132, 394
gyászruhás nő, A (*The Woman in Mourning Dress*) (play) 49, 414

Haarmann, Fritz 123
Hahn, Mihály (Michael Hahn) 49-54
Hale, Creighton 297
Hall, Gladys 290, 327
Hall, Henry 285
Halló (*Hello*, aka *Halló!*) (play) 12, 18-20

Halsey, Forrest 267
Hammerstein II, Oscar 343
Hampton, Hope 229
Hards, Ira 204, 216, 217, 418
Harrigan, Nedda 208, 209, 228
Harris, Mitchell 365
Haunted House, The (1917) (film) 125
Hawks, Howard 389
Hawks, Kenneth 352-354
Házasság a Lipótvárosban (*The Wedding in the Lipótváros*, 1916) (film) 57
He Who Gets Slapped (1924) (film) 115-118, 423
Head, Cloyd 141, 142, 417
Helene Pons Studios 179
Herbert, Holmes 301
Herbert, Victor 252
Herndon, Richard 141, 417
Hersholt, Jean 343, 345
Hervé, Paul 135
Heyersman, Herman 35, 41, 412
Hollywood Music Box (Los Angeles) 278, 281, 363
Holmquist, Sigrid 192
Horn, Camilla 277
Hopkins, Charles 178
Horthy, Miklós 24, 27-28, 31, 36
House of Usher, The (play) 205
How to Handle Women (1928) (film) 192-195
Howard, Leslie 109, 112, 113, 132
Hughes, Gareth 132
Humphrey, Mrs. Irene 66
Hunchback of Notre Dame (1923) (film) 117
Hungaria Restaurant 107
Huntley, Raymond 203-204, 277, 376, 377, 392
Hurn, Philip 356
Hyams, Leila 299, 302

Invisible Ghost (1941) (film) 192
Invisible Prince! Or, the Island of Tranquil Delights (play) 199

Isquith, Louis I. 159
Irving, Sir Henry 202, 206
Irving Place Theater (New York) 35

Januskopf, Der: eine Tragödie am Rande der Wirklichkeit (*The Head of Janus: A Tragedy on the Border of Reality*) (1920) (film) 224, 332
Játék az esküvővel (*The Wedding Game*) (film) 49, 414
Jazz Singer, The (1927) (film) 343
Jenkins, J. C. 359
Jolley, James 228
Jory, Victor 379, 381, 392
Joy, Colonel Jason S. 301
Juck und Schlau (*Juck and Schlau*) (1920) (film) 59
Jukes, Bernard 204, 205, 221, 225, 245, 279

Kaiser, Georg 105, 415
Kaméliás hölgy (*Lady of the Camellias*) (play) 20, 409
Karloff, Boris 38
Károlyi, Count Mihály 106, 363
Keith, Ian 267, 271, 394
Kende, Géza 279, 318, 363
Kernell, William 370
Kerrigan, J. M. 365
Kertész, Mihály (Michael Curtiz) 36, 173, 260, 331, 337, 342, 363, 418
Kessler, Julius 59
King, Bradley 356
King, Burton L. 127
King of Jazz, The (1930) (film) 336-338, 425
Király, Ernő 24-31, 36-37, 39, 167, 410
Kohner, Paul 331, 333-335, 337
Korda, Sándor (Alexander) 260, 267, 331, 363
Korda, Zoltán 363
Kovács, Kálmán 337
Királynőm, meghalok érted (*My Queen, I Will Die For You*) (play) 39, 341, 411

kisasszony férje, A (*A Young Lady's Husband*, aka *Almost Married*) (play) 16-17, 60, 408
Königin der Luft (*Queen of the Air*) (operetta) 59
Krajnyák, Aranka 335
Kun, Béla 23-24, 36, 167
Küry, Klára 63
Küzdelem a létért (*The Struggle for Life*, aka *A leopárd* [*The Leopard*]) (1918) (film) 54

La Plante, Laura 332
Laemmle, Sr., Carl 123, 193, 331, 335, 337, 387
Laemmle Jr., Carl 387, 388, 391-392, 394-395
Laemmle, Edward 331
Lanfield, Sidney 370
Lancaster, Richard 235, 278, 285
Landenberger, Captain 319
Last Performance, The (1929) (film) 331-337, 425
Laub, William B. 130
Laugh, Clown, Laugh (1924) (film) 177
Laugh, Clown, Laugh (play) 177
Lawrence, George A. 79
Le Picard, Marcel 192
Lebedeff, Ivan 262, 304
Lee, Lila 132-134, 277
Lederstrumpf (1920) (film) 92
Lengyelvér (*Polish Blood*) (play) 57
Leoni Leo (*Leo Leoni*) (1917) (film) 54
Lessing Theater (Berlin) 59
Lexington Theater (New York) 25, 30, 42, 410, 413
Lichtig, Harry 252-256
Lichtig and Englander 252, 253
Liliom (play) 35-39, 42, 45, 82, 106, 141, 365, 407, 411
Listerine Mouthwash 189, 190
Little Theater (London) 203
Liveright, Horace 201, 203, 214, 219, 221, 224, 235, 278, 284, 382, 418

Lobero Theater (Santa Barbara) 282, 419
Loder, Lotti 347
Loff, Jeanette 337
London After Midnight (1927) (film) 295
Lonesome (1928) (film) 331
Lőrincz, Kornélia (Cornelia Lőrinc) 14, 16, 408, 409, 410, 411
Lorna Doone (1922) (film) 129
Lóth, Ila 50, 52, 54
Lothar, Rudolf 108, 415
Lowe, Edmund 91, 93, 96, 304, 370
Lowell, Amy 123
Loy, Myrna 365, 367, 370
Lubin, Arthur 73
Lubitsch, Ernst 331
Luce, Claire Booth 365
Lugosi, Lillian Arch 204
Lugosi-Buchter, János "Béla" 23, 167
Lugossy, János (John Lugosi) 167-168
Lugossy Film 49, 51, 54, 413, 414
Lukács, Pál (Paul Lukas) 332
Luxury (1930) (film) 365
Lyceum Theater (New London) 208, 418
Lyceum Theater (New York) 31, 106, 412, 413, 414, 415
Lynch, John 124
Lynne, Sharon 356
Lytton, Arnold 192

MacDonald, Jeanette 370-373
MacFadden, Hamilton 370
MacGrail, Walter 265
MacKellar, Helen 159-162
MacKenna, Kenneth 365
MacQuarrie, George 125, 163
Mack, Helen 228
Madách, Imre 11, 41, 63, 413
Manhattan Opera House (New York) 61, 141
Mansfield, Martha 93
March, Fredric 177, 185
Mark of the Vampire (1935) (film) 36, 343

Mark of Zorro, The (1920) (film) 129
Mask, The (1929) (film) 118, 190-191, 195, 425
Matrimonial Bed, The (1930) (film) 342
Maywood, Robert Campbell 200, 201
McCarey, Leo 356, 357
McClellan, George 109, 416
McCrea, Joel 299
McDermott, Marc 299
McWade, Robert 177
Mercer, Beryl 342
Mehra, Lal Chand 299, 301, 308
Metro Goldwyn Mayer (MGM) 117, 129, 299, 301, 304, 305, 310, 363, 387, 423, 424
Metropol Theater (Berlin) 57
Mezei, Mihály 335
Midnight Girl, The (1925) (film) 122, 132-136, 169, 277, 424
Midsummer Night's Dream, A (play) 269
Millard, Helen 301
Miller, Gilbert 252, 254
Mingo Pictures 92
Modern Magyar Színpad (Modern Hungarian Stage) 14, 16-17, 18, 20, 24, 35, 408, 409, 410
Mohr, Hal 334
Molnár, Ferenc 35, 39, 141, 267, 269, 272, 277, 365, 407, 411, 419
Mon Homme (*My Man*) (play) 71, 81
Monroe Theater (Chicago) 95
Montagh, Ilona (Ilona von Montagh) 14, 16, 28, 37, 41, 57-69, 114, 127, 318, 408, 409, 410, 411, 413
Morosco, Walter 269
Morris, Chester 392
Motion Picture Producers and Distributors of America (MPPDA) 301, 308, 353, 370
Muni, Paul 392, 393
Murder By Television (1935) (film) 285
Murders in the Rue Morgue (1932) (film) 48, 49, 54
Murnau, F. W. 224, 277, 332, 385

Murphy, Dudley 391
Murray, J. Harold 363
Mystic, The (1925) (film) 295

Nagel, Conrad 124, 125, 299, 304
National Theater (New York) 147, 416
Neill, Terence 206
Nemzeti Színház (National Theater) 17, 18, 24, 39, 335
Nile Theater (Bakersfield) 282, 419
Nora Bayes Theater (New York) 85
Nosferatu (1922) (film) 224, 385-386
Nossen, Bram 178
Noy, Wifred 132, 133

Oakie, Jack 316
Oakman, Wheeler 304
Oh For a Man! (1930) (film) 365, 370-373, 426
Olcott, Sidney 331
Olivotti, Eva 332
Olt, Arisztid (Aristid) 54
Open House (play) 158-165
ördög, Az (*The Devil*) (play) 277
Orpheum Theater (Harrisburg) 77, 414
Ouanga (aka T*he Love Wanga*) (1936) (film) 129
Owen, Catherine Dale 352

Pantages Theater (Fresno) 282, 419
Pantages Theater (Portland) 284
Parker, Albert 125
Parsons, Louella O. 247, 277, 299, 394
Parsons Theater (Hartford) 418
Papp, István (Stefan Papp) 14, 408, 413
Pasedena Playhouse (California) 178
Pauker, Dr. Edmond 252-256
Pavey, Harold 194, 423
Penzer, Norwood 345
Peret, Leonce 297
Peterson, Dorothy 203-206, 216, 221, 228, 235

Phantom, The (play) 200, 202, 214
Phantom of the Opera, The (1925) (film) 117, 123, 388
Phelps, William Lyon 182
Philbin, Mary 331, 335
Philipp, Adolf 135
Phillips, Mr. and Mrs. Eddie 242
Physioc, Joseph 216, 251
Picard, André 71, 81, 414
Pickford, Mary 50
Pidgeon, Walter 343
Planche, James Robinson 201, 202
Playboy (1930) (film) 342
Play is the Thing, The (play) 352, 353
Playhouse, The (Wilmington, Delaware) 74, 79, 414
Pogány, Bella 41, 413
Pogány, Willy 35, 41, 108
Polidori, John 201
Porter, Edwin S. 177
Porter, Gerald 192
Prevost, Marie 331
Prisoners (1929) (film) 258, 267-273, 315, 424
Punchinello (1926) (film) 118, 189-191
Pymm, Frederick 278, 284, 290, 378, 380

Quatermaine, Charles 301
Queen of Sheba (1921) (film) 93

Rabok (*Prisoners*) (novel) 267
Radmirov Katalin (*Catherine Radmirov*) (1917) (film) 168
Rainsford, Billie 189
Rand School (New York City) 63, 408, 413, 416
régiséggyűjtő, A (*The Antiquarian*) (1917) (film) 52
Rátkai, Márton (Martin Ratkay) 28, 35-40, 45
Reade's Broadway Theater (New Jersey) 159
Reade's Savoy Theater (Asbury Park) 208, 418

Red Mill, The (play) 252
Recording Laboratory of America 191
Red Poppy, The (play) 70-89, 92, 108, 141, 154, 164, 185, 407, 414
Reed, Carl 206, 239
Reisman, Leo 346
Rejected Woman, The (1924) (film) 124-127, 252, 424
Renaldo, Duncan 189-191
Renegades (1930) (film) 365-370, 379, 425
Return of Chandu (1934) (serial) 356
Return of the Ape Man (1944) (film) 192
Rhodes, Gary D. 115, 117, 118
Right to Dream, The (play) 105
Rita, Selma 279
Roach, Bert 345
Road House (1928) (film) 356
Road to Mandalay, The (1926) (film) 299
Romberg, Sigmund 343
Roosevelt, Jr., Theodore 94
Rotoli, Francesca 278, 282
Roxy Theater (New York) 397
Rund um die Liebe (*All About Love*) (operetta) 61
Rubens, Alma 124-125, 264

Salomé (1918) (film) 93
Santel, Alfred 352
Sappho (1926) (film) 189-190
sárga liliom, A (*The Yellow Lily*) (play) 39, 106, 267, 363, 411
Savoy Theater (New Jersey) 208, 418
Scared to Death (1947) (film) 192
Scarface (1932) (film) 393
Schildkraut, Joseph 35, 193, 392
Schilling, Marion 205, 317
Schreck, Max 385
Schwartz, László 14, 20, 408
Schwarzwaldmädel (*The Girl from the Black Forest*) (play) 59
Second Cup, The (play) 348, 407

Segal, Vivienne 343, 345-346
Seiter, William A. 267, 270-271
Serrano, Vincent 112-114
Seven Faces (1930) (film) 392, 393
Seven Keys to Baldpate (play) 213
Shadow of Chinatown (1936) (serial) 285
Shadows (1922) (film) 129
She (1935) (film) 228
Sheehan, Winfield 351
Sheffield, Richard 115-117, 212
Sherlock Holmes (1922) (film) 125
Sherry, J. Barney 129, 199
Shore, Viola Brothers 370
Shostac, Percy 206
Shotwell, Mary 297
Show, The (1927) (film) 295
Show Boat (1929) (film) 332
Shubert, J. J. 108
Shubert's Theater (New Haven) 205, 418
Silent Command, The (1923) (film) 91-103
Silent House, The (play) 228
Silent Witness (1927) (film) 192, 195, 262
Silvers, Louis 343
Sinclair, Howard (aka Howard St. Clair) 379
Singer, Robert 226, 407
Siposs, Jenő 168, 416
Sjöström, Victor (Victor Seastrom) 117
Soanes, Wood 390
Son of Kong, The (1933) (film) 228
Sorina, Die (*The Sorina*) (play) 104-105, 415
Sorrows of Satan, The (1926) (film) 262, 267
Sothern, Sara 141-143, 154
Spanier, Anna 282, 285
Speed (1925) (film) 130
Spider, The (play) 236, 242, 245, 393
Spooks Run Wild (1941) (film) 192
Spreckels Theater (San Diego) 281, 419
Stamford Theater (Stamford) 109, 208, 415, 418
Standing, Wyndham 125
Stardom of Broadway (radio) 185, 227

Stilliti, Luigi 319
Stoker, Bram 23, 24, 32, 123, 137, 189, 201, 202, 203, 223, 242, 277, 281, 315, 316, 338, 377, 379, 385, 386, 387, 398, 418
Stoker, Florence 387
Strange Case of Dr. Jekyll and Mr. Hyde (novella) 332
Strauss, H. David 355
Such Men Are Dangerous (1930) (film) 352-356, 363, 365, 425
Summers, Montague 277, 290
Supernatural (1933) (film) 343
Sutter Theater (Sacramento) 283, 419
Swanson, Gloria 259
Swickard, Josef 192, 262
Székely, Zoltán 12, 20
Szmik, Ilona 11, 57, 318
Tanz auf dem Vulkan, Der (1920) (film) 91
Teck Theater (Buffalo) 109, 143, 415, 416
Terror, The (1928) (film) 345
Terror Aboard (1933) (film) 343
Terwilliger, George 129
Thew, Harvey 343
Thompson, Kenneth 265
Thirteenth Chair, The (1919) (film) 297
Thirteenth Chair, The (1929) (film) 124, 284, 294-313
Thirteenth Chair, The (play) 297
Thirty-Ninth Street Theater (New York) 16, 60, 408
Three Faces East (1930) (film) 393
Thury, Ilona 168, 173, 412, 417
Tietjens, Eunice 141, 142, 417
Tilden, William "Big Bill" 379, 392
Tora, Lia 261-264, 337
Tordai, Erzsi 28, 412
Tovar, Lupita 262
Törvény (The Law) (play) 24, 410, 411
Tóth, József R. 168, 416
Trader Horn (1931) (film) 190
Tragic 18 (play) 178

Trilby (1923) (film) 123, 242
Tryon, Glenn 192, 195

Unger, Gladys 108
Unholy Three, The (1925) (film) 295
Unholy Three, The (1930) (film) 388
Universal Pictures 54, 123, 192-195, 260, 262, 331-337, 363, 373, 387-388, 390-395, 397, 398, 423, 424, 425
Unknown, The (1927) (film) 295

Vajda, Ernest 260, 363, 415
Van Sloan, Edward 205, 221, 229, 245, 397
Vampire, The (1910) (film) 199
Vampire, The (painting) 199
Vampire, The, or the Bride of the Isles (play) 201
Vampyre, The (play) 201
Vampyre, The, A Tale (novel) 201
Vampires of the Coast (1909) (film) 199
Vampires of the Night (1914) (film) 199
Várkonyi, Mihály (Varconi, Victor) 173, 260, 418
Vasco, the Vampire (1914) (film) 199
Vass, Jenő 168, 416
Veidt, Conrad 260, 331-333, 336, 425
Veiled Woman, The (1928) (film) 260-267, 271, 272, 337, 424
Veiller, Bayard 297, 299, 301, 306
Vidor, Károly (Charles Vidor) 13, 37
Viennese Nights (1930) (film) 343-348
Vincenti, Paul 259, 260
Vitaphone Symphony Orchestra 271
Vitaphone System 351
Von morgens bis mitternachts (From Morn to Midnight) (play) 105
Von Stroheim, Eric 259, 331, 393
Voodoo Man (1944) (film) 133, 192, 285
Vörösmarty, Mihály 31

Waldmann, Emil 59
Waldron, Donnee 208
Walker, Harry 245, 246, 278, 282
Wallace, Ramsey 159, 161, 162, 163
Walsh, Raoul 394
Warfield, Ruth White 141
Warner Brothers 388
Warner, H. B. 206, 356, 365
Washington Irving High School Auditorium 49, 50, 51, 411, 413, 414
Watkins, Linda 177, 185
Weber, Harry 387
Weeks, Beatrice Woodruff 318-326
Weeks, Charles Peter 319, 320, 322, 325, 327
Werewolf, The (play) 108-115, 117
West, Roland 392, 393
West of Zanzibar (1928) (film)
Wheeler, Bert 229
Whitaker, Alma 241
White, Courtney 379, 380, 392
Whiteman, Paul 336, 337
White Zombie (1932) (film) 94, 336
Whitman Bennett Studios 129
Whitmore, Hazel 234, 235, 279, 285

Wiene, Robert 331
Wieting Theater (Syracuse) 144, 416
Wild Company (1930) (film) 356-359
Williams, John D. 204
Willis, W. F. 308
Winchell, Walter 323
Windsor Theater (New York) 160, 417
Winslow, Dick 345
Winwood, Estelle 71, 73, 76-80, 82-86
Wizard of Oz, The (1939) (film) 365
Women Everywhere (1930) (film) 118, 362
Woodruff, Commodore John S. 318
Woods, Donald 278
Woodward, Orville D. (O.D.) 235, 238, 242, 253, 254, 277-278, 281, 284-285, 419, 420
Woollcott, Alexander 184
Women of All Nations (1931) (film) 93
Wray, John 388
Wycherly, Margaret

Yeaman, Elizabeth 392

Zanuck, Daryl F. 343, 345
Zsolt, Ferenc 50, 414

www.ingramcontent.com/pod-product-compliance
Lightning Source LLC
Chambersburg PA
CBHW080539230426
43663CB00015B/2642